Blue Mountains Revisited

Blue Mountains Revisited

Cultural Studies on the Nilgiri Hills

edited by
Paul Hockings

DELHI
OXFORD UNIVERSITY PRESS
CALCUTTA CHENNAI MUMBAI
1997

Oxford University Press, Walton Street, Oxford OX2 6DP
Oxford New York
Athens Auckland Bangkok Calcutta
Cape Town Chennai Dar es Salaam Delhi
Florence Hong Kong Istanbul Karachi
Kuala Lumpur Madrid Melbourne Mexico City
Mumbai Nairobi Paris Singapore
Taipei Tokyo Toronto

and associates in
Berlin Ibadan

ISBN 0 19 563784 4

Typeset by Excellent Laser Typesetters, Tri Nagar, Delhi 110035
Printed at Rekha Printers Pvt. Ltd., New Delhi 110020
and published by Manzar Khan, Oxford University Press
YMCA Library Building, Jai Singh Road, New Delhi 110001

To
The People of the Nilgiri Hills

Preface

This volume logically follows on from *Blue Mountains: The Ethnography and Biogeography of a South Indian Region* (Oxford University Press, 1989). It also follows on more generally from the findings of a regional scientific and historical literature so extensive (Hockings, *A Comprehensive Bibliography for the Nilgiri Hills of Southern India* (forthcoming) that one could almost literally paper the Nilgiri district with the pages of its publications! Let us hope that does not happen.

Despite hundreds of existant anthropological studies dealing with the diverse people who make up Nilgiri society, and to a very considerable extent because of those works, the present volume is able to offer a variety of studies which in virtually all cases deal with topics that have never previously been touched upon.

Thus Frank Heidemann offers the first sociological examination of the immigrant labourers who today make up a sizeable part of the Nilgiri population, yet are scarcely mentioned in any earlier ethnographic study. Nurit Bird-David offers the first serious comparison of social organization on the Nilgiri Plateau and that on the lower Wynaad Plateau. Christiane Pilot-Raichoor gives the first comparative analysis of Badaga and neighbouring languages. Richard K. Wolf offers the first published analysis of Kota rain ceremonies. William A. Noble gives us the first technical study of contemporary Toda housing. Ulrich Demmer offers the first full account of the Jenu Kuṟumba hunter-gatherers in the Nilgiris. And the editor, Paul Hockings, reveals the existence of a virtually unknown body of Badaga epic poetry. One special contributor is Murray Emeneau, who writes on some problems of linguistics and botany, and who has now reached his sixtieth year of involvement in Nilgiri studies.

It is with real regret that we note the passing, in 1987, of David Mandelbaum, our friend and mentor in Nilgiri matters. His broad contributions to *Blue Mountains* helped make that book the landmark that it has become in Indian regional studies.

We are happy to note that Esha Béteille is again seeing our work, through the press, for which we thank her warmly.

PAUL HOCKINGS

Contents

List of Figures

List of Plates

Introduction

PAUL HOCKINGS

1

Introduction

When Alfred Tennyson wrote his oft-quoted (though not easily located) line about the Nilgiri Hills, invoking 'the sweet half-English Neilgherry air', he quite inadvertently proposed an agenda for late twentieth-century history and anthropology. To what extent are the Nilgiris 'half-English' today? Are the small Toda tribe—now, or at any time in the past—inmates of some colonial zoo, 'stall-fed aborigines', as someone once portrayed them? Has the British influence in this South Indian district faded away, as India approaches the half-century of its Independence, or is there still something quintessentially European about the economic geography and urban institutions of the place down to this very moment? What is the role of the English language itself, and of the local educational institutions that were in most cases founded during the years of imperial rule?

Such questions still call for definitive answers, and these may well come from social historians rather than social anthopologists, amongst whom are the majority of the authors contributing to this book. A more journalistic approach to the issues raised might be to ask such rhetorical questions as, what if the British had never settled in the Nilgiris, never constructed its roads, towns, and marketplaces? What if the Toda tribe, and to some extent the other ones too, had never enjoyed the legal protection of a live and let-live imperial administration? What if W.H.R. Rivers had never published his seminal study, *The Todas*, in 1906?

We will not reach answers to such questions by mere speculation: one needs a sound basis of ethnographic 'fact'. But who is to provide that? The authors of this book are indeed some among the numerous social scientists who have worked in the Nilgiris district and who have dispassionately, in a socially and politically uninvolved manner, disentangled the broad, the minute, and the sometimes arcane components that have gone to make up the experience of all the local people, that have indeed generated their society and history. No doubt any one of the chapters in the present book can and should be regarded as only one person's view of the subject, for it can never be seen as definitive. On the other hand it is not self-serving either, for it should be clear from their writing itself that none of these authors has a political agenda or a social formula to promote. We are all simply trying to record for posterity our informed (though never perfect) understanding of the state of things in late twentieth-century Nilgiri society.

I use the word 'society' in the singular because it seems to me that is what we are dealing with, a unitary thing. Yet the appearance of the terms Toda, Badaga, Jēnu Kuṟumba, Kota, in our chapter titles may well raise some doubts about this. Surely each of these is a discrete society? My answer (though perhaps it is not shared by all of my colleagues) is that each of these groups may well have been discrete societies with their own characteristic and very distinctive culture until mid-century; but that today, like the ethnic groups of the United States, they have all become players in a larger society. It is still true, for example, that the Badagas do not marry Todas—and so keep up some old distinctions, but on the other hand the degree of interaction between Todas and Badagas is much more subtle and at the same time broader than it was in the past. There was a time when the Todas provided the Badagas with a set of goods and ritual services, according to a formalized schedule that has repeatedly been described by anthropologists (Hockings 1980: 111–22). Today those obligations have passed away, but, as Noble shows in his chapter, we now find the Todas building themselves non-traditional houses that follow a Badaga model. Some Todas also work in a factory alongside people of many different cultural backgrounds. Clearly much has changed; and the change has been rapid, for most of the writers in this volume have been able to observe it at first hand during the course of their professional careers. We can safely assume that this cultural change will be even more rapid in the future, that the cultural boundaries between the different Nilgiri groups will become more and more obscure, and that the accounts we have published will quite literally become history, a view of things as they were but no longer are. There is in

India today a certain urgency about getting such ethnographic records as the present one published and into the public view.

The Nilgiris were not always a scene of perceptible change. They had been an isolated cultural backwater *vis-à-vis* the militaristic neighbouring states in the plains; until in 1820 the British founded Ootacamund and began to settle in the hills. At the beginning of the twentieth century, Rivers' now-classic account of the Todas, depicting them as a small transhumant tribe of buffalo pastoralists, gave us a lot more detail but hardly portrayed them as culturally changed from the days in 1602 when Father Fenicio gave us the first European account of these people.

Soon after the Badaga settlement on the hills, which must have begun after the break-up of the Vijayanagar Empire in 1565, their status began to change from that of landless refugees to a more dominant one, millet farmers who produced a food surplus that could be bartered with the neighbouring Toda, Kota, Kuṟumba and Irula tribes. This relationship developed into a viable economic and ritual symbiosis, one that was still in effect when the early generations of anthropologists began to put together the mosaic of ethnographic accounts from this district. By the eighteenth century, the Badaga population had become the largest of any on the hills, it would seem; certainly by the first rough census, in 1812, they had become numerically preponderant. Their mixed farming and cattle herding economy must also have been by then a dominant factor in the life of the district.

By comparison the other tribal groups were—and remained—very small. There were seven different groups of Kuṟumbas and one of Irulas, all of whom maintained themselves by a curious mix of jungle horticulture, hunting, and practising the craft of sorcery. The Kotas, living in just seven villages, had an economy more like that of the Badaga in that it was based on mixed farming and buffalo herding; but to these subsistence activities the Kotas had added the crafts of pottery-making, leatherwork, iron smelting, silversmithy, carpentery and building, as well as professional musicianship. These were crafts traditionally practised by no other Nilgiri groups, crafts which therefore gave the Kotas a crucial role in the lives of the other peoples.

In the lower Wainad Plateau the situtation was rather different, as Bird-David's paper makes it clear, Kotas, Todas and Badagas were present there too, with their usual economic activities; but they were in very small numbers as compared with the Chettis, Paniyas and Nayakas who occupied the land, and today the Todas may no longer be found there. These groups were mostly engaged in agriculture of one sort or another, and rice was capable of cultivation here, whereas it certainly never was on the Nilgiri Plateau. Groups like the Nayakas and Jēnu Ku̱rumbas had small garden plots, but also relied on hunting and foraging activities. Today most of such Nilgiri ethnic groups, who led an itinerant foraging life before, are employed on tea, coffee or rubber plantations.

Their lives have changed forever. The situation wherein the indigenous peoples of the Nilgiri Hills were long linked with each other has become of perennial interest among anthropologists because it exemplifies some classic ecological relationships. Each of these ethnic groups successfully exploited its particular ecological niche for some centuries, and the various forms of socio-economic exploitation complemented each other. So, just as in the ancient Near East and, in particular, the Old Testament, we found herders on the fringes of other people's farmland, and yet others—neither farmers nor pastoralists—working as artisans or traders either inside the numerous towns or moving between them: so too in the Nilgiris we find the Toda pastoralists linked with the other groups but spatially apart from them; the Badagas concentrating on growing millet and other staples (nearly all of Near Eastern origin); the Kotas acting as the artisans and exchanging products of all sorts for food; and the various Irula and Ku̱rumba groups living on the extremities, and surviving through a mixture of hunting, foraging, gardening, and magical practice. It is an age-old picture which survived until the middle of the twentieth century.

References

Hockings, P. 1980. *Ancient Hindu Refugees: Badaga Social History 1550–1975.* The Hague: Mouton.

The Nilgiri Tribal Systems: A View From Below

NURIT BIRD-DAVID

2

In 1980, the Nilgiris of Tamil Nadu were chosen to be India's first biosphere reserve under the 'Man and the Environment' programme launched by UNESCO (United Nations Educational, Scientific and Cultural Organization), in an attempt to conserve for study examples of characteristic eco-systems from each of the world's natural regions. Scholastic interest from a broad spectrum of disciplines has turned, therefore, to the Nilgiris, and it has become apparent that although the Nilgiris have been studied extensively, anthropological attention has been uneven and parts of the region have been grossly under-studied. This chapter intends to provide a foundation for filling this gap in the Nilgiri scholarship.[1]

Introduction

The tribal populations of the Nilgiri Hills of southern India have attracted massive ethnographic attention for over 150 years. In the *Bibliography for the Nilgiri Hills of Southern India,* (1978), Hockings listed 576 references to them, and additional work has since been published (Hockings ed., 1989). However, although the regional ethnography is extraordinarily voluminous for an area of only 984 square miles, the overwhelming majority of studies are concerned with the Nilgiri Plateau at the top of this mountainous region, and its tribal communities, the Toda, Badaga and Kota. Surprisingly few studies deal with the Nilgiri-Wynaad Plateau, which lies at a distinctly lower elevation a dozen kilometres down from the Nilgiri Plateau on the western slopes, or with its tribal groups which include the Mullu Kuṟumba, the Betta Kuṟumba, the Nayaka, the Paniya, and the Chetti. Anthropological studies conducted in the latter area, in fact, consist of Fürer-Haimendorf's brief investigation during the summer of 1948 of all the aforementioned five groups (1952); Misra's study of the Mullu Kurumba in Erumad for the Anthropological Survey of India (1971, 1972, 1989); and my own study of the Nayaka near Pandalur (Bird 1983a, b; Bird-David 1987a, b; 1988, 1989, 1990, 1992a, b).[2]

Since Keys (1812), observers and scholars have been particularly concerned with the system of relationships between the tribal communities of the Nilgiri Plateau. Several scholars have argued over the question of whether it should be regarded as an early tribal variant of the Indian caste system, and if so, what can be learnt from it (Mandelbaum 1941; Fox 1963; Gould 1967; Hockings 1980; and Walker 1986). At the same time, except for Misra's short article (1972), in which she describes intertribal relationships in her study-village, Erumad, there has as yet been no attempt to look at the nature and the form of intertribal relationships in the Nilgiri-Wynaad, and how they compare with the more well known ones of the Nilgiri Plateau.

The objective of this chapter is to fill this lacuna in the regional ethnography in a twofold way. This chapter examines, the Nilgiri-Wynaad intertribal world, and it will compare it with the well-known system of the Nilgiri Plateau. The comparison is between two regional social worlds with each of which tribesmen interact, or think they interact, with one another more frequently than they do with tribesmen in the other regional social world. It is therefore concerned as much with social representations as with intertribal interaction and, indeed, tribesmen in some cases have easier access to tribesmen whom they consider to be part of the other regional social world than to those they include in theirs. We are concerned, furthermore, with what twentieth century local people and their observers regard as the 'traditional' intertribal world, which encompasses the consequences of regional historical processes up until the nineteenth century, but ignores the considerable impact of British colonization.[3] The Badaga in this view are regarded as one of the Nilgiri tribes, although, as Hockings (1980) shows, they are descended from farming refugees who fled from Karnataka when the Vijayanagar Empire collapsed and arrived on the Nilgiris during the seventeenth and early eighteenth centuries. Similarly, the Chetti of the Nilgiri-Wynaad are viewed as an autochthonous land-owning people, while it seems they are composed of a variety of Kannarese and Malayalam speaking peoples who probably gradually emigrated from surrounding areas throughout preceding centuries and encroached on land in the Nilgiri-Wynaad (Richards 1932: 170). I shall use the past tense in the comparison, adopting the tense people usually employ when speaking about the 'traditional' way of things. However, part of what I describe as 'traditional' has bearing on their present thoughts and actions.

I shall first compare the Nilgiri Plateau (including the steep slopes and glens of the south-western, southern, south-eastern, and eastern slopes), focusing on the intertribal world of the Toda, Badaga, Kota and Kuṟumba,[4] on one hand, to that of the Mullu Kurumba, the Betta Kuṟumba, the Nayaka, the Paniya, and the Chetti[5] on the other. I, thereby show that there are significant differences between the two systems. I shall then consider the little-known isolated communities of the Toda, Badaga and Kota who live in the Nilgiri-Wynaad, and demonstrate that the relationships between these communities differ from those between their main respective groups, and instead bear the marks of the intertribal arrangements in the Nilgiri-Wynaad. For brevity, I shall call the two areas Region N and Region W, and the two intertribal worlds System N and System W, respectively.

Spatial Articulation

The first striking point of contrast between Region N and Region W is that the tribal people in Region N had, on the whole, distinct territorial riches, while in Region W they were interspersed, forming multi-ethnic clusters. Thus in Region N the Toda lived on Wenlock Downs on the western side of the Nilgiri Plateau, at elevations ranging from 2,000 to 2,400 metres (Walker 1986: 44). Badaga mainly inhabited the eastern half of the Nilgiri Plateau, at elevations ranging between 2,200 and 1,200 metres (Hockings 1980: 66). The small Kota population was interspersed amongst the Badaga, but there were no mixed villages of Badaga and Kota, nor of Kota and Toda, nor Toda and Badaga (Walker 1986: 23). Finally, Kuṟumba of various groups lived mainly on the steep slopes and glens of the south-western, southern, south-eastern, and eastern ranges of the Nilgiris, at elevations ranging from 1,600 to 600 metres (Kapp 1978: 169),[6] and their settlements furthermore appear to have been separated from the other tribes by an uninhabited zone of land between 1,300 and 1,400 metres above sea level (Hockings 1989: 11).

In contrast with Region N, in Region W tribesmen lived interspersed one village beside another. The Mullu Kuṟumba were concentrated in one area—the western Cherambod area (Misra 1971: 2)—but the Paniya, the Nayaka, the Betta Kurumba and the Chetti lived scattered throughout the Nilgiri-Wynaad—including the Cherambod area. Nayaka, for instance, were found in the northernmost flat Mudumalai sanctuary, in the southernmost Ouchterlony Valley, at the eastern border around Gudalur, and on the western side in Cherambod (Bird-David, fieldnotes). Fürer-Haimendorf reports that they 'did not possess a compact territory of their own, but share their habitat with several other tribes. It is said that even in the old times the Jen Kuṟumba [Ñayaka], lived in the same *jama* [the territory of a local group] as Betta Kuṟumba' (1952: 25).[7]

The scattered communities in Region W formed multi-ethnic localities. For example, around Erumad village there lived Mullu Kurumba, Betta Kuṟumba, Nayaka, Paniya and Chetti (Misra 1972: 3). In Thepakadu, at the eastern end of the Nilgiri-Wynaad, lived Betta Kurumba, Nayaka and Paniya.

Furthermore, the territorial division in Region N was anchored in folk history. A Kota folk story, for example, recounted that, upon their arrival on the Nilgiri plateau, the first Badaga refugees met a council of the three resident tribes—Toda, Kota and Kuṟumba—and pleaded for some land (Emeneau 1946: 157; cf. Ouchterlony 1848: 8). Badaga placenames, moreover, include names which bear reference to Toda and Kuṟumba placenames. The names probably bear witness to the displacement of Toda and Kuṟumba by the Badaga who immigrated into the area during the seventeenth century and, it seems, pushed Toda upwards and Kuṟumba downwards (Hockings 1980: ch. 2, especially p.65).

In Region W, by contrast, folk tradition concerning the location of tribal groups alluded to an absence of territorial divisions. Nayaka in the Pandalur area, for instance, related that at the beginning of time Nayaka pairs lived scattered throughout the Nilgiri-Wynaad area, and the scattered local groups of the present were descended from them (Bird-David, fieldnotes). The Chetti in Erumad said they had migrated several centuries before from the Madurai district in Tamil Nadu in search of land and—they to make no reference to other occupants—had settled where land had been found throughout the Wynaad (Misra 1972: 136).

Socio-economic Articulation

The second obvious point of contrast between Region N and Region W is that intertribal economic relationships were respectively dominated by what anthropologists commonly distinguish as 'gift' and 'commodity' relationships.[8] Thus in Region N families of the separate tribal communities were linked to one another by hereditary links which passed down from father to son, and formed the basis for traditional relationships of exchange between tribal communities. The Toda families provided their exchange partners with dairy food, the Badaga families with grain, the Kota families with utensils and craftware, and the Kuṟumba with forest produce.[9] According to the literature, the tribal communities in Region N did not provide one another with labour, nor did they engage in market transactions. Walker observes that 'economic exchange had ritual and social dimensions and took place not randomly in a market place but according to established relationships, mostly between families' (1986: 25).

The tribesmen in Region N also performed ritual and ceremonial duties for one another in exchange for ritual services and traditional exchange resources. The following example concerning the interchange between the Kuṟumba and the Badaga, has been widely recorded in the literature (Francis 1908: 154; Grigg 1880: 211; Hockings 1980: 125; Noble 1976: 118–20; Ward 1821: LXXVI). Each Badaga community had its own Kuṟumba 'watchman' with a lifelong and hereditary position. The Kuṟumba 'watchman' guarded the Badaga village from supernatural danger and in addition played a necessary role in Badaga ritual, acting as an accessory to the Badaga priest. During the Badaga sowing festival, the Kuṟumba 'watchman', for example, cut the first furrows with a plough or a ploughshare, and then sowed the first seed.

Furthermore, it seems that in Region N social interaction across the ethnic divide was mainly occasioned by, and channeled through institutionalized traditional links. As Emeneau maintained:

> communication between the symbiotic communities making up the local Nilgiri caste system is rigidly restricted to a very few channels. Members of one community

have certain well-defined rights and duties *vis a vis* members of the others. Beyond these contacts, communication hardly exists (1941: 167).

The tribal communities each had their own temples and celebrated their own festivals (Walker 1986: 23).

The literature which deals with Region W—anthropological and other—tells us little about the interrelationships between the local tribal communities. I would argue, however, that this is only because Region W lacked the kind of formal and rich ritual system of Region N, which fascinated observers. It seems that tribesmen in Region W engaged in mercantile exchange of commodities with one another. Nayaka, for instance, supplied a wide range of forest produce to meet changing demands. For example, they exchanged honey, firewood, bamboo and various spices, for rice, tobacco, metal knives, and clothes. Furthermore, tribesmen in Region W provided one another with labour in exchange for payment either in kind or in money. Paniya were engaged as agricultural serfs by land-owning peoples in the area, while other tribesmen occasionally worked for one another. In Erumad, for example, Mullu Kuṟumba worked in the fields of the Chetti, and Nayaka worked in the fields of both the Chetti and the Mullu Kuṟumba (Misra 1972: 32). Nayaka, moreover, were also employed as watchmen by other tribesmen, which brings to mind Kuṟumbas' employment of watchmen by Badaga in Region N (see p. 9). However, the difference between the two cases is striking, and it clearly illustrates the contrast I make between the two systems. While the Kuṟumba were employed as 'watchmen' to ward off supernatural danger, the Nayaka were employed to ward off predators and trespassers. While the employment of Kuṟumba was hereditary and for life, the employment of Nayaka was on a contractual payment basis, for a season and sometimes for a single day.

In contrast with tribesmen in Region N, tribesmen in Region W had common local temples and held common local celebrations. Chetti, Mullu Kuṟumba, Nayaka, Betta Kuṟumba and Paniya, for example, participated together in the celebration of the Vishnu festival in the *ambalam* (temple) of Erumad. A hierarchical order between these groups was expressed in seating arrangements as well as in dancing and ceremonial arrangements; nevertheless all the tribesmen attended and participated in the festival. They all walked in procession around the temple premises—Chetti first and after them the Mullu Kuṟumba, the Betta Kuṟumba, the Nayaka and the Paniya. In turn, they all danced around a ceremonial fire which was passed from one tribal group to the other (Misra 1972: 145-6). Multi-tribal festivals were also celebrated in the early nineteenth century. One such festival, for example, is described in Colonel James Welsh's *Military Reminiscences* (1830, cited in Raghavan 1929).

The Organizational Environment

The third feature which clearly distinguishes Region N from Region W is a uniform clan organization in the former and diverse social organizations in the latter. Thus the tribal groups in Region N, with their clear territorial and socio-economic boundaries, had similar intratribal social organization. They were divided into subgroups which were wholly or partly endogamous and were, in turn, divided into several exogamous units. Toda had two endogamous divisions; Badaga had nine relatively endogamous divisions; Kota comprised twenty-one exogamous particlans; and Kuṟumba were divided into two endogamous groups. (Walker 1986: 21, citing Hockings 1965: 44–69; Hockings 1980: 71–97; Verghese 1969: 143; Mandelbaum 1938: 574; Mathur 1977: 56–7; Nambiar and Bharathi 1965: 9; and Zvelebil 1979: 74. See also Kapp and Hockings 1989).

The tribal groups also had similar intratribal political structures. For example, the forest-dwelling Kuṟumba, who are contrasted below with the Nayaka of Region W, had an elaborate structure of offices hereditary in the patriline. In each settlement there was a village headman (*maniagara*), and a second head (*talevary*). They had two assistants (the *bandari* and the *kurudale*). Over and above the village structure, Kuṟumba had several pan-tribal offices: the priest (*mannugura*), the priest's helper (the *kanikuruma*), the diviner (*kanigara*), the exorcist (*devvagara*), and the sorcerer (*odigara* or *odia*) (Kapp and Hockings 1989: 4, 8).

Region W was markedly different. As Fürer-Haimendorf writes

> the social systems of the Wynaad tribes are diverse . . . and the social anthropologist is in the unusual position of finding within easy walking distance communities presenting several varieties and combinations of partrilineal, matrilineal and bilateral systems of descent and inheritance (1952: 36).

The Betta Kuṟumba had partrilineal exogamous clans known as *maga* (Fürer-Haimendorf 1952: 26). The Mullu Kuṟumba had exogamous matrilineal clans called *kula*, and, cutting across them, patrilocal and patrilineal kin-groups known as *kuṭumba* (Fürer-Haimendorf 1952: 28).

The Nayaka, about whom we are in a position to elaborate, were divided into territorially-based local groups: those who lived in a particular area (*jama*) constituted a group (*sime*, meaning relatives). The *sime* was highly fluid in composition. According to a bilateral pattern, individuals could associate themselves with the *jama* of either of their parents and with the *jama* of their spouses. The Nayaka had an egalitarian political organization similar to the organization found in other hunting and gathering societies, and considerably different from that of the food-gatherer Kuṟumba in Region N (see above). With two exceptions, the Nayaka had no official positions, and even the two exceptions were not political. The first was the *modale* (meaning the first to have come to the area). His main responsibility was simply to organize a festival in honour of the ancestors—a festival held every few years. The second was the shaman. This position was an achieved one and it was open to young and old, females and males. It carried no special rights and obligations outside the context of the shamanistic performance.

Social Representations

The fourth point of contrast between Regions N and W concerns the pan-regional social representation of constituent tribal communities. Communities in Region N were cast into distinct economic roles, although, as it now appears, they did not pursue exclusively the activities ascribed to them. Toda were known as pastoralists although they occasionally gathered food in the forest and took up cultivation (Walker 1986: 21). The Kota were known as artisans and musicians although, in addition to being smiths, leather workers and potters they also maintained some cultivated land and herds.[10] The Badaga were known as agriculturalists but kept some buffalo (Walker 1986: 21). Finally, the Kuṟumba were known as food-gatherers, but they also pursued shifting cultivation (Kapp and Hockings 1989), and even their 'ceremonial work' for the Badaga deviated from their stereotypical occupation in involving, as mentioned above, ploughing and sowing. The main consequence of this stereotypical representation, it seems, was to provide a basis for links of complementary specialization between the tribal communities, elaborated in the form of traditional exchange relationships.

While the tribal communities in Region N characterized themselves by accentuating differences, in Region W the differences were subdued. In terms of the Durkheimian class distinction—applied to the integration of communities within regional systems—it can be said that while System N was characterized by organic solidarity, System W was distinguished by mechanical solidarity. In marked contrast with Region N, the communities in Region W were described more uniformly as cultivators and food-gatherers, although there were significant differences in the extent to which they pursued the one or other activity. Mullu Kuṟumba, described as cultivators and hunters, were in fact settled plough cultivators who practised communal hunting only as part of their marriage celebration (Misra 1972). On the other hand, Nayaka, who were often described as food-gatherers and shifting-cultivators, planted vegetables and fruit only erratically, and then usually neglected them. On the basis of conversations with local informants, Fürer-Haimendorf writes that it was hard to establish the nature and extent of economic differences between the tribal communities.

The Nayaka in Region W and the Kuṟumba in Region N were both described as sorcerers. However, the descriptions were differently constructed; although the difference was subtle, it had morbid consequences. The Kuṟumba were viewed by their neighbours as occupying, in Turner's terms, a liminal position: they were described as being both humans and animals, within and outside the Nilgiri society; associated with danger and with sacredness. The Badaga, for instance, although they employed Kuṟumba as assistants to their priests (see p. 9), believed the Kuṟumba were able to change into insects of any sort and into mammals, that they killed and ate people and were capable of inflicting mortal epidemics.[11] Even in the 1960s, Badaga informants described incidents of Kuṟumbas turning into tigers which, they said, they saw with their own eyes; women were afraid of mice, lizards and insects, because they might have been Kuṟumbas, and everyone was afraid of walking alone in the forest (Hockings, fieldnotes).

In contrast with Region N, in Region W it was held that Nayaka behaved like animals—as opposed to turning into animals. Even in the 1970s, their neighbours related that Nayaka 'do not value shelters and, like animals, frequently sleep in the jungle', and that 'they show little concern for each other, eating like animals, food where they find it' (Bird-David, fieldnotes). Tribesmen did not fear the Nayaka. On the contrary, in what related to the forest world they made use of their knowledge and their expertise. Walking in the forest, for instance, they used Nayaka footpaths and crossed through their hamlets. They also approached Nayaka for natural medicines and for mediation with the supernatural realm, since they regarded Nayaka shamans as being very powerful.

The inordinate fear in which tribesmen in Region N held the Kuṟumba resulted in massacres of suspected Kuṟumba sorcerers. When a mishap struck Badaga or Toda, they attributed it to Kuṟumba sorcery. A Badaga party, often accompanied by one or two Toda, then took revenge on Kuṟumba families. Massacres, for example, were recorded officially in 1824, 1835, 1836, 1875, 1882, 1891, and 1900.[12] In 1835, no less than forty-eight Kuṟumbas were murdered (Thurston and Rangachari 1909: IV, 171); in 1875, six households of Kuṟumbas were massacred with axes (Hockings 1980: 200); and in 1882, one Kuṟumba family was impaled and burnt alive. A police report from 1890 describes the murder of an entire Kuṟumba family (Thurston and Rangachari 1909: IV, 171).

Silence is loud with regard to Nayaka in Region W. In official sources concerned with the Nilgiri region as a whole, there is, to my knowledge, no mention of any intertribal violence in the Nilgiri-Wynaad during the same period in which so many cases were record in Region N. Other sources make no mention of intertribal tension. We can make a case out of silence and suggest that intertribal tension, so prominent in Region N, was not found in Region W.

Finally—and symptomatic of the two systems—tribesmen in Region N spoke a great deal about 'the food-gatherer and sorcerer Kuṟumba', but knew little about the day-to-day life of the Kuṟumba people (Bird-David 1987a). While in Region W they knew a great deal about the daily practices of 'those food-gathering Nayaka who live in so-and-so place', they were reluctant to form any generalization about the Nayaka. In Region N, they regarded the local food-gathering people as *The Other*, and in Region W as others.

Regional Exceptions

Small communities of the Toda, Badaga and Kota also lived in Region W away from their main groups in Region N. The extensive literature on the Nilgiris contains only a few and scattered references to these isolated communities. However, once the references are collated and viewed as a whole, they show considerable differences between the two regions—evidence of, in all likelihood, the influence of the regional social milieu. They suggest that Badaga, Toda and Kota who lived in Region W probably adjusted themselves to their regional social world and accordingly deviated from customs and conventions of their main groups of affiliation.

One of the three divisions of the Toda's Piedr clan lived in Kavidi in Wynaad. From W. H. R. Rivers' seminal monograph on the Toda (1906)—a monograph in which this Cambridge-based founder of British Social Anthropology demonstrated the uses of the genealogical method—we can deduce that Kavidi differed from all other Toda villages in a number of ways.

Firstly, Toda normally saluted villages with a special gesture (*kaimvihkti*). Some villages were saluted by members of all the clans, and others only by members of their own clan. Only Kavidi, Rivers observed, 'had no sanctity whatever and was not saluted when seen from a distance' (1906: 703), not even by 'members of the clan to which it belonged' (1906: 420).

Secondly, it was generally believed that a deceased Toda went westward to Amnodr in the other world, crossing on their journey a river called Puvurkin, on the banks of which lived . . . 'people who belonged to all tribes' . . . (1906: 399). All Todas who were selfish, jealous and grudging during their lifetime, or who had committed any offence against the sanctity of the dairies, fell into the river, and were kept by the tribal people of Puvurkin, except for the Toda of Kavidi. 'They', wrote Rivers, 'run no danger from this source, however bad they may have been' (1906: 400).

Thirdly, Toda did not normally enter a Kota settlement for fear of being polluted. Rivers recorded only a single exception: Toda could, and did, enter the Kota village of Kalgas, near Gudalur, and even slept in that village (Rivers 1906: 636, 640). The Kota village was close to Kavidi and presumably it was the Toda of Kavidi who usually visited it. This deviant custom, furthermore, was credited to the cultural hero, Kwoten, who was the first Toda to visit the Kota village in Wynaad (Rivers 1906: 200).

Fourthly, customarily, when a man of either of the two other divisions of the Peidr clan (who lived in Region N) performed a certain ritual, a buffalo was given to the other division. However, if a man from Kavidi performed the ritual, the buffalo was given to either one of the two other divisions (Rivers 1906: 671).

Although Rivers mentioned each of these exceptions on its own, within its relevant thematic context, these deviations combine with one another to form a whole, which clearly invites consideration within a local context—i.e., the location of Kavidi outside Region N and within Region W. All these exceptions, I suggest, are evidence of a diluted presence of features characteristic of System N and are in apparent conformity with features that are characteristic of System W. The first item on the list, we can say, alludes to relative profanity; the second reflects on friendly and immediate relationships with undistinguished 'other tribes' who live in the same locality; the third further attests to intertribal friendly visits; while the fourth is an echo of a lax form of exchange ties.

A similar picture emerges from examining the Badaga Gauda of the Wynaad, who were distributed there in thirteen communities (Hockings 1980: 31, 130). They seem to have had no relationships with the Toda in the Wynaad. They did not fear Kuṟumba sorcery in a mythical way as did the Badaga in Region N, and did not accept the 'watchman' institution, so prominent in the communal life of Badaga in Region N (Hockings 1980: 130). Moreover, it seems that they did not believe that the Nayaka—their own local forest-dwelling, food-gathering people—were fearful sorcerers, and employed them, as well as other tribesmen, to work in their fields. Nayaka near Pandalur, for instance, related that during the early twentieth century they used to work in local Gauda fields (Bird 1983a: 36), and Paniya, Betta Kuṟumba and even the Kota probably did so as well (Hockings 1980: 130). Finally, the Badaga Gauda in Region W were not as strictly endogamous as they were elsewhere, and they did intermarry occasionally with the local agricultural Chetti (Hockings 1980: 32). Thus, these local variations of the Badaga tradition are in accordance with what is shown by the afore-mentioned local variations of the Toda tradition.

Conclusions

In drawing on diverse literary sources, as done in this analysis, there always remains the question concerning the credibility and completeness of data. Is our picture of the Nilgiri-Wynaad incomplete? Is it only for lack of data that there seems to be no institutionalized elaborate intertribal system in the Nilgiri-Wynaad, as was the case in the nearby Nilgiri Plateau? Or, on the other hand, is it that the projection of the complex intertribal system in the Nilgiri Plateau was exaggerated precisely because so many accounts concerned themselves with it. In each account references in previous studies were taken as evidence. The evidence provided the basis for further generalizations, and the generalizations, in turn, were taken as evidence in subsequent accounts. Thus, cumulatively—as Winnie the Pooh in search of the Heffalump—commentators further enriched the 'evidence' for, and the articulation of, the traditional intertribal system in Region N.

It is hard to know for certain. It is likely, in fact, that there is a grain of truth in both possibilities. However, the differences between the regional systems are remarkably consistent and, in the light of the comparison, each regional system seems in itself to be highly intra-consistent. On the one hand, in the Nilgiri-Wynaad (in comparison with the Nilgiri Plateau), we have an intertribal system wherein constituent ethnic groups are largely mingled. On the whole, they do not accentuate too much the economic differences between them, and they hold common local festivals. Moreover, by and large, in day-to-day life, tribesmen are linked to one another by informal ties. On the other hand, on the Nilgiri Plateau (in contrast with the Nilgiri-Wynaad) we have a regional system wherein constituent ethnic communities maintain clear ethnic boundaries: they each have their own festivals and emphasize their distinct economic occupations. In addition, they regulate intertribal interaction socially through institutionalized economic, political and ritual means.

I would further note that while it is true that we have only sparse sources on the Nilgiri-Wynaad, it is highly likely that a major contributory factor for that is precisely that there was no elaborate intertribal system there, as found in the Nilgiri Plateau. The pluralistic and fluid nature of intertribal relationships in the former area did not attract observers' attention—customarily inclined towards ritual-rich ceremonialism and formal structures—as did the structured and formal intertribal relationships in the latter area.

Thus, notwithstanding the aforementioned reservations, I suggest that there is a strong case for the existence of two kinds of intertribal worlds in the Nilgiris. They constitute two types of system which respectively dominated the ways in which local peoples and their observers constructed the 'traditional' intertribal worlds in the

Nilgiri-Wynaad and the Nilgiri Plateau. Whether these traditional worlds reflected accurately the actual, historical intertribal worlds in the two geographic areas is another question and one which deserves close scrutiny.[13]

The existent extensive literature on the Nilgiris has not been concerned with, let alone examined, the intertribal world of the Nilgiri-Wynaad. Perhaps this essay will encourage basic ethnographic research in the area, neglected for far too long in favour of the Nilgiri Plateau. It is hoped, furthermore, that in offering a systematic outline of the differences between it and the Nilgiri Plateau, the inquiry will provide an analytical matrix for the fluid and pluralistic intertribal world in the Nilgiri-Wynaad, as well as an impetus for broader regional examination which include the Nilgiri-Wynaad. When continuing research further explores the two Nilgiri intertribal worlds, the well-established Nilgiri scholarship will have to reconsider old questions,[14] and raise some new ones.

Notes

1. This essay was written during my stay in Cambridge as the Smuts Visiting Fellow in 1990–1. I am grateful to the Managers of the Smuts Memorial Fund for their assistance. I am also grateful to Paul Hockings for his generous help throughout the many years which have passed since I began my work with the Nayaka of the Nilgiris. This essay originally appeared is *Modern Asian Studies* 28 (1994: 339–55) and is reproduced here with slight corrections by kind permission of the editor and publisher of the journal.
2. The major spell of fieldwork was conducted during 1978–9, and was financed by grants from the Smuts Memorial Fund, the Anthony Wilkin Studentship, and the H.M. Chadwick Studentship. The return visit was financed by the Horowitz Institute for Research of Developing Countries, and the Jerusalem Foundation for Anthropological Studies.
3. On aspects of recent changes, see Bird-David (1992a), Hockings (1980), and Walker (1986).
4. The Irula are not mentioned much in the literature, but their position is accepted as being similar to that of the Kurumba. See Hockings (1980).
5. Except for the Nilgiri Plateau, the tribal population of the Nilgiris, especially of the Nilgiri-Wynaad, has been confusingly described under many names. We probably still do not know all its ethnic constituents, but see Zvelebil (1981) and Bird-David (1987a).
6. Hockings (1989: 11) positions the Kurumba at 1500 metres down to 450 metres above sea level.
7. Paniya and Chetti were scattered equally widely. See figures 2 and 4 in Richards (1932).

8. See Appadurai (1986) for a recent discussion of this distinction.
9. For recent discussion, see Walker (1986: chapters 1 and 3) and Hockings (1980: chapters 4 and 5).
10. Fürer-Haimendorf in fact describes them as 'substantial cultivators' who 'were probably the first agricultural population in the highlands' (1950: 126).
11. See Hockings (1980: 123), drawing on Harkness (1832: 84-5), Metz (1864: 116-17), Thurston and Rangachari (1909: I, 86) and Thurston (1912: 232-3).
12. Hockings (1980: 200), citing Breeks (1873: 65), Grigg (1880: 299, 411), Stokes (1882: *passim*), Francis (1908: 155), Thurston and Rangachari (1909: 1, 86), and Tignous (1911: 155). See below, pp. 296–300.
13. With respect to the Nilgiri see below, pp. 296–300. Plateau, see Bird-David (1987a) on the Kurumba.
14. For example, in speculating on the origin of the Toda, Rivers (1906, chapter 30) attached considerable importance to the fact that Toda did not show any reverence for the Toda settlement of Kavidi. He thought that it went against the hypothesis of their arrival on the Nilgiris from Malabar.

References

Appadurai, A. (ed.). 1986. *The Social Life of Things : Commodities in Cultural Perspective.* Cambridge: Cambridge University Press.

Bird, N. (subsequently Bird-David). 1983a. 'Conjugal Families and Single Persons: An Analysis of the Naiken Social System', Ph. D. dissertation, Cambridge University, UK.

——— 1983b. 'Wage-gathering: Socio-economic Change and the Case of the Naiken of South India'. *In* P. Robb (ed) *Rural South Asia: Linkages, Change and Development.* London: Curzon Press, pp. 57–89.

Bird-David, N. 1987a. 'The Kurumbas of the Nilgiris: An Ethnographic Myth?' *Modern Asian Studies* 21, 1, 173–89.

——— 1987b. 'Single Persons and Social Cohesion in a Hunter-gatherer Society'. *In* P. Hockings (ed.) *Dimensions of Social Life: Essay in Honor of David Mandelbaum.* Berlin: Mouton de Gruyter.

——— 1988. 'Hunter-gatherers and Other People: A Re-examination'. *In* T. Ingold, D. Riches, and J. Woodburn (eds.) *Hunters and gatherers I: History, Evolution and Social Change,* Oxford: Berg.

——— 1989. The Nayaka: 'An Introduction to the People and the Ethnographic Myth, *In* Paul Hockings (ed.), *Blue Mountains: The Ethnography and Biogeography of a South Indian Region,* New Delhi: Oxford University Press, pp. 249–80.

——— 1990. 'The Giving Environment: Another Perspective on the Economic System of Gatherer-hunters'. *Current Anthropology* 31(2), 183–96.

———— 1992a. 'Beyond The Original Affluent Society: A Culturalist Reformulation'. *Current Anthropology*.

———— 1992b. 'Beyond the Hunting and Gathering Mode of Subsistence': Culture-sensitive Observations on the Nayaka and Other Modern Hunter-gatherers'. *Man*.

Breeks, J. W. 1875. *An Account of the Primitive Tribes and Monuments of the Nilagiris*. London: India Museum.

Emeneau, M. B. 1941. 'Language and Social Forms: A Study of Toda Kinship Terms and Dual Descent'. *In Language, Culture and Personality: Essays in Memory of Edward Sapir*. Menasha, Sapir Memorial Publication Fund, 158–79.

———— 1946. *Kota Texts*. Pt. University of California Publications in Linguistics 11: 191–335.

Fox, R. G. 1963. 'Caste Dominance and Coercion in the Nilgiris'. *In Papers of the Michigan Academy of Science, Arts and Letters* 48, 493–512.

Francis, W. 1908. *The Nilgiris* (Madras District Gazetteers), Superintendent, Government Press.

Fürer-Haimendorf, C. von 1950. 'Youth-dormitories and Community Houses in India. A Restatement and a Review'. *Anthropos* 45, 119–44.

———— 1952. 'Ethnographic Notes on Some Communities of the Wynaad'. *Eastern Anthropologist* 6, 18–32.

Gould, H. A. 1967. 'Priest and Counterpriest: A Structural Analysis of Jajmani Relationships in the Hindu Plains and the Nilgiri Hills'. *Contributions to Indian Sociology* (n.s) 1, 25–55.

Grigg, H. B. 1880. *A Manual of the Nīlagiri District in the Madras Presidency*. Madras: E. Keys, Government Press.

Harkness, H. 1832. *A Description of a Singular Aboriginal Race Inhabiting the Summit of the Neilgherry Hills, or Blue Mountains of Coimbatoor in the Southern Peninsula of India*. London: Smith, Elder and Co.

Hockings, P. 1965. 'Cultural Change among the Badagas, a community of Southern India', Ph.D. dissertation, University of California, Berkeley.

———— 1978. *A Bibliography for the Nilgiri Hills of Southern India*. New Haven, Connecticut: Human Relations Area Files, vols I-II.

———— 1980. *Ancient Hindu Refugees: Badaga Social History 1550–1975*. The Hague: Mouton.

————(ed.) 1989. *Blue Mountains: The Ethnography and Biogeography of a South Indian Region*. New Delhi: Oxford University Press.

Kapp, D. B. 1978. 'Childbirth and name-giving among the Ālu-Kurumbas of South India.' *In* R. R. Moser and M. K. Gautam (ed.), *Aspects of Tribal Life in South Asia 1: Strategy and Survival,* Berne: Studia Ethnologica Bernesia 1, 167–80.

Kapp, D. B., and P. Hockings. 1989. 'The Kurumba Tribes'. *In* P. Hockings (ed.), *Blue Mountains: The Ethnography and Biogeography of a South Indian Region,* New Delhi: Oxford University Press, pp. 232–47.

Keys, W. 1812. 'A Topographical Description of the Neelaghery Mountains from a letter by William Keys, Assistant Revenue Surveyor to W. Garrows, Collector of Coimbatore.' *In* Grigg (1880) XLVIII-LI.

Mandelbaum, D. G. 1938. 'Polyandry in Kota society'. *American Anthropologist* 40: 574–83.

——— 1941. 'Culture Change among the Nilgiri tribes'. *American Anthpologist* 43: 19–26.

Mathur, P. R. G. 1977. *Tribal Situation in Kerala.* Trivandrum: Kerala Historical Society.

Metz, J. F. 1864. *The Tribes Inhabiting the Neilgherry Hills: Their Social Customs and Religious Rites,* 2nd edition. Mangalore: Basel Mission Press.

Misra, R. 1971. *Mullu-Kurumbas of Kappala.* Calcutta: Anthropological Survey of India.

——— 1972. Inter-tribal Relations in Erumad. *Eastern Anthropologist* 25: 135–48.

——— 1989. 'The Mulla Kurumbas'. *In* P. Hockings (ed.), *Blue Mountains: The Ethnography and Biogeography of a South Indian Region,* New Delhi: Oxford University Press, pp.304–18.

Nambiar, P. K., and Bahrathi, T. B. 1965. *Census of India* 1961, vol. IX, Madras, Part VI, Village Survey Monograph 20 Hallimoyar, Delhi: Manager of Publications, Govt. of India.

Noble, W. A. 1976. Nilgiri Dolmens. *Anthropos* 71: 90–128.

Ouchterlony, J. 1848. Geographical and statistical memoir of a survey of the Neilgherry Mountains, under the superintendence of Captain J. Ouchterlony 1847. *Madras Journal of Literature and Science* 15, 1–138 [1849].

Raghavan, M. D. 1929. 'Jain-Kurumbers: An account of their life and habits.' *Man in India,* vol. IX: 54–65.

Richards, F. J. 1932. 'Notes on the cultural geography of the Wynaad'. *Indian Antiquary* 61: 170–4, 195–7.

Rivers, W. H. R. 1906. *The Todas.* London: Macmillan.

Stokes, W. 1882. 'Mission Work amongst the Badagas and Other Hill Tribes on the Nilgiris'. *Harvest Field* 3: 169–70.

Thurston, E., and K. Rangachari. 1909. *Castes and Tribes of Southern India,* 7 vols. Madras: Government Press.

——— 1912. *Omens and Superstitions of Southern India.* London, Leipzig: T. Fisher Unwin.

Tignous, H. P. J. A. 1911. 'In the Nilgherries'. *Illustrated Catholic Missions,* 26: 99–102, 116–19, 154–7.

Verghese, I. 1969. 'The Kota', *Bulletin of the Anthropological Survey of India* 18(2): 107–82.

Walker, A. R. 1986. *The Toda of South India: A New Look.* Delhi: Hindustan.

Ward, B. S. 1821. 'Geographical and statistical memoir of a survey of the Neelgherry Mountains in the Province of Coimbatore made in 1821 under the superintendence of Captain B. S. Ward, Deputy Surveyor-General'. *In* Grigg (1880), LX-LXXVIII.

Welsh, James. 1830. 'Wynaud'. In his *Military Reminiscences; Extracted from a Journal of nearly Forty Years' Active Service in the East Indies;* 2: 12–17. London: Smith, Elder, and Co.

Woodburn, J. 1980. 'Hunters and gatherers today and reconstruction of the past'. *In* E. Gellner (ed.), *Soviet and Western Anthropology,* London: Duckworth.

Zvelebil, K. V. 1979. *The Irula (Erla) Language.* Wiesbaden: Harrassowitz, Neuindische Studien 6.

——— 1981. 'Problems of identification and classification of some Nilagiri tribes: Irula-Uralis, Kattu Nayaka/Jenu Kurumba, Solegas'. *Anthropos* 76: 467–528.

The Megalithic Graves of the Nilgiri Hills and the Moyar Ditch

ALLEN ZAGARELL

3

The Nilgiri mountains have represented a special problem for those interested in the Megalithic phase of South Indian development. Since the reports of individuals like Captain Congreve (1847) and finally the excavations of Breeks (1873), in the nineteenth century, the region has been of particular interest to archaeologists. At first glance the megalithic monuments which dot the crests of hills in the upper reaches of the Nilgiri mountains were thought to have been simply variants of the widely dispersed Megalithic cemeteries found throughout much of southern India—the so-called 'Pandukal' tradition (Leshnik 1974). However, increasingly, the Nilgiri graves come to be seen as a phenomenon unto themselves, different from the so-called Pandukal Megalithic tradition (Gururaja Rao 1972: 104). These cemetery complexes were viewed as extraordinary, corresponding to the remarkable indigenous inhabitants of this mountain zone. These indigenous mountain peoples, especially the Toda buffalo pastoralists, were seen as something unique. They were romanticized as holdovers from a more glorious past. They were compared to the lost tribes of Israel, to the Romans, to the Sumerians of southern Iraq (Walker 1991, Peter 1951, Francis 1910:138) and remnants of the ancient buffalo herders of neolithic South India (Allchin 1963). The assumption of the antiquity, the primitiveness of the highlanders was contained in the suggestion that the well-known economic and ritual symbiosis of the various highland communities, the agriculturalist Badagas, the pastoral Todas, the crafts-oriented Kotas, the hunting/gathering Kuṟumbas and Irulas, possessed a *jajmani*-like relationship. These groups were seen as being proto-like in form. Yet, unlike the castes of the lowlands, the participating groups were not believed to have been integrated through the presence of coercive groups, by state or urban authorities (Fox 1962). Thus, the unique nature of the Nilgiris, along with their distinctive monuments, and the extraordinary relationships of its inhabitants, was understood as the consequence of the relative isolation of the Nilgiri region. The singular character of the upper Nilgiri people was the result of an island-like isolation (Hockings 1980: 7). Hockings testifies to the regional isolation of the Nilgiri mountains. He describes the Nilgiri life as relatively peaceful, the tribes possessing 'no militia or weapons of war', and which operated 'a complicated system of intertribal economic and ritual exchange that was based firmly on trust' (Hockings 1989: 365). He suggests that malaria-causing Plasmodium parasites, which can reach up to the 1400 metres mark, caused there to be an uninhabited zone around the hills, creating the island-like character of the Nilgiri Massif (Hockings 1989: 369).

This area was seen as developing on the periphery of Indian civilization, relatively untouched by broader South Indian culture. Most scholars do not suggest that the Nilgiris were totally untouched by lowland events but that these connections were not viewed as long-lasting or as basic to Nilgiri traditions. For example, Walker (1989:187) notes the 'long isolation of the Nilgiris from centres of South Indian learning, and the former lack of writing among all the Nilgiri peoples . . .'. In his monograph on the Todas, Walker notes that the extreme physical contrasts between the Nilgiri highland and the surrounding plains afforded the Toda and other Nilgiri peoples a marked though never total isolation from the mainstream of Hindu society (Walker 1986:20). Mandelbaum writes 'that the Nilgiri system [was not] supported by a state and guarded by a panoply of rulers and lawgivers. In pre-British times, the Nilgiri peoples occasionally paid taxes, irregular tribute may be a better term, to one feudal lord or another from the environing gentry, but the hand of the government was not otherwise felt in the hills' (1989:182). Despite the enormous knowledge, scholarly ability and erudition of those cited above, this view is certainly wrong. I will show that the upper hills had extensive, long term relationships with surrounding state and complex societies. Indeed, the inhabitants of the upper plateau were seen as particularly interesting to 'historical evolutionists' because of the island-like isolation of the region (Walker 1991: 27, citing Rooksby 1971), giving insights into earlier societies through the supposed more pristine-like conditions prevailing in the Nilgiris.

As the inhabitants of the hills were unique, the supposed consequence of relative isolation, so too did the peculiar inventory and types of the Nilgiri Megalithic monuments appear to give testimony to the relative isolation of the region. The Megalithic monuments were understood, quite early, as diverging from the types typifying much of the remainder of South India during the Megalithic period (Breeks 1873). Highland cemeteries were broadly recognized as later in time than the Megalithic structures dotting much of South India (Naik 1966, Leshnik 1970 and 1974, Hockings 1976, among others, in this regard). Given the supposed isolation of the area, much of the research into the region's ancient monuments emphasized the search for the indigenous Nilgiri ethnic group responsible for constructing these monuments. This search for ethnic authorship can already be read in Congreve (1847: 77 *et passim*). Breeks suggested the Todas as most likely responsible for Nilgiri Megaliths (1873: 97 *et passim*). Indeed, archaeological concern for ethnic origins was typical of world archaeology during the nineteenth and early twentieth century (Trigger 1989), but this interest has continued to dominate Nilgiri scholarship. Quite recently, there has been a reaffirmation of the Toda responsibility for the construction of the monuments (Noble 1976, for example). The graves have also been ascribed to Kuṟumba groups from the north (Metz 1864, Shortt, and Ouchtelony 1868, Naik 1966, Hockings 1976). On the other hand, Kapp has assembled considerable evidence for the current Kuṟumbas as the creators of much of the Nilgiri Megalithic culture (Kapp 1985).

The search for ethnic responsibility for the construction of the Megalithic complex is not the main concern of this essay. Rather, the goal is to gain some insight into the organizational, social and ritual significance of these graves. In general little attention has been given to the symbolism inherent in these megalithic cemeteries or their societal and historical context. Clearly the regional graves and cemeteries are burial places, but they are certainly much more. As suggested below, they are centres for multi-faceted community ritual, and therefore are congealed community symbolism. Based upon information from these cemeteries, I will attempt to give some insights into the type of society that built some of these monuments, and the regional context in which the Nilgiri cultures developed.

The Geographical Context

The Nilgiri mountains create a powerful impression when viewed from the plains. The green, forest-covered slopes seem to disappear into the clouds. From certain directions the massif appears unscaleable, sheer cliff reaching to the heavens. The traditional area is approximately 2,400 square kilometres and rises 2,636 metres in height (Lengerke and Blasco 1989: 21). Along its upper stretch it deceptively transforms itself into rolling hills, surrounding verdant, fertile valleys, intermittent forest and green pasture. The upper area is rich with moisture, receiving up to 5000 millimetres of precipitation, although amounts vary considerably from area to area. Much of the Moyar Ditch, along the northern rim, receives 1000 millimetres or less (Lengerke and Blasco 1989: Fig. 3.3). The Plateau itself had a high agricultural potential. Indeed, the successes of agriculturalists in the highlands give some indication of what might have been possible. The upper areas were the homes of the Todas, Kotas and Badagas when first described by British scholars in the nineteenth century. The hill slopes, on the other hand, are heavily forested, less amenable to intensive agriculture,and historically the home of the Kuṟumba and Irula hunting/gathering/shifting agricultural economies. Much of the Nilgiri mountain region is surrounded by rivers, emanating from the mountains themselves. The south, southeast, and eastern zones are separated from the plains by the Bhavani river. The Nilgiri side of the river is still thickly covered with forest, in stark contrast to the cultivated fields to the south and east. The lowlands immediately to the south of the Nilgiris represent one of the few openings through the Western Ghats, a mountain spine that runs along the southwest coast. The Palghat gap connects Kerala and the western coast with the plains of Tamil Nadu and eventually the east coast of India. This gap was one of the major historic thoroughfares for trade, integrating India with large parts of world.

Immediately to the north of the Nilgiris is the Moyar Ditch, a depression bounded by the Nilgiri mountains and the Mysore Plateau. It is traversed by the Moyar river, which runs along the entire length of the northern Nilgiris, joining the Bhavani river along the northeast. From Mangalipatti eastwards the Moyar flows through the heart of the ditch, close to fields potentially quite suitable for agriculture. West of Mangalipatti, the river sits within a gorge, separated by hills from the village areas, until Hundi Moyar, where it runs along the edge of the plain around Masinagudi. The ditch is extremely well-watered by a series of vigorous streams and rivers, including the Sigur river, the Kedar Halla (Anikatti), the Kukaltorai behind Tengumarahāḍa, the Gundegal Halla, east of Halimoyar, the Kotagiri and Pattikambai Halla near Kallampaliyam, among many others. The region, as a whole, has a very high potential for agriculture, although the western half of the Ditch does not give the impression of being potentially as rich as the eastern half. Today this area is the home of Irula and Kuṟumba groups, various hunting/gathering/less intensive agricultural peoples. It is in this area that I carried out much of my work. Research was done over a period of four seasons of archaeological survey, two of which were concentrated in the Moyar Ditch.

The western border of the Nilgiris consists of a series of descending hills, called the Wynad, leading to the heartland of Kerala. The Wynad had close ties historically to the Nilgiri area and peoples. As stated above, many researchers believed that the Nilgiri Hills were only tangentially influenced by events in the plains. When the British arrived they found much of the footland area and the lower slopes overgrown, largely abandoned, except for tribal peoples, and menaced by malaria and other epidemics. Most drew the conclusion that this reflected earlier conditions. This belief in the marginality of the region tended to be continued by researchers. As I will show, the northern Moyar Ditch area was inhabited by relatively large populations for extended periods of time, who abandoned the region comparatively recently. Moreover, the northern Moyar Ditch must be understood as closely tied to the upper Nilgiris, It is crosscut by traditional 'tribal'/community pathways up the mountain—these include pathways from Kallampaliyam, Tengumarahāḍa, Halimoyar, Anikatti, below Ebanadu, and along the Sigur river. Most routes take a few hours to climb. I have regularly seen people doing so. Malarial conditions could not have stopped the Moyar populations from climbing the hills, since they were already inhabiting potentially malarial areas. Not only could contact have taken place, I will show that there is much evidence of contact throughout the Megalithic period and beyond (Zagarell 1993 for inscriptional and narrative evidence of contact). Indeed, it is impossible that regularized contact did not take place.

Megalithic Culture in the Greater Nilgiri Region

The upper Nilgiri region has several Megalithic grave types. Breeks describes the grave types of the Nilgiris as consisting of

a) cairns are a circular enclosure formed by rough stone walls or heaps, or by single stones. These include a type peculiar to the Nilgiri mountains, the draw-well type. These are corral-like structures, built up of varied sized stones, or small boulders, open in the centre.

b) barrows consist of a mound of earth encircled by a ditch or sometimes by one or more circles of stone.

c) cists are constructed of large stone slabs, closed on every side, occasionally with a 'porthole' in one of the walls. It may or may not be surrounded by a stone circle or tumulus (cairn). Breeks states that these cists are called 'Moriary Mane' by the Badaga inhabitants of the region.

d) azarams, which are simple stone circles in which relics preserved from the Toda green funerals are burnt (Breeks 1873: 77).

Cairns, barrows and azarams are said to be the most common forms. Cists are rare, only reported from Udairaya Fort below Kotagiri, along the eastern section of the hills. The reports generally do not offer much to differentiate the types according to grave finds. Finds include various crudely made vessels of orangish or reddish ware. Many of these vessels are unique in Indian circles, including vessels resembling multiple stacked vessels. (See Naik 1966 for a description of forms and types).

Figurines, which are common, include anthropomorphic and zoomorphic forms. Mounted and armed males wearing conical head-dresses and cross belts over their chests, and women with simple skirts and bangles typify the figurines. Males have clipped beard and moustache, and males and females are characterized by hair combed upwards into a bun (Leshnik 1970: 90). Animal figurines comprise both wild and domestic animals, including multiple buffalo figurines, often decorated with garlands, vestments and wearing of bells around their necks. Other domestic animals include the horse, often mounted by riders. Objects of iron, copper, bronze and gold accompany the other small finds. These metal objects include iron swords, knives, spearheads, and arrowheads. They also include iron billhooks, sickles, razors, shears and beautifully constructed bronze vessels. Additional grave goods include jewelry and beads. While the pottery is thought to be locally produced, the bronzes are believed likely to have been imported (Leshnik 1974: 261). That most of these sites were graves is evidenced by the frequent appearance of burnt bone.

Clearly the 'burials' were not of an entire individual, but appear to represent selected parts of individuals. Several graves appear to have consisted of multiple interments (Leshnik 1970: 88 for apparent multiple urns containing bone). Also note the grave 'Toda and his two wives', five kilometres west of Kotagiri, to the north of the Ootacamund/Kotagiri road, in the central plateau area where multiple cist-like graves are found.

What can these graves tell us? We will take a preliminary look at some aspects of construction, contents and spatial distribution of the graves and cemeteries on the upper plateau. We shall then compare them with the monuments of the Moyar Ditch and will then attempt a broader analysis of their significance.

Most researchers dealing with the region agree that the graves are to be dated somewhere during the first millennium AD (Naik 1966, Leshnik 1970 and 1974, Noble 1976, Hockings 1976), although the range suggested within the first millennium varies considerably. In general I accept the range offered by Leshnik (from the fourth through the sixth century; the Gupta Period) although I do not automatically exclude the later dates. However, to a significant degree the later dates rest upon a single ^{14}C date (Hockings 1976). Clearly, a single ^{14}C date cannot be overly relied upon without confirmation from other sources. Contamination is quite possible given the possibility of roots and other carboniferous materials intruding into the grave. Nevertheless, it seems certain that megalithic practices and specifically grave construction continued for a considerably longer period in the Nilgiri highlands than in most areas displaying the typical 'Pandukal' megalithic inventory. As will be suggested below, the megalithic cult appears also to have continued in the Moyar region, intimating some degree of contemporaneity.

The grave goods indicate a society much more complex than any other society reported upon by early British researchers. In fact, I suggest that if we did not have the ethnographic reports, researchers would have been more likely to ascribe the finds to organizationally complex societies, more state-like than the acephalous or weakly led groups characterizing historic Nilgiri life. Well armed individuals on horseback, iron technologies, military weapons, and luxury bronze vessels imply a complex society. Certainly, whichever ethnic group or groups may have been represented in the complex of Megalithic graves, these groups did not resemble the societies presently occupying the Nilgiris. Even the multiple buffalo figurines, found in connection with the burials, which have led many to look to the Todas as the group responsible for the graves, do not necessarily suggest nomadic groups *per se,* but only a society with a sizeable pastoral aspect, typical of several upper Plateau groups. As we shall see, the evidence below indicates real leaders and an administered society.

The upper plateau does seem to have represented some broad form of cultural unity. Clearly, most of the graves must have belonged to peoples sharing closely certain cultural beliefs. The orientation of most of the graves north-east/south-east (Breeks 1873: 93, 99) implies a cultural optimum, which separates these builders from those of the neighbouring lowlands (where an east-west orientation for megalithic graves is the norm). Similarities in pottery and burial objects, metal types, styles of figurines, depiction of human types, etc., also indicate a broad cultural homogeneity. And yet there are significant variations in grave types and cemetery layouts.

Breeks first noted a basic difference in distribution of Megalithic graves in the upper plateau. He divided the graves into three groups, suggesting the typical and richest group in contents is found in the central area of the Nilgiris, in the region around Tuneri. Another group is found west of the Sigur road, along the western Nilgiris. There the pottery was cruder, more poorly fired and the figurines more clumsily made. The cairns in the west appear to be the most poorly constructed, he noted. In the region to the east, between Kotagiri and Kodanad (Peranganad) the cairns were thought to be quite similar to those near Tuneri. However, the figurines were stated to be smaller, rougher and darker in colour, and the pottery varied in detail from other sites (Breeks 1873: 94-6). Thus Breeks suggested regional variation corresponding to the agricultural potential of the region, which certainly implies an agriculture-oriented society, not a fully nomadic one. Similarly, in the southwest area, the Kundas, relatively few graves were found, indicating significant regional variation. Indeed, in my view, it suggests the builders of the megaliths were not strictly nomadic or operating under other social or political restraints. One wonders why more graves are not found in that area, which is still least attractive for agriculture, if we are dealing with strict pastoral nomads. Most of the Megalithic sites are found along the northern section of the plateau. Moreover, most sites sit atop hills. It has been suggested that the high average elevation for such graves corresponds to the elevations utilized by the Todas. But the elevations utilized simply reflect the fact that the crests of hills are being utilized for burials. These graves are often immediately above agricultural communities, but a half hour's walk to the top of the hill. The total number of graves appear to have been relatively high (Gururaja Rao 1972: 107); hundreds were reported in the Ootacamund area alone, although each cemetery is small, apparently never more than seven graves (barrows/cairns/draw-wells) as opposed to the much larger cemeteries in the lower areas. Moreover, graves generally form a straight line along the crest of a hill, rather than the larger, somewhat more dispersed type of the Moyar region.

There are many other variations in the context of broad cultural similarities discussed above. Some draw-well graves apparently differ from simple cairns and, indeed, there are even variations among the draw-well graves themselves. For example, above Kilkotagiri, overlooking the Moyar Ditch, is a line of seven draw-well graves (Noble 1976: 95)—or perhaps eight if one counts the smaller, much cruder (newer?) circle further down the hill. These seven circles are literally covered with fragments of figurines, overwhelmingly buffaloes. These poorly baked figurines appear to have been intentionally smashed. The fragments are placed under stones making up the circle. Horns, legs, torsos, skulls, perhaps well over a thousand cover the surface. Among the fragments are also less numerous potsherds of the same ware (Fig. 3.11).

A similar situation could be seen at Kalhatti, where several graves had been destroyed. Covering the surface of the field were hundreds of figurine fragments of domesticated buffalo (Fig. 3.12).

On the other hand, a site like Ammalle, a draw-well site above Havvur, has only rare bits and pieces of pottery nearby. Clearly, very different activities must have taken place at these sites, and, it seems fairly certain that these sites fulfilled different functions despite similarity in form of monument. One suspects that the sites covered with large numbers of figurine fragments may have been the focus of rituals performed over an extended period of time. Significantly, the stone circles at Seven Fort Hill were called corrals by one Kota informant. This individual, an inhabitant of the nearby Kota community of Kilkotagiri, also claimed that activities in connection with these circles were held regularly by the local Kotas approximately fifty years ago. This was, however, vehemently denied by another member of the community, Kambutan, a Kilkotagiri priest.

On the crest of a hill is another draw-well-like site, the 'Toda and His Two Wives', five kilometres west of Kotagiri, which has multiple (three) chambers nearby, suggesting the name of the site. The grave is quite dissimilar to most Nilgiri cemeteries. Moreover, these chambers built off to one side are much more finely built than the simple cists of the lower region. Also a short walkway leads to the centre of the grave. Another variant can be found on the extreme northeast of the plateau, near Udairaya Fort, where there is a series of cist graves. These sites are said to be oriented in an east-west direction, similar to the typical lower-level/Moyar Ditch site. Breeks reports that a very different pottery is found at the cist sites than in those excavated from most Nilgiri megaliths. The pottery is said to carry a thick glaze (Breeks 1873: 106). It may be that this handful of sites contained red wares similar to that found in the lower regions, although that must remain speculative (Noble 1989: 114). Another variant is a group of sites observed at Havvur, near the Lingayat temple on the crest of the hill. Facing east are two large, undecorated dolmens, called *Mauriya Mane* by the local population. Approximately nine metres directly to the west we find small stones (menhirs) which seem to provide an entranceway forty centimetres wide. Shortly before I arrived the local people had uncovered and dismantled two large stone circles (the exact type is unclear) while clearing an area for a tea plantation. The boulders were piled nearby and the surface covered with sherds typical of the Nilgiri Megalithic. At this site the ritualized nature of the place and its connection with dolmens, normally thought unconnected with grave complexes, indicate that these sites are not only graves, but may represent foci of more regularized ritual activities.

Although it has been suggested that the Nilgiris were first settled approximately around AD 100 (Noble 1976: 98), there is very strong evidence for an earlier utilization of the hills. At Valerie Kombai, on the eastern hill slopes, facing Mettupalaiyam, is a rock face whose upper section is painted with anthromorphic and zoomorphic representations in a 'Mesolithic style' although not necessarily of

Mesolithic date (Brooks and Wakankar 1976, Neumayer 1982, for descriptions of the various styles). The lower face, to the northeast, is painted in Chalcolithic style. At Kuṟumban Alai, along the northeastern Nilgiri slope, above the Sigur river, is a small cave site, whose outer face is decorated with figures in a Neolithic style. Neolithic settlement of the Moyar region is also suggested by the appearance of ground stone axes reportedly discovered in the Masinagudi vicinity (pl.7). Moreover, crushed within the Kuṟumban Alai cave is a black polished vessel and, nearby, below and to the southeast, is an undecorated shelter covered with polished blackware sherds, similar to wares discovered at some of the megalithic sites along the Moyar Ditch. More significantly, along the slopes above Tengumarahāḍa, to the north, at the painted shelter site of Wananga Pazham, are found sherds of typical black-and-red ware, characteristic of the megalithic of the Moyar Ditch. Clearly the slopes were being utilized at a time preceding the AD 100 suggested range and apparently were utilized during the zenith of the Pandukal Megalithic period. This all suggests that the Nilgiris experience is historically connected with events unfolding in the lower region.

Extraordinary evidence, relating to the Nilgiri megalithic phase, may be found at the small rock shelter of Wananga Pazham (Fig. 3.10). At this site a few shards of standard lowland black-and-red ware appear. But most importantly, the site is decorated with multiple paintings of animals and humans. These paintings relate to the Nilgiri Megalithic period. The paintings, however, were not all applied at one time, and therefore all are not contemporary. There are possible hints of red paint at one point, underlying white-painted layers of figures. Among the earliest depictions are squares with stylized figure-like representations within. There are also occasionally wild animals underlying the later paintings. The major scene is a huge battle scene, with armed soldiers mounted upon elephants and horses. Those painting the pictures seemed to have identified with the elephant riders. A hero stands upon the back of an elephant. In his left hand he holds a battleaxe, on which the wrapped material hafting can still be seen. The hero wears a turban-like head-dress and about his neck hangs some sort of emblem on a chain—most likely a lotus-like pendant. He may be naked, although that is uncertain. Another smaller figure on the left-hand rock face also wears a turbaned cap, although he does not appear to be of the same importance as the mounted individual. The major figure, in the centre of the painting, is also an elephant rider. He sports a special, rounded cap, and has a pig-tail(?) trailing behind. He carries something in his left hand, which I cannot interpret—possibly a shield or symbol. In his waistband is a knife, the handle of which can be seen. His elephant, like the others represented, also wears a turban-like head dress. Significantly, these figures appear very similar to those in the Nilgiri reliefs. Thus they are quite possibly individuals from the north—from the Mysore plain. These individuals face in the opposite direction to the horse-rider between them. He holds the reins of his horse in his right hand. Interestingly, he wears a pointed cap, quite distinct from the elephant riders. Moreover, he seems to have a short beard. Thus he looks quite similar to the figurines found in the Nilgiri graves.

The connection to the upper Nilgiri Megalithic graves is still more evident in the form of several decorated animals and objects. Towards the right side of the cave are several figures which are decorated with a series of dots, similar to the punctuation marks on the Nilgiri figurines. Among the figures depicted are the head and an outstretched leg of a cow/bull, similar to Nandi depictions; another rectangular figure, which might represent a boar's head; and some kind of emblem, near the cattle head, part of which resembles a tower-like structure found on top of a Nilgiri grave vessel. Dots are also used at several other points. Certainly earlier than the fighting figures are a series of six and eight armed figures surrounded by dots. They are painted with a darker cream-like white paint, underlying the brighter white of the fighting figures. These figures, interpreted as possible cattle at other sites, are certainly human-like figures, as they can be seen to be walking on two feet. Their multiple arms suggest, however, that they are gods, rather than humans. One eight-armed figure is either pierced with a sword or is carrying one at his waist. A very similar figure can be seen at Akkathangachimoruvar, another rock shelter somewhat west of Wananga Pazham, along the Kukkaltorai.

The Wananga Pazham site also contains several other peculiar representations which connect this site with the Nilgiri Megalithic. At two points on the rock face there are depictions of hut-like constructions. One on the lower right hand section is painted in the earlier cream white, whereas the second, slightly above and to the left, is chalk white in appearance. Within these structures are small circles. Significantly, within one of those circles, and most probably within the second, is the drawing of a prone figure. I assume these figures are individuals fallen in battle who are being buried—in something which appears similar to Megalithic circles. Other circles appear without the hut-like representation, at least one of which clearly contains the figure of an individual. Others have something within the circles but whether they are human figures is unclear. These burials suggest and depict battle and the death of a hero; but what we see at Wananga Pazham is a type of hero-stone—the depiction, mourning and celebration of an heroic death.

The peculiarities of this site do not end here. On the second row to the left side of the scene, just to the right of a figure riding a horse or possibly a horned animal, is a painting of a rather stylized elephant. To its right is the figure of another animal, which seems to be tethered to a large standing stone. The figure is crude and, although it appears more cat-like at first glance, may depict a cow or bull. Although any interpretation must remain speculative, tying of an animal to such a tethering stone is typical of local animal sacrifices, common in the region when first encountered by the British. There are other strange goings-on. On the extreme lower right is a row of what appear to be crudely rendered dancing figures (notice the legs on some of the stick figures) before an open section of an otherwise enclosed area—or possibly a raised structure. Within the area is a square structure open on one side. Is this a dolmen or a 'temple-like' structure found commonly among present villagers?

Towards the bottom of the site is the skull of a bull, sitting on what seems to be a stand, facing another horned animal, which stands before a cart-like structure. This depiction reminds one of the descriptions by Francis of some elements of Kota funerals, although I am not suggesting a direct correspondence. He writes that at Kota funerals a wooden cart decorated with cloth is placed in front of the dead man's house and a buffalo is killed and the flesh distributed. Several practices remind one of Kota practices—but there is no suggestion that the painting itself has anything to do with the Kotas *per se*—simply that certain practices were already in vogue. Again, several of the scenes indicate a death scene and a representation of heroism. There are paintings of a much later date having a large bird-like creature in the middle of the painting.

The Moyar Ditch Megalithic

The lower region, along the Moyar Ditch, appears to have been utilized at least since the neolithic period. A ground stone axe in the possession of the proprietor of the Bamboo Inn near Masinagudi indicates a possible Neolithic population (pl. 7). This is supported by the shelter Kuṟumban Alai which contains neolithic-style paintings on a stone block along the Sigur slopes. Clearly there was utilization of this region before the advent of the Megalithic period of settlement. Nevertheless, the Megalithic period appears to be the best represented period. Over thirty-five sites within the Moyar area have been located. These sites surely do not represent all the Megalithic sites in the Moyar Ditch area. I feel certain that more intensive work would lead to a discovery of new sites. Still, the number of cemeteries, their distribution, size, and diversity, tell us some important things about Megalithic life along the northern border of the Nilgiri mountains.

Most of the Megalithic sites are found along or near rivers or along seasonal stream beds. This may not be a true representation of real distributions. Many of the sites discovered are within a few kilometres of inhabited villages. These sites are more likely to have been known to villagers than sites at greater distances from the villages. However, the tribal inhabitants travel widely in the Ditch area, and are likely to be aware of the larger cemeteries distributed within the broader Moyar region. Therefore, I suspect, I have located a significant number of the larger cemeteries, while many smaller sites almost certainly remain to be found.

The fact that many sites are located along rivers, within the range of fertile fields, indicates that these people had an agricultural component. Many of the sites are near areas either presently irrigated, or suitable for simple irrigation regimes. This is furthermore supported by the fact that areas that are dry and unsuitable for simple irrigation show few Megalihic sites—for example, much of the area north of Masinagudi seems to be devoid of Megalithic sites, except along the Sigur river area. The large cemeteries at some of the prime agricultural areas indicate sizeable populations, perhaps connected to real village life. For example, near Tengumarahāḍa, several grave sites exceeding 200 graves each can be found (TM 1 and 2) as well as several other smaller cemeteries. On the other hand, no villages have been located dating to this period with certainty. This lack of village sites does make an agricultural interpretation less likely. Nevertheless, I strongly suspect that we are dealing with communities carrying out some agricultural activities, similar to what appears to have been the case in other areas (Begum 1991: Ch. 2), This is not to deny the probability of a strong pastoral component, utilizing the slope and riverine resources. Indeed, the appearance of Megalithic pottery on the Nilgiri slopes, connected with several rock shelters, would indicate this to have been the case.

Approximately 3,000 graves have been located (based upon a mixture of firm count and estimates). As stated, there were certainly more cemeteries in the past (several cemeteries seen have experienced considerable destruction), and many remaining to be found. Moreover, many of the graves have multiple cists, strongly suggesting multiple interments. Megalithic graves appear to be more common than Irula cemeteries distributed about the same region, thus suggesting populations larger than present-day tribal levels. Population levels would therefore appear to have been comparatively high, although the time element—how long such cemeteries were being constructed—would clearly be important to determine. And indeed there is some reason to believe that a Megalithic grave cult continued somewhat later in the Moyar region than in some other neighbouring regions.

The layout of the cemeteries tells us something about the societies involved in constructing them. There are indications that we are dealing with some sort of a segmented society. Although some of the cemeteries are quite large (with over 200 graves), the cemeteries do not appear to have been constructed as single units, simply expanding over time. Rather than a cemetery which starts at a particular point and then expands outward as time goes on, the Moyar Megalithic cemeteries appear to have been constructed out of several small groups of graves separated from one another by negative space. Over time some of these spaces were filled in by other groups of graves. Some of the cemeteries found (although rare) consist of little more than one small group of three to six graves, while others such as Thottapatti 1 are clearly made up of several spaced but related groups of cairns and capped cists (see Fig. 3.9). Indeed, many of the cemeteries appear to have been broken up into larger groups of graves, with negative spaces left between them (McConkey 1992; see Vazhaithottam 4, Vazhaithottam 1, and Tengumarahāḍa 2, for example).

The layout of the cemeteries suggests that we are dealing with segmented groups, probably kin-related groups, where close family members are grouped together in various sections of the cemetery. This closely corresponds to the burial practices of some of the Irulas. The Irulas are the tribal people who presently dominate the Moyar Ditch area. They were hunter/gatherer/extensive cultivators when reported upon by the British. The Irulas are divided up into several clans, each having a familial burial ground. Individuals are brought back to these ancestral family grounds to be buried, from wherever they die. Nuclear and extended family groups are buried together or near one another under small cairns. The family section, at one site viewed in the Moyar area, is marked by a memorial stone which faces east. The burial sector of the clan covers a still larger area. In other localities, near some of the Mariamman temples, belonging to various villages, there are simple stone circles where individuals have been buried. Space always separates the various clan burial grounds.

Interestingly, the Thottapatti (TP1) cemetery, although broken into several clearly discrete groups, does seem to have had a unity which encompassed the entire cemetery. At the extreme western end of the cemetery are two very large adjacent graves. These two graves (both are 12 m in diameter) are as large as any of the other graves. They are similar to the two very large adjacent graves found bordering the site of Tengumarahāḍa 2 on the extreme east. Again both sites are approximately the same size, 22 m each. Similarly, at the site of Vazhaithottam 1 (VZ 1), three very large, adjacent graves form a line down the middle of the site. This may have once been the border of the site (McConkey 1992). This suggests a symbolic significance for the larger bordering graves, perhaps identifying the cemetery with significant community or kin figures.

The identification of the cemeteries with different groups, with somewhat different traditions, appears obvious. Many of the cemeteries are characterized by varying grave types. Several sites are divided into different spatial areas characterized by Megalithic grave complexes. This is particularly clear in the case of VZ 2, where the site consists of two relatively equal halves. The northern half of the site consists only of stone circles; the southern half is entirely made up of cairns and capped cists. Similarly, at Chokanali (VZ 4), east of the village of Vazhaithottam, the site again is divided between cairns and circles. At Kallampaliyam 3, to the west of Kallampaliyam, near the Doddamariamman cave, are two closely connected sites. Indeed, in this case the two sectors are separated by negative space. To the east are simple cairns. To the west are cairns, with dolmen-like structures, cists, caps, but many of the graves are surrounded by tall menhirs surrounding the site, forming an arch above several of the graves (pl. 6 and Fig. 3.16). Again at Mangalipatti we see the spatial division of types. On the eastern side of the river, the area is divided into two major areas. The southern section has large number of small stone cairns—simple stone piles (which are probably later than the larger cairns). Perhaps a hundred metres separate this area from the main area of the cemetery where one finds cairns, cists and capstones. On the western side of the river, directly across from Mangalipatti 1, in Mangalipatti 2, one finds large stone circles constructed with huge boulders. These graves include cists and capstones.

Further suggesting the segmented nature of Moyar area settlement patterns is the fact that many cemeteries consist of a single type of grave. For example, Tengumarahāḍa 1 is made up of circles, often surrounding barrows, frequently with cists and capstones as well as dolmenoid cists. The stones making up the circle are often huge boulders, up to 1.4 m tall. On the other hand, the graves found in the nearby cemetery of Tengumarahāḍa 2 are generally cairns, with cists and caps. There are no boulder and barrow graves in Tengumarahāḍa 2. Note the quite different distributions of the mapped sites characterizing otherwise similar and large cemeteries (Fig. 3.21). Comparable stone circles are found alone at Budykupee, along the northeastern fringe of the Moyar Ditch. Another fact suggesting an ethnic basis for grave construction is the concentration of similar but distinct types in various sections of the plains. For example, the standing megaliths surrounding many graves are concentrated exclusively in the Kallampaliyam area. However, to the east of Halimoyar, in the direction of Kallampaliyam, are several sites, some of which have small menhirs in the centre of the graves.

These sites are certainly not only simple cemeteries that were destined just for burials. Many of the cemeteries seem to have had a more extensive ritualized symbolic nature. The most significant example of this symbolism is found at the site of Vazhaithottam 4 (Chokanali). At that site, within the cemetery, along its western corner is a clear dolmen, 75 cm high and 87.5 cm in length. The dolmen must have once faced west. The dolmen is surrounded by a wall, creating a rectangular open area 13.6 by 9.4 m. The rectangle is divided in half by the remains of a raised area towards its east, on part of which stand the remains of the dolmen. This rectangular structure appears very similar to structures found at many contemporary Irula as well as Kuṟumba cemeteries. These structures and the dolmens within them hold small boulders representing the dead of the particular community clan. Not insignificantly, the structure and its dolmen at VZ 4 are connected with a compact group of graves to the south of the site, clearly separated from other graves. To the north, seemingly more connected with a northern group of graves, is a menhir. A third standing stone appears with a small group of graves to the east (McConkey 1992). Although menhirs occasionally mark urn burials these menhirs should be compared to several Irula cemeteries where menhirs represent family groups (see above). Another such rectangular structure is found at the cemetery site of Thottapatti (TM 1), although free of a dolmen. A dolmenoid cist, however, can be seen directly opposite the rectangle (Fig. 3.9). Small dolmens, probably related to rituals connected with these graves, can be found at several other sites including Kallampaliyam 3 with its canopies of menhirs (see Sami Koil Mukkai, Fig. 3.6). Similarly at Makupatti, not far west of Anikatti, a dolmen bordering a Megalithic cemetery to its north can be found. Additional dolmens in close proximity to Megalithic cemeteries can also be found at Sedapatti (discussed later).

Several other sites contain other clearly symbolic elements. At Tengumarahāḍa 2, at Padathottapatti (TP 3), Vazhaithottam 3, and Thatakurlipatti are lines and low walls of stone separating the outside from the inside of the site. The remaining lengths of these walls range up to 100 m at some sites (VZ 3, for example, although not noted on McConkey's map). The existence of such low walls, often no more than a line of stones, implies that these cemeteries are sacred areas, separate from a secular outside. At one of these sites, Padathottapatti (TP 3), there is an added element: all the graves at this site are cairns, except for one circle, which sits atop a hill, just west of the remainder of the graves. This circle contains a dolmenoid cist, 1.8 by 1.07 m in width, facing southeast rather than east-west as do the cists of the other circles. This layout leaves the impression that the circle had a symbolic, ritual function, raised above and differentiated from the other monuments.

Two sites, Thatakurlipatti, northwest of Tengumarahāḍa, already mentioned in connection with walls surrounding the site, and Kotai Moollai, near Kallampaliyam, stand out from other sites with regard to clear ritual evidence (Fig. 3.8). Thatakurlipatti, along the northern bank of the Moyar river, has a single, very large, dolmenoid cist, surrounded by a stone circle constructed of boulders, standing in the middle of a broader area. Nearby are foundations of a series of former structures, and a row of menhirs towards the centre of the site. These structures certainly relate to this central, dolmenoid grave. Use of the site is reflected in the massive distributions of medieval pottery found over much of the surface. Further to the north is the major cemetery area, where a series of modestly-sized cairns, devoid of cists and caps, can be found. The site appears to have been once surrounded by walls, the remains of which can still be discerned. Certainly, there was something about this grave which was worthy of special attention and veneration.

Kotai Moollai is still more remarkable. This site consists of several very large rectangles of dressed menhirs (Fig. 3.7 a.b). These rectangles range up to 19.5 m in diameter. On their surface (at least areas 1 and 2) are found much loose brick and large amounts of sherdage. These are otherwise rare on the site. The bricks suggest once standing structures and the proliferation of pottery points to activities occurring on these squares, apparently ritual in nature. There are lines of stone, forming walkways at various points within the site and the remnants of a taller wall which cross-cuts the site. Moreover, in the extreme northeast corner of the site are concentrated a sizeable number of small stone cairns, similar to those in the southern section of Mangalipatti and perhaps Thatakurlipatti, noted above. At Kotai Moollai are the remains of low walls or walkways near the small cairns. Both these sites are certainly more than simple cemeteries. Both certainly were the venues of complex ritual activities. There are reasons to believe that these sites, at least in part, are considerably more recent than the other Megalithic sites discussed. Both were covered with massive amounts of pottery lying on the surface—quite distinct from the remainder of Megalithic sites. The pottery also varied from those typical of the Megalithic period. The pottery was of a medieval type found at many other Moyar Ditch sites.

The Moyar cemeteries, although largely of the cairn, cist, and stone circle genre, show considerable variation. The two sites of Thatakurlipatti and Kotai Moollai stand out—but they are not alone—in their distinctiveness. Two others—one at Sedapatti, and another nearby cemetery, across from Sedapatti, at Vazhaithottam itself—manifest considerable differences from other sites.

The Sedapatti site occurs in conjunction with a village. The remains of fallen huts and piles of small stones packed in the mud plaster cover the hillside. The pottery at the site largely consists of grey slipped and self-slipped wares, including spouted vessels, otherwise not found at any site. Also badly corroded pieces of metal (iron), including hinges for boxes, were found near the surface. To the extreme north of the site is a graveyard made of stone circles and cairns, as well as two sizeable dolmens, just south of the graveyard. The dolmens, strangely enough, point north, rather than opening to the east, as is typical of most of the area's dolmens. Just north of the dolmens is a simple large circle, 10.20 m in diameter, made up of numerous small boulders. In its centre are four small stones forming the corners of a square. This appears quite different from most of the circular graves or stone circles of the lower region, and may have an entirely different function than the typical graves. Immediately adjacent are a series of small cairns, some with capstones. Although these more closely approximated the typical Moyar Ditch cairns, they seemed smaller than most graves at other cemeteries.

A second site, which was certainly not typical, is no longer standing, apparently destroyed by road-builders. Just southeast of Vazhaithottam there were a series of small, white, quartzite circles. These were near the present village of Vazhaithottam and in the vicinity of a series of dolmens, one of which carried an inscription of the fifteenth century (which I assume date much later than the burials—although the graves might have been quite late). One of the other dolmens carries a relief probably dating to the Vijayanagar dynasty. Within the area are the remains of a temple also dating to that broad time span. These graves indicate a long tradition of Megalithic structures, which I suggest, overlap to some significant degree the graves of the upper Nilgiris.

Dating the Moyar Megalithic

The pottery found scattered among the many plundered graves indicates a date consistent with the mainstream Indian Megalithic tradition—the so-called Pandukal tradition. The pottery types include typical black-and-red wares, black polished ware, and a cruder red, sometimes polished, ware. At several sites together with this pottery there were found cruder red buff wares, similar to some of the cruder pieces collected from the upper Nilgiri region. The cruder red wares often seem to belong to larger, multi-footed vessels, possibly urns. The pottery was not evenly distributed. Most of it was found in connection with disturbed graves. However, most sites contained no disturbed graves and, therefore, offered no pottery for collection. The cemeteries were generally free of any surface pottery not emanating from illegally excavated graves. However, at Kallampaliyam 3 and 2, red ware could be found distributed over much of the surface while the graves did not appear to have been tampered with. This might indicate that some activities occurred there after the dead were interred, which did not occur at other sites. Pottery is of course also found at sites like Kotai Müllai and Thatakurlipatti which does appear to have been utilized for some sort of ritual activity, although it seems to be considerably later than most sites.

Moyar Megalithic Society

What can we say about the organizational structure of Moyar Ditch society? No clear habitation sites have been discovered, which indeed seems odd, given that the distribution of cemeteries suggests an agricultural orientation. Sedapatti and Makupatti represent possible settlements. But neither contain the black-and-red ware, polished black ware, not the polished red wares connected with standard Moyar Megalithic sites. Both these sites might be quite late. I have suggested that the Moyar Ditch Megalithic economy may have combined pastoralism and agriculture. More certainly, however, the cemeteries and the graves indicate a segmented, kin-based society (as discussed above, similar to the social organizational forms noted for the Kuṟumbas and Irulas). The relatively large cemeteries suggest a similarly high level of corporateness if my guess about the form of community is correct. The areas occupied by individual segments, I have suggested, are relatively limited in size, again implying something less than fully specialized, undifferentiated nomadic groups. There are also indications that the society is socially ranked, to some degree. The differences in grave size suggest differential labour input in grave construction. The extreme cases such as the high cairn grave of Kalala Mirda, southeast of Hundi Moyar (see Fig. 3.6), 19.5 m in diameter on the top of the grave, up to 22.5 m at the base, sharply contrast with simple stone circles, frequently no more than 1 m in diameter at many sites. This particular grave, sitting on the very top of the hill crest, was clearly special. This cairn with cist grave on top is quite large, but still within the range of the very largest graves at other sites. However, the grave is surrounded by thirty-six dressed, rectangular slabs, forming a circle along the outer rim of the cairn. Moreover, the entire surface of the grave is covered with white quartzite boulders. This grave is extraordinary and represents a particularly high concentration of expended labour. Similarly, the very large graves along the outer edge of some sites (Tengumarahāḍa 2, Vazhaithottam 1, and Thottapatti 1) also suggest differences in labour input and presumably status, as does the singular prominent circle grave of Thatakurlipatti, with the apparent ritual attention paid to it. The Vazhaithottam 1 site, with its three very large graves topped by huge capstones up to 2.7 m in diameter, again indicates that labour was not evenly expended on the various graves.

The suggestion of significant status hierarchy among Moyar Megalithic peoples is further supported by the rather skewed distribution of grave sizes at many Moyar Megalithic sites. Although some sites show simple bell-curve-like distributions (K4), this is not the case at most other sites (Figs. 3.15–3.22). If grave sizes are simply a function of a natural range of variation, disparity in size is not necessarily an indicator of status, authority or class differences. Bell-curve distributions indicate a range of distributions, some of which are simply on the far end of the curve. However, most sites indicate skewing of the curve. The vast majority of graves are concentrated in the small to very small categories. The larger sites decrease quite rapidly in frequency, but small numbers of quite large graves extend the graph's range considerably. Moreover, there is often an interruption in the flow of site size, suggesting that the very largest of graves are in a class of their own, clearly separated from the large number of small and simple graves of most cemeteries. This in turn implies a conscious construction of particularly large graves, and a probable symbolic function for them.

There are very significant differences between the cemeteries of the upper and lower regions—although there may indeed have been some span during which Moyar and upper Nilgiri Megalithic activities coexisted. Certainly the specifics of grave construction, orientation, and probable grave goods differ considerably. This may have simply reflected the ethnic differences between the two regions. But significantly, the cemetery systems of the two areas demonstrate wide divergences. Most important, according to me, is the fact that the upper Nilgiri cemeteries consist of only a small group of graves. While their number may go up to seven, generally we are speaking of considerably fewer graves in any cemetery. This contrasts with cemeteries of well over two hundred graves in the Moyar region. Rarely does one find a cemetery consisting of so few graves—and then, one presumes, they were in the process of increasing in size. While the Moyar cemeteries are often constructed of smaller, compact units, which I have suggested are smaller (minimal) kinship units and which could conceivably reflect similar conditions to those underlying the upper Nilgiri situation, they soon blossom into much larger complexes of such units. This never seems to happen in the upper regions.

The grave goods of the upper Nilgiris certainly relate to domestic concerns, reflecting household economies, minimal kinship units, which would seem at first glance to tie the lower and upper Nilgiri Megalithic societies together organizationally. But the fact that these units are not combined into supra-household cemeteries on the Plateau indicates that the upper and lower Nilgiris were organized differently. Moreover, it hints at the possibility that the Nilgiri graves have a very different symbolic significance than do the lower cemeteries. As discussed above, apparent variation in upper Nilgiri graves indicates that such graves had more than one symbolic role in earlier society. The lone grave sitting atop a prominent hill, one of the several dotting nearby hills, implies something much different than a simple burial-place for some lone individual, although I am presently unable to suggest the particular functions of various grave constructs. A modern form potentially analogous to these lone graves might be a monument constructed on one of the upper Nilgiri hills, near Denadu. The monument consists of a foundation, a small stela, on top of which a fire is periodically burnt. It supposedly represents one of the Badaga clans in the region. Do some of the upper Nilgiri sites represent kin symbols, community corporateness, regional and territorial claims, similar to the Akka Bakka stones of Badaga communities? Clearly, in form the upper graves are similar to—although significantly different than—the Moyar Valley sites. Grave goods and proximity to contemporary Megalithic traditions and complex societies suggest contact, perhaps some aping of lowland high-status traditions.

The lower region certainly represented an important area. During the Pandukal period, it was intensively utilized. Shortly thereafter, it was inhabited by state organized or influenced society. During the period suggested for the upper Nilgiri cemeteries the Moyar region was a civilized, stateorganized centre. Sites like those of Sitarampatti on the southern edge of Tengumarahāḍa which include statuary and architecture from the seventh to the ninth century, and inscriptions from the tail end of the first millennium, and southeast of Hundi Moyar with an inscription from the ninth century, suggest that the Moyar Ditch was an important region either during or shortly after the period of upper Nilgiri Megaliths. Thus an area clearly within sight of the upper Nilgiri inhabitants—sitting just below Kodanad and Ebanadu—was a complexly organized entity during the proposed Nilgiri Megalithic period. Tribal tracks connecting ditch and heights demonstrate the relative closeness of the two regions.

It appears quite probable that the upper Nilgiri Megalithic culture did not develop in a vacuum. Rather the region seems to have been in direct and significant contact with neighbours. Indeed, the possible coexistence of some of the Moyar Megalithic complexes and the upper Nilgiri graves has been considered. Moreover, there is strong evidence that areas immediately bordering on the Nilgiri hills were already integrated into state level society during the major period of high plateau Megalithic construction. This is attested to by trade routes, temple complexes and Megalithic cults in the Moyar. Furthermore, the Wananga Pazham material suggests real leaders, members of complex societies, leading major forays (at the very least) into the Nilgiri Megalithic phase. While there are many paintings of 'Chalcolithic' or Early Historic date which indicate such intervention (Totinalai, Sigur I, Valerie Kombai, and Akkathangachimoruvar have such themselves), Wananga Pazham appears to relate to the Nilgiri Megalithic more directly.

The picture that seems to emerge is not of an isolated region so often assumed in works about the Nilgiri mountains, but rather a region and a people regularly and significantly pulled into the orbit of complex political structures. This is certainly true of later periods. There is no reason to assume that the symbiosis of Nilgiri groups, the exchange of community products, is simply the autonomous creation of local groups, but rather the interplay of kin-based groups and state societies creating caste-like relations. Certainly, local upper Nilgiri traditions seem to remember little concerning earlier contact. However, as I have discussed elsewhere (Zagarell 1993), those memories are faulty. There is now strong documentary evidence demonstrating regular state intervention in the region. Much work remains to be done despite the several projects carried out in the area. There are many surprises to come.

Notes

1. I would like to thank the Fulbright Foundation, the Smithsonian, and the American Institute of Indian Studies for variously funding aspects of my research during the years 1983, 1984, 1988, 1991. I am furthermore grateful to Western Michigan University for providing me with equipment and research grants and for putting at my disposal computer facilities adequate to deal with my data. But most of all I would like to thank my many Indian colleagues and friends who have helped me carry out my work within the Nilgiris. Dr. Gururaja Rao, Professor of Archaeology at Mysore University, has been an important source of advice and inspiration. Dr. K.V. Ramesh has given me invaluable help in the gathering of the inscriptions and in providing translations of the texts. Special thanks go to my dear friend Professor Basavalingam of the Government Arts College, Ootacamund, who has inspired me with his dedication to Nilgiri history and on whom I always could rely. I would also like to thank friends and colleagues Mr. Kuruvilla and Mr. Pungadan, as well as the people of Moyar and the Nilgiris, without whose help this work would have been impossible. Thank you.

REFERENCES

Allchin, F.R. 1963. *Neolithic Herders of South India.; A Study of the Deccan Ashmounds.* Cambridge: Cambridge University Press.

Begum, Shanawaz, M.E. 1991. 'The Megalithic Culture of South Karnataka'. Doctoral thesis, for Department of Ancient History and Archaeology, Manasagangotri: University of Mysore.

Breeks, J.W. (ed. S.M. Breeks) 1873. *Primitive Tribes and Monuments of the Nilagiris.* London: India Museum.

Brooks, R.R., and V.S. Wakankar. 1976. *Stone Age Painting in India.* New Haven: Yale University Press.

Congreve, Harry 1847. 'The Antiquities of the Neilgherry Hills, including an Inquiry into the Descent of the Thautawars or Todars.' *Madras Journal of Literature and Science,* 4. pp. 77–146.

Emeneau, M.B. 1946. *Kota texts.* Berkeley, Los Angeles: University of California Press.

——— 1984. *Toda Grammar and Texts.* Philadelphia: American Philosophical Society.

Fox, Richard. 1962. 'Caste Dominance and Coercion in the Nilgiris'. *Papers of the Michigan Academy of Science, Arts and Letters,* 48.

Francis, W. (ed.) 1908. *The Nilgiris.* Madras: Superintendent of Government Printing.

Grigg, H.B. (ed.) 1880. *A Manual of the Nilagiri District in the Madras Presidency.* Madras: E.Keys, Government Press.

Gururaja Rao, B.K. 1972. *The Megalithic Culture in South India.* Mysore: Prasaranga Press.

Harkness, H. 1832. *A Description of a Singular Aboriginal Race inhabiting the Summit of the Neilgherry Hills, or Blue Mountains of Coimbatoor, in the Southern Peninsula of India.* London: Smith, Elder.

Hockings, P. 1989. *Blue Mountains: the Ethnography and Biogeography of a South Indian Region.* Delhi: Oxford University Press.

——— 1976. 'Paikara: An Iron Age Burial in South India'. *Asian Perspectives,* 17–18: 26–50.

——— 1980. *Ancient Hindu Refugees: Badaga Social History, 1550–1975.* New Delhi: Vikas.

Kapp, D. 1985 'The Kurumbas' Relationship to the "Megalithic" Cult of the Nilgiri Hills South India' *Anthropos,* 19: 1985: 493–534.

Lengerke, H. von, and F. Blasco. 1989. 'The Nilgiri Environment' in P. Hockings, (ed.) *Blue Mountains: the Ethnography and Biogeography of a South Indian Region.* Delhi: Oxford University Press.

Leshnik, L.S. 1970. 'A suggested Dating for the Antiquities of the Nilgiri Plateau, South India'. *Acta Praehistorica et Archaeologica* 1.

——— 1974. *South Indian 'Megalithic' Burials, The Pandukal Complex.* Wiesbaden: Franz Steiner Verlag GMBH. [Appendix A: The Date of the Nilgiri Antiquities].

Mandlebaum, D.G. 1989. 'The Kotas in their Social Setting' in P. Hockings, (ed.) *Blue Mountains: the Ethnography and Biogeography of a South Indian Region.* Delhi: Oxford University Press.

McConkey, D.K. 1992. 'A Survey of a Number of Megalithic Complexes in Tamil Nadu, Southern India'. Unpublished MA Thesis for Anthropolology, Western Michigan University.

Metz, J.F. 1864. *The Tribes Inhabiting the Neilgherry Hills: Their Social Customs and Religious Rites.* 2nd edition. Mangalore: Basel Mission Press.

Naik, Iqbal Abdul Razak 1966. *The Culture of the Nilgiri Hills with its Catalogue Collection at the British Museum.* London: Ph.D. dissertation, University of London.

Neumayer, E. 1982. *Indische felsbilder.* Vienna: E. Neumayer.

Noble, W. 1976. 'Nilgiri Dolmens (South India)'. *Anthropos,* 71: 90–128.

——— 1989. 'Nilgiri Prehistoric Remains' in P. Hockings ed. *Blue Mountains: the Ethnography and Biogeography of a South Indian Region.* Delhi: Oxford University Press.

Peter, H.R.H. 'Possible Sumerian Survivals in Toda Ritual.' *Bulletin of the Madras Government Museum* 6 vol.1 pp. 1–24.

Ritti, S. 1990. *South Indian Studies.* H.M. Nayak, B.R. Gopal (eds.). Mysore: Geetha Book House.

Rooksby, R.L. 1971. 'W.H.R. Rivers and the Todas'. *South Asia,* vol.1 pp. 109–21.

Shortt, J., and J. Ouchterlony. 1868.

Trigger, B. 1989. *A History of Archaeological Thought.* Cambridge: Cambridge University Press.

Walker, A.R. 1986. *The Toda of South India: A New Look.* Delhi: Hindustan Publishing Corp.

——— 1996 'The Western Romance with the Toda'. [See below, pp. 106–135.]

Zagarell, A. 1993. 'Folk Traditions and State Rule in the Nilgiri Mountains of South India.' Presented at the Annual Meeting of the Michigan Academy, Western Michigan University, March 5–6, 1993.

Pottery Figures

figure 10:
a-c; heavy mineral tempering on surfaces, orange-buff surfaces, brown-black core, poorly baked.
d; handmade, quartzite temper, buff ware, red-brown slip, very uneven surfaces, black inner surface, black core.
e; handle and part of vessel, mineral temper, very uneven surfaces, brown surface, black core.
f; jar, hand/wheelmade?, heavy mineral tempering, pocked internal surface, brownish-buff, black core, poorly baked.
g; handmade, badly weathered, heavy mineral on surface, brownish buff, hints of red slip, poorly baked, black core.
h; handle?, orangish buff, heavy mineral temper, internal surfaces very uneven.
figure 12:
Lower Mangalipatti; wheelmade, heavy mineral, black and quartzite temper, brown surfaces, brick red core.
Kallampaliyam; large grit temper, much mineral on inside, pitting on outside surfaces, orange ware, hints of red slip, thick black core.
Lower Mangalipatti; wheelmade, mineral temper, purplish surface.
Wananga Pazham; wheelmade, very fine quartzite and larger black mineral temper, red polished outside, inside uneven black polished, some black on rim.
VZ2 gr18; handmade?, grit temper, reddish brown ware, poorly baked, black core.
Lower Mangalipatti; jar rim, heavy mineral temper, reddish purple surfaces, reddish brown core,
TM2 gr7; wheelmade, quartzite and grit temper, black polished ware, hard baked.
TM2 gr63; wheelmade, quartzite/grit, black-polished ware, hard baked.
TM2 gr63 as above.
Kallampaliyam; much large to fine grit/red and glitter, orange ware, red slip outside, black core.
figure 13:
a; wheelmade, very fine glitter (quartzite?) temper, red slip inside and outside surfaces, black core.
b; very fine glitter (quartzite?) temper, orange ware, reddish slip outside, black-gray inner surface.

c; wheelmade, very fine glitter temper, reddish brown ware, red brown slip inside and out.
d; wheelmade; very fine glitter, light brown ware, red slip on both surfaces, black-brown core.
e; wheelmade, quartzite/grit temper, reddish brown surfaces, hard baked.
f; wheelmade, very fine fibre temper, red ware, thick black core.
g; jar cover, wheelmade, very fine glitter, purplish on outside, brown/gray core.
h; wheelmade; very fine quartzite, red brown ware, red slip.
i; wheelmade, fine quartzite temper, red brown ware, purplish outside, redder inside surface, black core.
j; wheelmade, very fine glitter, red brown ware, red polished slip on outside, light brown core.
k; wheelmade, quartzite temper, brown/red inside, black/dark red outside, well baked.
l; mineral and very fine fibre, very brown ware, completely black core.
m; handmade, some mineral on outer surface, uneven outer surface, orange crude ware, black inside surface, scraping on inside surface, black core.
n; wheelmade, quartzite temper, reddish brown in colour, well baked.
o; wheelmade, minerals on surface, orange surfaces, blackened on upper, hand perforation.
p; wheelmade, quartzite temper, reddish brown surfaces, well baked.

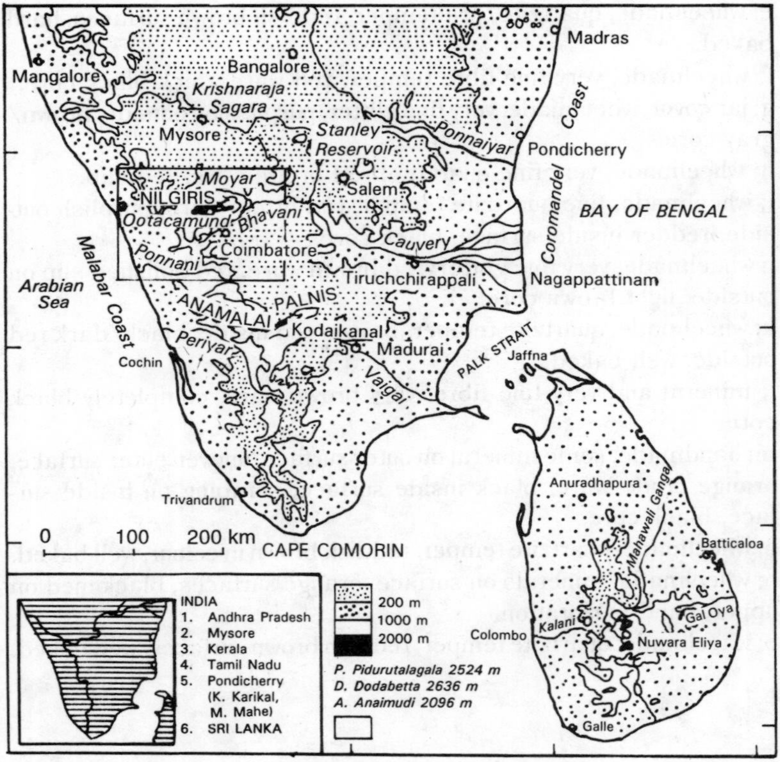

Fig. 3.1 Location of the Nilgiris in South India

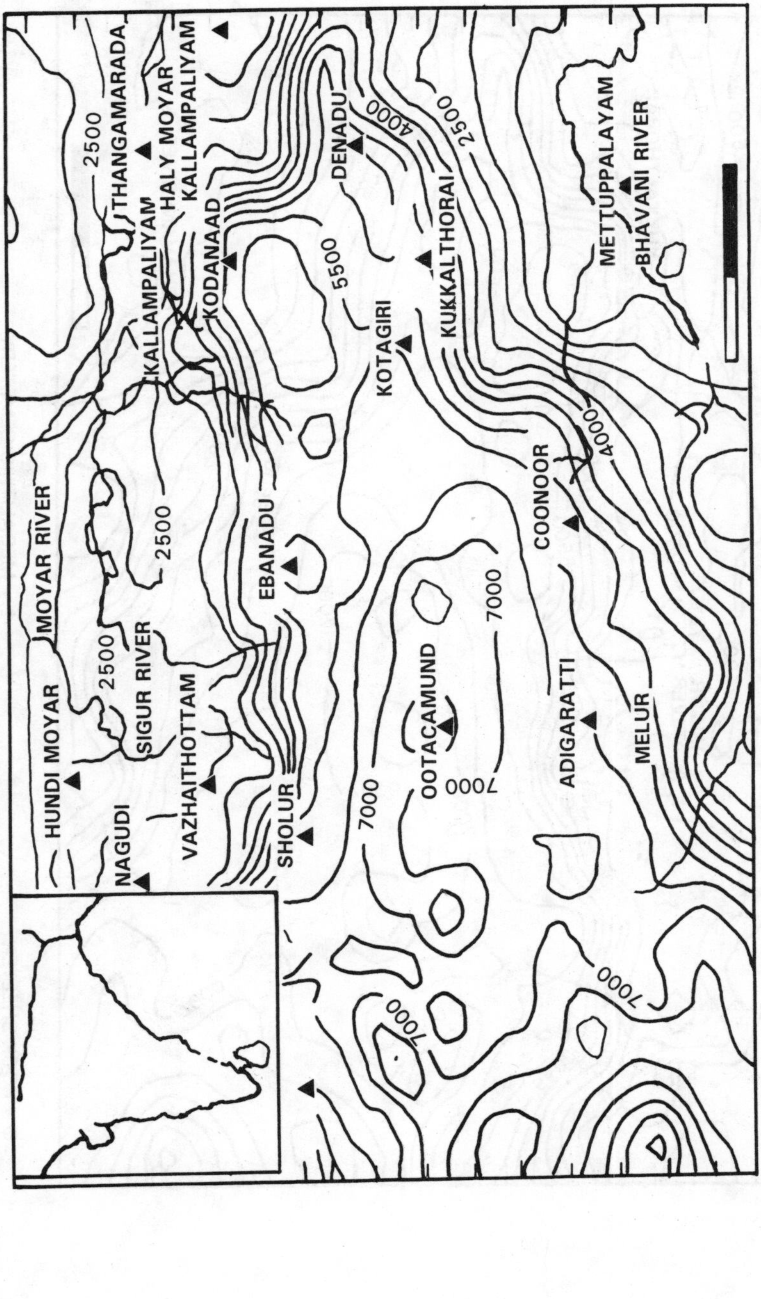

Fig. 3.2 Sketch of the Nilgiri Region

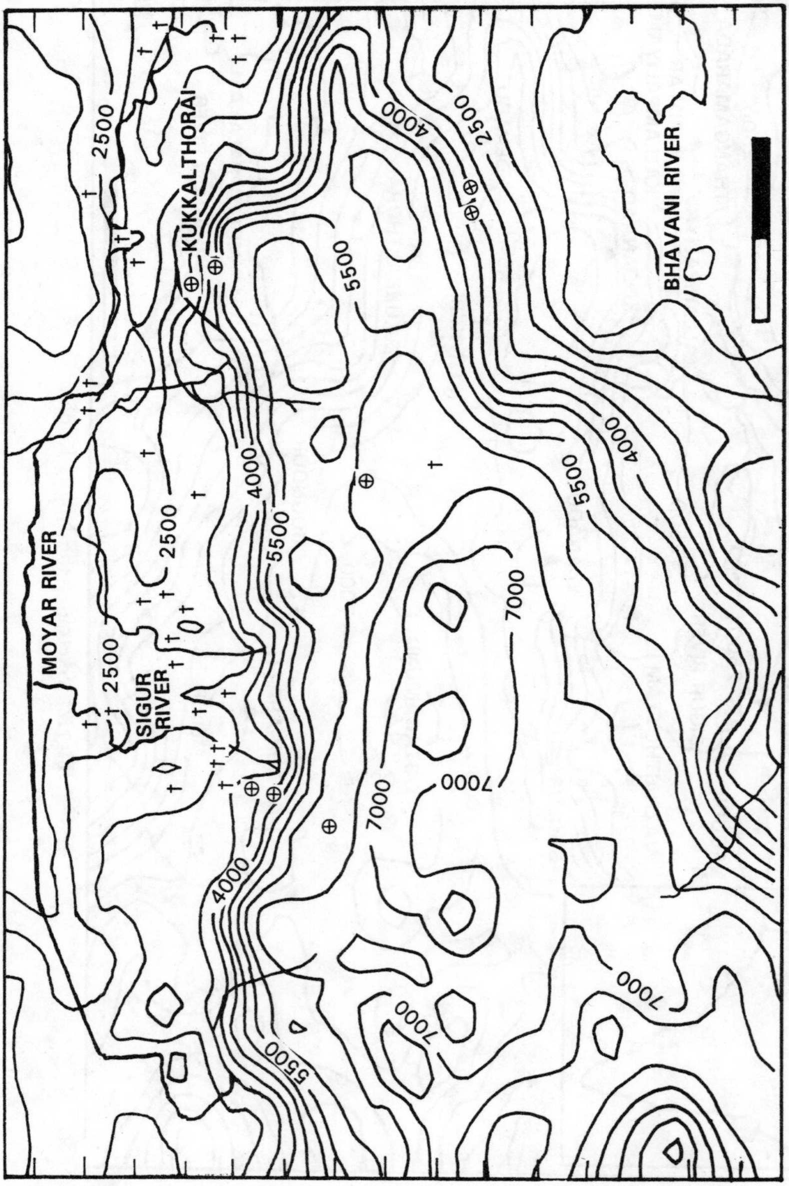

⊕ – ROCK SHELTER　　† – MEGALITHIC CEMETERY

Fig. 3.3 Moyar Ditch Megalithic Cemeteries and Rock Shelters

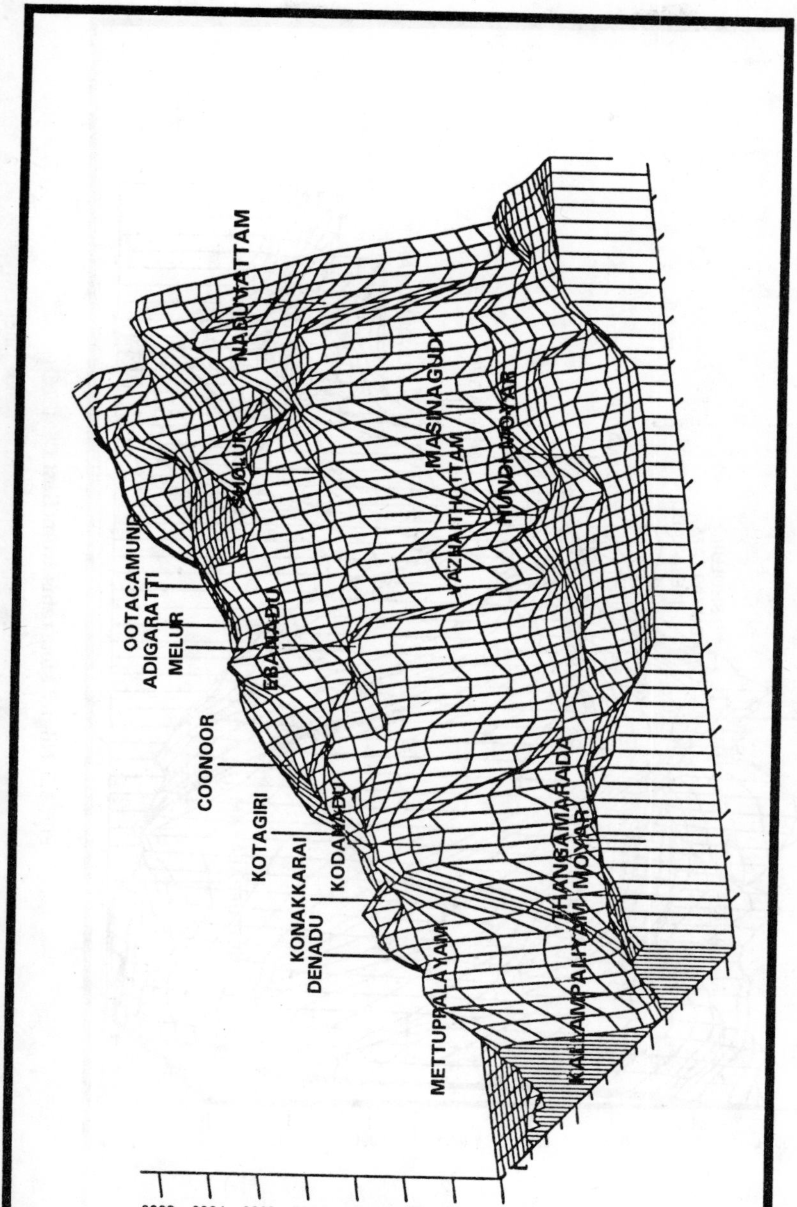

Fig. 3.4 Nilgiri Mountains from North

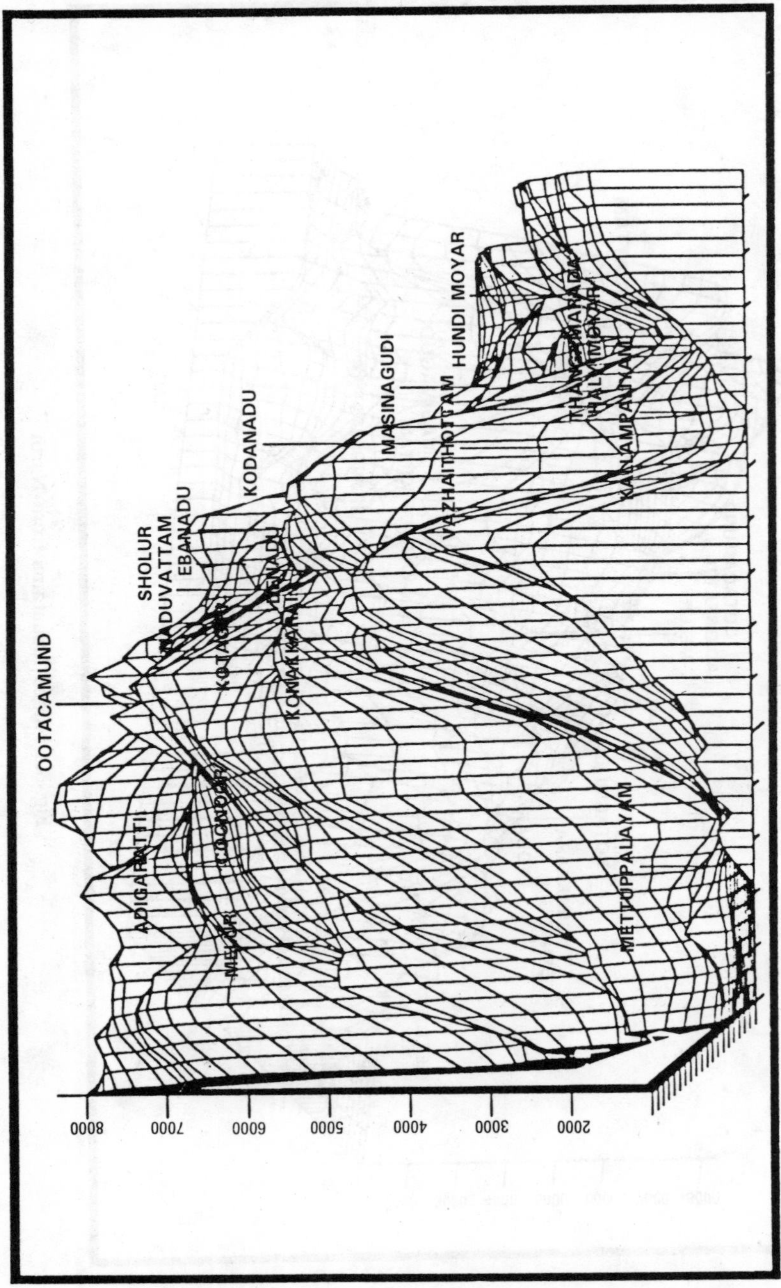

Fig. 3.5 Nilgiri Mountains from East

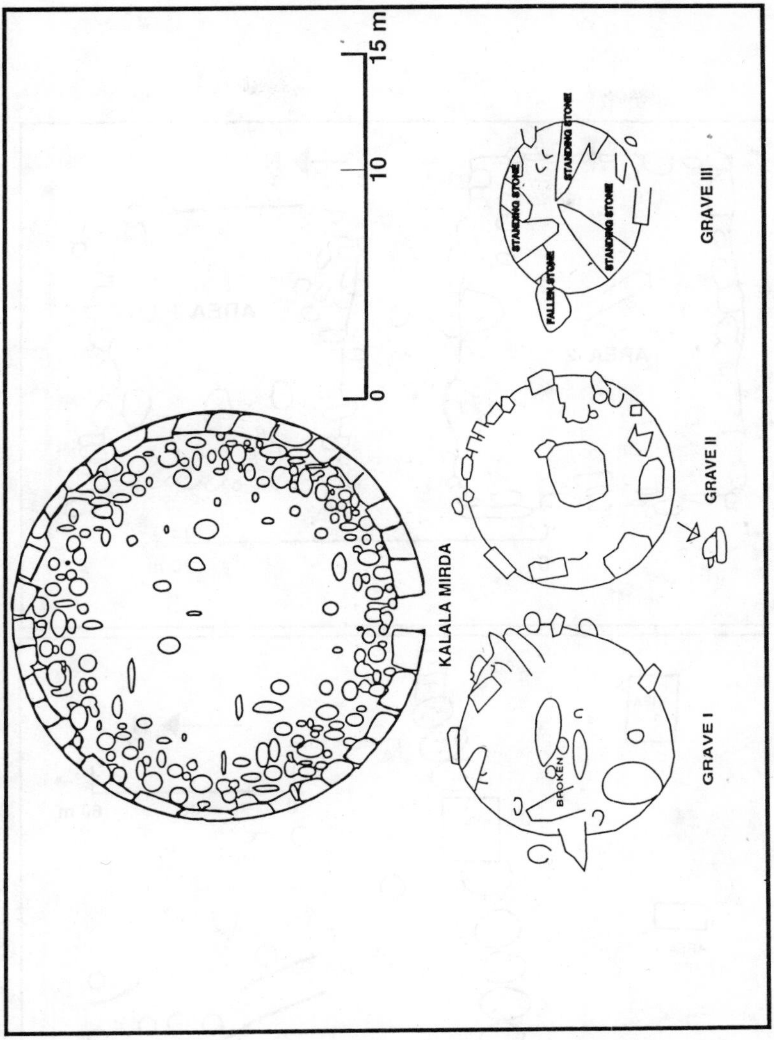

Fig. 3.6 Sami Koil

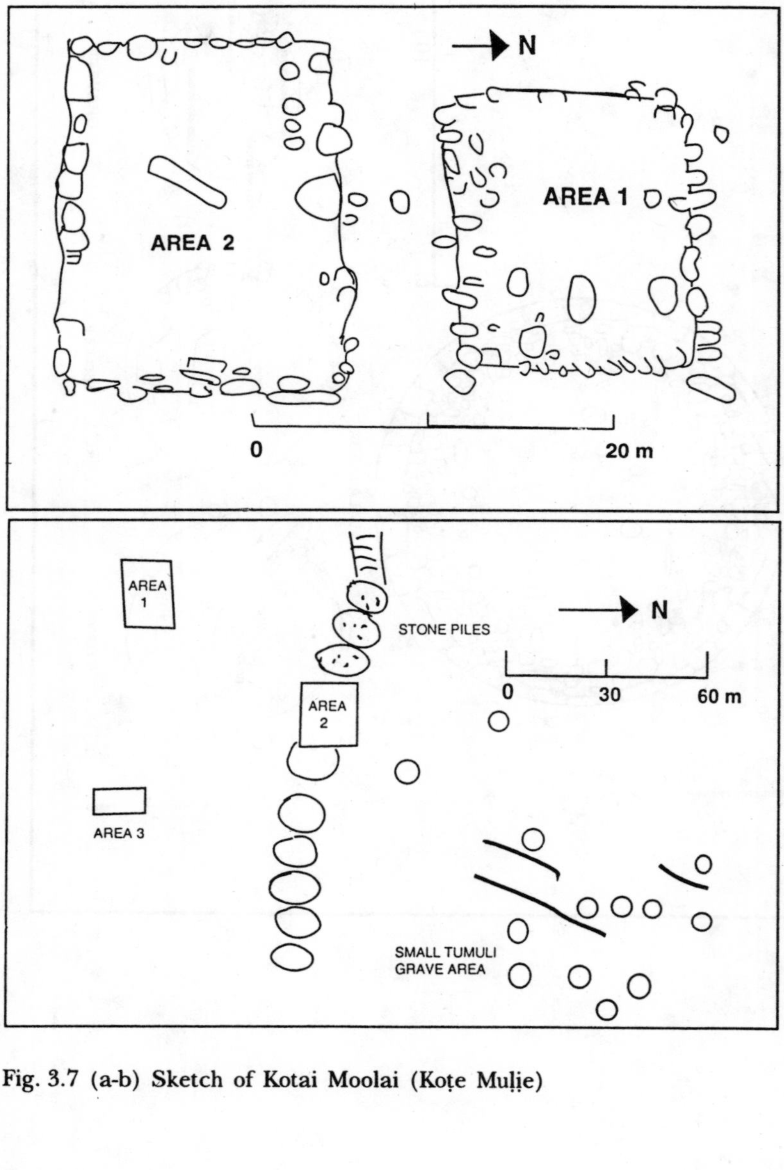

Fig. 3.7 (a-b) Sketch of Kotai Moolai (Koṭe Muḷịe)

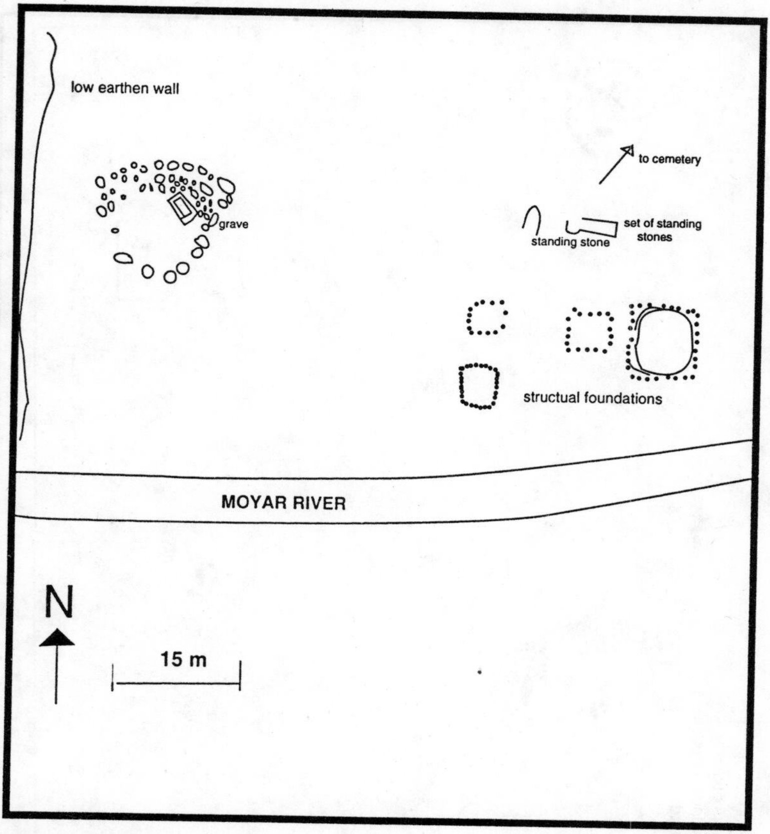

Fig. 3.8 Thatakurlipatti

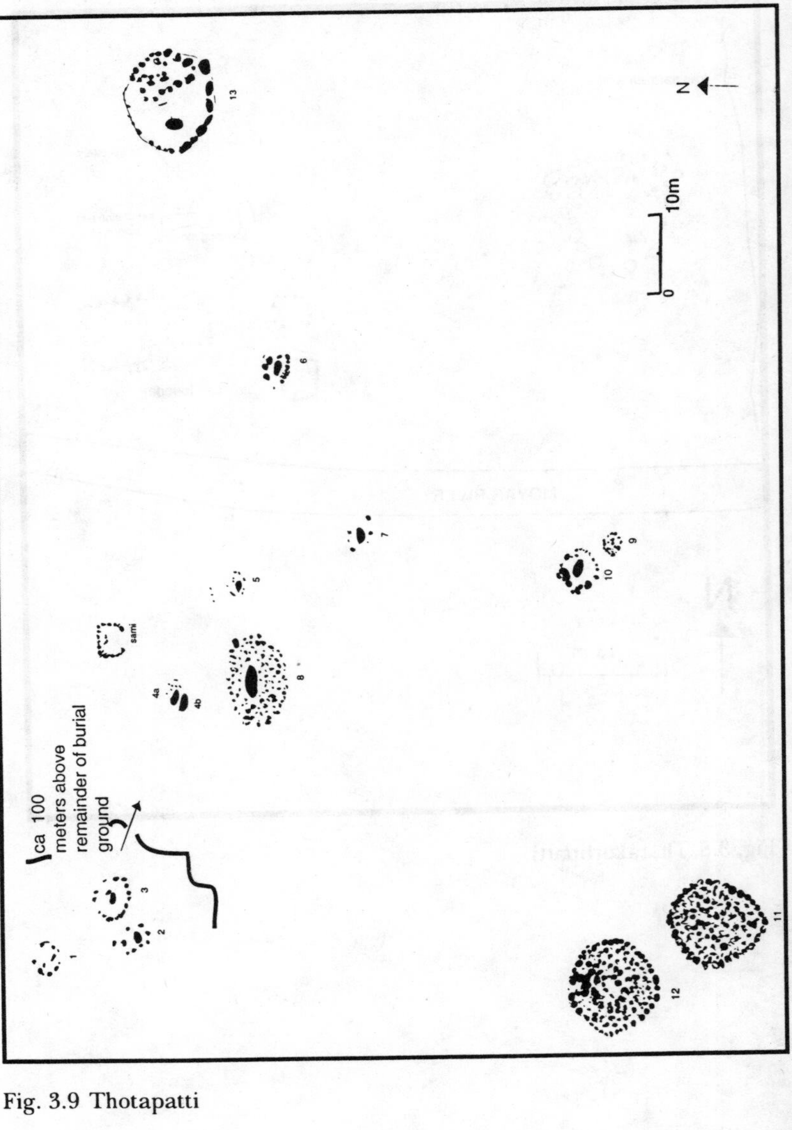

Fig. 3.9 Thotapatti

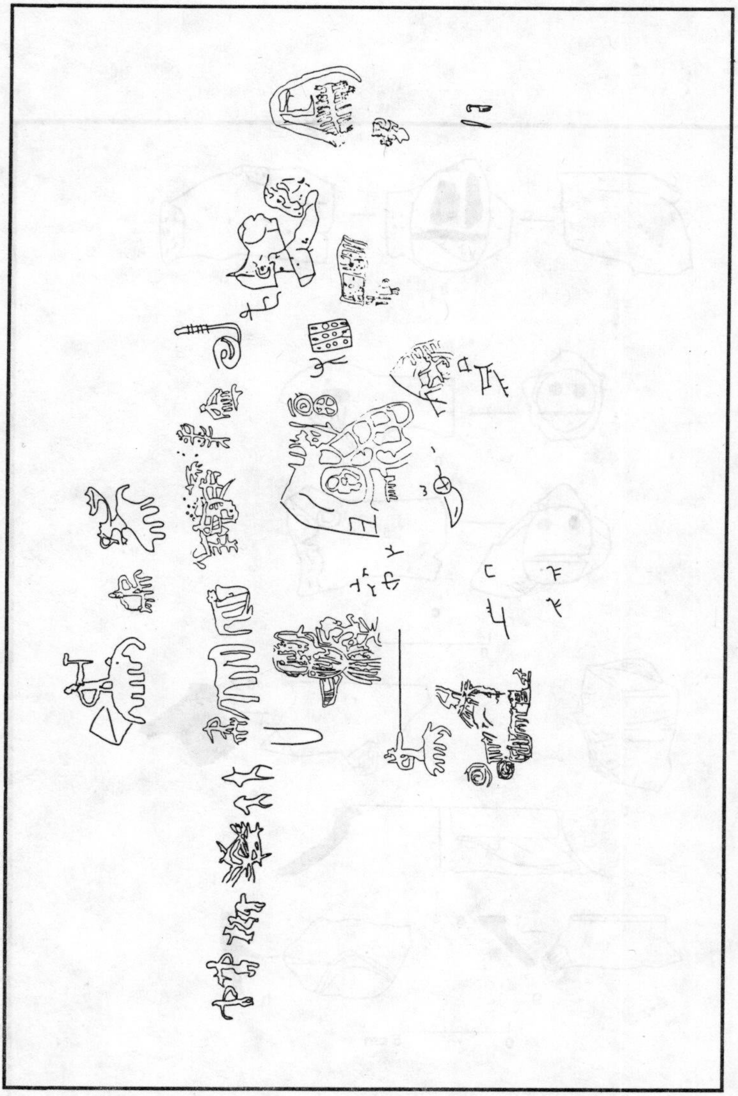

Fig. 3.10 Wananga Pazham. Rock Shelter Southwest of Thangamarahada (Tengumarahāḍa)

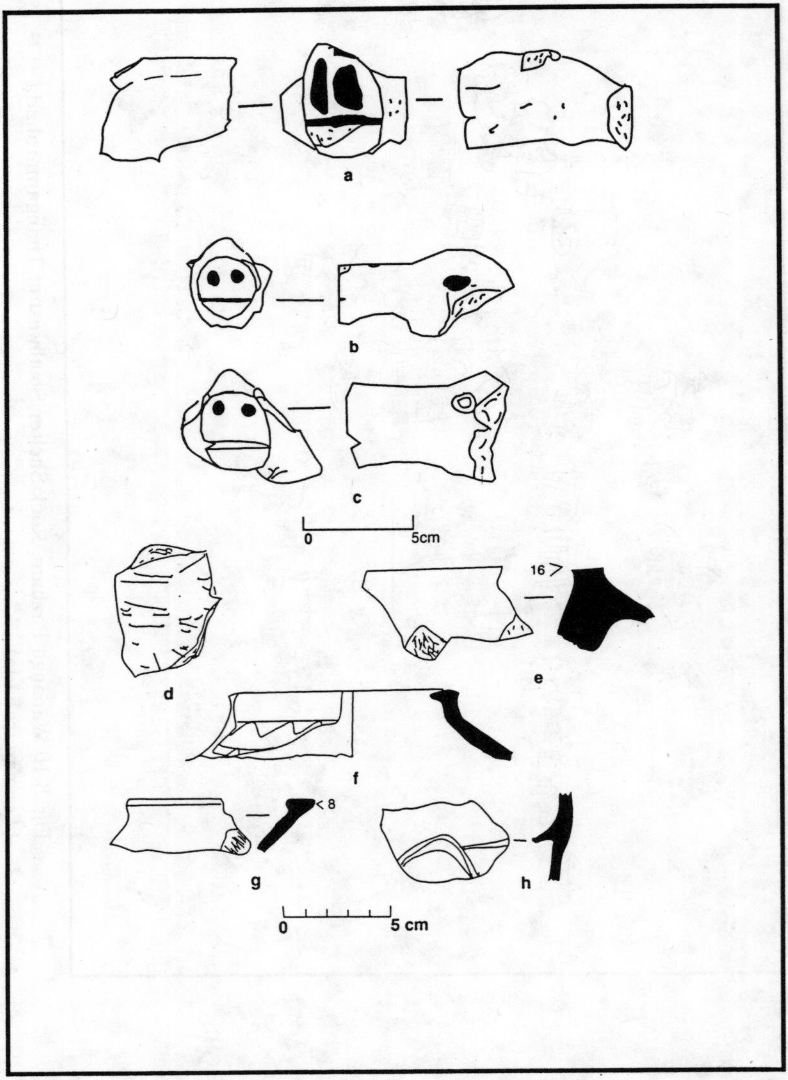

Fig. 3.11 Figurines and pottery from Seven Fort Hill

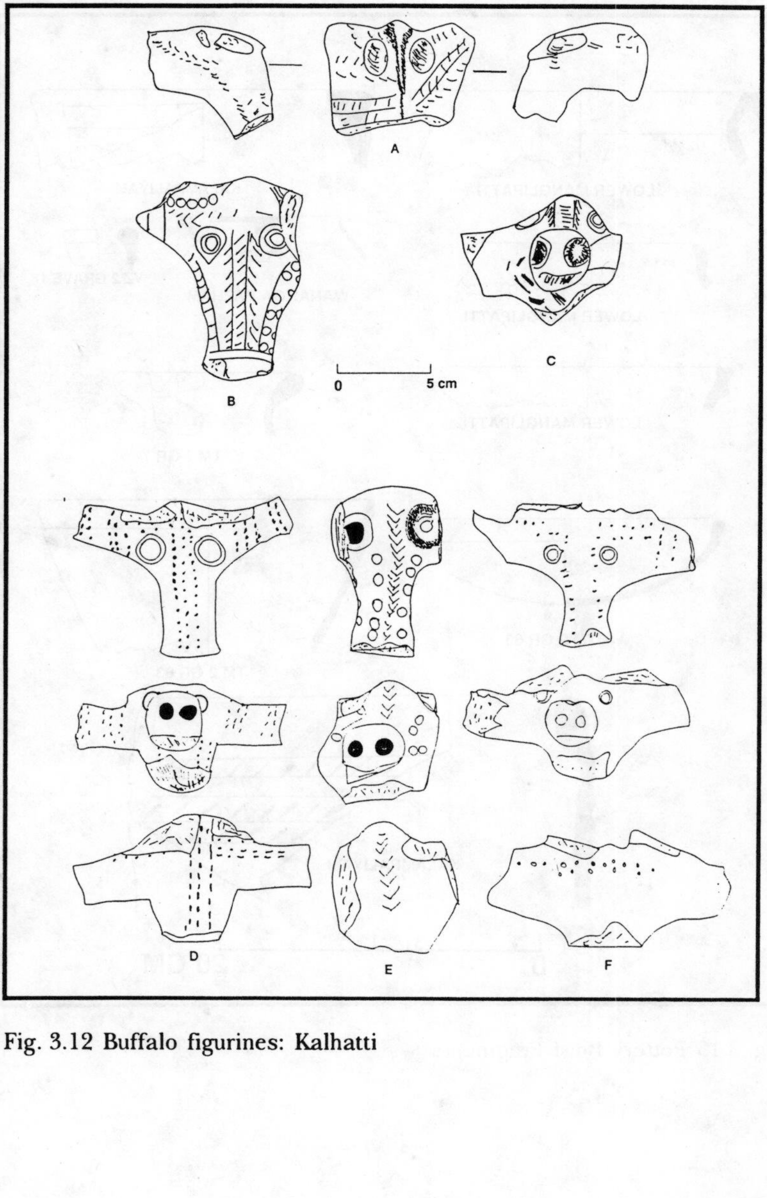

Fig. 3.12 Buffalo figurines: Kalhatti

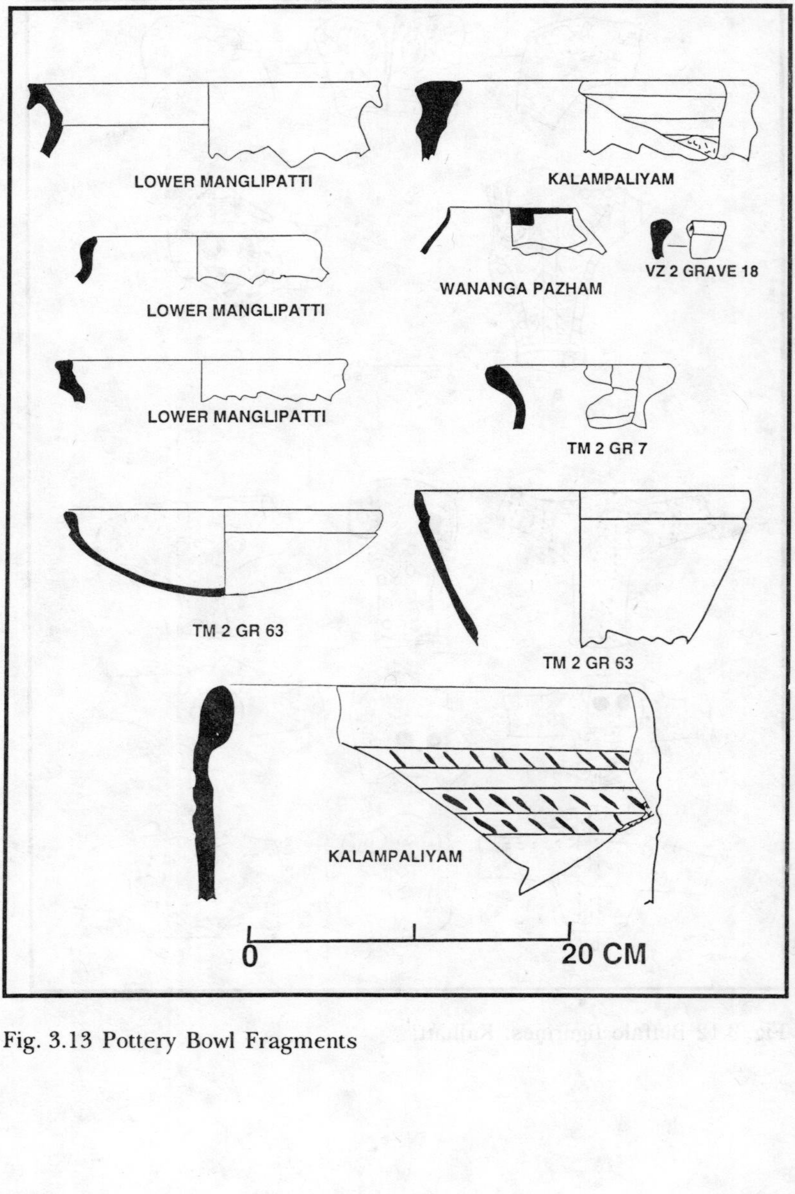

Fig. 3.13 Pottery Bowl Fragments

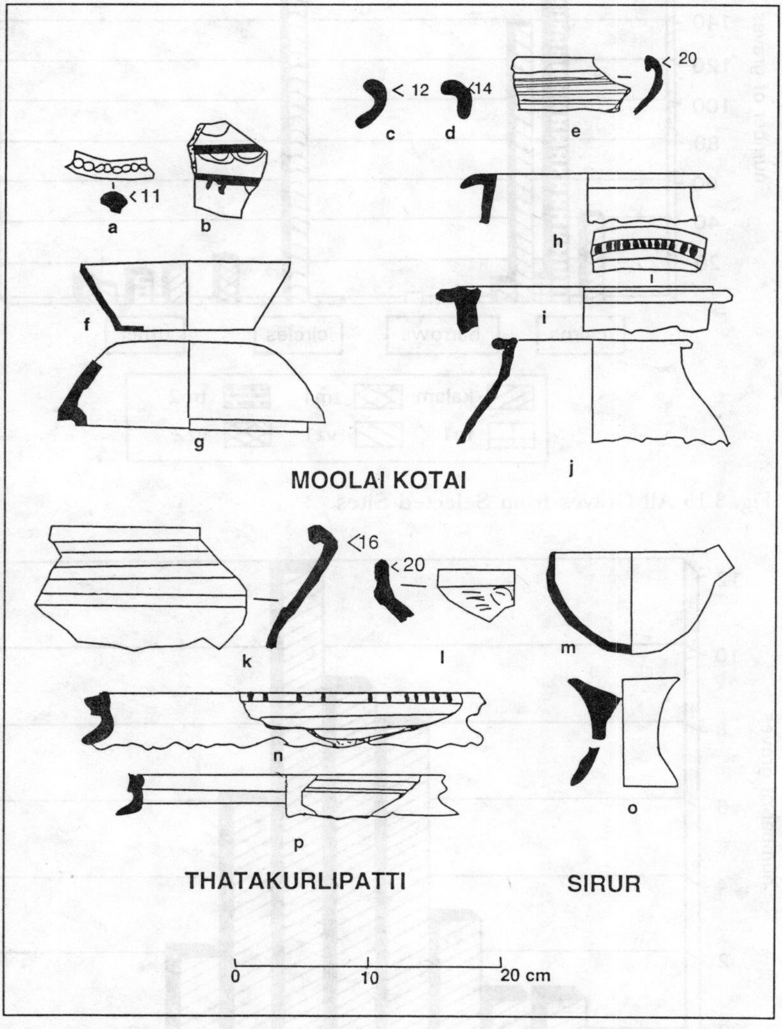

Fig. 3.14 Pottery Bowl Fragments

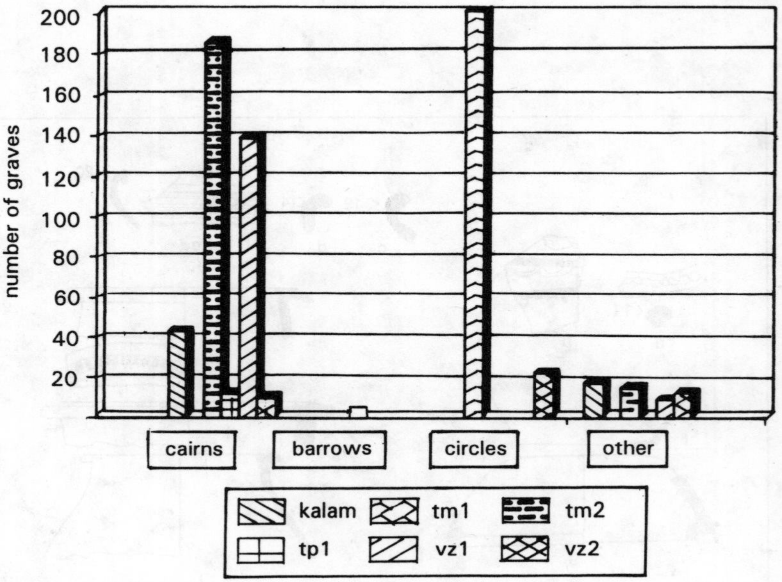

Fig. 3.15 All Graves from Selected Sites

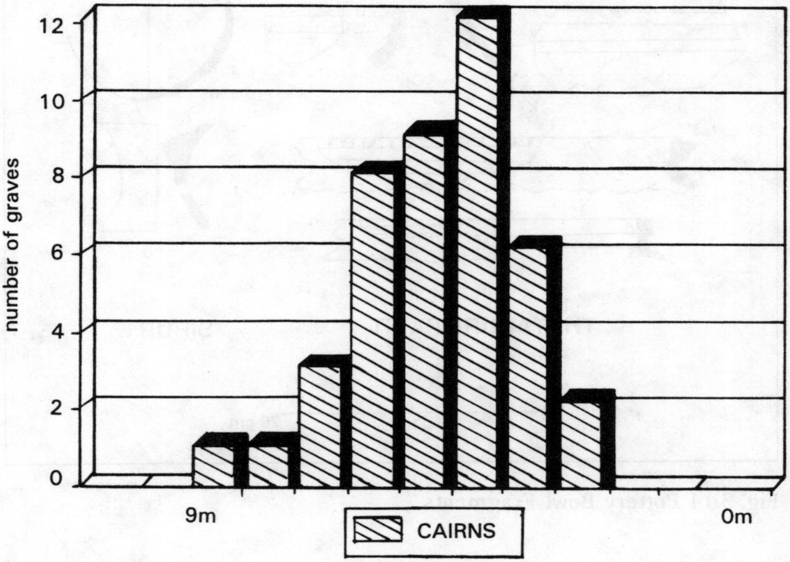

Fig. 3.16 Kallampaliyam 4 Grave Distribution

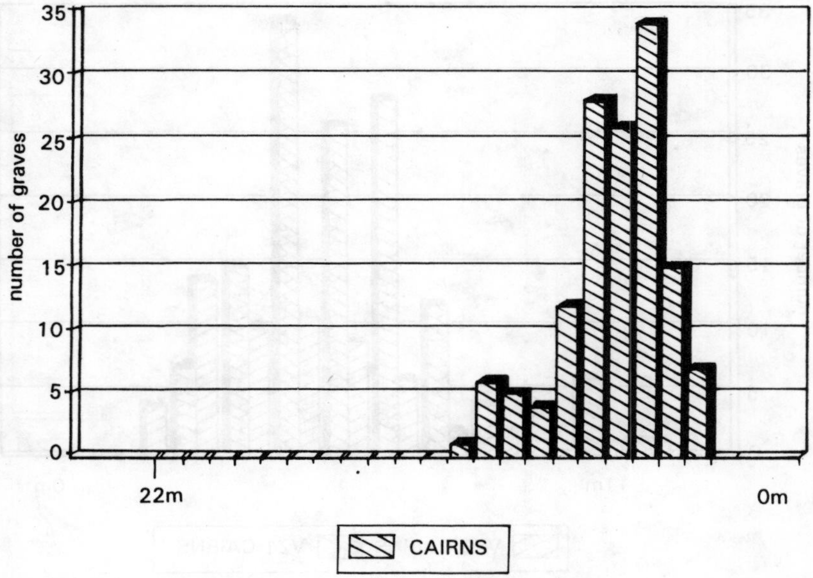

Fig. 3.17 Vazhaithottam 1 Grave Distribution

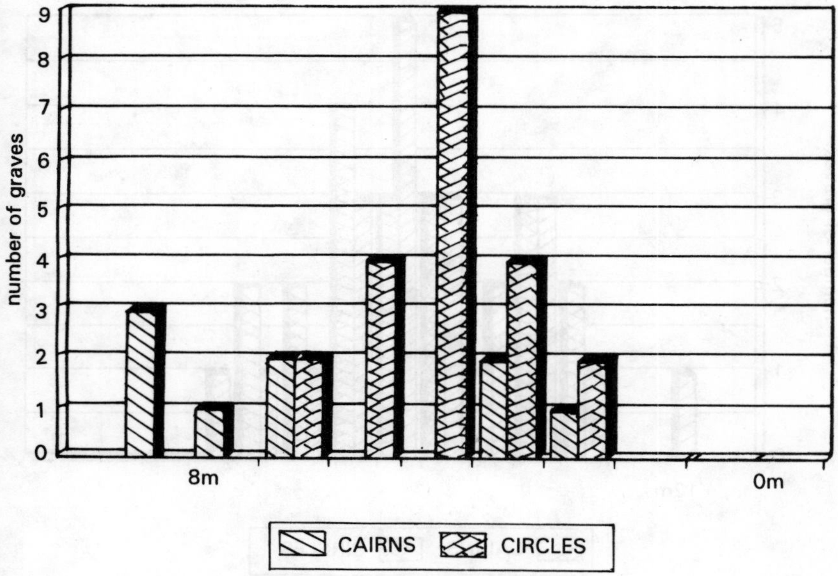

Fig. 3.18 Vazhaithottam 2 Grave Distribution

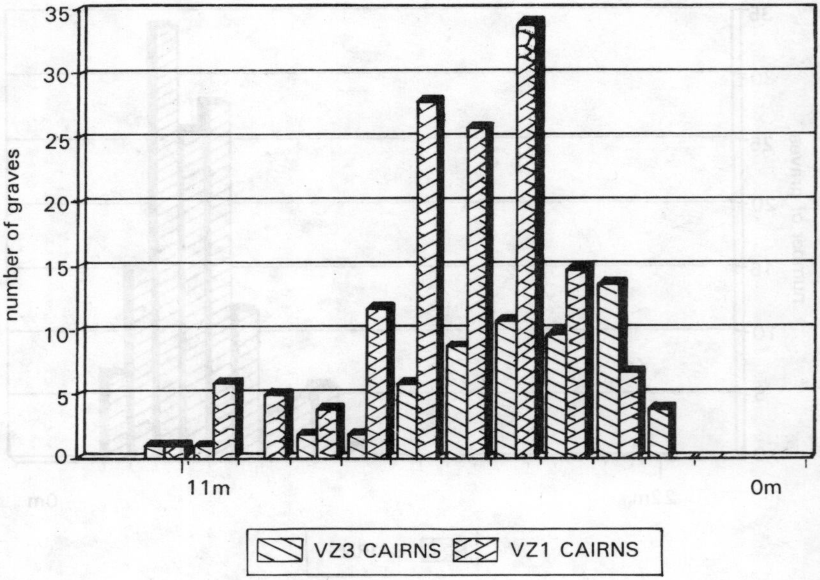

Fig. 3.19 Vazhaithottam 1 and 3 Grave Distributions

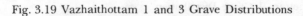

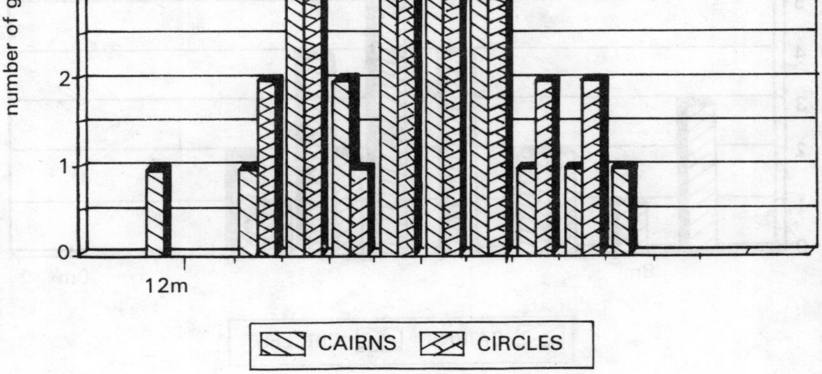

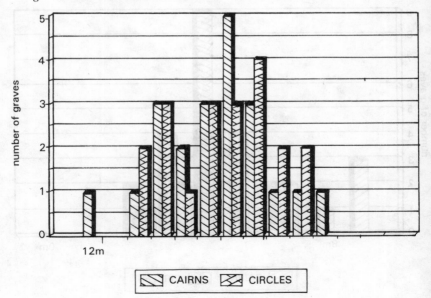

Fig. 3.20 Vazhaithottam 4 Grave Distribution

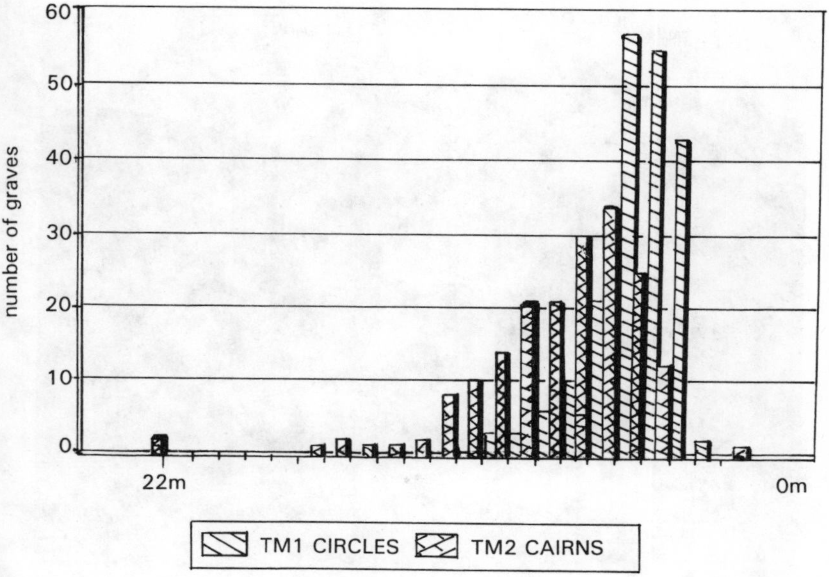

Fig. 3.21 Thangamarada 1 and 2 Grave Distributions

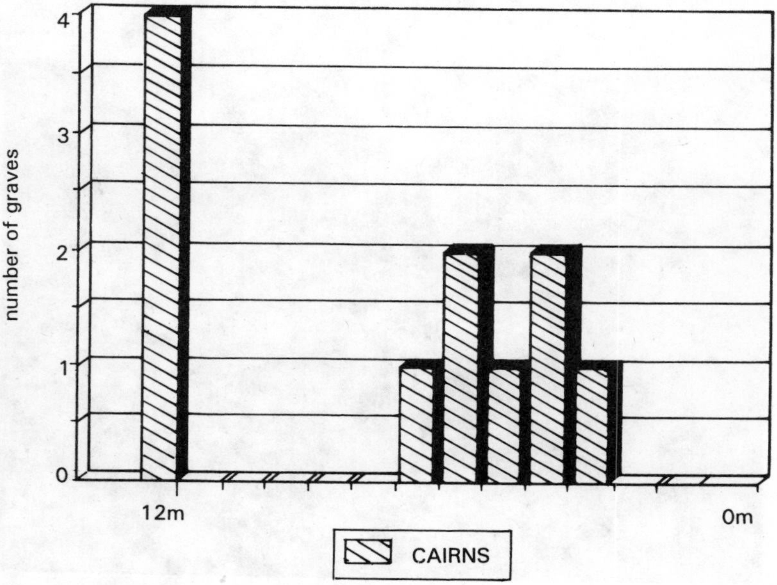

Fig. 3.22 Thottapatti 1 Grave Distribution

Pl. 1: Thatakurlipatti Grave

Pl. 2: Vazhaithottam Cairn

Pl. 3: Cist grave on Vazhaithottam 1 Cairn

Pl. 4: Stone Circle Thangamarada 1

Pl. 5: Budykupee Stone Circle

Pl. 6: Kallampaliyam Stone Circle and Menhirs

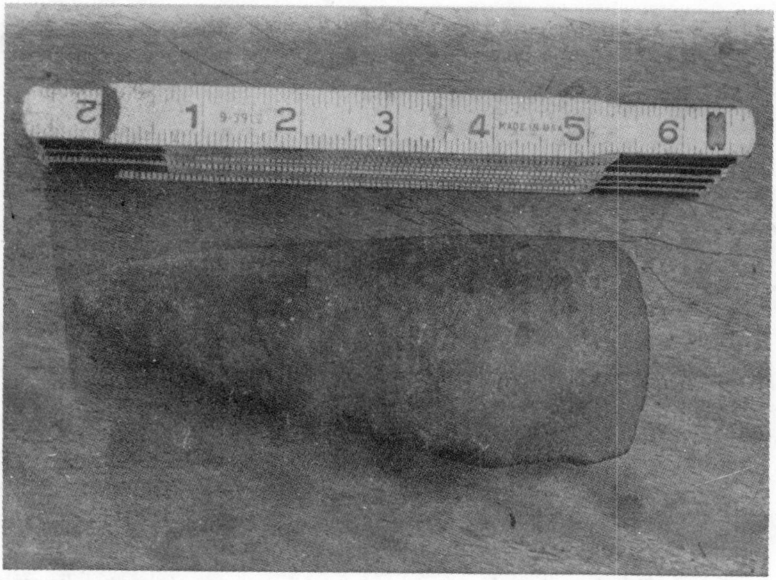

Pl. 7: Ground-stone Axe/Celt reportedly from Masinagudi

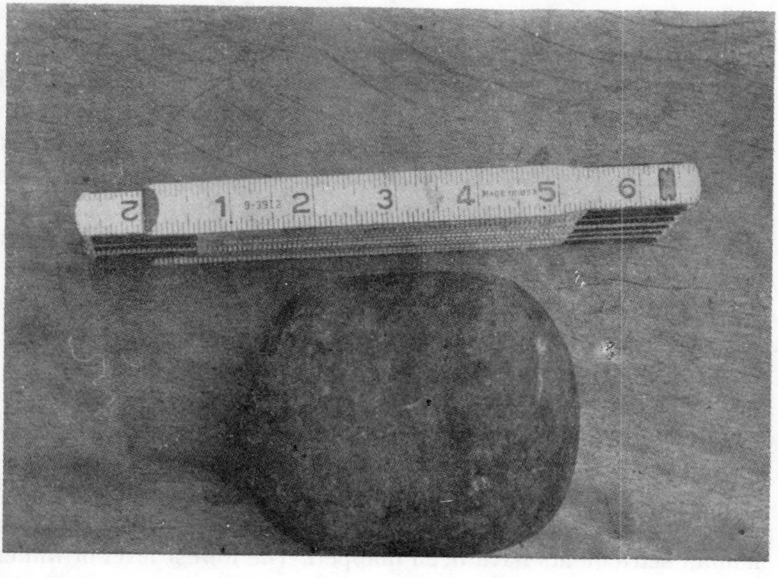

Pl. 8: Grinding stone reportedly from Masinagudi

Linguistics and Botany in the Nilgiris

M. B. Emeneau

4

Why the Nilgiris? For the uninitiated, it should be explained where and what they are and, among other things, why they have been of peculiar interest and have offered some peculiar difficulties to the anthropological linguist (or, indeed, to the anthropologist).

The word is an anglicization of their Sanskrit name 'Nīlagiri' [Blue Mountain(s)], a mountainous plateau of South India. The two mountain ranges which run down the western and the eastern coasts of the Indian peninsula, known as the Western Ghats and the Eastern Ghats, form a junction at about 11° latitude north of the equator. This junction rises spectacularly, in general through heavily jungled, steep escarpments and foothills to the mountainous plateau of the summit. The surrounding areas are generally lower, even much lower, than 1,000 metres (3,281 feet) in elevation. The plateau itself, an area of roughly 40 by 20 miles, is generally over 1,800 metres (5,905 feet) in elevation, the central, most densely inhabited area being over 2,134 metres (7,000 feet). However, the eastern and north-eastern sections of the plateau are in part somewhat lower, and the Wynaad to the west of the western mountainous rim of the plateau varies in elevation from 1000 metres down. The whole plateau is cut up by numerous valleys and ranges with peaks that rise over 2,500 metres (8,202 feet), the highest being Doddabetta, 2,636 metres (8,649 feet). The Nilgiri Plateau at such an altitude has a climate greatly different from that of the lower plains around, being especially cooler. It has been characterized (by geographers, von Lengerke and Blasco in Hockings 1989: 3) as 'a cold tropical island rising above the warm tropical sea of South India'. It has now become evident too (Hockings 1989; 369) that ecologically there is a gap of about 200 metres (about 650 feet) between the elevation of 1,200 and 1,400 metres (3,937 and 4,593 feet) where only four human settlements have been mapped. The lowest level of winter frosts is 1,400 metres and 'it is also the highest level at which the malaria-causing Plasmodium parasites can survive, that being the limit for their Anopheles mosquito vector'. The Nilgiri Plateau is indeed an 'island', surrounded at a lower elevation by an uninhabited *cordon sanitaire* and, even lower, by jungle, malarious and infested by elephants, tigers, cobras, pythons, and other dangers.

That the climatic differentiation between the Plateau summit and the lower levels of the Nilgiris should be seen also in differences of vegetation has been known since botanists from the West appeared there and undertook Linnaean taxonomy. It has become a matter of general statement (Hockings 1989: 46) that 1,800 metres (5,905 feet) of elevation is the dividing point. The high levels of the Plateau are in their flora different from the plains; the lower levels (around 1,800 metres or slightly lower) show some transitions/ambiguities. Such botanical details will form a major subject of this chapter.

SECTION 1

For many centuries the Nilgiri climate, the jungles of the surrounding foothills and the escarpments made the Plateau uninviting to inhabitants of the plains. Before the British came, beginning in 1821, we know that a general in a Kannaḍa inscription of AD 1117 recorded that he invaded the Nilgiris (and saw the Todas). Thereafter we know of the Jesuit priest Fenicio who in 1603 visited the Nilgiris, saw enough of Todas and Badagas to write a short account of them, but decided that the missionary efforts located in Malabar could be pursued more profitably.

However, on linguistic grounds we speculate that about two millennia ago, and before Tamil and Malayalam (as we now know them) underwent the palatalization of proto-Dravidian initial velar stops before front vowels (an approximate statement), two communities related in a caste-like way came to the upper Nilgiri Plateau. Whether there were already settlers there, we do not know, though archaeological remains on the Nilgiris suggest that possibly there were (but there are other theories in the field with regard to these remains). These two invading communities became the entities that we know as the Todas and the Kotas. They were indeed related in a caste-like way which, being so like what we know of the caste relations of the Hindus of the plains of India, must be thought of as something that they brought with them in their invasion.

The Todas subsisted on their herds of water-buffaloes and ritualized to a daunting degree the care of the animals and the dairy practices involving their milk; they lived in tiny settlements of a few families each, on the pasture lands scattered all over the Plateau. The Kotas supplied the Todas with some food grain, with pots and iron tools, with funeral music, and received in return the carcasses and hides of buffaloes that had died or had been slaughtered at funerals; they lived in seven villages that in effect were scattered enclaves in the Toda pasture lands. The economic exchanges (and also ritual presence of Todas at some Kota ceremonies) were passed down from generation to generation between traditionally related lineages in the two communities. Other rather minor types of interchange were held between these two groups and other much more marginal groups, who led hunter and food-gatherer lives in the marginal jungles of the Plateau and in the jungles of the precipitous areas leading up to the Plateau—Kuṟumbas of various affiliations, Irulas, Sholegas, etc. Of these and their languages we still know all too little, though work has been published in recent years on the Irulas and the Ālu Kuṟumbas and their languages.

A third community, the Badagas, appeared on the Plateau in the sixteenth century, having come up from the Mysore plains to the north, apparently in part at least because of Muslim persecution. They were agriculturalists and, finding it possible to cultivate some areas of the Plateau's open spaces that were not in immediate use by Todas or Kotas, their population grew rapidly so that they were the majority community when the British arrived (about 2,200 in the first census of 1812) and by now number between 150,000 and 200,000. In contrast the two communities that might be termed 'aboriginal', the Todas and the Kotas, during the period when they have been known to non-Nilgirians, have each numbered below or just over 1,000 members. After the Badagas joined the two earlier groups on the Plateau, the three communities further developed intercaste relationships of the type already sketched as holding between Todas and Kotas. There were, however, so many differences between the three Nilgiri communities and the familiar caste structure and relationships of Hindus of the plains, that it was long before the Nilgirians were recognized as being in fact marginally Hindu in most respects of their social structures, religions, economic organization, etc. (Walker 1986).

It will be noted that I have used the past tense in writing of the three communities. Most of their interrelationships, and in the case of Todas and Kotas, much of their basic economy and all the social and other structures that had depended on the economy, have either completely gone or been seriously undermined and impoverished. This is so because in the past half-century the economy of the Nilgiris has been modernized out of all recognition from what it was a century and a half ago (Walker 1986).

From the beginning of the British incursion ethnographic description has gone on in the Nilgiris. The conspicuous aberrancy of the Todas attracted most attention, and was done full justice to in the culminating account by W. H. R. Rivers (1906). The jungle communities received least attention because of the obvious contact difficulties, but the latter half of the twentieth century has seen some serious work on them.

SECTION 2

So far I have not mentioned the conspicuous linguistic differentiation between the communities mentioned. In India all types of difference between castes tend to be preserved and even emphasized; 'intra-community solidarity' is one of the phrases used to characterize the situation. This has seldom been carried as far linguistically as it has been in the Nilgiris. There each of the well-known communities speaks a different language, all being mutually unintelligible: it is thought, and known in part, that this statement is true of the jungle communities too. Little serious linguistic work was done in the area until towards the middle, actually the thirties, of this century. The Toda and Kota languages are by now published with some degree of accuracy (Emeneau 1984 for Toda, 1944–6 for Kota), as are Irula (Zvelebil 1973–82) and Ālu Kuṟumba (Kapp 1982). The Badaga language now begins to be well-known.[1] There exists unpublished material from several other Kuṟumba languages, and even from Sholega. How many separate languages there are is still unknown, but ten is probably not an overestimate.

It is, however, certain that all are Dravidian languages, belonging to the South Dravidian sub-group. Toda and Kota are fairly close to Tamil and Malayalam; Irula is very close to Tamil; Badaga started as a dialect of Kannaḍa but is now probably to be recognized as a closely related, but a separate, language. The exact placing of the other languages is still uncertain, but they are not to be separated from the neighbouring languages. In fact, as soon as intensive study of the Nilgiri languages became possible, it became clear that these were geographically separated members of the Dravidian family and were to be treated as a linguistic microarea according to the methodology of areal linguistics (Emeneau 1980, collected work that began to be published in 1956). Structural criteria were identified as marking off the area linguistically from the Dravidian languages of the surrounding plains, and these criteria were joined by areal lexical items as soon as Dravidian etymological work was done in the etymological dictionary prepared by Burrow and myself between 1949 and 1984 (*DED* and *DEDR*). The microareal treatment was begun by Zvelebil in 1980 (Emeneau 1989 and Zvelebil 1990).

The etymological dictionary work soon identified numerous lexical items which were peculiar to the Nilgiri languages or which showed peculiar Nilgiri developments of general Dravidian lexical material. Inspection of botanical lexical items discovered many such items. We could hardly have expected floral nomenclature to be otherwise, given that the Nilgiri Plateau is botanically differentiated from areas of lower elevation. When the earliest Dravidian speakers settled on the Plateau, their floral vocabulary must have been quite inadequate for what they found there. What, then, was their procedure? Did they adapt their old vocabulary items because of botanical similarities or because of other similarities? Some such items are identified below. It may be suggested that there were other, even many other, such items which can no longer be identified as such because of loss (or non-recording so far) of the pertinent items in the other languages of the family. Or did they invent new terms on the basis of non-botanical criteria? Several such are identified. Or did they pluck new terms out of thin air? Or, since 'out of thin air' is most unsatisfactory, did they borrow terms from prior Nilgiri inhabitants? This, the positing of non-Dravidian-speaking aborigines, has been suggested, especially by Zvelebil (1990: 64). He is following the tempting path taken by many earlier scholars in many parts of the world and F. B. J. Kuiper in dealing with languages of north India. But we have, in fact, apart from the words we are trying to explain, no evidence of a linguistic kind for such aborigines in the Nilgiris. The only basis for such speculation would be the racial mixture that is alleged to be evident in south India (as also in the rest of the subcontinent). Without other linguistic evidence, to posit non-Dravidian origin for our pertinent items is a completely circular procedure.

What I have just written of possible aborigines and have reported earlier of the prehistory of the Todas and Kotas as it can be reconstructed on linguistic evidence, should be supplemented by a very brief statement of what the Todas and Kotas say themselves. I have recorded (and published, in the references given in Section 10) that each of these communities has a story of how Todas, Kotas, and Kuṟumbas were created in the Nilgiris by a god (different ones in the two accounts). In these myths 'they' are aboriginal. One of the botanical items to be treated below was part of the aboriginal diet in these myths (Section 2, 10, p. 88 below).

SECTION 3

The remainder of the chapter examines a number of botanical lexical items for which statements can be made relevant to the questions that we have just asked. Unfortunately, few of the problematic items have yielded solutions. Part of the problem is the difficulty of making exact botanical identifications during linguistic fieldwork, and then the difficulties offered by the botanical taxonomic publications themselves. It is necessary to outline these problems in some slight detail before attacking specific cases.

I had occasion during my rather extensive fieldwork on the Toda and Kota languages to record many items of the flora, both as elicited isolated forms and as words in texts of various sorts, accounts of cultural activities, folktales, myths, songs (especially in the Toda language), anecdotes, etc. To establish identifications within the botanists' taxonomy in the field was a problem. My practice was to have my informants, on occasion, bring me armloads of specimens. To these I attached the Toda and Kota names. I was more fortunate than many, if not most, field-workers in that Ootacamund, the chief English-established town of the Nilgiris, was the hot-weather government centre for the (British) Madras Presidency. An adjunct of the centre was the Government Botanical Gardens. The offices of the Gardens had been made the depository of a large collection of excellent coloured plates of flora, which had been produced over the years by several ladies (including Lady Bourne, the wife of a former official in the government); these were labelled with the Latin nomenclature of the items. As best as I could (and at times with the aid of Mr. Butcher, then Curator of the Gardens), I matched my specimens of vegetation with the plates and recorded the botanical labels. Years later during work on the etymological dictionary I attempted to reconcile these recordings with the synonymy that is provided in the botanical taxonomic works.

There has been much effort expended on the botanical classification of the flora of the Nilgiri Plateau, beginning already in the early years of the nineteenth century. Hooker's work of 1875–97 is a synopsis of all the earlier work for all of the Indian subcontinent and contains much on the Nilgiris. Gamble's three volumes, printed in 1915–35 (reprinted in 1957 and again in 1967), on the flora of the old Madras Presidency, contained advances on Nilgiri flora. Fyson's three-volumed work of 1915–20, (reprinted in 1974–5), contained new description and classification; it concentrated, as its title shows, on the flora of 'the Nilgiri and Pulney hill-tops [above 6,500 feet (roughly 2,000 metres)] ... round the hill-stations of Ootacamund, Kotagiri and Kodaikanal'. His 1932 work, (reprinted in 1977), contained further observation and classification. Of more recent botanical works than Fyson and Gamble, one may say that the one by Matthew (1983) is of value to the Nilgirian, even though his special area is what he calls the 'Tamilian Carnatic', which borders on, but does not include the Nilgiri summit. In fact, however, some of the lower hill areas covered by Matthew are over 1,500 metres, and many of the Nilgiri species are found in his work.

The non-botanist must be warned that during the nearly two centuries of the botanists' taxonomic work they have produced numerous reclassifications, and many of these have involved changes in the Latin nomenclature. These changes are recorded in the more ambitious botanical works in what are referred to as 'synonymies'. Matthew's 1983 work provides the most recent of such synonymies (if, that is to say, my non-competence in such matters has not caused me to neglect some recent publications). It is necessary to mention these synonymies because it should be evident that, in general, linguistic scholars who have attempted to give botanical taxonomic equivalents for the flora names that they elicited from native speakers have worked in different periods and have had easy access to botany books of different periods. Their botanical identifications have, almost without exception, been not by synonymies but by the single Latin label given in the accessible botanical work.

Even worse, definition has often been by an approximation to a vernacular name or by an Anglo-Indian or approximate English label. Consequently, attempts to equate these definitions, as in an etymological dictionary, produce the difficulties that are recorded in such works as *CDIAL* or *DEĐR*. The examples that are presented in this paper show how great such difficulties may be.

SECTION 4

Some attempt was made by botanists in South India to provide the vernacular names of the species they identified. Of these Lushington (1915) is the most ambitious. However, his work was linguistically so badly based and his sources so haphazard (I think this not an unfair judgement) that Burrow and I were unable to make much use of his three large volumes in our etymological work; e.g., for Tamil nomenclature the *Tamil Lexicon* (1924–39) was so great an advance and linguistically so accurate that it superseded Lushington in almost all his linguistic details, even though at times it recorded items as given by him. The botanical works on the Nilgiris made little contribution to the early recordings of names in the vernaculars, by which of course I mean our special concern, the Nilgiri vernaculars. Both Gamble and Lushington made sporadic notations of Badaga names, so a phonetic reconstitution of their generally wretched recordings is sometimes possible. Their Badaga sources, as well as sources of names in the literary languages, seem not to have been already published material, but rather the colloquials of their various native-speaker contacts. In this paper I attempt to use items that can be salvaged from Lushington and Gamble (and later Matthew) to add to my old Toda, Kota, and occasional Badaga material. I gratefully add Hockings and Pilot-Raichoor's new Badaga material, as well as Zvelebil's Irula and Kapp's Ālu Kuṟumba material.

SECTION 5

In the following thirteen sections fourteen species are presented, which are either found only in the Nilgiris, or, if found elsewhere, show peculiarities of Nilgiri nomenclature.

Sections 6 and 7 of the paper deal with species which do not grow on the Nilgiri summit but are known to the summit communities and have Nilgiri names with general Indian or South Dravidian etymologies. Sections 8 and 9 have Nilgiri species related to those of the plains; the Nilgiri names are related to more general Dravidian etyma; in addition the Toda name in §8 is unique. In sections 10 and 11, Nilgiri species have names related to etyma which have no botanical reference. Sections 12 to 17 contain Nilgiri species which are not closely related to species elsewhere and which are denoted by names with only Nilgiri etymologies and no etyma elsewhere; it is these (along with the Toda item in §8) which offer acute problems as to how they originated—from Dravidian names which were lost elsewhere in the Dravidian family, or through borrowing from non-Dravidian-speaking aborigines; it is not even possible to speculate further on these items with any profit. Section 18 deals with two unrelated species which have three groups of names, two of the groups with no etyma elsewhere than in the Nilgiris; the details of the data are very difficult.

SECTION 6

A fruit-bearing tree, known in the English of South India as the jack-tree (< *DEDR* 2275 *cakkay, Tamil cakkai and forms in several other South Indian languages), is botanically *Artocarpus integrifolius*, Linn. = *A. heterophyllus*, Lam.[2] In some botanical works this is separated from the breadfruit (e.g. *A. incisus*, Linn.); in others the two are said to be only one species. Linguistic vocabularies consequently show confusion as to whether both botanical equivalences are intended by the same vernacular word (e.g. for the Malayalam word in *DEDR* 2275), or which English equivalence should be given (e.g. *CDIAL* 7781 gives only 'breadfruit' for the Sanskrit panasá and its Indo-Aryan continuants). We need not attempt to unravel this confusion, nor to settle the relationship of the 'jungle jack', 'wild jack', *A. hirsuta* = *A. pubescens*, to the other two (or one) species. Gamble makes it clear that for him 1,219 metres (= 4,000 feet) is the upper limit at which *Artocarpus* grows, i.e. (as is seen in section 1) roughly the upper limit of the escarpment jungles. The jack-tree, then, could be known to the communities of the summit Plateau only through forays that they might make down to jungle areas from, e.g., the slightly lower, northeast corner of the Plateau or over the western mountain range to the Wynaad. Since it is known that there was immediately pre-modern establishment of a few Toda hamlets and a Kota village in the Wynaad (followed by an early modern withdrawal to the Plateau), there is no insuperable problem as to where the summit communities might have gained knowledge of the jack-tree and words denoting it.

The jack-tree is known in Indo-Aryan as Sanskrit panasa- (Māhābhārata), Hindi panas, Marathi paṇas, etc. (*CDIAL* 7781), and in Central Dravidian languages Telugu (also Kannaḍa, by borrowing from Telugu) as panasa, Parji penac, Kuwi paṇhā (*DEDR* 3988). It has been thought that the Dravidian forms with –n– are the source of an Old Indo-Aryan borrowing (so, with little doubt, Mayrhofer 1963: 209, s.v. panasáḥ).[3] South Dravidian, however, has forms with l rather than n, and though these two consonants do appear in some etymologies in allomorphic variation (e.g. *DEDR* 1407 *kan–/*kal– 'dream'), it cannot, with quite complete certainty, be ruled out that the Central Dravidian languages owe their n or ṇ to borrowing from Indo-Aryan, whatever the origin of Sanskrit panasa–may be. The South Dravidian languages including Kannaḍa with palasa and Tulu with pila, pela, all have –l– forms. It is certain that the first phones are *pal–. Malayalam and also colloquial Tamil (Subrahmanyam 1983: 246) have plā– by aphaeresis. The longer from with suffixal –v(u) also has aphaeresis in Malayalam. Both Tamil and Malayalam preserve both consonants pl– by secondary insertion of –i– (in feature analysis i and l are closer than a and l); Tulu has pila by borrowing from Malayalam. The following schema is probably nearly correct:

*palā (Tamil palā, Malayalam plā-kkāyi; Irula [Zvelebil 1982: 103] pala· ł here rather than with *palāv–); secondarily *pilā (Tamil pilā, Tulu pila, pela)

> *palāv(u) (Malayalam plāvu, Kota pala·v, Toda pas̲of); secondarily *pilāv(u) (Malayalam pilāvu).

It is to be noted that Kota and Toda provide the only straightforward evidence for *palāv(u); Malayalam plāvu involves a further aphaeresis (Subrahmanyam 1983: 246). It is unclear whether (as I have assumed) –v– is a development to 'protect' a suffix –ā (for which suffix see a suggestion in Subrahmanyam 1983: 23), or is a substitute (rather than –y–, Subrahmanyam 1983: 333) for the *c seen is Koḍagu palaci, Kannaḍa palasa, palasu (modern Kannaḍa and Badaga halasa) and in the n–forms of Central Dravidian, Telugu (and Kannaḍa) panasa, Parji penac, Gadaba paṇasa, Kuwi paṇhā (< *panVcā). From all this detail we may, for our special

Nilgiri interest, abstract the statement that Kota and Toda in (presumably) pre-Kota-Toda had the same form which is evidenced in detail only by pre-Malayalam (unless indeed there is a similar form not yet recorded from modern dialectal Tamil); this may possibly be an argument for finding that these Nilgiri communities originated from the west in what is now the Malayalam-speaking area. The Irula form and the Badaga are of different non-Nilgiri origins.

SECTION 7

The banana (plantain), *Musa paradisiaca,* Linn. = *M. sapientum,* Linn. (Hooker), is extensively cultivated, but not at as high an elevation as the Nilgiri Plateau (listed in Matthew, but not in Fyson). In addition there is a 'wild plantain, hill plantain', *M. superba,* Roxb. (Hooker), recorded by Gamble as growing in 'W. Gháts...1,000-5,000 feet.' Only *M.p.* = *M. sapientum* is recorded in *DEDR* 5373 with South Dravidian language names, from Tamil to Tulu, all representing **vāṟạy* (for Telugu, *DEDR* 205). Badaga (Hockings) has entries for both species: ba·ye/be·giḍu (giḍu 'plant, bush') '*M. superba*' and baḷe haṇṇu (haṇṇu 'fruit') 'M.p.' The source for the latter is apparently a proverb (Hockings 1988; 379, no. 748) from Bühler's collection made in the middle of the nineteenth century. Hockings says the form ba·le is 'archaic', and probably this is so, a retention in the proverbial context and with reference to the plains species. Otherwise the word for the hill species shows the normal development for *ṟ in the dialect recorded by Hockings. That this is so is clinched by Hodgson's (i.e. Metz's) writing of the word as bláé-(haṇṇu); this represents what would have been in the dialect that I recorded (if I had recorded the word) bá·e or bắ·e, or the like (with retroflex/retracted vowel). Kapp records for Ālu Kuṟumba ba·e (-aṇṇu) 'Banane' and ba·e-mara 'Bananenstaude' with a botanical name *Ensete superbum,* a term, which I have not found elsewhere,[4] and by which the wild/hill plantain must be intended; the phonology of the form, close as it seems to be to the Badaga form, is the correct development within this language. Similarly, the Irula forms va·/va·e (Zvelebil 1973: 56), vä·/va·e (id. 1982: 103) for banana/plantain are regular developments within the language (note *v– retained regularly, as against b– of the languages Badaga and Ālu Kuṟumba); which of the species is intended is not specified. Of the other two languages of the Plateau, Toda has pa·w and Kota va·y vaṇ (Kolme·l dialect; paṇ 'fruit'); only 'banana' was recorded as the meaning. The forms can only be regular continuants of the reconstructed form *vār̤ay; no influence from any of the neighbouring languages (or Tamil, Malayalam, Kannaḍa) can be identified (note among other details Kota v– as against b– of Badaga or modern Kannaḍa, and *r̤ > Malayalam r̤, modern Tamil and Kannaḍa). Another Kota form was recorded as of the Kurgo·j-Kala·c dialect, viz. va·g, which is reconstructed by Subrahmanyam (1993: 430, no. 1194) as from pre-Kota *vāl̠k (i.e. in *DEDR*'s and my writing *va·r̤k). The historical circumstances leading to the retention in Toda and Kota of continuants of the reconstructed form elude us, but they must be similar to those assumed for the jack-tree.

SECTION 8

A large taxonomic family known as *Myrtaceae* is divided into a number of genera, of which several are well-known in India as yielding fruit (and timber). A rather large genus included within the *Myrtaceae* was in one classification known as *Eugenia*; so it appears in Fyson and contains, he says, over 700 species. This is subdivided by others into 'sub-genera' and here there appears, to this non-botanist, to be wild confusion. *Jambosa, Syzygium,* and *Eugenia* appear in Hooker and Gamble; in some taxonomists, e.g. Fyson 3, *Syzygium* seems to replace *Eugenia* in the nomenclature of the species in which we are interested; Matthew includes very few of the species in which we might be interested and separates them between the two generic terms. In several of our *DEDR* entries both *Eugenia* and *Syzygium* are replaced by *Calyptranthes,* a term which has eluded discovery in any of the botanical treatises to which I have had access, except that Lushington lists it in his index with reference to his entries under *Eugenia.* In *DEDR* 2914 and 2917 various botanical terms are recorded for one species, as they were given in our dictionary sources; our two entries have a linguistic relationship which eluded us in detail and which I am still unable to solve. The species is known in Indian English as the 'jamoon plum' (< Hindi jāmun) or the jambu (< Sanskrit jambu-), the nev/wel (< Tamil nāval, Malayalam ñāval), or the rose apple. The botanical synonymy is: *Syzygium jambolanum,* DC. (Fyson 3, Gamble) = *Eugenia jambolana,* Lam. (Hooker) = *Calyptranthes caryophyllata,* Pers. (probably also *C.*

caryophyllifolia, Swartz), to which Gamble adds *Eugenia caryophyllifolia,* Lam. (also Wight), and Matthew (as his accepted term, probably the term to be used now) *Syzygium cumini,* Skeels. For this species the Central Dravidian languages, plus Malayalam, Kannaḍa, and Tulu, use names derived from *DEDR* 2917 *ñā/ēṟVi- (or the like); cf. Badaga (Hockings) ne·raḷu '*S.c.*' Tamil and Malayalam have forms from *DEDR* 2914 ñāval.

Although this species grows (Gamble:340, s.v. *S.j.*) in the plains and the hills up to 6,000 feet, a species with similar characteristics growing in the Nilgiris above 5,000 feet is identified as *Syzygium montanum,* Gamble (Fyson 3) = *Eugenia montana,* Wight (Fyson 1), and is given the English name 'Nilgiri mountain black plum' or (Hooker) 'jamboo'. Its Badaga name is (Lushington, Hockings) pu·na·ge (in Gamble poo nagay), i.e. 'flower(y) nāge'. The element nāge is to be connected etymologically with *DEDR* 2914 Tamil nākai (pronounced in the colloquial [nāhe] or, in some dialects, [nāge] or [nāγe]); this was listed in *DEDR* with Tamil-Malayalam *ñāval, as only a possible etymon.[5] But it any case it seems most likely that the Badaga word is a borrowing from Tamil.

Another closely related species is *Syzygium Arnottianum,* Walp. (Fyson 3, Gamble) = *Eugenia Arnottiana,* Wight (Hooker, Fyson 1) = *Syzygium densiflorum,* Wall.; Gamble: 'at high levels, rarely lower than 5,000 feet.' For Tamil, Gamble gives nāval and nākai of *DEDR* 2914 (which corresponds fairly closely to the data of *Tamil Lexicon*). Badaga (Hockings) for *S.A.* has ne·ri, which corresponds closely enough to Kannaḍa nēṟil of *DEDR* 2917. Hockings gives ne·raḷu, corresponding to Kannaḍa nēṟaḷu of *DEDR* 2917, for 'jamoon, black plum', which he identifies botanically as *Syzygium cumini,* which we found to be Matthew's and probably the modern accepted term for *S. jambolanum* = *Eugenia jambolana* of the older sources. Of the other Nilgiri languages, Kota has ne·rl for *E. A.*, corresponding to Kannaḍa nēral(e) for *E. jambolana*. For Ālu Kuṟumba Kapp (388) records në·ṟi-(mara) 'the tree Eugenia jambolana,' i.e. the plains and lower hills species; the vowel development is normal. The Irula form recorded by Zvelebil (1982: 104) as no·ra-pammu (pammu 'fruit') for *E. j.* presumably belongs in *DEDR* 2917, though the vowel [o·] is still a problem.

Finally, Toda has for *E.A.* the form kö·s̱, for which there are no etyma so far. Rivers identified as *E.A.*, Wight, what he wrote 'kêrs', noting (1906: 344) that it provided fuel for funeral pyres.[6] This word should be from an unattested * kēl–. My *Toda Texts* 1984; 305 ff., text 112, sentence 31), but especially the frequently occurring song formula kö·s̲ far̲ł 'kö·s̲ fuel (par̲ł)' (1971: 866), agree that kö·s̲ is the source of fuel for the pyre, and add (1984: 208 ff., text 18, sentence 25) that the fruit is eaten. The song formula paired with kö·s̲ far̲ł is kö·n dït 'funeral pyre' (tït 'fire'); this may have in kö·n an attribute form kö·s̲-n (then 'fire of kö·s̲ wood') with simplification of the consonant cluster s̲n > n (cf. 1984: 45 f., section 1. 9.4.3 end).

SECTION 9

The 'olive', 'wild olive', or 'mock-olive' is both botanically and linguistically a grand mishmash, and I am not sure that I have disentangled it correctly. What is clear is that whatever species (one or more) is/are involved, the habitat is at a high elevation, over at least 4,000 feet. In section 15 it is recorded that several botanists equated *Olea* species ('olive') and *Ligustrum* species ('privet'). Hooker indicated that *Olea* species and *Ligustrum* species were hard to classify; Matthew (886) writes that the *Ligustrum* genus is in urgent need of revision.

One group of Nilgiri names for these 'mock-olives' is *DEDR* 5419: Kota viky 'olive', viky-marm '*Olea Bournei,* Fyson(?)', Toda pïšky 'wild olive, *O.B.*' In section 15 we state that for Fyson the genus name *Olea* is 'olive' and that he separated *O. Bournei* from *O. glandulifera,* even though others (Gamble, Matthew) combine these two as synonyms. The matter is complicated by Hockings recording for Badaga bikke 'mock-olive, Malabar wild olive, saw-leaved olive linden, *Elaeocarpus serratus*' (also other *E.* species with various attributes before bikke), and Kapp's recording for Ālu Kur̲umba as bïkki-mara '*Elaeocarpus oblongus* (?)'. Fyson 1 (48) lists *E.o.*, Gaertner (and Hooker), with the English meaning 'Nilgiri mock-olive' and a notation: 'Fruit an Olive-like drupe'. Gamble (88) lists *E. serratus,* Linn. and *E. oblongus,* Gaertn. as separate species, as does Hooker. For *E.o.* Gamble gives Tamil bikki, which he must be incorrectly quoting from Lushington, no. 338, where for *E.o.*, under Tamil (and Kannaḍa) the name bikki is given as Badaga (and not Tamil or Kannaḍa). Matthew (178) has the synonymy *E. serratus,* Linn. = *E. oblongus,* Gaertner.

It seems that, unless my botanical identifications for the Kota and Toda words were mistaken, two genera are involved merely because of a likeness of their fruit (cf. Fyson's notation above)—which is certainly not impossible (cf. section 11, where *nelli is used for several species because of their similar fruit tastes). Proceeding further in the same way, to his entry Ālu Kuṟumba bïkki-mara with its queried *E.o.* identification, Kapp added that for Kannaḍa Kittel recorded bikke, bil̤ke [my bir̤ke] 'n. of a small tree with eatable fruits, *Gardenia gummifera'.* Matthew (704 f.) notes that the habitat of this species is 'hills, above 1,000 m.' It is not in Fyson, but Lushington for several *Gardenia* species gives Telugu bikki, Kannaḍa bikke; Gamble lists for four *Gardenia* species Telugu bikki with differentiating attributes, and for one of them (*G.g.*) Kannaḍa bikke.

Using only the Kota and Toda forms, Subrahmanyam (1983; 399, no. 1141; the Toda form is misprinted as pišky instead of pïšky) produced a reconstruction *viri(k)ki, with Toda š < *r before k. Now that we add Ālu Kuṟumba bïkki, in which the vowel change (*i > ï) requires that a retroflex consonant was lost, and noting that the combination of *Gardenia* species with *Olea* and *Elaeocarpus* species allows us to use the Kannaḍa form bir̤ke in the reconstruction, we reconstruct as vir̤k- or vir̤i(k)ki/ay, since Toda š < *r̤ before k is in order (Subrahmanyam 1983; 434 ff., section 37.5.5), as is the vowel ï < * i. The word appears in Telugu and Kannaḍa (in the plains), but otherwise as a Nilgiri name for two different local Nilgiri species with similar fruit. Kota and Toda agree on one species, Badaga and Ālu Kuṟumba on another (there is no record yet for Irula);[7] the third appears only in the plains and languages there.

SECTION 10

A species which grows only on the high Plateau, and which has mythic importance for Todas and Kotas, has a name which was recorded in three of the languages. Search for its etymology in both Dravidian and Indo-Aryan languages has resulted in a non-botanical word which is very plausibly the origin of the name of the species. This is *Ceropegia pusilla* (Wight Hooker). Gamble records it as growing 'on the grassy downs above 7,000 feet', and it is recorded in Fyson also for that area and given an English name 'little lantern flower'. Strangely, Lushington does not include this species among the *Ceropegia* (henceforth *C.p.*) species that he lists. Matthew says that the various species have not been adequately studied and does not list this species for his 'Tamilnadu Carnatic', although he found it in 'Salem' (1981: 261).

It is a low plant with a notable flower ('lantern flower'), but to the Nilgiri tribes it is notable especially for its edible tuberous root (bulb) about one inch in diameter. It is this bulb that is named (*DEDR* 1343) by the Kotas kavḷ and the Todas kafïḷ (–f– = [v]). A Kota story (Emeneau 1944: 39, text 1, sentence 1, and 41, text 2, sentence 1) tells of the origin of the three Nilgiri communities (Toda, Kota, and Kuṟumba) from the previous more primitive undivided people who lived in the jungle or caves and ate gathered jungle produce, including specifically kavḷ bulbs. In a parallel Toda story (Emeneau 1984: 212, text 21, sentences 7–9) the creator goddess of the Todas created a Toda, a Kota, and a Kurumba, and food, viz. honey, fruit, and jungle produce including kafïḷ. These the Todas ate, but the other two, not knowing about them, eventually ate meat. These stories are paralleled in Irula accounts (Zvelebil 1982: 26) of their primeval state when they were given tubers (two especially) by the gods as their food. Though *C.p.* is not one of these two tubers and Zvelebil has not recorded an Irula name for *C.p.*, there is obvious parallelism between all three legends, and we must find in them a Nilgiri areal cultural feature, presumably of some age.

From Badaga an etymologically related name for *C.p.* was recorded by me as kā̈vve (the vowel ā̈ is evidence for *ḷ in an earlier Kannaḍa form of the word); it is recorded in Hockings as kavve (or kauve). Since there is no record of a Kannaḍa kavaḷe (or the like) for a tuber, it seems probable that the Kota-Toda word (*kavVḷ-) was borrowed by Badaga, and presumably that the retraction of vowel (*a > ā̈) and deletion of *ḷ took place at some time between the arrival of the Badagas in the Nilgiris (sixteenth century) and the present; the most generally spoken Badaga dialect has lost retraction of vowels, hence *kavve.*

Repeated search of the etymological dictionary material has found no extra-Nilgiri designations of flora that might be related to the Nilgiri *kavVḷ–. However, Tamil-Malayalam kavaḷam, Kannaḍa kavaḷa, kabaḷa, Telugu kabaḷamu all mean 'mouthful', as do Sanskrit (Māhābhārata) kavala–, Pali kabala–, kabaḷa–, Prakrit kavala– (*CDIAL* 2960). All these items, Dravidian and Indo-Aryan, are listed in *DEDR* 1222 under the verb *kapp– 'to seize with the mouth (as e.g. a dog, tiger, etc.), eat greedily, gulp down', whence also longer forms, especially nouns and expressives, with –v– replacing –pp–

(e.g. Kannaḍa kavakk- 'with the sound of gulping quickly', Kui kavali giva 'to chew the cud'). Whatever may be the exact direction of the various borrowings of items between Dravidian and Old Indo-Aryan (stated very cursorily in *DEDR* 1222 and in Mayrhofer 1956: 186-7, s.v. kavala–), it seems at least worth suggesting that the names of the Nilgiri *C.p.* bulb (*kavVḷ–) might be derived from the 'mouthful' words of Tamil or Kannaḍa (*kavaḷa–), especially when it is remembered that this bulb is said to be about one inch in diameter. This, however, is the sort of etymology that cannot be proven; it is a matter of faith, but possible, even plausible. If it were found acceptable, it might be argued that the Badagas imported the word into the Nilgiris in the modern Kannaḍa form with ḷ and it was borrowed from them by the indigenous communities. I should think, however, that the prominence of *C.p.* in the Nilgiri myths argues for a considerably older presence of the word in the Nilgiris and the borrowing direction that I first suggested.

It may be noted that Badaga (Hockings) also has kavve ga·su '*Curculigo orchioides*, Gaertner', named by Fyson in English as 'yellow ground star', which grows in the hill areas. It is quite different from *C.p.*, but has an edible root, which however is not a bulb but a 'long thick root', rather carrot-shaped. This shape of root is denoted by Badaga ga·su 'root, tuber, rhizome; potato'. My recording of this latter word was gá·su 'potato'. The retracted vowel of my recording is evidence of its derivation, with *ṟ, from Old Kannaḍa geṇasu, (*DEDR* 1578; cf. Tamil kiṟaṅku, Kannaḍa geṇasu, Telugu genasu, etc.). It is evident that the Badagas found no difficulty in using kavve for both species.

SECTION 11

In *DED* 3115 *nelli, two species were combined, *Phyllanthus emblica* (English: 'emblic myrobalan') and the tamarind, both chiefly plains species; *DED* 3114 recorded a Nilgiri species, *Fragaria nilgerrensis*, Kota nel, Toda niṣ̲, which presumably looked to a form without the final *i of *nelli. It was recorded for Toda that the fruit (niṣ̲ ko·y) is a berry which tastes very sour, but when water is drunk, it immediately tastes sweet. It was pointed out by several Indian scholars that since this is the taste effect of the fruit of all three species, the two entries should be united; consequently, they were united in *DEDS* and then in *DEDR* 3755. New material is now to be added from other Nilgiri languages, but there still remain problems in uniting the two original entries.

The botanical synonymy is fairly simple for the species which is often defined with the English 'emblic myrobalan' or 'Indian gooseberry'. Hooker has *Phyllanthus emblica*, Linn. = *Emblica officinalis*, Gaertner, Wight; Matthew uses the first, Fyson and Gamble the second; several other terminologies are rarely used. The species is *nelli in Tamil, Malayalam, Koḍagu, Kannaḍa, Tulu, Telugu, and Gondi. In Parji it was recorded nella; the final vowel cannot represent *i, but in all probability is < *ay (this I hope to demonstrate elsewhere). The species is not found on the Nilgiri summit; Badaga (Hockings) does not record it. Ālu Kuṟumba, at a somewhat lower elevation, has nelli-mara '*Phyllanthus emblica* (Baum, mit essbaren Beeren-früchten)', and Irula, also at lower elevations, has nelli '*P.e.*, emblic myrobalan, gooseberry tree' (Zvelebil 1979: 86; 1982: 26). Although Toda as primary meaning for nis̱ ko·y has the sour/sweet berry which must be identical with Kota nel baṇ '*Fragaria nilgerrensis*', two Toda songs were recorded, whose setting is the lower elevation (the Badaga village Sholur, the Mariamma temple at Bokkapur) at which respectively a buffalo (Emeneau 1971: song 115, vs. 7) and the goddess Mariamma (ibid.: song 204, vs. 3) drank (verb uṇ– [uḍ–]) nis̱ ko·y ni·r 'the juice of the *P.e.* berry'. My original Toda recording of the item also had nis̱ ko·y me·ṇ (me·ṇ 'tree'); since the nis̱ ko·y 'berry' is low on the ground, the 'tree' must be *P.e.* of the lower elevation.

The meaning 'tamarind' is recorded for *nelli in the Central Dravidian languages Konḍa, Kui, Kuwi. This need not be investigated further.

Botanical details for the *Fragaria* species are as follows. Hooker records *Fragaria indica*, Roxb., Wight = *F. nilgirica*, Zenker, 'red strawberry' with bright red fruit, and *F. nilgerrensis*, 'white Nilgiri strawberry' with fruit 'white with pale pink tint'. The small *Fragaria* genus is found 'only in temperate and alpine climates' (Fyson), apparently not in the Indian plains; Gamble records both species, above 1800 metres (= roughly 6000 feet); they are at an elevation not included in Matthew's work.

Three Nilgiri languages are now on record for (presumably) the two strawberry species: Kota nel baṇ (paṇ 'fruit'), Toda nis̱ ko·y (ko·y 'unripe fruit'), Badaga (Hockings) nela muḷḷi (I muḷḷi 'thorn, bramble'; both species are listed). None of these three can be equated with *nelli, since they show no trace of *i. My Kota informant equated nel with nelm 'ground, soil', as Hockings does Badaga nela with nela (= Kota nelm); my Toda recording made no connection of nis̲ with any other word, certainly not with neln 'ground, earth', which appears also as nes̲n in the song-unit: nes̲n bïḍΘfïs 'it has fallen to the ground'. Both the Kota and the Badaga connections seem good; it is even plausible to interpret b in Kota baṇ (< paṇ) as due to the original final m of nelm (this sandhi development has not yet been completely worked out for Kota). It is difficult, however, to equate Toda nis̲ with its neln, nes̲n 'ground, soil'. Subrahmanyam, in his searching treatment of vowels in the Nilgiri languages, especially Toda, found that the Kota and Toda forms for the *Fragaria* were to be derived from *nel– (1983: 126, item 417), no other reconstruction for the Toda form apparently being possible within the conditioning factors that he stated. It is, in fact, uncertain whether for the words for 'earth, ground' (*DEDR* 3676) the reconstruction should be *nilam, as seems to be required by its placing in *DEDR*, or *nelam. The word is found, with the exception of one language, only in South Dravidian. The vowel –a– in the second syllable in these languages produces this indeterminacy in the first syllable (as has been demonstrated long since, especially by Bh. Krishnamurti 1958 and 1961). Subrahmanyam (1983: 220) in dealing with Tulu dialect variation in this word assumed (I think from the placing in *DEDR*) that *nilam is to be reconstructed, perhaps thinking too of derivation from *DEDR* 3675 *nil- 'to stand'. However, the suggested (but queried) listing in *DEDR* 3676 of Parji nendil 'earth, ground' would point to the reconstruction *nelam, but the Parji formation is anything but clear. Comparison in *DEDR* of 3676 *ni/elam with 2913 *ñā/ēl- id. is much more probable, the latter producing Tamil ñālam 'the earth' (apparently only this equivalent of Sanskrit loka–), Telugu nēla 'land, earth, soil, ground', Gondi nēl, nēli 'field, earth, ground', etc. Relationship of the noun bases *nēl– (< *ñā/ēl–) and *nel– presents no insuperable problem; parallels, though somewhat rare, are to be found listed in Subrahmanyam 1983: 176 f., §14.1.6, e.g. item 663 (*DEDR* 3679) Tamil niṟal, nīṟal 'shadow, reflection' (cf. also Burrow 1945: 607). We can conclude then that Toda nis̲ '*Fragaria*' < *nel-is, like the Kota and Badaga forms, derived from *nelam 'ground, earth', and that there is no connection with *nelli of *DEDR* 3755. The separation in *DED* was correct; *nelli, as applied to trees, cannot semantically be a derivative from the 'ground, earth' form.

As to the Toda use of nis̲ ko·y for both the strawberry species and the fruit of the tree *Phyllanthus emblica*, the similar taste must have allowed the Todas to identify the nelli of some other Nilgiri language(s) with their nis̲, even though incorrectly.

SECTION 12

Of the items of flora which are found only on the Nilgiri summits and which have linguistic labels without non-Nilgirian etyma, the first one presented is the tree *Meliosma pungens* = *M. Wightii* ('hill mango'). It is notable as being treated by Todas, Ālu Kur̲umbas (? also Pālu Kur̲umbas), and Irulas as most sacred, its bark being used by all these communities in producing ritual purity; Zvelebil (1982: 25 ff. and 157) identifies it as a most conspicuous Nilgiri culture-areal feature. Linguistically, its name is a lexical areal feature with no etyma elsewhere (Emeneau 1989: 141): *DEDR* 3377 *tūṭay, Kota tu·ṛ, Toda tï·ṛ, Ālu Kur̲umba tu·ḍe, Badaga (Hockings) tu·ḍe (Lushington's toḍe can be ignored); Badaga must, of course, have borrowed from one of the others. The only difficulty is that of connecting the Irula name, tukḍe or tūkḍe, with the others. It can be suggested that the long vowel ū in *tūṭay is a contraction of *–ukV– (Subrahmanyam 1983: 305, §22.2.2, for some examples of this development; cf. *ukir > Kota u·r 'fingernail'); exact treatment of Irula details is not yet possible (e.g. Irula k for *–k–, which should not yield voiceless k; note too the uncertainty about the length of vowel); reconstruction of * tukVṭay does not lead to any further non-Nilgirian etymology.

SECTION 13

One of the genera included within the *Myrtaceae* family (section 8) is the small genus *Rhodomyrtus*. It is represented by one species in South India and Sri Lanka (as well as in Malaysia), viz. *R. tomentosa*, Wight (Hooker, Gamble, Fyson); Gamble records it as growing above 5,000 feet, and consequently it is not in Matthew. Its names are: *DEDR* 3112 *tavuṭṭay, Tamil taviṭṭu, Kannaḍa tavuṭe, Kota tavṭ, Toda tafïṭ, to which we can now add Badaga (Hockings) tauṭe and tavuṭi (which latter may be from Lushington), and Ālu Kur̲umba tavuṭe-mara; Indian English knows it as 'hill gooseberry, hill guava'.

This is practically free from linguistic problems, except the question as to the source of Tamil and Kannaḍa terms for a tree at that elevation. The source in the *Tamil Lexicon* is a modern dictionary of mountain flora with medicinal uses, and it seems highly probable that the term is derived from a Nilgiri source (Kota or Toda, or something comparable) without a final vowel (whence Tamil restored a final –u, rather than –ai < *–ay which is represented by –e in some of the other languages). Kittel's dictionary is unrevealing as to the source of the Kannaḍa word. On the other hand, the terms in the Nilgiri languages are all obviously related, and it may well be that we are dealing with a Nilgiri lexical item without etyma elsewhere.

SECTION 14

A Nilgiri species, the name of which has been recorded in only two languages, is prima facie easy of identification botanically. Rivers (1906: 738) listed 'Kîâz Litsaea Wightiana, Benth. and Hk. f. [i.e. Hooker]'; he wrote: 'The wood...is used when making fire for most sacred purposes' (1906: 435), referring to the firesticks, which are said (1906: 438, 582) to be of kiaz or keadj. My field recording was ke·ʐ (ʐ = [dz]). In a note (Emeneau 1984: 330, text 132, sentence 2) I discussed the identification, noting Lushington's English equivalent 'betel-nut laurel' and a Nilgiri vernacular name kenju recorded in an unidentified language by Brandis 1906. Toda ke·ʐ should be < *kēñcu [kēnju], or possibly < *kēñci if Subrahmanyam's rule (1983: 133), PDr. *e: > To·e:/—(C)y, is to be invoked (otherwise *e: > To·ö· is to be expected). The identity of Brandis's language is still unclear, even though the Badaga name of the species is now at hand. It must be ke·nji; this is given in Gamble (866), spelled keynjee, and by Lushington in his Canarese index (vol. II-B, p. 60): 'Kenji; B[adaga]... 2479 [correct to 2469] *Litsaea Wightiana*'; Hockings ke·nije seems somehow incorrect. Could this Badaga word be the origin by borrowing of Toda ke·ʐ? In fact, however, we should expect the borrowing to have been in the other direction, and this should not be ruled out, since the phonetic equivalence would not have been too difficult for Badaga speakers to recognize.

My slight reservation on the botanical identification results from difficulty in pinning down the synonymy satisfactorily. Gamble has: *Litsaea Wightiana,* Hooker = *Cylicodaphne Wightiana,* Nees; Fyson 1

(349) lists *L. W.*, Wall., Hooker. Lushington has *L. W.*, Wall., but with a cross-indexing for this species under *C. W.*, Nees, and *Tetranthera Wightiana*, Bedd., which last Gamble gives as a synonym for *Litsaea floribunda*, Bl., which in Hooker was somehow related to *L. W.* I am unable to resolve this tangle. Matthew does not have our species, but the three related species he lists have both *Litsaea* and *Tetranthera* in their designations.

SECTION 15

In section 9 a beginning was made in the identification of several trees denominated 'wild olive, mock-olive', but it was clear that the botanical nomenclature so far defies solution. Linguistically, the Nilgiri terms were related to etyma found in plains languages. In this section analysis is attempted of 'wild olive' terms found in three Nilgiri languages and related to one another, but with no etyma elsewhere.

DEDR 1602, Kota kiḏ, Toda kïḏ, was identified as *Olea robusta* (Rivers 1906; 738, has for Toda 'kiḏ probably *O. r.*', which I probably was able to confirm in Botanical Gardens records). To these we now add Badaga (Hockings) *kunde* 'glandular-leaved olive, wild olive, *Olea glandulifera*'. Lushington had recorded for *O. g.*, Wall., that the Badaga name was kuṉde (his spelling; 1915: 110, no. 1787); in the botanical index (275) he records *O. robusta*, Wall., with reference to no. 1795, which is *Ligustrum robustum*, Blume, a privet species (no Badaga name given); if this were a misprint for no. 1785, that is *Linociera intermedia*, Wight, 'common hill olive', with a subspecies *L. Roxburghii*, for which he gives Badaga kuṉde. Gamble (1967: 559) lists *Olea glandulifera*, Wall. = *O. Bournei*, Fyson, with a Badaga name which he spells '*Kunthay*', intending Badaga (Hockings) *kunde*, (Lushington) *kuṉde*; he has (558) several *Linociera* species—*L. intermedia* and *L. Wightii*, C. B. Clarke = *Olea linocieroides*, Wight. Finally, Gamble (560) lists *Ligustrum Roxburghii*, C. B. Clarke = *Olea robusta*, Wight. Hooker had listed *Ligustrum robustum*, Blume = *Olea robusta*, Wall. Cat.; he has no *O. Bournei*. Matthew (892) gives a synonymy *Olea glandulifera*, Wall. = *O. Bournei*, Fyson, and has no *O. robusta*; however, under *Ligustrum Gamblei*, T. P. Ramamoorthy, he puts synonyms *L. robustum*, Beddome (*non* Blume) and *L. Roxburghii*, C. B. Clarke, Hooker. Fyson 1 (278–9) lists *Olea Bournei*, Fyson, and says: 'allied to *O. glandulifera* Wall.'; he lists no *O.*

robusta; he distinguishes (278) the genus *Olea* 'olive' from the genus *Ligustrum* 'privet'. To solve the botanical riddle is beyond my competence; there is obviously an 'urgent need of revision' (Matthew: ibid.).

The three Nilgiri names listed above, Kota kid̲, Toda Kïd̲, Badaga kunde, for what is in all probability *Olea glandulifera* = *O. robusta* = *O. Bournei* (or whatever the most modern botanical revision is or will be), are reconstructible as *kun̲t̲ay. Badaga *kunde* is clear. Kota kid̲ has regular developments: *n̲t̲ > d̲; *u[CC]ay > i (Emeneau 1969); *–ay > *e > zero (short vowel lost in non-initial syllable). In Toda a change from *u to ï (after k–) is expected only before a labial followed by *a (Subrahmanyam 1983: 94 ff.); ï is so much an exception in this word that it is perhaps indicated that the word is borrowed from Kota kid̲, since pre-Toda *i > Toda ï is regular (except when followed by c, č, or s or preceded by *c-, Subrahmanyam 1983: 76-81). *DEDR* 1602, by its position implying the vowel *i, should be changed to a position near entries 1864-65 with vowel *u.

One other Nilgiri language, Ālu Kur̲umba, has (Kapp 1982: 326) kunde for a tree, but the species is unidentified, and one can only guess that it is the one that we are concerned with. *DEDR* 1865 *kun̲t̲i includes a number of trees or climbers (none in the Nilgiris), and there seems to be no possibility of connection with *kun̲t̲ay.

SECTION 16

DEDR 2245 records kōli as Tamil 'sp. privet, *Ligustrum Perrotettii*' and Kannaḍa as this species and *L. neilgherrense*, and with a query Toda kwï·s̲y (which is < *kōli) as merely an unidentified 'sp. plant'. The *Tamil Lexicon* entry, on reexamination, reveals that the source is Lushington, and Lushington reveals that the language he recorded under Tamil was really Badaga for *L. n.*, but Tamil (and not Badaga) for *L. P.* Lushington's entries for the two species give under the Kannaḍa (Canarese) heading both C. (Canarese) and B. (Badaga); however, in his 'Canarese index' he lists 'Kōli' twice (for the two species), but in each entry indicates that the word is only Badaga; Kittel's Kannaḍa dictionary does not have kōli for a *Ligustrum* species. The two species, as listed in Hooker (and Lushington), were later classified as only one: *L. P.*, D. C. = *L. n.*, Wight; so it is indicated in Fyson 1 (280; the genus is not listed in his index), and then in Gamble and Matthew. It is clear that this is found only in the hills, especially (Gamble) the Nilgiris, at 6,000–7,000 feet (Gamble; = roughly 1800–2134 metres), (Matthew; 1000–1500 metres = 3281–4921 feet).

Linguistically, then, Tamil and Kannaḍa give no evidence for the word kōli for this species. For Badaga (attested in Lushington, as above), Hockings gives ko·li 'Nilgiri privet, wax tree, *L. P.*' For Ālu Kuṟumba Kapp recorded ko·li as '*Ligustrum*-Art'. Toda kwï·s̲y may well be this species. I recorded (1974: 82, man's name 812) a name Kwï·s̲yxwï·ṛ, which is 'branch(es) (kwï·ṛ) of the kwï·s̲y tree', one of the trees in front of the dairy at Koḷem, the man's mund (hamlet). The word for this Nilgiri tree is only found in this microarea, Kota not being in the record, unless the unidentified ko·j 'sp. tree' is < *kōli (see fn. 15). Badaga must have borrowed from one of the other languages, but otherwise nothing can be said.

A complication is found in the listing in Kittel's Kannaḍa dictionary of kōli for a quite different species, *Zizyphus jujube*, Lam. This is not found in the Nilgiris, nor is there any place in *DEDR* for this Kannaḍa word for *Z. j.* Kannaḍa kōli for a *Ligustrum* species was a mistake (as determined above) based on Lushington. Whether the Nilgiri word *kōli (for *L. P.*) is to be connected etymologically with the Kannaḍa kōli (*Z. j.*) cannot be determined; for the latter, see further *CDIAL* 3358.

SECTION 17

The numerous *Strobilanthes* (English: 'conehead') species of the Nilgiris have been much written about, because of their conspicuous periodical flowering and because of their place in tribal lore (e.g. in reckoning age by the Todas, s.v. pyu·f xaṭ below). Apart from the listing of the species in the general works which include the flora of the Nilgiris (Hooker, Fyson, Gamble, Matthew 1983), there have been mention and special treatment of the *Strobilanthes*, both botanical (Matthew 1970, Bremekamp 1944) and cultural (e.g. Zvelebil 1982: 24–5; 1988: 35–6; Emeneau 1989: 141).

While there has been much botanical observation and classification of the numerous species, such accounts as Matthew's (1970, 1983) say that the taxonomy still needs working out on the basis of 'careful field studies',[8] and particularly of long-range observations of the periodical flowerings of the different species. So far as I can discover, it is only *Strobilanthes Kunthiana's* twelve-year periodicity that is really vouched for (Matthew 1983: 1205). Of the many species four appear by name in my fieldnotes for Toda. For these I give the synonymies that I have been able to arrive at from study of the varying accounts. Whether the radical revision by Bremekamp (1944) is generally accepted by other botanists is unknown to me even after careful examination of Matthew's much more recent presentation of the species of an area ('Tamilnad Carnatic') bordering on the Nilgiris. Essentially I retain the Latin terminology otherwise used, basing myself chiefly on Matthew (1983). Although *Strobilanthes* was at times treated as masculine when adding adjectives to it, Matthew finds this unacceptable; I give only the feminine forms.

Strobilanthes foliosa, T. Anderson (Hooker, Fyson, Gamble, Matthew) = *Nilgirianthus foliosus,* Bremekamp = *Endopogon foliosus* or *capitatus,* Wight.

S. Zenkeriana, T. Anderson (Hooker, Fyson, Gamble) = *Goldfussia Zenkeriana,* Nees = *Xenacanthus Zenkerianus,* Nees, Bremekamp = *Endopogon strobilanthes,* Wight, Gamble; Fyson (93) finds *S. f.* and *S. Z.* very similar, and *S. Z.* is not in Matthew.

S. Kunthiana, T. Anderson (Hooker, Fyson, Gamble, Matthew) = *Phlebophyllum Kunthianum,* Nees, Bremekamp.

S. consanguinea, C. B. Clarke (Hooker, Fyson, Gamble, Matthew) = *Phlebophyllum spicatum,* Roth, Bremekamp; Matthew finds the recording so uncertain and complex that he would leave this species unnamed until further research is done.

In Tamil literature, where *Strobilanthes* (of the mountain area) appears from the earliest poetry on, the name is kuṟiñci (*DEDR* 1849, with related words in Malayalam and Kannaḍa, according to Lushington). The Nilgiri linguistic microarea does not have any name related to this, but has a name, *DEDR* 1154 *kaṭṭay, recorded nowhere else, plus another unique word generally used in connection with *kaṭṭay. The names derived from *kaṭṭay are: Kota kaṭ (my fieldnote: 'apparently different species are not distinguished', Toda kaṭ ('any species'; *a > Toda a/– *ay, Subrahmanyam 1983: 54, Section 4.2.1.ii), Badaga (Hockings) kaṭṭe '*Strobilanthes* spp.', Ālu Kuṟumba kaṭṭe '*Strobilanthes*-Art'.

The related word appears in the record in several ways. In Kota there was recorded peb 'a big flowering of *Strobilanthes*' (an elicited sentence was: kaṭ peb (p)acuko·, 'there was a big flowering of *S.*', probably 'the *S.* held/had a big flowering'). Badaga (Hockings) has, as well as kaṭṭe, hebbu kaṭṭe with the same meaning '*Strobilanthes* spp.'. Irula has ebbukaṭṭe 'Strobilanthes'. Ālu Kuṟumba has, as well as kaṭṭe for any *S.* species, ebbu-kaṭṭe '(üppig blühende) *Strobilanthes*-Art', i.e. (Zvelebil 1990: 69) 'profusely flowering kind of conehead'.

For Toda I recorded kaṭ with three different attributes as different species (but I certainly cannot guarantee the correctness of my identifications):

mo·f xaṭ '*S. Kunthiana*' (mo·f 'open space away from mund, e.g. where buffaloes are pastured, or people defecate';[9] Fyson on *S.K.*: 'the common *S.* of the open hill-sides, covering large areas');

twa·s̲ xaṭ '*S. consanguinea*' (twa·s̲ 'grove, thicket', *DEDR* 2891; Matthew reports that *S. c.* is found in 'dense thickets, especially in ravines', hence probably the Toda name);[10]

pyu·f xaṭ '*S. foliosa* and *Zenkeriana*' (these were said to flower every eighteen years,[11] and old Toda formerly reckoned, and perhaps still reckon, their age by the number of times they saw the profuse blooming of *S.*, using eighteen years as the interval).

The etymology of pyu·f has been a puzzle. However, systematic investigation of the rather small number of instances of the Toda combination (-)yu·-,[12] and realization that Kapp (1982: 302) had suggested for Ālu Kuṟumba ebbu- (to which must be added Kota peb) *per-pū 'many flowers', have yielded the solution. The combination *-r-p- has resulted in -bb- in a number of the languages including most of the Nilgiri languages; e.g. starting with *per 'big', *per-pāmpu 'big snake' > Kannaḍa hebbāvu 'boa', Ālu Kuṟumba ebba·vu 'python' (*DEDR* 4085 *pāmpu 'snake'); Badaga (communicated by Hockings) ebba·te 'big cockroach' < *per-pāṟṟay, cf. *DEDR* 4123 Malayalam pāṟṟa, Toda pa·ṯ, Koḍagu pa·te, Kannaḍa hāte 'cockroach'; Badaga (communicated by Hockings) hebbaṭṭe/ebbeṭṭu beralu 'thumb' < *per-boṭṭu viralu 'big + finger, thumb, big toe + finger' (Kannaḍa hebbaṭṭu 'thumb, big toe'; cf. *DEDR* 4493).

On the Toda side, there are clear instances of -r-p- (< * -r p-, or *-r v-) yielding f (between vowels phonetically [v]); e.g. pe fï·t 'ham' < per + pï·t 'flesh, muscle' (*DEDR* 4588, cf. Kota po·t 'flesh, meat'); pe fe·ḻ 'thumb' < per + pe·ḻ 'finger, toe' (*DEDR* 5409 *viral/ḷ); pe fiḻy 'big silver ring' < per + piḻy (*DEDR* 5496 *veḷi); pe fiḻy 'great shout of triumph' < per + piḻy *DEDR* 5433 *viḷi); ka fo·n 'the (black) sky' (several examples in Emeneau 1971; 849, s.v., and also in prose) < *kar + *vān (*DEDR* 5381; for *kar → ka, Emeneau 1984; lll f., §VI.4.10).[13] The combination suggested by Kapp for peb and ebbu, viz. *per-pū, would be for Toda *per-pu·f which would yield *pe fu·f, phonetically *[pevu·f]. In investigating the origin of yu·, it was realized that kyu·ḍ 'deafness, deaf' is < *kevuṭu (*DEDR* 1977c, Kota kevṛ, cf. Tamil ceviṭu, Kannaḍa and Badaga kivuḍu).[14] Then, closely parallel, *[pevu·f] 'profuse flowers' yields pyu·f. This is a particularly pleasing areal etymology, because of the aberrant-seeming Toda form—but it is no more aberrant than Toda's many other aberrancies.

SECTION 18

The rhododendron, a conspicuous feature of the Nilgiri landscape above 1524 metres [5000 feet] and related of course to the rhododendron of the Himalayas, is identified botanically by Gamble as *Rhododendron nilagiricum*, Zenk. = *R. arboreum*, var. *nilagirica*, C. B. Clarke. Fyson gives only *R. a,*; Matthew does not list it (his area is too low); Lushington lists *R. a.* (*nilagirica*), essentially as Gamble (and Hooker).

Examination of the linguistic material should, for the moment, leave aside the entries in *DEDR* 4553. New and straightforward material is now at hand: Badaga (Hockings) billi (*R. n.*), Ālu Kuṟumba bille-mara (*R. a.*), and, from recent research in my records, Kota viḷy (*R. n.*). These forms easily yield a reconstruction *villi (*villay for Ālu Kuṟumba).[15] There are no non-Nilgiri etyma for these forms; nothing is so far recorded for Irula. If Toda had a derivative of *villi, it would be pïs̲y. This is not what I recorded; my records have pïs̲x. A recent suspicion that I might have misheard the voiceless y that would have been heard in pïs̲y (very like the fronted velar fricative of German *ich*) and identified it rather as the back velar fricative x (like that of German *ach*), has proved groundless; fresh observation[16] has yielded a statement that there is no pïs̲y, but that the rhododendron is pïs̲k varying with pïs̲x (the unexpected pïs̲k introduces a further problem into the reconstruction, which I solve elsewhere). My Toda record, then, for the rhododendron (*R. a.*), pïs̲x, can only be connected with the other Nilgiri forms derived from *villi/ay by a reconstruction *vil(l)Vṅk- [*v- > Toda p-; *i > Toda ï, except before or after *c; *l or *ll > Toda s̲; *ṅk > Toda x, after vowel in second syllable (Subrahmanyam 1983: 314 ff., section 22.7.2)]; this would certainly be possible, even though it is Toda alone that would require this reconstruction (alongside of *villi/ay);

the new recording would require *vil(l)Vkk-, whose relation to *vil-(l)Vṅk- is unexplained.

However, there are disturbing details not yet treated. For Toda it was recorded that pïs̱x preceded by pum 'fruit' (*DEDR* 4004) or by tö·n 'honey' (3268) denotes a quite different species, *Elaeagnus latifolia*, whose fruit has a pleasant taste (Fyson 'pleasantly acid', Gamble 'edible'), and which Lushington names in English 'wild olive'. Gamble has the synonymy *E. i.*, Linn. (Hooker) = *E. Kologa*, Schlecht, and Matthew uses the latter, which is now apparently the approved nomenclature. The species is recorded as growing 'above 5000 feet.' Rivers (1906: 739) gives purs for both rhododendron and *E. 1.* Apart from Toda pis̱x, Kota polg was recorded for *E. 1.* So far no Badaga name has been identified (in Hockings) Lushington records huḷige for Kannaḍa, but this is not in Kittel. Since prima facie p- in both Kota and Toda requires reconstruction of *p- (rather than *v- of *villi 'rhododendron'), the only way to save a reconstruction of *vil- (l)Vṅk- for Toda pïs̱x '*E. 1.*' would be to posit that Kota borrowed the initial from Toda. Certainly both Toda -s̱x and Kota -lg look to *-l(l)Vṅk-. However, it has not yet been possible (using Subrahmanyam's 1983 statements of development) to connect the vowels Kota -o- and Toda -ï-. No connection is yielded by his statement (94, Section 8.2.3), /*u > Toda ï/ labial– *a, unless a way is found either to motivate *u > Kota o, or to allow *o to become Toda ï (since *o > Toda wa when a non-nasal alveolar, here *l, follows [Subrahmanyam 1983: 140, §12.2.1], and Toda wa loses w after a labial). Lushington's Kannaḍa huḷige is no help. The problem of the relationship of these words must be left unsolved for the moment.

Notes

1. I am greatly indebted to Paul Hockings for a copy of the draft of his and Christiane Pilot-Raichoor's new Badaga dictionary (1992, referred to as Hockings). I should note that my fieldwork on Badaga was concentrated not on the dialect of the majority of the community, but on a minority dialect (probably now near extinction) which is archaic in that it has vowels with two degrees of retraction/retroflexion, which result from ḻ, which is present in the parent modern Kannaḍa and has been almost completely lost in the major Badaga dialect. An account of these vowels was published in Emeneau (1939), with numerous examples. In the present essay items with such vowels are quoted from the 1939 paper and from my still unpublished notes. In quoting Ālu Kuṟumba forms I have omitted accent markings, which are in general placed

according to rule. This essay in general owes much to Zvelebil's proposal of treatment of the Nilgiris as a linguistic microarea. I must acknowledge here the help and advice in botanical matters that have been given me over the years by Lincoln Constance, Professor Emeritus of Botany, University of California, Berkeley.

2. The botanists have at times decided that the Latin gender should be feminine, and have written *A. integrifolia* and *A. heterophylla*; so it is found in some lexical entries. But they seem to treat *Elaeocarpus* always as masculine.
3. For some remarks on the matter, *see* Burrow 1970: 52.
4. Lushington lists *Musa ensete*, giving Abyssinia as its habitat.
5. Subrahmanyam 1983: 305 finds examples of *-k- > -v- in a few instances in Telugu and some colloquial dialects, but it cannot be pushed in *DEDR* 2914.- Hockings suggests derivation of the Badaga na·ge from Sanskrit nāga- 'snake', but the correspondence with Tamil nākai is against this, since Tamil -ai, Badaga -e find no place in such a derivation.
6. My field identification of kö·s̱ as *Lisgustrum lucidum*, a Chinese species introduced into the Nilgiris, was wrong, and all my argumentation (notes on 1984: 208 ff, text 18, sentence 25, and 328 ff, text 132, sentence 2) unnecessary, Rivers' identification was correct, but his writing kêrs (also kers and even, p. 286, kiars) was unrevealing of the phonetics of the word and for some time threw me off the correct track. See also the name of a kö·s̱ tree at a particular mund in Emeneau (1974: 54, name 99). Fyson 1, 152, on *Eugenia Arnottiana*, finds 'berry...juicy but *quite inedible*' (my italics)!
7. Kittel gives for Kannaḍa bīgaḍa mara '*Elaeocarpus lanceaefolius*, Lam.' Whether this is to be related to bikke, biṟke, I cannot determine.
8. Bremekamp's 1944 monograph seems to have been based on an insufficient study of Indian material; he seemed more closely interested in the Indonesian and Malaysian species.
9. *DEDR* 4780 *mā(vu); the meaning is basically 'deer, i.e. (wild) animals of all deer species', whence Toda mo·f 'deer', mo·f ma·ṛ 'jungle animals'; *ā > Toda o·, except when *ay follows in next syllable (Subrahmanyam 1983: 65, section 5·2·1). The meaning 'to go driving (buffaloes) to pasture' for the phrase mo·fa·r fe·ṭ o·ḍ- seems to be literally 'to hunt among the wild animals (or, deer)'.
10. Zvelebil 1982: 25 quotes this identification from Emeneau 1971: 853, s.v.kaṭe θešk 'loops of *Strobilanthes*', where I noted that loops of *S.* 'were used in thatching instead of the tef bamboo now used'.
11. Since an interval of twelve years has now been observed for the profuse blooming of *S. Kunthiana*, eighteen may well be an exaggeration.
12. To be presented elsewhere.
13. There are also examples of *-r t- > θ and *-r k- > x. A more general treatment is in Emeneau 1984: 40, section I.8.5.(1).
14. The only weak point in the etymology is that, corresponding to Tamil -ṭ-, Kannaḍa -ḍ-, Kota -ṛ we should expect Toda -ṛ, i.e. kyu·ṛ. Contamination with the corresponding word in one of the other languages, e.g. Badaga, may be invoked as explanation. Or could there have been interference from (and avoidance of) Kyu·ṛ, the name of a mund (hamlet) of Kï·wïṛ clan, which has a high degree of sanctity (cf. Emeneau 1974: 73, mund name K128 Kyu·ṛ and

mund name K 140 Mo·lkuṣ, the latter being the mund used by women of Kyu·ṛ when they are pregnant or suffering childbirth pollution, i.e. ritually impure)? Of course, no etymology is known for the name Kyu·ṛ.

15. For the Kota form with ḷ, see my forthcoming paper 'Some origins of Kota j (–)'.

16. I must thank Professors Peter Ladefoged and P. Bhaskara Rao for kindly gathering this information for me during their recent phonetic investigations, especially of Toda, in the Nilgiris. —As for *Elaeagnus latifolia*, treated in the last part of this section, their informants did not recognize either pum bïs̠x or tö·n bïs̠x; they gave only pïs̠k pum "the fruit of the pïs̠k tree."

References

Brandis, Dietrich 1906. *Indian Trees.* Dehra Dun: Bishen Singh Mahendra Pal Singh.

Bremekamp, C. E. B. 1944. Materials for a monograph of the Strobilanthinae (Acanthaceae). *Verhandelingen der Nederlandsche Akademie van Wetenschappen, Afd. Natuurkunde,* Tweede sectie, 41.1, 306.

Burrow, T. 1945. 'Dravidian studies V'. *BSOAS* 11.595–616.

——— 1970. 'Notes on some rare words in Sanskrit and their etymology'. *BSOAS* 33.46–54.

Burrow, T., and M. B. Emeneau 1961. *A Dravidian Etymological Dictionary,* (*DED*). Oxford: Clarendon Press. [*DEDS* = 1968. Id. Supplement. *DEDR* 1984. Id. 2nd edition.]

Emeneau, M. B. 1939. 'The vowels of the Badaga language'. *Language* 15. 43–7.

——— 1944–6. *Kota Texts.* (University of California Publications in Linguistics, 2–3.) Berkeley and Los Angeles: University of California Press.

——— 1969. 'A Kota Vowel Shift'. *Journal of Tamil Studies* 1.1.21–34.

——— 1971. *Toda Songs.* Oxford: Clarendon Press.

——— 1974. *Ritual Structure and Language Structure of the Todas.* (Transactions of the American Philosophical Society 64.6.) Philadelphia: American Philosophical Society.

——— 1980. *Language and Linguistic Area.* Stanford, CA: Stanford University Press.

——— 1984. *Toda Grammar and Texts.* (American Philosophical Society, memoir 155.) Philadelphia: American Philosophical Society.

——— 1989. 'The languages of the Nilgiris'. In Paul Hockings. (ed.) *Blue Mountains: The ethnography and biogeography of a South India region.* Delhi: Oxford University Press.

Fyson, P. F. 1915–20. *The Flora of the Nilgiri and Pulney Hill-tops (above 6,500 feet) . . . round the Hill-stations of Ootacamund, Kotagiri and Kodaikanal.* 3 vols.; xxviii, 475; 286; xx, 581. Dehra Dun: Bishen Singh Mahendra Pal Singh; Delhi: Periodical Experts, 1915, 1915, 1920 (reprinted 1974, 1974, 1975). [Vol. 1 contains his earlier taxonomy, and vol. 3 later additions and corrections; they are referred to when necessary as Fyson I and Fyson 3; Fyson without numeral refers to vol. 1.]

——— 1932. *The Flora of the South Indian Hill Stations . . .* 2 vols. Madras: Superintendent, Government Press. [Reprinted New Delhi: Today and Tomorrow's Printers and Publishers, 1977].

Gamble, J. S. 1967 [1915–35]. *Flora of the Presidency of Madras.* 3 vols. Calcutta: Botanical Survey of India. [Since pagination is continuous in the three volumes, page reference when necessary is given without year or volume reference.]

Hockings, Paul. 1988. *Counsel from the Ancients: A Study of Badaga Proverbs, Prayers, Omens and Curses . . .* (Trends in Linguistics, Documentation 4.) Berlin: Mouton de Gruyter.

——— 1989. *Blue Mountains: The Ethnography and Biogeography of a South Indian Region.* Delhi: Oxford University Press.

Hockings, Paul, and Christiane Pilot-Raichoor. *A Badaga-English Dictionary.* Berlin: Mouton de Gruyter.

Hooker, J. D. 1875–97. *The Flora of British India.* 7 volumes. London: L. Reeve and Co.

Kapp, Dieter B. 1982. *Ālu Kuṟumba Nāyann: Die Sprache der Ālu Kuṟumbas.* Neuindische Studien, 7. Wiesbaden: Otto Harrassowitz.

Krishnamurti, Bh. 1955. 'The history of vowel-length in Telugu verbal bases'. *JAOS* 75.237–52.

——— 1958. 'Alternations i/e and u/o in South Dravidian.' *Language* 34.458–68.

——— 1961. *Telugu Verbal Bases.* (University of California Publications in Linguistics, 24.) Berkeley and Los Angeles: University of California Press.

Lushington, A. W. 1915. *Vernacular List of Trees, Shrubs and Woody Climbers in the Madras Presidency.* Vols. 1, 2:A, 2:B. Madras: Superintendent, Government Press.

Matthew, K. M. 1970. 'The flowering of the Strobilanth (Acanthaceae)/(Strobilanthinae *sensu* Bremekamp)'. *Journal of the Bombay Natural History Society*, 67: 502–6.

——— 1981. *Materials for a Flora of the Tamilnadu Carnatic.* Tiruchirapalli: Rapinat Herbarium, St. Joseph's College.

——— 1983. *The Flora of the Tamilnadu Carnatic.* 3 vols. Tiruchirapalli: Rapinat Herbarium, St. Joseph's College.

Mayrhofer, Manfred. 1956. *Kurzgefasstes etymologisches Wörterbuch des Altindischen.* Bd. I: A-TH. 1963. Bd. II: D-M. Heidelberg: Carl Winter Universitätsverlag.

Rivers, W. H. R. 1906. *The Todas.* London: Macmillan and Co.

Subrahmanyam, P. S. 1983. *Dravidian Comparative Phonology.* Annamalai University, Department of Linguistics publication no. 74. Annamalainagar: Annamalai University.

Tamil Lexicon, 1924–39. 6 volumes and supplement. Madras: University of Madras.

Turner, Ralph. 1966. *A Comparative Dictionary of the Indo-Aryan Languages.* [CDIAL]. London: Oxford University Press.

Walker, Anthony R. 1986. *The Toda of South India: A New Look.* Delhi: Hindustan Publishing Corporation.

Zvelebil, Kamil V. 1973. *The Iruḷa Language.* Neuindische Studien, 2. Wiesbaden: Otto Harrassowitz.

——— 1979. *The Irula (Ërla) Language*, part II. Neuindische Studien, 6. Wiesbaden: Otto Harrassowitz.

——— 1980. 'A Plea for Nilgiri Areal Studies'. *International Journal of Dravidian Linguistics,* 9: 1–22.

——— 1982. *The Irula of the Blue Mountains.* Syracuse, NY: Syracuse University.

——— 1990. *Dravidian Linguistics: An Introduction.* Pondicherry: Pondicherry Institute of Linguistics and Culture.

The Western Romance with the Toda

ANTHONY R. WALKER

5

Introduction

In a largely Western-generated ethnographic record, certain groups seem to stand out as having been especially attractive to European observers.[1] People, for example, like the Maasai of East Africa, the Plains Indians of North America, the Nagas of the Indo-Burma frontier and the Balinese of Indonesia. Among the ranks of 'most-favoured peoples', we must surely include the Toda of south India. Of all the Nilgiri communities, they are the ones who have attracted by far the greatest attention. In the 'ethnology' section alone of Paul Hockings's *Bibliography for the Nilgiri Hills of Southern India 1602–1978* (1978), over a quarter of the entries (not solely the works of Westerners, of course) deal exclusively with the Toda; a great many more deal substantially with them (along with other Nilgiri or non-Nilgiri peoples). By contrast, a mere 8 per cent of the entries focus exclusively on the region's dominant ethnic group: the Badaga (despite Professor Hockings's [1980a, 1980b, 1988] yeoman service to rectify the imbalance). But more than this, the Toda, for the most part, are also the ones who have received the greatest admiration.

Let the words of William Yeatts, officer-in-charge of the Madras Presidency volumes of the 1931 Census of India, set the background for this essay.

> More has been written about this tribe, more theories have been evolved about its origin and more prophecies about its future, than about any other tribe or even caste of South India. Rivers's treatise, exhaustive and almost wearisome in its detail, is in itself an indication of the interest this people has aroused and that so many amateurs should have forced themselves to labour through his not very inviting pages is another. That the Todas should arouse such interest is not surprising for in the first circumstance of all, outward appearance, their departure from all South Indian types is marked. Even the most Gallio of Europeans observes the Toda, or at least the Toda male, as something different. The greater stature, the erect carriage, the

luxuriance of hair and beard, the clear and generally lighter skin, the almost Semitic cast of face, the distinctive garment, the easy shepherd's gait that comes from generations of walking over springy down grass, all form a type that even the most unobservant could hardly fail to register. When peculiar customs, uncertain origin, unusual houses set almost always in beautiful surroundings are added and also the melancholy interest that attaches to alleged decay and approaching extinction, it would be strange if the Todas were not a Nilgiri institution. They are known far beyond India and the undesirable side of this fame is shown by the Todas near Ootacamund having sunk to be a globe-trotters' showpiece (Yeatts 1932: 387).

Certainly the Toda were the focal Nilgiri community for the first Westerner known to have climbed these mountains, now almost 400 years ago; and I suspect there can be little argument that, even now, they attract the greatest attention from casual visitors—Western or Indian—to this corner of South India. The (undated) guide I picked up on my most recent visit to the mountains begins its description of the Toda as follows: 'When the Toda men stalk along the countryside roads twitching their mantles, the effect is startlingly patriarchal. They are most dignified in their bearing with well marked facial features' (Halayya 1988: Ch. 6. 2; the first sentence, incidentally, is copied verbatim from page 22 of Mollie Panter-Downes's [1967] book *Ooty Preserved: A Victorian Hill Station*!) More than once I have heard Indian anthropologists talk of avoiding Toda research because, so they say, these people have been 'spoilt rotten' by excessive Western interest. But this is a view that is neither particularly new nor, for that matter, confined to those of Indian nationality. The epitome of nineteenth century British orientalists, Sir Richard Burton, wrote in his book *Goa, and the Blue Mountains*: 'Covetousness is now the mountaineer's ruling passion: the Toda is an inveterate, indefatigable beggar, whose cry, *Eenam Juroo*, "give me a present!" no matter what, –money, brandy, cigars, or snuff–will follow you for miles over hill and dale . . .' (1851: 351–2). And a couple of decades later, Dr John Shortt of the Madras Medical Service could write: 'the Toda, as a class, are much spoiled, so much so, that nobody now-a-days can go to see them without paying a *douceur*, which, if not gratuitously offered, is sure to be asked for and expected as a right . . .' (1869: 230).

This essay details and analyses the history of relations between the Toda community and various categories of Westerners (in the Toda language, generically *ars*, the original meaning of which was 'king' [cf. Tamil-Malayalam, *aracan*; Kannada *arasa*] with whom they have been associated over the past four centuries). Particularly,

I am interested in exploring Western attitudes to the Toda. The focus is not so much the socio-economic and cultural changes the former have so frequently helped propagate among the latter, a subject I have dealt with at some length elsewhere (Walker 1986: 240-93). Because the first Westerner known to visit the Toda was a Christian priest, the study begins with the Christian missionaries. The next Europeans to come to the Nilgiris, several centuries later, were officials in the employ of the British East India Company; then, not long after them, a whole posse of explorers, adventurers, and amateur ethnologists. The reactions of some of these men and women are examined. Finally, a brief analysis of the academic interest in the Todas is offered.

Western Missionaries and the Toda

In 1584, a twenty-year-old Italian Jesuit priest, a native of Capua, arrived in Malabar, where he was destined to remain until he died nearly half a century later, in 1632 (Ferroli 1939: 250, 390–1). His name was Giacomo Fenicio, and because he wrote his missionary reports in the dominant secular language of the Roman Church in the India of his time, he is often mistakenly credited with Portuguese ethnicity. Fenicio is a very important figure in the history of the Toda. Not only was he the first Westerner to report on these people, but his was the first substantial ethnographic account of them from any source whatsoever. In a very real sense, Toda history (*contra* proto- and pre-history) begins with this Jesuit priest's 1603 visit to the Nilgiris. Fenicio, then based in Calicut, climbed up the high Nilgiri Plateau at the command of the Bishop of Angamale, following a less-than-fully satisfactory 1602 expedition to these mountains by a Malayali priest and deacon. The clerics were investigating rumours circulating among the Roman hierarchy in Malabar that living in these Nilgiri mountains was a lost community of backsliding Christians of the Malabar Syrian rite (Whitehouse 1873: 132). A translation of Fenicio's report, from a manuscript presently in the British Museum (Fenicio 1603), appears as Appendix 1 of W.H.R. Rivers's classic study (1906). Fenicio met and conversed with a *poḷo·ḷ* the highest-ranking grade of dairyman-priest (Rivers 1906: 83-122; Walker 1986: 149-56) and visited a Toda hamlet. His largely descriptive report provides us with valuable data on the

Toda as they were at the beginning of the seventeenth century: on the institution of the *poḷo·ḷ*, on the Toda's buffalo-based economy, their eating habits, their marriage and funerary customs, and on their political subordination to Badaga headmen. It is a pity, however, that he says so little about his personal reactions to the Toda. It is clear, of course, that the Jesuit's interests were essentially evangelistic and his observations, as one might expect, thoroughly coloured by his own religious ideology. When the *poḷo·ḷ* asks after Fenicio's welfare, he replies: 'well and all the better for meeting him for it proved to me that God was my guide, since I had come so far to see the Thodares and immediately met with their chief.' (Rivers 1906: 724). He describes the *poḷo·ḷ* as 'a huge man, well-proportioned, with a long beard and hair *like a Nazarene'* (emphasis added); he takes the opportunity to show the dairyman-priest his Christian icons and Bible. Later he preaches to a party of Toda, but is clearly not sufficiently enthused by their response as to wish to embark on any programme of active evangelism. On the contrary, he advises his superiors not to undertake work in these hills: 'I do not think that the present is a suitable time for the Company to undertake such out-of-the-way enterprises', he writes, 'since it cannot attend to others of *greater importance* which are close at hand for want of workers' (Rivers 1906: 729, emphasis added). This advice, incidentally, was to give the Toda community a two-and-a-half-century-long reprieve from evangelistic Christianity.

The next Christian propagandist to strive for 'Toda souls' was more earnest than Father Fenicio, but no more successful. He was the German Protestant, Johann Friedrich Metz, who worked for the Swiss-based Basel Evangelical Mission Society, which in 1846 established a base for its itinerant preachers in the Badaga village of Ketti (Hockings 1980a: 188). Hockings sketches a nice portrait of Metz 'tramp[ing] from village to village—a different one almost every day—preaching as he went'. 'Arrogant[ly] self-righteous', Hockings writes, Metz's 'contempt for . . . [the people to whom he preached] bordered on paranoia'. And Metz's own, far from endearing comments on the Toda certainly seem to vindicate Hockings's charge. Winning not a single convert among the community, he was obviously frustrated and writes of the people as being 'virtually atheists, leaving nearly all religious concerns to their priests, and never giving themselves the smallest trouble about them' (Metz 1864: 133). Listen to this account of his visit to a *poḷo·ḷ* at his *ti·* dairy-complex and reflect then on how very much more charitable was his Roman predecessor, two-and-a-half centuries earlier:

A visit to the abode of one of these ascetics enabled me to see what a life of useless self-abnegation they are constrained by their customs to lead. My object was to deliver to him the gracious message of Salvation by faith in Jesus Christ, and to induce him to return to his family and friends . . . . I endeavoured to persuade the youthful Palaul of the utter futility of his endeavours to secure favour of a spotless God towards himself and his kinsmen by a mere act of self denial, while his sins remained unpardoned and the wrath of God rested upon him (Metz 1864: 39–41).

Sometime during Metz's missionary career in the Nilgiris, other men of the cloth, spiritual heirs of Fr. Fenicio, were also in contact with the Todas. Unfortunately, I have failed to track down any of their writings and have to rely on a notoriously unreliable though certainly entertaining source, the famous theosophist and mystic, Madame Blavatsky (more on her own reactions to the Toda later on). She talks of Jesuit priests with their 'habitual shrewdness' establishing 'good friendship' with the Toda and discovering:

to their great joy—for they detest the Protestants still more than the pagans . . . that Metz might have lived with them for centuries in the most intimate friendship [somewhat unlikely given what we know of his character] without making the slightest impression upon them.

'The white man's language resembles the chattering of the maina or the gabbling of monkeys' [said the Toda to the Jesuits] . . . 'We listen, and we laugh . . . What need have we of your gods while we have our great buffaloes?' (Blavatsky 1930: 103).

Well, accurate or not (much of Blavatsky's Nilgiri work is clearly not, the sentiments and buffalo allusions seem to ring true, even though, as it happens, Metz was a rather fluent speaker of Badagu (Hockings 1989: 354), a language which the Toda men of that time would certainly have known. Blavatsky's book appeared first in her native Russian in 1893, and she writes (1930: 104) that 'these events took place about ten years ago'; she goes on to comment that, 'since then, the missionaries of the two religions have abandoned their efforts' having 'finally realized that their endeavours would mean nothing but a loss of time' (shades of Fenicio 250 years before).

As a matter of fact, there was to be only a temporary cessation of Christian proselytism. Indeed, even before Blavatsky's book had gone through press, another, and this time much more successful, missionary onslaught had begun: that of the Church of England Zenana Mission Society. In the Nilgiris, this mission is inseparably linked with the name of Miss Catharine F. Ling. Sometime during the final years of the nineteenth century, this dedicated woman had set up a school for Toda children and, from among its pupils, in 1904, she had won her first convert. Labouring for forty-three years among the Toda, Ling succeeded where others had failed, and to this day there exists a small Christian Toda community, with three of its own 'traditional' (in that they are located on ancestral Toda lands) villages, but with members widely scattered and intermarried throughout the district, state, country and even overseas. But that is another, if connected, story (Walker 1986: 263–74). Here I am interested only in Miss Ling's personal reactions to the Toda. Like so many Westerners before and after her, she was struck by the people's physical appearance: 'a fine race, taller and fairer than the people of the plains', she writes in her book, *Dawn in Toda Land* (1910: 5), and repeats much the same comment in her *Sunrise on the Nilgiris* (1934: 4), 'a fine race, tall and well proportioned and capable of travelling long distances on foot'. And of the Toda character, Ling writes (with an enthusiasm and empathy markedly different from those of our old acquaintance Brother Metz) that:

> They have certainly a great charm, a sort of natural refinement, a sense of humour to which one can appeal and which often turns an otherwise serious situation into an occasion for laughter . . . Kind-hearted and loyal to their own, they will never give away a friend . . . Generous to a fault and hospitable, the Todas would consider it an insult to ask anyone to pay for entertainment (Ling 1934: 4).

Although Miss Ling avoids any explicit comparison, except with regard to the colour of skin, I would guess that here she is, at least subconsciously, contrasting her Toda friends with peoples of similar socio-economic background both in the Nilgiris and on the plains below them. But Miss Ling's appraisal of Toda character is not entirely positive. In *Sunrise on the Nilgiris* (1934), she writes: 'They do not love work, and there is a lack of perseverance and continued effort'; and cites an assertion by 'a candid friend' that the Toda character is like Reuben's blessing: 'Unstable as water, thou shalt not excel.' These are surely ethnocentric remarks based on a 'Protestant ethic' which obviously excludes from the rubric 'work' the admittedly rather leisurely male task of herding buffaloes, well used to roaming the Nilgiri grasslands on their own; the hours which women spend embroidering shawls and other cloth items (while chatting to one another) under a shade tree; and the many more hours that both men and women devote to the preparation and performance of ritual. Come to think of it, I might be prepared to argue that the truly 'original affluent society' was not that of the gatherer-hunters (Sahlins 1972: 1–39), but rather of the Toda pastoralists; and, unlike Miss Ling, I am delighted for them!

Other Westerners of the missionary persuasion came into contact with the Toda, particularly during the first half of the present century, but none, to my knowledge, has left us with so detailed a record of their work and views on this people, as have Johann Metz and Catharine Ling. Besides, I suspect that these two, though they were of a vastly different character, provide us with a relatively accurate overview of that profession during the mid-nineteenth to the mid-twentieth centuries. Convinced of the correctness of their cause, they determinedly devoted their lives to the conversion of these 'benighted pagans'. But, beyond this central conceit, they varied greatly in the degree of empathy they were able to achieve with the people amongst whom they had chosen to spend their lives. It seems unlikely that Metz's departure from the Badaga Christians would have caused such dismay as did Catharine Ling's from the Toda. This is part of a song composed by her Christian converts when she retired to England:

> There is no relative at all to help us.
> We have become like children on the lap.
> We have become like calves in the calfpen (Emeneau 1971: 632–3).

Emeneau, who was with the Toda shortly after Miss Ling's retirement, vividly describes the situation:

> The Toda Christians who had turned to her for settlement of all their difficulties now found themselves without strong and sympathetic guidance, and dissatisfaction with those who succeeded her and quarrels among themselves . . . produced in the community what may only be regarded as disintegration (Emeneau 1939a: 95).

Representatives of the Company and Raj (At Work and On Leave)

The Honourable East India Company acquired the Nilgiris in 1799 as part of the lands annexed from the territory of Tipu Sultan, the

Muslim ruler of Mysore, whom the Company's troops had defeated that same year at his capital city of Seringapatam (Thurston 1913: 178, 180). But another couple of decades were to pass before the first Englishmen would set eyes upon a Toda. These were assistant revenue surveyor William Keys, and his apprentice, C. McMahon, in 1812, apparently the first Westerners to reach the high plateau since the Italian Jesuit twenty-one decades before. Keys remarks on the 'uncommonly rude appearance' of the Nilgiri highlanders, 'more especially the Thothavurs', apparently because of the soiled condition of their clothing and the abundance of their hair (Keys [1812] in Grigg 1880: xlix); his minimal ethnographic observations are certainly no match to those of Fenicio a couple of centuries before him.

The Toda themselves seem long ago to have forgotten Fenicio and even Keys and McMahon. They talk (and sing) of John Sullivan, Collector of Coimbatore and founder of Ootacamund, as the first Englishman to meet with them. Sullivan first came to these mountains in January of 1819 and climbed up again in March of the same year (Francis 1908: 108; Hockings 1973). An anonymous letter 'from a subscriber' dated 23 February 1819 and published in the *Madras Courier* of 30 March of that year was probably penned by Sullivan himself. The writer paints a reasonably accurate picture of Toda habitations and pastoral economy; he also mentions their polyandrous marriage institution. More generous than Keys with his remarks on Toda appearance, he describes the menfolk as 'robust and athletic, with a marked expression of countenance, Roman noses, and handsome features.' But he is less enthusiastic about the womenfolk, whom he reports as having 'anything but a prepossessing appearance: their features are coarse and their mouths unusually wide . . . . Their dress consists of a single cloth, which completely envelops their persons, and effectually conceals any grace of figure they may possess'. He remarks that 'Both men and women are fair—fairer perhaps than the fairest Mohamedans' (Anonymous [1819] in Grigg 1880: liv). By contrast to the Toda, he reports (ibid.) the Kota as 'more diminutive, their complexions darker, and their features less expressive'.

During his second visit to the mountains in March 1819, Sullivan was accompanied by a French naturalist, M. Leschenault de la Tour, who reported not only the polyandrous marriage institutions of the Toda, but also their custom of permitting formal sexual relations between members of the otherwise endogamous subcastes. And Leschenault remarks of the Toda that 'the symmetry of this race of people is beautiful, and their countenances are fine' (English translation in Hough 1829: 7).

Following Sullivan and Leschenault, sundry nineteenth-century British officials, military men, clerics and travellers wax eloquent over the physical appearance and general demeanour of these people. And many of them like to credit this linguistically Dravidian and sociologically thoroughly south Indian community with a foreign origin. Let just a few examples suffice.

In a letter from Coimbatore of 3 Nov. 1826, and addressed to the *Bengal Hurkaru*, an English-language newspaper published from Calcutta, the Rev. John Hough, a chaplain on the Madras establishment, describes the Toda with what seems today quaint (at best) Victorian hyperbole:

> in appearance, a noble race of men, their visages presenting all the features of the Roman countenance very strongly marked, and their tall athletic figures corresponding with the lineaments of the face. Some of them stand upwards of six feet high, and differ, in every respect, from all the tribes of Asiatics with which we are at present acquainted . . . I cannot but think that they may be found to be the remains of an ancient Roman colony . . .
>
> Their bodies are well proportioned, and their limbs remarkably muscular, possessing herculean strength. . . . It is beautiful to observe the agility with which they bound over the hills, shaking their black locks in the wind, and as conscious of liberty as the mountain deer, or any true-born Briton. They are remarkably frank in their deportment; and their entire freedom from Hindoo servility is very engaging to the Englishman, and cannot fail to remind him of the 'bold peasantry' of a still dearer land. When before you, they are constantly smiling, and are addicted to immoderate laughter. If amused with anything they have heard or seen, they will retire to a short distance, throw themselves on the ground, and laugh till they seem literally convulsed.
>
> The women, with the exception of the mouth, which is wide, possess handsome features, and their complexion is fairer than that of the men. Their teeth are beautiful, which is quite an anomaly in India, and great vivacity sparkles in the eye. . . . I cannot imagine the ancient Roman (if we except the quality and cleanliness of their habiliments) to have presented a finer figure than those of some of the Thodawurs (Hough 1829: 63–8).

Having devoted one whole letter to the Toda, the following week (10 November) he wrote another, in which he summarily dealt with all the remaining Nilgiri peoples! If length alone does not suggest his bias, listen to what he had to say of the Badaga: 'They are an inferior race to the Thodawurs; being, with a few exceptions, very diminutive . . . the visages of some of the elder women are frightful' (Hough 1829: 89–90). And of the Kota, 'their dress is the same as that of the Thodawurs, but worn less gracefully . . . their front and side locks point in all directions, and give them a wild, shaggy appearance' (Hough 1829: 101). The Kuṟumba and Irula he pretty much summarily dismissed as 'wild inhabitants of the mountain's side' (Hough 1829: 109).

Some forty years after Hough, another member of the Madras establishment, the medical officer John Shortt, accounted for current Western attitudes to the Toda in the following words:

> In physique by far the most prepossessing [of the Nilgiri peoples] . . . it is this superiority of personal appearance . . . [and their] bold and self-possessed deportment and unique social and domestic institutions, that have at all times attracted for them the greatest share of attention and interest from Europeans (Shortt 1869: 236).

Captain Harkness of the Madras Army, in his book with that splendidly nineteenth century title, *A Description of a Singular Aboriginal Race Inhabiting the Summit of the Neilgherry Hills, or Blue Mountains of Coimbatoor, in the Southern Peninsula of India*, remarks of the Toda appearance:

> A large, full, and sparkling eye, Roman nose, fine teeth, and pleasing contour; having occasionally the appearance of great gravity, but seemingly ever ready to fall into the expression of cheerfulness and good humour, are natural marks, prominently distinguishing them from all other natives of India (Harkness 1832: 7).

The Captain, of less speculative bent than some of his civilian colleagues, ends his still rather informative work, not in the manner so typical of his time 'THE END', but rather—and still in capital letters—'WHO CAN THEY BE?'

Government surveyor John Ouchterlony, writing of his 1847 survey of the Nilgiri Hills, had no qualms about suggesting an answer to just that question. Remarking that 'In form and countenance the appearance of the Todas is striking', he further writes that 'their bold independent carriage, and finely moulded and sinewy limbs attest that they can be sprung from no effeminate eastern race.' (Like my Chinese colleagues working on imperial Chinese reports of the minority peoples in the southwest of their country, I too cannot but feel some embarrassment at the language of my imperialist forefathers!) Rather, Ouchterlony avers:

Femme toda. —Dessin de P. Fritel, d'apres un croquis de M. Jaaseen.

their aquiline nose, receding forehead, and rounded profile, combined with their black bushy beards and eyebrows, give them so decidedly Jewish an aspect, that no beholder can fail to be impressed with the idea that they must, in some way, however remote, be connected with one of the lost and wandering tribes of ancient Israelites. (Ouchterlony 1848: 51)

And if one is to be embarrassed by the language of nineteenth century imperialism, let's make it clear that the men of religion were often no better than their secular contemporaries. Listen to the words of the Rev. C.F. Muzzy, a one-time resident of the Nilgiris, published from Madras in an 1844 number of the *Christian Instructor and Missionary Record*:

The Todas, or Todavas, are another tribe, differing, not only from their immediate neighbours, but from all the tribes in this part of the world . . . Their appearance is very prepossessing. Generally they are above the common stature, athletic, and well made; and their open and expressive countenances and bold and manly bearing form a striking contrast with the stupid, pusillanimous, cringing appearance of the natives of the plain. (Muzzy 1844: 360)

Another military man, Captain Harry Congreve, was more restrained with his comments on Toda character and appearance—'an inoffensive pastoral race', he writes of them in his paper 'The Antiquities of the Neilgherry Hills, including an Inquiry into the Descent of the Thautawars or Todars' (1847: 77)—but not so in his enthusiasm for their origins:

It is possible that a remnant of one of the Scythian tribes, driven from place to place by the hostility of the inhabitants of the country they invaded, at length found shelter and tranquillity in the mountain fastnesses of the Neilgherries; a region probably more resembling in climate and altitude the steppes of their own country, than any other in India, and in which their posterity may have since continued, or the Thautawars of Scythian descent, were the aborigines of the plains prior to the Hindoo invasion before which they fled to the mountains.

In the sequel I shall produce strong and numerous proofs to this hypothesis of their descent . . . [and am] confident that I shall be able to establish satisfactorily the fact that a relationship subsisted between the Thautawars and the Scythians of Europe and Asia (Congreve 1847: 77–8).

To be fair, not all nineteenth century Western commentators were quite as ready to jump to Jewish, Roman, or some other equally improbable theory of Toda origins. Sir Richard Burton writes in his book that:

As the Toda race is, in every way, the most remarkable of the Neilgherry inhabitants, so it has been its fate to be the most remarked. Abundant observation has been showered down upon it; from observation sprang theories, theories grew into systems. The earliest observer remarking the Roman noses, fine eyes, and stalwart frames of the savages, drew their origin from Italy–not a bad beginning! Another gentleman argued from their high Arab features, that they are probably immigrants from the Shat el Arab, but it is apparent that he used the subject only to inform the world of the length and breadth of his wanderings . . . . Captain Congreve determined to prove that the Todas are the remnants of the Celto-Scythian race . . . . He has treated the subject with remarkable acuteness, and displayed much curious antiquarian lore; by systematically magnifying every mote of resemblance, and, by pertinaciously neglecting or despising each beam of dissimilitude, together with a little of the freedom in assertion allowed to system-spinners, he has succeeded in erecting a noble edifice, which lacks nothing but a foundation (Burton 1851: 339-40).

Such spinners of theories (and their critics) aside, generations of British officials who served in the Nilgiris seem, almost to a man, to have had a 'soft spot' for the Toda. 'It is impossible not to like them', wrote Commissioner James W. Breeks, the first civilian officer in charge of the newly-constituted Nilgiri district (not yet a collectorate) in his book posthumously published in 1873, 'if only for their independence and good-humour.' Breeks, as a matter of fact, was one of the more perceptive observers of Toda physique, less prepared than most to proclaim their complete physical difference from other Indians. 'The facial peculiarities of the Todas are not so great as they at first sight appear', he wrote. 'When they shave and wear turbans, which many now do, they are hardly to be distinguished from other natives.' But Breeks goes on to remark that:

Their frank bold manners are, however, entirely peculiar to themselves, and very attractive. A Toda laughs without disguise or restraint at anything in an Englishman that strikes him as ludicrous, and generally seems to consider himself as an equal or superior. (Breeks 1873: 7)

Breeks, like Catharine Ling who was to arrive in the Nilgiris some years after his death, was not impressed with the Toda capacity for work, at least outside that relating to their buffaloes; but neither was he inclined to moralize over it. Instead he relates a charming tale:

Labour of any kind they hardly ever attempt; indeed so entirely incomprehensible is the notion to them, that when, on one occasion, an unlucky mistake about the ownership of some buffaloes committed an old Toda to jail, it was found impossible to induce him to work with the other convicts, and the authorities, unwilling to resort to harsh measures, were compelled to save appearances by making him an overseer (Breeks 1873: 9).

In summary, the impression one gains from reading their numerous reports is that the reactions of the expatriate servants of the Raj to the Toda community were primarily coloured by the striking physical appearance and open behaviour of these people. That these reactions were ethnocentric is abundantly clear for, in both these dimensions, the Toda reminded the British of their own kind rather than of other Indians, an observation made almost *ad nauseum* in the early Western writings on this community. Those who were prepared to go beyond personal appearances were also fascinated by the apparent uniqueness of Toda social custom, particularly their sexual mores and their more-or-less exclusive devotion to their buffalo herds, from both economic and ritual perspectives. Most observers, it is probably true to say, did not delve very deeply into these matters. But there were notable exceptions. Harkness's *A Description of a Singular Aboriginal Race,* Marshall's *A Phrenologist amongst the Todas,* and Breeks's *An Account of the Primitive Tribes and Monuments of the Nilagiris* arguably rank among the classics of nineteenth century ethnography. More important yet, these books may still be read with advantage by students of Toda society (who, needless to say, must exercise caution with them, as well as thoroughly digest more recent work).

Daughters of Russia: Mystic and Socialist

During the three-quarters of a century between 1893 and 1969, two daughters of Mother Russia wrote books in large part devoted to the Toda. Even the titles are rather similar: in English translation, 'Enigmatic Tribes on the Blue Mountains' (1893) and 'The Secret of the Tribe of the Blue Mountains' (1969). Moreover, despite the vastly differing ideological persuasions of these two Russian women, there are yet some interesting parallels between the writings of the nineteenth-century theosophist, Elena Petrovna Blavatskaia (or H.P. Blavatsky, the form she usually used in her English-language publications) and the twentieth-century teacher of Russian, Liudmila Vasilevna Shaposhnikova. Both women, for example, are vociferous in their distaste for British colonialism, as also in their contempt for Christian missionary activity. At all periods of history the British 'prestige' had to proclaim aloud its presence, otherwise it might possibly be forgotten, writes Blavatsky (1930: 23), and continues

(p. 26) 'Official Anglo-India created an abyss between herself and the natives, an abyss so profound that milleniums cannot bridge it'. And with particular regard to the Toda, she writes:

Profiting by the fact that the 'masters of the mountains' had reserved for themselves the highest peaks of the Nilgiri [*sic.*] for the pastures of the 'sacred buffalo', the English usurped nine-tenths of the Blue Mountains. . . . Although the 'fathers' of the Company—and after them the government bureaucrats—continued, on paper, to bestow upon the Todds [*sic.*] the title of 'legal proprietors of the ground,' they as always, acted like 'lords toward barons.' (Blavatsky 1930: 94–5).

'India's gaining her independence was essentially the salvation of the Todas,' Liudmila Shaposhnikova (1969: 26) opines.

As for the missionaries, we have already noted something of Blavatsky's views. She writes (1930: 95), too, that, 'The missionaries, who would not let the opportunity slip by, mocked at the natives and their faith in the gods and the spirits of the mountains.' Shaposhnikova's attacks against missionary enterprise are more virulent still. Writing of Dunmere, a Christian school and 'industrial centre' in Ootacamund, she says:

The school isn't the only place in 'Dunmere' where you can meet the Todas. The industrial centre for the Todas is here. It was created by the energetic Catherine Ling in her day. The Toda women come to the Centre and get work—pieces of cloth with a design marked out on them. These are future tablecloths and napkins. For a gracefully embroidered tablecloth, the missionaries pay the women 5 rupees, and they sell it right here at the Centre for 25 rupees. For a napkin the makers get 2½ rupees, and the mission—10 rupees. In this way the missionaries rob about fifty Toda women every week, forgetting about the 'depravity' and sins of the tribe. Money has no religion.

The robbery for the embroidery, of course, is the most innocent. The mission took tens and hundreds of acres of land away from the Todas . . . . When you see the villa 'Dunmere', don't believe its peaceful and decorous atmosphere. Its inhabitants are stealing not only the souls of the Todas, but also the very last thing that the tribe has (Shaposhnikova 1969: 180).

Of missionaries Metz and Ling, Shaposhnikova writes:

Metz's stories about Christ were soon effaced from the memory of the people in the tribe . . . but a little while later a more sinister representative of the Christian army reminded the Todas of the alien God—the English Miss Catherine Ling . . . hers was a strong character, 'larded with' hysterical religiosity and fanaticism. These were just the kind of 'soldiers' that the church of the British Empire needed. Catherine Ling was worth ten Father Metzes. And she had even greater support—the colonial authorities and police (Shaposhnikova 1969: 182).

But, however much they may agree on the evils of British imperialism and the Christian missionary enterprise, one would not expect Blavatsky, the theosophist, and Shaposhnikova, the socialist (and, from her Morgan-like explanation of the Toda matriclans as indicators of a former matriarchy [1969: 126], I would guess theoretical Marxist as well) to react to the Toda in an identical light. And, of course, they don't.

The views of Blavatsky, who is rather charmingly described by a Danish reviewer of my own book on the Toda as 'that dubious high priestess of Victorian mysticism' (Pedersen 1988: 144), probably represent the ultimate nineteenth-century flight of fancy, so far as Western writings on the Toda are concerned. Little bothered, indeed even contemptuous, about her contemporaries' more mundane search for Toda origins, she claims for the community supernatural powers 'of which our savants have no conception' (Blavatsky 1930: 118); she puts these words into the mouth of her Nilgiri host, General Henry Rhodes Morgan, the planter and retired military man, whose wife seems also to have been of theosophical bent. Blavatsky writes that:

> All these peculiar [Toda] ceremonies, these rites belonging in a philosophy obviously secret, lead people versed in ancient Chaldean, Egyptian, and even medieval magic, to think that the Todds [Toda] are cognizant, even if not of the whole system, at least of a part of the veiled sciences, or occultism . . . . According to us—and it is our unshakable conviction—the Todds are the disciples—half unconscious, perhaps, of the antique science of *white* magic, while the Moulou-Kouroumbas [Mullu Kurumba] remain the odious offspring of *black* magic and sorcery (Blavatsky 1930: 185–6).

Shaposhnikova, as befits a modern Soviet humanist, is more temperate in her reactions, but by no means bereft of flights of fancy—if only of a social evolutionary bent. And (if the English translation I have at hand is any indication) she writes much better than Blavatsky:

> The Toda and I were people from different worlds. Thousands of years lay between us, and this barrier had to be overcome. The Todas live according to a tribal system, and I had come from a country in which a socialist system had been formed. We understood everything in different ways, but the time came when the ordinary human mutual understanding, which is peculiar to all people, even very different ones, came to us . . . .
>
> For some strange, and, at present, not easily explained reason, life has thrown this fragment of an ancient people into the modern world . . . . And so, in order to get into the past, one doesn't have to invent a time machine. Modern means of

transportation, specifically, the 'Nilgiri Express', are entirely suitable for this purpose. History has made a generous gift to men of the atomic age. It has preserved, almost inviolate, the customs, traditions, and social organization of a tribe which can claim more than a thousand years of existence. And, this, by the way, in the center of a region in which capitalist cities have been built, in which the poles of high-voltage transmitters march along the mountains, in which electric stations and dams are erected. But the Todas stubbornly refuse to yield to the influence of civilization and continue to live as their forefathers lived in far-off times. And already a second century of scholars is struggling with the riddle of the Todas.

In the style of Edward Burnett Tylor and Lewis Henry Morgan, but, oh, so much better written. Would that Rivers had peppered his prose just a little, in the style of this daughter of Soviet Russia!

Western Travellers from Many Lands

Already we have heard descriptions of the Toda from the pens of an Italian, a German, many Britons, and two Russians. When we turn, anon, to the anthropological community, we will hear from two more Britons, two Americans and a Greek. But none of these can be described as a 'globe trotter' pure and simple. All, in one way or another, have been committed, for greater or shorter periods of time, to India. There is yet another genre of writing which comes from those Westerners who have visited the Toda, more or less briefly, during their Indian peregrinations. I do not intend to examine it in much detail. One or two samples must suffice.

Marguerite Milward was a sculptor by profession and one particularly interested in portraying heads of different racial types. For eight months during 1935 to 1936 she roamed the Indian subcontinent, mostly in the so-called 'tribal belts,' in search of subjects for her artistic endeavours. Late in 1936 she exhibited the result of her Indian travels at India House, London. She also wrote a book, *Artist in Unknown India* (1948), about her Indian adventures. Not surprisingly, Milward came to the Nilgiris and, of course, she sculpted a Toda man and woman (Milward 1948: plate facing p. 50). Her comments on her search for Toda subjects are interesting. She writes:

The difficulty of choosing the best type of Toda was very great. The faces of the men are most striking; they had long well-shaped noses, moustaches, and long beards, thin faces covered with hair; while their silky curls in a ring showed the shape of their heads and gave a classic effect to their features. . . . [They had a] fine carriage and proud bearing. I met them daily swinging along the roads of the Downs; heads bare, hair windblown, each one draped in a heavy mantle and carrying a shepherd's crook. I used to stop in wonder to gaze at such an unusual and distinguished-looking people (Milward 1948: 102).

Early in 1951 there arrived in the Nilgiris a group of young men calling themselves 'Expedition Tortoise', which included four French architects from the School of Fine Arts in Paris and a mechanical engineer, the latter described as a 'British subject'. Since a full-length travel book, *Expedition Tortoise* (Rambach *et al.* 1957) and a superb photographic book, *Primitive India* (de Golish *et al.* 1954), were the outcome of this expedition, I shall, for the purposes of this paper, let these men represent the thousands of young Westerners who, since the great post-Second World War boom in world travel, have visited the Nilgiris and seen for themselves something of the Toda community. In their travel book (Rambach *et al.* 1957: 243), they describe five Toda guests at a Badaga fire-walking festival: 'it was impossible to ignore their presence for an instant. Their stature marked them out in the crowd', they say, and continue:

Their proportions and athletic build seemed to suggest some link with the type depicted in Greek statues. Sometimes we had the strange feeling of being confronted with so many Aristophanes or Pericles. The natural dignity, the innate majesty of these sages living far from the world was remarkable . . . (Rambach *et al.* 1957: 247).

The Frenchmen, by no means the first nor last of the men from the West (or, for that matter, East—another story), were quickly carried from reality by their Nilgiri experience. They declare the Toda 'a disconcerting example of a people living in the twentieth century in exactly the same way as people lived about 5000 BC; . . . they are a mystery and an enigma' (Rambach *et al.* 1957: 248). And our new 'experts', after admitting (ibid.: 246) to a knowledge of but one word of the Toda language—*mund* (actually not Toda, but an anglicization of the Badagu *mandu*; the Toda word is *mod*)—proceed to declare that the Toda language has 'nothing in common with the other languages spoken in India' and so gives 'no real indications as to their origins' (ibid.: 250)!

The modern travellers are impressed, as were almost all others, by the striking physical appearance of the Toda. And some of them, it seems, can be as free with their unfounded speculations as any nineteenth-century visitor!

Professional Anthropologists and the Toda

Professional anthropologists have added their share to the wealth of published data on the Toda. Indeed, it is often thought that the community has been swamped by anthropologists. But I scarcely need to remind this readership that, in reality, the anthropological profession is a very small one. As far as the Toda are concerned, their first meeting with a professional anthropologist (or professional anthropologist-to-be, according to one's point of view) came in 1901. This, of course, was the year when William Halse Rivers (1864–1922) came to the Nilgiris. Since his time, only four other trained anthropologists and/or linguists from the West have spent substantial time with the community. Murray Emeneau (b. 1904), a linguist but, as a student of Sapir naturally very concerned with cultural materials as well, was with the Toda in the mid-1930s. Prince Peter of Greece and Denmark (1908–80) in 1939 and also in 1949; myself (b. 1940) in 1962–63, with continuing short visits through the '70s and '80s; and David Mandelbaum (1911–87) in the late 1960s and into the 1970s, all worked professionally with this community. David Mandelbaum's Nilgiri work—focusing particularly on the Kota—of course goes back much earlier, to the late 1930s.

It is not my purpose here to review the contents of the professional anthropological and anthropological-linguistic record on the Toda generated by these persons. My interest focuses rather on the professionals' reasons for studying the Toda and, if I have been able to discover them, their reactions to this community.

In the history of anthropology, W.H.R. Rivers's name is as indissolubly linked to the Toda as is Boas's to the Kwakiutl, Malinowski's to the Trobriand Islanders, Evans-Pritchard's to the Nuer and Firth's to the Tikopia, and this even though Rivers spent more time in Melanesia than in South India; and even though, after his major publications on them in 1905 (his seventy-five-page paper 'Observations on the Senses of the Todas' for the *British Journal of Psychology*) and 1906 (his famous 755-page monograph, *The Todas*), he scarcely mentioned these people again. There is a word on them, for comparative purposes, in his 1907 article, 'The Marriage of Cousins in India', and an entry, 'The Todas' (1922) for Hastings' *Encyclopaedia of Religion and Ethics* and that's about it; hardly matching, for example, Evans-Pritchard's writings on the Nuer!

Curiously, also unlike all the other above-named mentors of our discipline, we cannot be quite certain why Rivers chose to study the people with whom his name is most frequently associated in anthropological circles. Certainly, he had no prior personal experience of the Toda or, for that matter, of India. Obviously, while still in Cambridge, he had read a good deal about them, for he comments in his 'Introduction' to *The Todas* (1906: 1–2) on the 'very large literature [that] has accumulated about the Todas and their customs', noting also, however, that:

> A review of the literature . . . showed me that there were certain subjects about which our information was of the scantiest. This was especially the case in matters connected with the social organisation. Little was known of the system of kinship, and it was not known whether there was any definite system of exogamy. The Todas furnish one of the best examples of the custom of polyandry, but scarcely anything was known about the various social regulations which must be associated with such a practice (Rivers 1906: 1–2).

Richard Rooksby (1971: 112–13) has suggested some of the reasons which *might* have influenced Rivers's choice of the Toda. Rivers had been a member of the 1899–1900 Cambridge University Expedition to the Torres Straits. During his work in the demographically small and territorially demarcated island societies, Rivers discovered the great value, both for his psychological and sociological studies, of collecting from his informants detailed genealogical data (Rivers 1910). This 'genealogical method of anthropological inquiry', as he himself termed it, Rivers was to utilize again, and with extraordinary success, among the Toda, also a demographically small and territorially-discrete society, whose Nilgiri homelands had some of the isolating natural characteristics of an island and whose 'moieties' and polyandry were particularly interesting to historical evolutionists among whom Rivers then counted himself. But I doubt whether we may positively assert, with Rooksby (1971: 112) that it was with the specific purpose of testing his 'Method' that in 1901 Rivers set out for South India to conduct a second field study, this time among the Toda.

It is quite evident that when Rivers arrived in the Madras Presidency during the 1901–2 cool season, he had no intention of devoting his entire research effort to the Toda. Accompanied by Edgar Thurston, superintendent of the Madras Government Museum, enthusiastic collector of ethnographic data and editor-to-be of the seven-volume *Castes and Tribes of Southern India* (1909), Rivers headed for the Nilgiris, yes, but not at first for the Toda. Instead the two men focused their attention on two of the forest-dwelling peoples of the lower slopes: the Urali and Sholega, dividing their labours so that Rivers involved himself with 'psycho-physical work' which he published in the *Bulletin of the Madras Government Museum* (Rivers 1903), while Thurston studied the 'customs and physical characteristics of the people' (Thurston 1903). Only subsequently did Rivers proceed (without Thurston's company) to the upper Nilgiris, where he focused exclusively on the Toda. Whether his personal delight in the community had anything to do with his decision to concentrate all his attention on the Toda cannot be inferred from Rivers's own writings. Confirmed scientist that he was (a practising physician and psychologist), all he has to say is:

> I had not worked long among the Todas before I discovered the existence of many customs and ceremonies previously undescribed, and I was able to obtain much more detailed accounts of others which had already been repeatedly recorded. I found that there was so much to be done that I gave up an intention of working with several different tribes, and devoted the whole of my time to the Todas (Rivers 1906: 2).

That he was impressed with the Toda is reasonably clear. True, his book provides little of personal anecdote. But he does conclude his introductory section of Chapter Two, 'The Toda People', with the following remarks:

> The characteristic note in the demeanour of the people is given by their absolute belief in their own superiority over the surrounding races. They are grave and dignified, and yet thoroughly cheerful and well-disposed towards all. In their intercourse with Europeans, they now recognize the superior race so far as wealth and the command of physical and mental resources are concerned, but yet they are not in the slightest degree servile, and about many matters still believe that their ways are superior to ours, and, in spite of their natural politeness, could sometimes not refrain from showing their contempt for conduct which we are accustomed to look upon as an indication of a high level of morality (Rivers 1906: 23).

Although most people (and I include myself amongst them) will probably agree with David Mandelbaum (1980: 295) that Rivers's Toda monograph gives no quarter to skimmers—may even concur with Yeatts concerning its wearisome detail and not very inviting pages—nonetheless several commentators have noted the 'humanistic component in the monograph,' to borrow Mandelbaum's (1980: 284) words again. Rivers' modern-day biographer, the Canadian anthropologist Richard Slobodin, an Inuit specialist for whom the Toda and the Nilgiris are presumably very remote, can nonetheless write:

> Although Rivers is by no means an examplar [*sic*] of the 'waving palm trees' genre of ethnographic writing, the Todas, as people, do come alive. For one thing, all the adults and some of the children are named. . . . The reader . . . comes in time to learn a good deal about many of the Toda personalities whose doings are chronicled. When I took up *The Todas* in recent years, it had been at least a quarter of a century since I had looked at the book. Yet I had no trouble recognizing by name such men as Kurolv of Kuudr and Karnoz of Melgarsh, and that much-married lady, Puvizveli of Kusharf . . . . It is extraordinary how much of the rich and strongly reinforced detail one remembers or recognizes (Slobodin 1978: 104–5).

Rivers must have been a man who really admired the Toda. And it is for this reason that I shall once again, as I have done before (Walker 1986: 4–5), take to task the American anthropologist David Banks (1976: 22) for his ungracious and unfounded remarks about Rivers's 'fieldwork methods . . . produc[ing] the maximal status differential, he being the superordinate and his Toda informants wards of the Crown . . . it appears that establishing distance between himself and those he studied was part of Rivers' research strategy.' 'Fiddlesticks', as Margaret Mead was wont to say!

Murray Emeneau is another scholar who went to the Nilgiris to study much more than the Toda—and in this he succeeded mightily. But who will say that the Toda (to whom he dedicated his monumental *Toda Songs* [1971]) were not his favourite Nilgiri people? And among the epigrams he chooses for his dedication page are two from the *Rig Veda*: 'Shining beauty is imprinted upon their speech' (RV 10.71.2d) and 'One sits making to blossom a multitude of verses' (RV 10.71.11a). Like Rivers before him, Murray Emeneau tolerates little padding in his scholarly writings, packed with a wealth of linguistic and ethnographic detail which will doubtless engage scholars of the Toda for generations to come. Leaving aside, then, his three marvelously valuable books *Toda Songs* (1971), *Ritual Structure and Language Structure of the Todas* (1974) and *Toda Grammar and Texts* (1984), not to mention the more than a dozen hugely valuable ethnographic papers (see Emeneau 1967), I turn instead to a popular piece he wrote more than half a century ago for clues to Emeneau's personal feelings about the Toda. In an article for the New York-based journal *Asia*, entitled 'The Singing Tribe of Todas' and published in 1939, Emeneau describes his

Toda friends as 'most attractive in appearance, sturdy in physique and aristocratically upstanding in bearing.' And he concludes his short but fascinating account of Toda religion, social structure and oral poetry by saying: 'The Todas are indeed an attractive people. The student of languages whose lot it was to work among them intermittently for three years and to make friends among them can count himself a lucky man.' (Emeneau 1939b: 332).

Prince Peter of Greece and Denmark, who studied both psychology and anthropology (the latter under Malinowski at the London School of Economics), was drawn into Toda research as part of a study of polyandry in South Asia, which took him also to the Indo-Tibetan border and to Kerala and Sri Lanka (Peter 1955, 1963). His first visit to the Nilgiris, in July and August 1939, involved a more-or-less general ethnographic survey of the Toda. But on his return ten years later, from May through August 1949, his focus was a single polyandrous family at Meḷga·s (Peter 1949, 1953a, 1963: 275–300), that so well-known Toda hamlet above the Ootacamund botanical gardens. Prince Peter is not, in print at least, particularly forthcoming about his personal reactions to the Toda. He has the standard comments on Toda physical appearance: 'The men are tall and handsome. They have grave, patriarchal faces, and wear their hair and beards long. The women are good-looking, slim and well-built, with always a gay smile on their faces' (1953b: 59). Prince Peter's personal commitment to these people is clear from his reports concerning their welfare, especially their land problems and, above all, their declining population in the decades from 1930 to 1950 (Peter 1949; 1953b; there was also a 1939 report to the then British Governor of the Madras Presidency, Lord Erskine, but I have never been able to see a copy). He appealed to Prime Minister Nehru to do what he could 'to help keep the Todas from total extinction' (1953b: 68) and in August 1949 he wrote a report to the Governor of Madras State (as Tamil Nadu was then called) outlining his suggestions regarding government recognition of Toda land rights (1949: 7–8), the provision of medical assistance to the community (ibid.: 8), the development of a dairy industry (ibid.: 9) and the implementation of educational services (ibid.: 12). The Prince prefaced his report by saying that he was submitting it 'In my eagerness to assist people who in every way have contributed enormously to my anthropological store of knowledge' (ibid.: 1), and he concluded as follows:

The Toda community is a very small one—especially in relation to the enormous population of India.

It is however an extraordinarily original one, renowned throughout the world for its curious customs, its way of life and for the mystery of its origins (possibly Babylonian). In anthropological circles at least, the Todas are probably the best known people in the world, and many of their institutions have given birth to classical terms in ethnological literature.

India is privileged in having these people inhabiting her soil. Now she is free, the eyes of the world are upon her, watching what she is going to do with her newly-found independence. And one of the things which are going to attract critical world-attention is the way she will care for her minorities.

The fate of the Todas, so well known outside the boundaries of India, is thus sure to be followed with concern by very many, and it is therefore important that India show herself worthy of the trust, and even improve on what was done for these people by the previous administration (Peter 1949: 12).

And so to David Mandelbaum, whose recent death has left his profession in general and in particular our small fraternity of Nilgiri specialists with so deep a sense of loss. We all know that his major Nilgiri researches were conducted among the Kota. Most of us know that it was in order to set those Kota within their wider Indian context that Mandelbaum began his major study of Indian society, which was to culminate in his monumental two-volume work *Society in India* (1970), a precious compilation and analysis of sociological work on India up until 1970 and an invaluable teaching aid. Many of us who have worked in the Nilgiris were intrigued by David Mandelbaum's return to the field in the late 1960s, not to take up his Kota research again, but to begin anew on the Toda. (Needless to say he already possessed a huge working knowledge of the literature on the Toda and had had some prior contacts with the people themselves.) I never learned why he turned to the Toda. What I do know is that he did so with great enthusiasm, and he expressed to me often his admiration for them. His untimely death has, thus far at least, prevented most of us from reading the results of his Toda work.

In conclusion some autobiographical notes. Why did I study the Toda? Why do I keep going back to the Nilgiris? I first heard of the Toda, not as an anthropologist, but while I was a student of Indology at Osmania University in Hyderabad. A friend and fellow student, A. Gopala Krishna, had written his master's thesis on social change among the Toda (Gopala Krishna 1960). He showed me his work and his photographs and he promised to take me to the Nilgiris and introduce me to his Toda friends, especially to Naricane, to Mutnars,

Paksin and Sodamalli, to Pellican and Muthicane, all of them soon to become dear friends. We went for a week in 1961. It was a marvellous experience and I carried back with me to Hyderabad most of the stereotypes (I like to think the better ones) of my countrymen of bygone years. The proud, elegant and friendly people, the fascinating domestic and religious architecture, the magnificent herds of long-horned hill buffaloes, Narican's obvious delight in showing off his buffaloes, his ability (to me nothing short of amazing) to call one of them out from a herd of thirty or more grazing animals (her name was Kemosh and I remember the occasion as vividly as if it were yesterday), the extraordinary prettiness of the Wenlock Downs (those were the days before the massive reafforestation and extensive potato cultivation which sometimes bring old-timers close to tears). It was a romantic view, but I am not ashamed of it; it brought me back to the Toda in the following year and kept me in the hills from October 1962 to September 1963. The Toda, in turn, are the people who brought me to anthropology and a career I would exchange for no other. And how close indeed was I to my predecessors when, more than a quarter of a century ago, I concluded the second chapter, 'The Toda People', of my master's thesis for Oxford University with the following words:

> In concluding these opening remarks on the Todas . . . [let me] mention . . . the imposing dignity of these people. The Todas are indeed proud of their traditional ways and by no means prepared to adopt a servile attitude to outsiders. I have had some, although limited, experience of another small-scale south Indian society, the Chenchus of Adilabad in Andhra Pradesh. The differing attitudes adopted by Todas and Chenchus to my presence among them was too striking to ignore. Among the Todas I was accepted as an equal and by the older members of the community as simply a young student interested in their ways. A number of Toda children accorded me the kinship term *oṇa.*, elder brother. The few Chenchus whom I met appeared to adopt the attitude that they were so inferior that their customs could scarcely be of interest to a European 'sahib' . . . I vividly remember and even recorded in writing, my impressions of the dignity of the Todas during my very first days among them (Walker 1965: 44).

I do not now particularly care for the prose; but I feel no embarrassment for the sentiments expressed.

Scholars from the West, through prior reading of the Nilgiri and comparative anthropological literature, may have an academic edge over others who come to these mountains. In the twentieth century, and more especially in the era of independent India, they are hopefully less prone to the gross ethnocentrism of their nineteenth-century forebearers. But it seems that they are just as susceptible to Toda charm and Toda good looks as any of their fellow countrymen in this century or before. Would not all the *ars* (or certainly the great majority) add their voices to those of the *o.ɬ* when they sing:

We fixed our eyes on beautiful buffaloes.
We laid our hands on beautiful places.
(Emeneau 1971: 508)

The stone temple, how beautiful is the temple!
The buffaloes of Kïwïr clan, how beautiful are the buffaloes!
(Emeneau 1971: 77)

Glossary of Toda Words

Item	Per Rivers (1906)	Meaning
Amuno·ṛ	Amnòḍr	the land of the dead
ars		European
Kïwïr	Kûûdr	name of a patriclan; also of the chief hamlet of that patriclan
Melga·s̲	Melgârs	name of a patrician; also of the chief hamlet of that patrician
mod̲	mad	Toda hamlet; can also mean 'patriclan', 'dairy complex set apart from a hamlet,' 'funeral place' and, by extension, any special place which is at some time the scene of Toda customary activity
o·ɬ	ol	'The people', i.e. the Toda
oṇa	anna	elder brother, in address
poɬo·ɬ	palol	highest ranking grade of dairyman-priest
ti·	tî	highest grade of Toda dairy

NOTE

1. This paper was first presented at a colloquium on the Nilgiri hills organized by Professor Paul Hockings under the aegis of the 1991 annual South Asia Conference at Madison, Wisconsin. The present revision purposely retains something of the informal flavour of the original presentation. My thanks to Paul Hockings for stimulating me to write this paper, at a time when my thoughts were rather more focused on the Lahu people of Yunnan province in China; also to my wife, Pauline, for her usual, and timely, editorial skills.

I dedicate this paper to the memory of Naricane Toda of the Meḻga·s̱ people,
whose journey to Amuno·ṛ began on 21 May 1991.
They say: 'My friend has let go my heart'.
They say 'My friend has butted my eyes.
We have come to have our dwelling in two different places'.
'We have come to have our buffaloes in two places'.
(Emeneau 1971: 39).

References

Anonymous 1819. Letter from 'A Subscriber' (possibly John Sullivan). *Madras Courier*, 23 February 1819. Reprinted in Henry B. Grigg, *A Manual of the Nílagiri District in the Madras Presidency*. Madras: E. Keys, Government Press.

Banks, David J. 1976. 'Rivers' Tent in Southeast Asia: Ethnicity, Relative Status, and Empathy in Fieldwork,' in David J. Banks ed. *Changing Identities in Modern Southeast Asia*, 21–41. The Hague: Mouton.

Blavatsky, Helene Petrovna 1930. *The People of the Blue Mountains*. Wheaton (IL): Theosophical Press. (Trans. of *Zagadochnyîa Plemena na 'Golubykh Gorakh'* [1893].)

Breeks, James Wilkinson 1873. *An Account of the Primitive Tribes and Monuments of the Nilagiris* (edited by his widow). London: India Museum.

Burton, Richard F. 1851. *Goa, and The Blue Mountains; or, Six Months of Sick Leave*. London: Richard Bentley.

Congreve, Harry 1847. 'The Antiquities of the Neilgherry Hills, including an Inquiry into the Descent of the Thautawars or Todars', *Madras Journal of Literature and Science*, 14: 77–146.

de Golish, Vitold, Pierre Rambach and F. Hébert-Stevens. 1954. *Primitive India: Expedition 'Tortoise' 1950–1952, Africa—Middle East—India*. Nadine Peppard, trans. London: George Harrap.

Emeneau, Murray B. 1939a. The Christian Todas. *Proceedings of the American Philosophical Society*, 81: 93–106.

——— 1939b. 'The Singing Tribe of Todas.' *Asia* 39: 461–4.

——— 1967. *Dravidian Linguistics, Ethnology and Folktales: Collected Papers*. Annamalainagar: Annamalai University, Linguistics Department Publication no. 8.

——— 1971. *Toda Songs*. Oxford: Clarendon Press.

——— 1974. *Ritual Structure and Language Structure of the Todas.*

(Transactions of the American Philosophical Society (ns) 64. no. 6.) Philadelphia: American Philosophical Society.

——— 1984. *Toda Grammar and Texts.* Philadelphia: American Philosophical Society.

Fenicio, Giacomo (also Jacome Finicio). 1603. Letter to the Jesuit Vice-Provincial in Calicut (in Portuguese). British Museum Add. MS 9853. A, trans. de Alberti In W.H.R. Rivers 1906: 721–30.

Ferroli, D. 1939. *The Jesuits in Malabar.* Bangalore: The Bangalore Press.

Francis, Walter 1908. *Madras District Gazetteers. The Nilgiris.* Madras: Superintendent, Government Press.

Gopala Krishna, A. 1960. 'Problems of the Modern Toda: A Sociological Study'. MA thesis, Osmania University, Hyderabad.

Grigg, Henry B. 1880. *A Manual of the Nílagiri District in the Madras Presidency.* Madras: E. Keys, Government Press.

Halayya, M. 1988. *An Encyclopaedic Tourist Guide: Ooty, Coonoor, Kotagiri, and Gudalur.* Coimbatore: Kalaimani Printing Industries.

Harkness, Henry 1832. *A Description of a Singular Aboriginal Race Inhabiting the Summit of the Neilgherry Hills, or Blue Mountains of Coimbatoor, in the Southern Peninsula of India.* London: Smith, Elder and Co.

Hockings, Paul E. 1973. 'John Sullivan of Ootacamund'. *Journal of Indian History*, Golden Jubilee Volume: 863–71.

——— 1978. *A Bibliography for the Nilgiri Hills of Southern India 1602–1978.* HRAFlex Books Bibliographical Series no AW 16–001. New Haven: Human Relations Area Files.

——— 1980a. *Ancient Hindu Refugees: Badaga Social History 1550–1975.* New Delhi: Vikas; The Hague: Mouton.

——— 1980b. *Sex and Disease in a Mountain Community.* New Delhi: Vikas.

——— 1988. *Counsel from the Ancients: A Study of Badaga Proverbs, Prayers, Omens and Curses.* Berlin: Mouton de Gruyter.

——— 1989. 'British Society in the Company, Crown and Congress Eras' in Paul Hockings (ed.), *Blue Mountains: The Ethnography and Biogeography of a South Indian Region*; 334–59. Delhi: Oxford University Press.

Hough, James 1829. *Letters on the Climate, Inhabitants, Productions, etc. etc. of the Neilgherries, or Blue Mountains of Coimbatoor, South India.* London: John Hatchard & Son.

Keys, William 1812. 'A Topographical Description of the Neelaghery Mountains'. Reprinted in Henry B. Grigg, *A Manual of the Nilagiri District in the Madras Presidency,* Madras: E. Keys, Government Press.

Ling, Catharine F. 1910. *Dawn in Toda Land: A Narrative of Missionary Effort on the Nilgiri Hills, South India.* London: Morgan & Scott.

——— 1934. *Sunrise on the Nilgiris: The Story of the Todas.* London: Zenith Press.

Mandelbaum, David G. 1970. *Society in India.* Berkeley and Los Angeles: University of California Press, 2 vols.

——— 1980. '*The Todas* in Time Perspective'. *Reviews in Anthropology*: 7: 279–302.

Marshall, William E. 1873. *A Phrenologist amongst the Todas or The Study of a Primitive Tribe in South India: History, Character, Customs, Religion, Infanticide, Polyandry, Language.* London: Longmans Green & Co.

Metz, Johann F. 1864. *The Tribes Inhabiting the Neilgherry Hills: Their Social Customs and Religious Rites.* Mangalore: Basel Mission Press.

Milward, Marguerite 1948. *Artist in Unknown India.* London: T. Werner Laurie.

Muzzy, C.F. 1844. 'Account of the Neilgherry Tribes'. *Christian Instructor and Missionary Record* (Madras), 2: 358–66.

Ouchterlony, John 1848. 'Geographical and Statistical Memoir of a Survey of the Neilgherry Mountains'. *The Madras Journal of Literature and Science,* 15: 1–138.

Panter-Downes, Mollie 1967. *Ooty Preserved: A Victorian Hill Station.* London: Hamish Hamilton.

Pedersen, Paul 1988. 'Review of *The Todas of South India: A New Look,* by Anthony R. Walker'. *Ethnos,* 33: 143–4.

Peter, H.R.H. Prince of Greece and Denmark 1949. 'Report on the Todas.'(typescript pp. 12).

——— 1953a. 'Melgarsh–The Study of a Toda Polyandrous Family' in Rudolph M. Loewenstein (ed.), *Drives, Affects, Behavior,* 37–67. New York: International Universities Press.

——— 1953b. 'The Problem of Toda Survival', *Vanyajati,* 1, no. 3, 59–68.

——— 1955. 'The Polyandry of South India: The Todas of the Nilgiris', *Actes du IV Congrès International des sciences anthropologiques et ethnologiques,* 2: 171–3. Vienna: Verlag Adolf Holzhausend Nfg.

———1963. *A Study of Polyandry.* Mouton: The Hague.

Rambach, Pierre, Rahoul Jahan and François Hébert-Stevens 1957. *Expedition Tortoise.* London: Thames and Hudson (translated from French by Elizabeth Cunningham).

Rivers, W.H.R. 1903. 'Observations on the Vision of the Uralis and Sholagas', *Bulletin of the Madras Government Museum,* 5: 3–18.

——— 1905. 'Observations on the Senses of the Todas'. *British Journal of Psychology,* 1: 321–96.

——— 1906. *The Todas.* London: Macmillan & Co.

——— 1907. 'The Marriage of Cousins in India', *Journal of the Royal Asiatic Society of Great Britain and Ireland,* 1907: 611–40.

——— 1910. 'The Genealogical Method of Anthropological Inquiry', *Sociological Review,* 3: 1–12.

——— 1922. 'The Todas', in James Hastings (ed.), *Encyclopaedia of Religion and Ethics,* 12: 345–57. New York: Charles Scribner.

Rooksby, R.L. 1971.'W.H.R. Rivers and the Todas', *South Asia,* 1: 109–21.

Sahlins, Marshall 1972. *Stone Age Economics.* New York: Aldine.

Shaposhnikova, Liudmila Vasilevna 1969. *Taina Plemeni Golubykh Gor* [The secret of the tribe of the Blue Mountains]. Moscow: Akademia Nauk S. S. S. R.

Shortt, John 1869. 'An Account of the Hill Tribes of the Neilgherries', *Transactions of the Ethnological Society of London* (ns), 7: 230–90.

Slobodin, Richard 1978. *W.H.R. Rivers.* New York: Columbia University Press.

Thurston, Edgar 1903. 'Uralis, Sholagas and Irulas', *Bulletin of the Madras Government Museum,* 4: 202–13.

——— 1909 (with K. Rangachari.) *Castes and Tribes of Southern India.* Madras: Government Press, 7 vols.

——— 1913. *The Madras Presidency with Mysore, Coorg and Associated States.* Cambridge: Cambridge University Press.

Walker, Anthony R. 1965. 'Toda Social Organization and the Role of Cattle', M.Litt. thesis, Oxford University.

——— 1986. *The Toda of South India: A New Look.* Delhi: Hindustan Publishing Corporation.

Whitehouse, Thomas 1873. *Lingerings of Light in a Dark Land: Being Researches into the Past History and Present Condition of the Syrian Church of Malabar.* London: William Brown & Co.

Yeatts, William W. M. 1932. *Census of India,* 1931. *Volume XIV. Madras Part I, Report.* Calcutta: Government of India, Central Publications Branch.

Badaga and Its Relations with Neighbouring Languages

CHRISTIANE PILOT-RAICHOOR

6

The Badaga community is not an autochthonous tribe but has been mentioned in a report of a missionary, Father Fenicio, as inhabiting the Nilgiris since the begining of the seventeenth century.

For at least four centuries this community has lived in close connection with the other mountain tribes—the Todas, the Kotas and the Kuṟumbas. From the beginning of the twentieth century, due to its population growth and its economic dynamism, the Badaga community has become one of the dominant social units of the Nilgiris.

Despite this fact, the Badagas—compared to the other Nilgiris tribes—have not attracted much scholarly interest during the past decades. Their social organization and their cultural traditions are known thanks to the numerous and detailed studies of the community by Hockings (1980, 1988, 1989).

Their language, long classified as a 'dialect of Kannada', has never been thoroughly studied until now. Some linguists, devoted to other Nilgiri languages, did some fieldwork on the Badaga language 'on the side', but very little was published. The first publication in modern linguistics was the important article of M. B. Emeneau on the retroflexion of vowels, 'The Vowels of the Badaga Language', in 1939, and then only at the beginning of the 'seventies was some work done in Annamalai University, leading to two articles: 'The Nouns of the Badaga Language' by Agesthialingom and 'An Outline of Badaga Phonology' by Swaminathan, both published in 1972.

That was the situation when I began my own fieldwork on Badaga (in the late 'seventies) and it has not changed much since. The description I produce here is not a full account of the Badaga language in all its varieties but can only be taken as representative of the Badaga dialect spoken by the Gauda Badagas around

Ootacamund; this is, however, the actual form of language spoken by a large section of the population.

The descriptive analysis of this language revealed so many differences from the Kannada language that I was led, first, to question seriously whether Badaga is a dialect of Kannada, as it is still usually acknowledged (cf. Emeneau 1989: 137); and, secondly, to emphasize the typological similarities among the Nilgiri languages, particularly between Badaga and Ālu Kuṟumba.

Points of divergence from Kannada

In the following pages, I shall try to give some evidence which leads, us to ascertain that present day Badaga differs markedly from Kannada.

Actually, the differences pertain to all aspects of the language, its phonology, morphology, syntax and lexicon, but I will only mention some of the most striking differences in the phonological and morphological domains.

PHONOLOGICAL DIFFERENCES

In terms of segmental units, the Badaga system does not differ very much from the Kannada one. Their vocalic systems—at least in the varieties I studied[1]—are identical, with five vowels: a, e, i, o, u, and a distinctive length. Some differences appear in the consonantal system. A strong reduction of the voiceless fricative set of phonemes can be noted: out of the six phonemes of Kannada, the strident fricatives (/s/ alveodental, /§/ retroflex, /S/ prepalatal) and affricates (flat /c/ and aspirated /cʰ/) and the laryngeal fricative /h/, the Badaga language has retained, on the phonemic level, only two units /s/ and /c/, the fricative /s/ being the only possibility in initial position.

		Kannada	*Badaga*
e.g.	'gold'	cinna	sinna
	'dry ginger'	suṇṭi	suṭṭi
	'year'	varṣa	barisa, etc.

As for the laryngeal /h/, compared to K. *heṇṇu* 'girl', we have in Badaga such variants as: *heṇṇu/eṇṇu/yeṇṇu* (in this last variant, the on-glide y-appearing before the front vowel e-, as before any initial e-, attests to the complete loss of phonemic /h/.

The main differences from Kannada do not lie in the set of phonemes itself but in the constraints and specific processes which affect the linear organization of phonemes.

For instance, both Badaga and Kannada have voiceless occlusive stops: p, t, ṭ, k, but while in Kannada there is a phonemic contrast between single and geminated voiceless stops, e.g. *kate* 'story' vs. *katte* 'donkey',[2] in modern Badaga this contrast is lost and the single or geminated pronunciation is often conditioned by the syllabic pattern (i.e. geminated pronunciation in disyllabic words: *appa* 'father', *makka* 'children', etc.), so that a Kannada word like *paṭu* 'clever, skillful' of I.A. origin (cf. Emeneau and Burrow (1962), *DBIA* 245) will be pronounced in Badaga as *baṭṭu* (with geminated ṭ). In other positions, single and geminated pronunciation freely vary: *arupu* ~ *aruppu* 'thirsty', *arake* ~ *arakke* 'prayer', etc.

But the most striking differences between the two languages result from the peculiar evolution of the retroflex lateral ḻ. Though Badaga does have a retroflex lateral phoneme in its phonological system, it clearly appears, on comparative ground, that intervocalic ḻ disappeared in most of the contexts:

		Kannada	*Badaga*
compare:	'dirt'	koḻe	koe
	'bull'	gu:ḻi	gu:i

The fall of intervocalic ḻ created many vocalic groups (unknown in Kannada) which in some cases have been affected with subsequent changes, either reduction in a long vowel: 'rain' Ka. *maḻe*, Bad. *me:*, 'inside' Ka. *oḻage*, Bad. *o:ge*;
or by a new syllabification: Ka. *kaḻi* 'to spend' (time)', Bad. *kai* ~ *kayyi* (cf. Pilot-Raichoor 1990).

The result of these changes is that, despite a nearly identical set of phonemes, the actual shape of the words in Badaga can make them quite 'unrecognizable' when compared to the corresponding Kannada words.

MORPHOLOGICAL DIFFERENCES

More than the phonology, the morphology of Badaga presents deep, structural differences from Kannada.

Here again, I will take only a few examples concerning the nominal and verbal morphology[3] to illustrate the differences.

The Badaga case system is, on the whole, rather Kannada-like, but in their details most of the case-forms differ from those of Kannada.

For example, in Kannada, the DAT case has several variants: -*ke, -ge, -ige*, but Badaga presents only one variant: *-ga*;

	Kannada	*Badaga*	
cf.	mane.yige	mane.ga	'to the house'
	kelsa.kke	gelasa.ga	'for work'

For LOC suffix, Kannada has retained the suffix *-alli*, but in Badaga we find a LOC suffix *-o:ge,* derived from the Kannada *olage* 'inside'.

Most interesting is the comparison of GEN and ACC caseforms of the two languages.

The variants of the GEN are similar in Kannada and in Badaga, basically formed with the vowel -a preceded, or not, by some linking consonant:

Kannada	appa	'father'	GEN	appana (Ka. & Bad.)
	mane	'house'		maneya (Ka. & Bad.)
	kelsa	'work'		kelsada (Ka.), gelasada (Bad.)

For the ACC case-form, Literary Kannada presents the suffix *-annu*: *appanannu, maneyannu,* etc. in Modern Kannada, this suffix has evolved into *-anna*, often reduced to *-an, -na* or just *-n*; e.g. *maravanna* ~ *mara:n(a)* 'tree+ACC'.

In Badaga, the ACC suffix occurs only in the short form *-a*. As a result it has become, in most of the paradigms, identical with the GEN suffix:

		Kannada			*Badaga*	
e.g.	GEN	appana	ACC	appanannu	GEN/ACC	appana
		maneya		maneyannu		maneya

(though they have remained distinct, in Badaga, in some paradigms: 'tree' mora GEN mora*da* ACC mora*va*).

This formal confusion of GEN and ACC case-forms is not devoid of syntactical impact.

Remaining in the nominal morphology, the comparison of the Kannada and Badaga sets of personal pronouns will reveal important structural differences. Except for the neuter forms sg. *adu*, pl. *ave* which are identical, and for the 1st and 2nd sg. person forms which are similar:

	Kannada	*Badaga*
'I'	na:nu	na:
'you'	ni:nu	ni:

all the other forms differ, cf.:

		Kannada	Badaga
3rd pers. sg.	Masc.	avanu	ama
	Fem	avaḻu	ava
3rd pers. pl.	M/F	avaru	avaka
2nd pers. pl.		ni:vu	ninga

but the main difference appears in the 1st pers. plural where, opposed to the only form *na:vu* in Kannada, we find in Badaga two different forms, the one *nanga* expressing a 'we (inclusive, i.e. 'we and you'), the other *enga* being exclusive 'we but not you'.

Even if we refer to the same distinction in Old Kannada, having *na:vu* for inclusive 'we' and *a:m* for exclusive 'we', the Badaga forms cannot be directly derived from these forms.

The third point taken as an example of deep difference between Kannada and Badaga concerns the verbal system.

On the whole, the verbal system has been completely redone in Badaga, but the most interesting innovation lies in the indicative mood forms.

In modern Kannada, there are three tenses, a present/future, a past tense and a contingent tense[4]. The differentiations are made by two sets of tense markers past/present and three sets of personal endings, e.g. Kannada:

	Pres./Fut.	*Past*	*Contingent*
'to do'	ma:ḍti:ni	ma:ḍde	ma:ḍye:nu
'to eat'	tinti:ni	tinde	tinde:nu

In Badaga, the indicative mood has been completely renewed under the stimulus of the Nilgiri languages Toda and Kota. As in these languages, both the Present and Past tense are built on to the so called 'past stem' or more precisely, on the S 2 as M. B. Emeneau (1967) has labelled it.

		present/future		past	
1°	(na:)	*gi:.d*-an.e	'I (shall) do'	*gi:.d*-e	'I did'
2°	(ni:)	*gi:.d*-ar.e	'you (will) do'	*gi:.de*-e	'you did'
3°M	(ama)	*gi:.d*-an.a	'he (will) do(es)'	*gi:.d*-a	'he did'
3°F	(ava)	*gi:.d*-iy.a	'she (will) do(es)	*gi:.d*-a	'she did'
3°N	(adu)	*gi:.d*-ar.a	'it (will) do'	*gi:.d*-a/*gi:d*-atu	'it did'
I°ex.	(enga)	*gi:.d*-an/euo	'we (shall) do'	*gi:.d*-eyo	'we did'
I°inc.	(nanga)	*gi:.d*-an.o	'we (shall) do'	*gi:.d*-o	'we did'
II°	(ninga)	*gi:.d*-a:ri	'you (will) do'	*gi:.d*-i	'you did'
III°M/F	(avaka)	*gi:.d*-a:ra	'they (will) do'	*gi:.d*-aru	'they did'
III°N	(ave)	*gi:.d*-ar.o	'they (will) do'	*gi:.d*-o	'they did'

From these paradigms, some details must be pointed out.

(1) As for Toda and Kota, too, which have only one set of personal endings (expressing person, gender and number—PNG—variations), the Badaga personal endings are mainly identical in Present/Future and Past paradigms;

(2) It may also be noted that, as in Kota and Toda, for the 1st plural person, the inclusive/exclusive distinction is also present in the verbal paradigms (inclusive PNG (*-o*) vs. exclusive PNG (*-eyo*);

(3) Finally, an important difference between Badaga and these other two languages must be stressed. While in Kota and Toda it is the past paradigm which is marked by a special tense affix—their structure being S2 + PNG in the Present Tense and S2 + Past marker + PNG in the Past Tense—in Badaga, it is the Present Tense which is marked by a special affix inserted between S2 and the PNG endings.

This last feature can be taken as a typical illustration of the process of individualization that the Badaga language has gone through:

Out of the speech forms, which undoubtedly were mainly varieties of the Kannada language, the speech forms of the Badagas have been deeply modified under the influence of the other Nilgiri languages. Under the stimulus of these languages, specific structural features have been introduced, like the inclusive/exclusive distinction, the use of the stem S2 as the basis of the indicative mood . . . to mention only the features discussed previously, but we could also add features like the transitive/intransitive distinction which has been presented by M. B. Emeneau in his article 'The South Dravidian Languages' (1967).

What is remarkable is that, in all these cases, the Badaga language has not directly borrowed or copied the actual forms offered by the neighbouring languages; it has only retained the necessity of distinguishing between, for example, inclusive vs. exclusive, or transitive vs. intransitive, etc., and it has modified its own material or developed new forms to express these distinctions which appeared to be fundamental in the speech of the surrounding people.

Whatever were the causes which created these changes, either mere 'natural' evolution—as can be seen in most of the phonological differences—or innovations due (or not) to the pressure of the neighbouring languages, the Badaga speech form is nowadays typologically very different from Kannada and cannot anymore be labelled a 'dialect of Kannada', but must be recognized as a separate language.

Typological Convergences between Badaga and Ālu Kuṟumba

This statement can be further reinforced if we turn our attention to other neighbouring languages.

It has been mentioned in the beginning that Badaga people lived in close contact for a long time with the Kotas, the Todas and the Kuṟumbas. Until very recently only two of these languages, namely Toda and Kota, had been precisely described, but detailed data were missing for Badaga and Kuṟumba. Thanks to Kapp's description (1982) the gap is filled for Kuṟumba and due to Hockings' book on the proverbs (*Counsel from the Ancients*, 1988), and to my own description, the Badaga language is now better known.

This new data will undoubtedly modify the older picture of the linguistic situation on the top of the Nilgiris. What has now appeared fully evident is that the Badaga language and the Kuṟumba language are actually very close. (This was rightly suggested by M. B. Emeneau in 'The Languages of the Nilgiris', 1989: 138). Though they are probably derived from different backgrounds, Ālu Kuṟumba being originally more 'Tamiloid' and Badaga being more 'Kannadoid', they have both evolved in the same direction and they now look very similar in all domains: phonological, morphological and lexical.

The typical phonological processes which have been stressed to differentiate Badaga from Kannada are also present in Ālu Kuṟumba. So, as in Badaga, we find:

• reduction of the voiceless fricative/affricate consonants to only one unit in initial position /c/ (*ca:re* 'near', *ca:vu* 'death', etc.) and two units in the intervocalic position /c/ and /s/ (e.g. *manuca* 'man' /c/ = [t] or [s], *kisuṇa* 'Krishṇa /s/ = [s];

• lack of the contrast between simple and geminated voiceless stops (cf. Kapp 1982: 31);

• loss of intervocalic /ḻ/, leading to the creation of many vocalic groups.

What is particularly interesting is that, in terms of process, the Ālu Kuṟumba, in most cases, lieș just one step behind the Badaga language. For example, in the case of the reduction of the strident fricative/affricate consonants, Ālu Kuṟumba actually retains in initial position only the affricate /c/. In Badaga nowadays only /s/ occurs in initial position, but a quick survey of the old records of Badaga clearly shows that Badaga also passed by a stage of free variation of /s/ and /c/ and generalization of initial /c-/ (cf. for example, the notation *ca:vu* 'death' in Bühler's manuscript[5] before it stabilized in /s/).

The same observation can be made in the case of deletion of intervocalicḻ:

(1) Ālu Kuṟumba still retains retroflexed vowels (/ï/, /ï:/, /ë/ and /ë:/; cf. Kapp 1982: 3 sq.) which were noted in Badaga by M. B. Emeneau in his article 'The vowels of the Badaga language' (1939), but which have now disappeared in most varieties of Badaga.

(2) Ālu Kuṟumba generally preserves the original vowel cluster due to the loss of intervocalic /ḻ/and does not show cases of assimilation and reduction to a long vowel as can be observed in Badaga, cf.:

AKu.	*Bad.*		
koalu	*ko:lu*	'flute'	(*DEDR* 1818 T. *kuḻal*)
ba:e	*be:*	'banana'	(*DEDR* 5373 T, *vaḻai*)

The Ālu Kuṟumba morphology also reveals some striking similarities with Badaga.

The pronominal system is particularly interesting. Out of ten forms, seven are strictly identical:

AKu. and Bad.:	*na:*	'I'
	ni:	'you (sg.)'
	ava	'she'
	adu	'it'
	ninga	'you (pl.)'

but also note the two specific forms of 1st plural person:

nanga	'we (inclusive)'
enga	'we (exclusive)'

which are not found in any other language with this distinctive meaning.

The 3rd singular masculine form of Ālu Kuṟumba *ava* 'he' is slightly different[6] when compared to the Badaga form *ama,* and the 3rd plural masculine/feminine form is *avaru* which is identical to the Kannada form but not to the Badaga form *avaka* 'they'. Lastly, Ālu Kuṟumba is lacking a proper 3rd plural neuter form (but it may be noted that the Badaga form *ave* 'they (neuter)' is rarely used today).

The verb system is also very similar in Ālu Kuṟumba and in Badaga.

The verb classes distinguished by Kapp (1982: 122–126) are nearly the same as those set for Badaga (cf. Pilot-Raichoor 1991: 434-44) except that class 2 of Badaga, with past marker *-d-*, is split into classes 2 and 4 in Ālu Kuṟumba (on the basis of AKu class 2 having a *-n-* variant; cf. Kapp 1982: 124).

The indicative mood is—as for the Badaga, Toda and Kota—built on stem 2 for present as well as past forms (Kapp 1982: 127, 129), but the set of personal endings is more reduced in Ālu Kuṟumba (no gender distinction in the 3rd singular person, pres. *-a/-adu,* past *-tu/-atu,* and no inclusive/exclusive distinction in 1st plural person endings, pres. *-o:no,* past *-o* (cf. Kapp ibid.).

The other verbal forms, either participial or modal, are very similar to the Badaga ones, for example:

AKu.	*na: i: gelaca (na)*	*ma:ḍo:ngu muḍia*
(Kapp 1982: 146)—		(ma:Do:dugu p.64)
Bad.	*na: i: gelasa (va)*	*ma: ḍo:duga muḍiya*
	'I cannot do that work'	

We even found in Ālu Kuṟumba the same peculiarities as in Badaga. I shall just take two examples out of many.

(1) the verb *ba:* 'to come' presents in both languages the same irregularities of having two stems in the present paradigm:

AKu.	*Bad.*	
na: bann.e:nu	*bann.e*	'I come'
ni: band.are	*band.are*	'you (sg.) come'

(Kapp 1982: 128)

(2) the special use of the old negative form *ka:ṇa* (of the verb *ka:ṇu* 'to see') in the meaning of 'is not present, has disappeared' (cf. Pilot Raichoor 1991: 632) is also present in Ālu Kuṟumba:

makka (*na*) *ka:ṇe* 'the children have disappeared'

(with the same optional use of the Accusative marker *-na* for what is translated as the 'subject').

From this quick comparison it should not be inferred that Badaga and Kuṟumba have any kind of genetic relationship. Many features show that Kurumba is more 'Tamiloid' or more archaic than Badaga; (contrast between simple and shrill *ir* (Kapp 1982: 23–24), a case system (Kapp 1982: 76) quite different from that of the Badaga and more Tamil-like).

What these similarities express is the quick diffusion of certain features among the Nilgiri languages (most probably due to the multilingual situation), so that, independently of their genetic affiliation, they do exhibit very strong clusters of isoglosses.

As far as the languages of the Nilgiri summit are concerned, irrespective of any social or ethnic affiliation, we are led to modify the picture of linguistic repartition and to propose, parallel to the Toda/Kota linguistic group, a Badaga/Ālu Kuṟumba linguistic grouping.

The development of micro-areal linguistics and the careful study of the diffusion of certain Nilgiri features—those pointed out by Zvelebil (1980: 14–19) or by Emeneau (1989: 138–40)—but also many others offer an important task to pursue.

Notes

1. Paper presented at the 20th Annual Conference on South Asia, Madison, Wisconsin, 3 November 1991.
2. That is, excluding the varieties which contain retroflex vowels as described in Emeneau (1939).
3. cf. U. P. Upadhyaya (1972), *Kannada phonetic reader*, p.45.
4. Data concerning Kannada are taken from Schiffman (1979).
5. cf. the description of the Kannada verbal system in Schiffman (1979: 51–67).
6. Some examples taken from the manuscript reproduced in Hockings (1988) have been presented in Pilot-Raichoor 1991: 243–50.
7. In a previous paper (Pilot-Raichoor 1990: 327) we suggested that this nasalized pronunciation of the pronoun might also have occurred in Badaga as an intermediate stage.

References

Agesthialingom, S. 1972. 'Nouns of Badaga Language'. *Journal of the American Oriental Society* 92: 276–9.

Burrow, T and Emeneau, M. B. 1984. *A Dravidian Etymological Dictionary:* 2nd ed., Oxford: Clarendon Press.

Chidambaranatha Pillai V. 1978, *A Grammar of the Kasaba Language.* Annamalainagar: Annamalai University.

Emeneau, M. B. 1939, 'The vowels of the Badaga language'. *Language* 15: 43–7.

——— 1944–6, *Kota Texts.* (I–IV). UCPL, Berkeley and Los Angeles: University of California Press.

——— 1957, 'Toda, a Dravidian language'. *Transactions of the Philological Society.* 15–66.

——— 1967, 'The South Dravidian Languages'. *Journal of the American Oriental Society,* 87. 365–413.

——— 1984, *Toda Grammar and Texts.* Philadelphia American Philosophical Society (Memoirs 155).

——— 1989, 'The Languages of the Nilgiris', *in* P. Hockings (ed.) *Blue Mountains: the Ethnography and Biogeography of a South Indian Region,* 133–43. New Delhi: Oxford University Press.

Emeneau, M. B. and Burrow, T. 1962, *Dravidian Borrowings from Indo-Aryan,* Berkeley and Los Angeles: University of California Press.

Hockings, P. 1980a, *Ancient Hindu Refugees: Badaga Social History 1550–1975,* New Delhi: Vikas.

——— 1988, *Counsel from the Ancients: A study of Badaga Proverbs, Prayers, Omens and Curses.* Berlin, New York, Amsterdam: Mouton de Gruyter.

——— 1989, *Blue Mountains. The Ethnography and Biogeography of a South Indian Region.* Delhi: Oxford University Press.

Kapp D. B. 1978 'Palu Kurumba riddles'. *Bulletin of the School of Oriental and African Studies* 41. 512–22.

——— 1982, *Alu-Kurumbaru Nayan: die Sprache der Alu-Kurumbas.* Wiesbaden.

Perialwar, R. 1978, *A Grammar of the Irula Language.* Annamalainagar: Annamalai University.

Pilot-Raichoor, C. 1990, Le badaga, une approche historique et comparative'. *Bulletin de la Société de Linguistique de Paris,* 85, 1: 311–36.

——— 1991, 'Le badaga, langue dravidienne (Inde). Description et analyse'. Ph.D. disseration in Linguistics, Paris III.

Schiffman, H. 1979, *A Reference Grammar of Spoken Kannada.*

Swaminathan, S. 1972, 'Badaga language. A descriptive Phonology', *in* Subramoniam, V.I. (ed), *Proceedings of the First All-India Conference of Dravidian Linguists.* (Trivandrum, 1971). 450–8. Trivandrum: Dravidian Linguistic Association of India, University of Kerala.

Zvelebil, K. 1979, *The Irula (Erla) Language, part II.* Wiesbaden: Otto Harrassowitz.

——— 1980, 'A plea for Nilgiri areal studies.' *International Journal of Dravidian Linguistics*, 9: 1–22.

——— 1985, 'The Body in Nilgiri Tribal Languages. A Contribution to areal linguistic studies', *Journal of the American Oriental Society* 105: 653–674.

Immigrant Labourers and Local Networks in the Nilgiris

FRANK HEIDEMANN

7

Immigrant labourers constitute a significant section of the Nilgiri population, and their daily labour is the backbone of the contemporary economy. The impact of their migration was both demographic and economic, with introduction of trade unions and changing ethnic relations. As Francis observed at the beginning of the twentieth century, the Nilgiris became 'the most polyglot area in the [Madras] Presidency' (Francis 1908: 124). The labour migration strengthened the link to the surrounding plains and introduced new ideas and ideologies. This, however, was more a quantitative than a qualitative change because links had always existed (Mandelbaum 1989: 19), and the labour immigration from the plains constitutes a recent link in the cultural continuity. The immigrants' share of the total population and their impact on the local society have been growing since the migration started. However, no separate study focusing on this group has as yet been published.

The term 'labourer' refers to those who work for wages, that is a category of people who occupy a distinct position in economic interaction; labourers are usually defined as a section of society. But in the Nilgiris, and I suppose in many localities in India, 'labourer' refers rather to a particular type of relationship. Therefore it is likely that a labourer is to be distinguished from others according to his kind of work and work-relationship. The evaluation of these particular circumstances is not always easy as some labourers work part-time and are self-employed in addition, others act as money lenders, receive a small side income from a minor property, or take the chance work-contracts and act as employers. Moreover, the kind of work and the quality of a relationship can change according to chance or season. For the purpose of this essay, I shall consider the main source of income and include all individuals who basically earn their living by physical work (usually on a daily wage).

After their arrival the labourers developed sets of local networks including social, political, economic, and religious organizations. I will try to show that immigration, the different types of work relationship, the places of residence and the local networks are interconnected; labourers and their dependents will be considered in their particular context.

Immigration from the South Indian Plains

In the nineteenth century, labourers on coffee and tea plantations were the principal day-labourers in the Nilgiris. In the 1830s the tea and coffee were planted for the first time, in the 1840s coffee was fully established, 'and by the year 1863–4 there were probably forty estates in various parts of the district' (Grigg 1880: 483).

Compared to coffee, which was planted on about 4,000 acres in 1880, tea was produced on a smaller scale—300 acres in 1869 and the acreage rose to between 3,000 and 4,000 acres in 1897 (Tanna 1970: 21). Labour was in abundance with, 'the neighbouring provinces of Malabar, Mysore and Coimbatore supplying *coolies* in sufficient number to meet all demands, and at all seasons of the year' (Ouchterlony, quoted from Grigg 1880: 484), and many Badagas too were available for this kind of work.

The labour recruiter, called *maistry* or *kangany* (Heidemann 1992: 5–9), played a crucial role in the migration process and became a central figure among Tamil labourers on plantations. Prior to his plantation job, he had some connection with British officials or planters and recruited mainly from his own or his wife's village or from the local market towns. Therefore the labour force of a plantation originated from the surroundings of the *kanganies*' native villages, which were scattered in the plains. Most labourers were thus recruited from various Tamil districts. Other plantations attracted labourers from other regions: for example Kodanad Estate, located on the northern slopes, employed a significant number of families from the Kannada-speaking districts, while other estates attracted Malayali-speaking labourers as well (Heidemann and Mizushima 1985: 166–70). As in other parts of India, many migrants left their families behind, visited their homes annually, and considered their stay in the Nilgiri Hills as temporary (Francis 1908: 128; Omvedt 1980: 190–2, 200).

In the nineteenth century, most of the plantation labourers lived rather isolated lives on small estates scattered over the Plateau or located on the slopes going down to the plains. On the plantation, social relationships and marriage alliances were continued as per the social system of the plains. The work relations, however, were based on an administrative or military model of hierarchy, similar to other plantation systems in South Asia (Bhowmik 1981: 9–15). In many places the immigrants worked together with Badagas from the Plateau, or with Irula or Kuṟumba people from the lower elevations. On some estates Badagas became foremen, supervising both Badagas and immigrant labourers, or took contracts for field and construction work.

The opening of the plantations and the construction of roads, the advent of telecommunication, railways and concrete buildings required numerous labourers from the South Indian plains; others came as washermen, rickshaw-pullers, domestic servants. Two decades after the immigration had started there were more labourers from the plains than original inhabitants.[1]

Most of the stonemasons had been settled in Coimbatore district before they came to the hills, and spoke Telugu. Tanna mentions a further group, but their descendants cannot be traced in the contemporary Nilgiris: 'Chinese prisoners were brought to India from China in 1859 and 1869 and jailed on the Nilgiris in two camps, one at Naduvattam, and one in the Thaishola Reserve Forest . . . there is a local legend that the Chinese prisoners gave instructions to the Planters in the cultivation of tea and its manufacture' (Tanna 1970: 17–18).

At the turn of the century more than 40 per cent of the people included in the census were not born in the Nilgiris district; the growth rates from 1891 to 1901 for Ootacamund and Coonoor taluk (including the Kotagiri region) were 22 per cent and 20 per cent respectively, against the whole Madras Presidency average of 7 per cent. 'Hindus and Animists', as they were called in the official records, constituted 81 per cent of the population, 13 per cent (including the British) were Christians, and 5 per cent were Muslims who controlled the local markets (Francis 1908: 123–4, 334).

In the course of immigration a spatial pattern came into being which reflects the history of immigration and the economic and social relations. The Aravenu area, perhaps the most commercialized micro-region in the rural part of the eastern Plateau, illustrates this process. Here, within a radius of one kilometre around Aravenu, labourers are settled on a plantation, in a bazaar, in field-huts and in 'colonies'.

Aravenu is the name of a Badaga hamlet, two and a half kilometres as the crow flies southeast of the Kotagiri bazaar. The road from Kotagiri to Mettupalaiyam, the only link in the eastern Plateau to the surrounding plains, passes a hundred metres below the hamlet. In 1820, the first workers were brought to the Nilgiris, when '[t]he bridle path up to the hills was made from Sirumugai near Mettupalaiyam to Kotagiri. . . . Pioneers and convict labour from Coimbatore and Salem were utilized' (Francis 1908: 109). At the latest by 1840, Rob Roy, one of the first plantations in this region, was founded, in the valley just below the Aravenu hamlet.

In Rob Roy, as in other plantations in the Nilgiris, development of the local networks was influenced by the organizational structure of the plantation and by the networks which existed in the labourers' places of origin. Labourers maintained agnatic and affinal links to their native villages but the daily interaction, most of the face-to-face relations, were confined within the boundaries of the plantation. An increasing number of marriages took place within the group of plantation labourers, religious festivals were celebrated within the plantation, and the labourers' headman too was usually a foreman in the plantation. The local networks did not exist independently of the plantation; the social, economic, and religious organization of the plantation were adapted to the residential pattern and work organization of the plantation. The membership of an individual in the group was determined by the work relationship. Outside the plantation the labourers were identified according to their work-place and thus their position within the local society was also ascribed according to the work-place.

In the following decades, a bazaar developed at the roadside between Rob Roy Estate and the hamlet. Muslims and Chettiars opened shops, Malayalis sold tea and ran bakeries, and other traders from Mettupalaiyam sold vegetables at a weekly market. The rather small number of bazaar labourers were either attached to a particular business or worked independently. Those working for the merchants or artisans were usually paid on a weekly basis and received a gift annually and sometimes a bus fare to their native village. These dependent bazaar labourers often originated from the same region as their employer; in some cases their relatives worked for the employer's family in the plains, or the labourers continued the work of their forefathers. The 'independent' bazaar labourers usually were members of a dependent labour-family or of a poor self-employed household, like a *dhobi* (washerman) or cobbler. They worked as helpers or porters in the bazaar, occasionally in a tea factory, and until the forties as rickshaw pullers they waited for British clients and took them down the slopes to Mettupalaiyam.

In the eastern part of the Plateau bazaars grew in Donnington, Eelada, Kil-Kotagiri, Sholurmattam, next to Pandian Park, in Kattabettu, and more recently in other places. The labourers who settled around the bazaar were not recruited from the plains, they immigrated one by one. Some came to visit their relatives working on a plantation and remained in the hills searching for employment, others knew relatives of the traders before and came up with a recommendation, and a few immigrated with the intention to build up their own business; they will be subsumed under a second category, the bazaar labourers. The local networks in the bazaars were rather weak organizational structures; they linked small groups of individuals together, usually those from the same place of origin. There was no leadership and no common worship; bazaar labourers, however, had no separate set of networks.

Near the Aravenu bazaar, Badagas had settled in more than a dozen hamlets; they were agriculturalists and, until the beginning of this century, they predominantly produced for their own consumption; only a few Badaga families employed day-labourers. In the first decades of the twentieth century the wealthy among this landowning community built field-huts for their non-Badaga labourers. The labourers worked and lived isolated in the fields, were employed all year round, and this economic relationship was often continued by the following generation. This economic relationship was of advantage for the landlords, since the crop (mostly coffee in this region in the first decades of the twentieth century) was thereby safeguarded against thieves and wild animals. The daily wage was lower than remuneration in the plantations, and labourers were usually indebted and bound to the landowning family. Labourers expected a loan free of interest and a gift for annual festivals or for important rituals. Thus field labourers worked and lived under conditions different from other labourers and formed the third category in this context. Their networks were comparatively vague structures, and primarily linked labourers to their employers. Among the field labourers, however, there was no separate leadership and, like the bazaar labourers, they did not celebrate an annual cult independently.

After independence a strong tea economy developed in the Aravenu area; besides Rob Roy and a few other plantations there were private tea factories, so-called bought-leaf factories, which processed tea leaf from smallholders. An industry supplying the local factories with tea chests, firewood dealers and various workshops started their business; later, a post and telegraph office, a *panchayat* office and two banks have opened. Aravenu shops and the weekly market were supplied by traders based in the plains. Until Independence bullock carts came up from the plains everyday. Today cars and jeeps are available for hire and lorry transport agents offer their service, buses shuttle to Kotagiri and reach Mettupalaiyam in one hour and Coimbatore in almost two hours.

The expanding economy encouraged more people to settle in this region. On a steep slope, just above the Aravenu bazaar, labourers built their huts. After Independence the DMK government granted small plots to the landless day-labourers and financed a housing scheme for so-called Harijans. In the 'seventies Sri Lankan repatriates moved in and extended the settlement, which is today one of the biggest colonies in the region.[2] These labourers enjoyed more autonomy than others and could fetch higher wages in peak seasons. But at the same time they were exposed to a higher degree of uncertainty and had to hunt for a job in slack seasons. Some of them opt for regular work, others offer their labour on a daily basis in the Aravenu bazaar. When work is scarce or better wages can be expected elsewhere, labourers walk the three-kilometre shortcut to Kotagiri, where they meet labourers from other colonies. Local farmers, foremen from big estates or contractors come to the same spots in search of labour.

The construction of a colony—the granting of land and housing to members of a minority—has to be understood as a political act. The settlers were involved right from the beginning in a process which created leadership, in many places opposition, and occasionally factions. The labourers in colonies were cut off from their former (often vague) networks and utilized the chance to develop their own organizational structures. They built small shrines and founded new local cults, and they set up colony councils and elected their own leaders. Leadership was mainly confined to internal matters, and for external interaction the settlers usually depended on their own initiative. However, a crucial aspect is the fact that the local networks in the colonies were, like the colonies themselves, independent of work relationships.

Over the course of years, the immigrant labourers and indigenous people became familiar with their new neighbours' culture, they paid mutual visits on annual festivals or attended weddings and funerals. Badagas showed interest in particular temples in the plains and some undertook pilgrimages there. In the 'sixties there were four categories of labourers in the eastern Nilgiri Hills: recruited labourers who worked in the microcosm of a plantation; labourers who individually (or with family) settled around bazaars; field-labourers who took up work in the coffee and later tea fields of local smallholders; and finally those who shifted to the labour colonies.

In the first half of the twentieth century, the size of many plantations and the number of workers increased. The infrastructure improved, plantation labourers visited the weekly market more frequently, and further small bazaar centres came up in various parts of the district. The internal organization among the labourers and the relationship of labourers and employers, however, remained basically unchanged: labourers constituted a heterogeneous class of people, they originated in numerous regions, belonged to various castes and spoke different languages. *Kanganies* (or *maistries*) mediated between labourers and the planters, and—as the senior planter of Glenmorgen Estate puts it—'(t)rade unions in plantations being unheard of practically until independence' (Tanna 1970: 54).

The Repatriates from Sri Lanka

In the early 'seventies the immigration of the so-called repatriates started, and in the following two decades they became, in local terms, the largest section among the Nilgiri labourers. They are Tamils but can be distinguished by their appearance: they have a liking for a particular fashion and hairstyle and speak with a distinct accent. The repatriates lived before on plantations in Sri Lanka, where caste and the concept of purity have—compared to the villages from where the early immigrants of the Nilgiris came—a different, less relevant meaning. On the plantations more secular values developed and trade union activities reached into most spheres of social life. The workers were socialized as class-conscious people who treated employers as representatives of an antagonistic interest. To understand the changes they caused after their arrival, their history will be briefly reviewed.

In the nineteenth century the forefathers of the repatriates were recruited from several coastal districts of the Madras Presidency to work on plantations in British Ceylon. They were either Harijans or belonged to one of the agricultural *Shudra* castes. The overwhelming majority was Tamil-speaking, but with regard to caste and place of origin they formed a heterogeneous plantation population. Unlike the plantation workers in the Nilgiris, these labourers in Ceylon were cut off from their ancestors' villages, in the beginning just by physical distance and the passage across the Palk Strait; and later, after 1939, by a ban on migration from India. This isolation and strong trade union movement contributed to the fundamental change of basic values. On the plantations in Ceylon, where the labourers were born and buried, space was not structured according to concepts of purity: Brahmans were absent; wages, water supply and accommodation were not based on a concept of caste and status; and authority rested on secular pillars. The more secular ideology, which emerged in the up-country of Ceylon, was to encounter opposition later in the south Indian villages and in the Nilgiri Hills (cf. Heidemann 1992: 42–7, 75–86). On the basis of two Indo-Ceylon Agreements of 1964 and of 1974 more than 450, 000 up-country Tamils from Ceylon (since 1972 Sri Lanka) were deported to India (Kumar 1977: 47–91). They were eligible for rehabilitation, but these state-run schemes left them de facto homeless and jobless. Only a minority among this expelled people were able to settle in their ancestral village, and the overwhelming majority sojourned elsewhere in south India (cf. CRNIEO 1983: 22–55; Fries and Bibbin 1984; Heidemann 1989: 124–64).

It is no surprise that the Nilgiris with a growing tea-industry and climatic features similar to the up-country in Sri Lanka attracted more repatriates than any other district. The only successful rehabilitation scheme, the Tamil Nadu Tea Plantation Corporation (TAN TEA), opened plantations in various parts of the district, and employed about 2,700 families (i.e. less than 3 per cent of the families repatriated to India). These families communicated with other repatriates in the plains and relatives in Sri Lanka and contributed to the further immigration of families. In the first decade of repatriation, most of these unfortunate families dwelt weeks or years in the plains after their arrival; in the 'eighties an increasing number migrated directly from the reception camp in Mandapam to the Nilgiris. In 1984, when the physical repatriation from Sri Lanka to India came to a standstill, I estimated the number of repatriates in the Nilgiris at over 100, 000; ever since the number has been growing, as more families move from the Tamil plains to the Nilgiris.

Besides the repatriates employed by TAN TEA there were hardly any families which were employed on plantations. In the Kotagiri taluk repatriates initially found work on the smallholdings of the local Badagas. Most Badagas, however, cultivated their little holdings themselves until the 'seventies. Then the tea-growing business encouraged more smallholders to plant more tea and to intensify production. They started to use fertilizers, to prune the bushes every five years, and some replaced old tea bushes with new varieties. As this process was coincidental with the immigration of repatriates, Badagas easily found labourers skilled in tea cultivation, and so more repatriates were encouraged to settle in this region.

In the first phase of the immigration they lived mainly in field-huts, rather scattered over the Plateau, but a few years after their arrival repatriates started to build their own colonies. This was a major transition, because for the first time repatriates could develop their own networks and a new social organization. The networks in the repatriate colonies were influenced, like other networks described earlier, by the background of the migrants as well as by the new social environment. The difference between the networks in the new colonies and those in the Nilgiris was due to the underlying ideology which originated in the history of the repatriates. The social and political networks in Sri Lanka were linked to a trade union organization which could not serve as a model after their arrival in the Nilgiris. In the new colonies, however, a social and political framework based on the ideal of equality was realized, and the settlers tried to reconstruct the old pattern of social relations (cf. Heidemann 1989: 182–230).

Most settlers gave up their rather safe jobs in a Badaga field, because they felt, in this inter-personal relation, unfree and bound, and preferred to rely on the 'free' labour market and on their own bargaining capacity. In the new colonies they gained a feeling of security, they could rely on neighbours, and the colony council could take up their internal and external problems. Settlers in each colony built small shrines or temples, and one or two settlers became the priests, and so annual cults commenced. Colonies created a new aura, a new era had started, and many of those repatriates in the colonies were for the first time since their forced departure from Sri Lanka determined to start a new life.

In the Kotagiri taluk there were 481 workers and their families employed by TAN TEA, and according to my own estimate in the year 1984 more than six thousand repatriates lived in the twenty-two colonies within the boundaries of the taluk, and approximately double that number outside the colonies. According to the revenue inspectors the total number of repatriates is almost ten thousand, and in the public opinion, repatriates constitute 'almost half of the Kotagiri taluk population', which amounted to 87, 831 in the 1981 Census report.

The relationship between Badagas and repatriates was in one way rather cooperative: the former gained access to a labour force and the latter found work. But in other ways, both sides considered the relationship problematic and antagonistic in interest. Implicit and explicit discord and in a few instances even physical fights were caused by disputes over wages in general, the form and time of remuneration or quality of work in particular, encroachment on land for colonies, and accusations of minor theft, etc. One of the major sources of tension which could not be solved by a compromise was different cultural concepts. To cite just one example, different ideas about honour or respect (*mariyadu*) caused severe inter-communal tensions. Repatriates were used to adjusting interpersonal interaction to either 'on-duty' or 'off–duty' situations and the latter required less respect towards a higher ranking position (cf. Hollup 1986: 200); but in the Nilgiris as well as in rural Tamil Nadu rules of respect have to be observed regardless of this distinction.

The relationship between repatriates and Badagas is influenced by two major processes. The first (historically) is adaptation: in the course of years face-to-face interaction became the basis for a mutual understanding, and the relationship between individuals became smooth, and more cordial. The second is polarization: the growing number of repatriates in many localities, the construction of colonies and their internal social structure, and the impact of voluntary associations representing either repatriates or Badagas in public, contributed to a stronger self-consciousness, to more participation in the political arena and to an increasing polarization.

From the point of view of the Badaga people as well as from the view of the repatriates themselves we can distinguish at least three categories, which also correspond to spatial concepts. First, repatriates employed by TAN TEA live rather isolated lives on tea plantations and are hardly involved in the inter-ethnic discourse; their local network corresponds to the organization of the plantation. Second, those living in the scattered field-huts of local landlords (or as individual families in bazaars), many of whom came early, contribute more strongly to the process of adaptation; their local network has a rather weak structure. Third, the repatriates settled in colonies, including most of the families which arrived later, change their employers, negotiate for wages; they are active members of repatriate organizations and demand their rights. The local networks in these colonies consist of a set of social, political and religious organizations independent of the work relationship.

Networks and Identity

Labourers in the Nilgiris immigrated from various places over a period of 170 years and occupy different positions in the local economy. In this essay they have been classified historically as well as according to their residential pattern, because this corresponds to the kind of work they do and, more importantly, people in the eastern Nilgiris classify individuals along these lines too. We distinguished early immigrants and repatriates respectively on plantations, in bazaars, in field-huts and in colonies. But it goes without saying that there are also local categories such as those of religion and language which classify people as Hindus, Christians and Moslems or as Tamils, Malayalis, Telugus and Kannadigas. Caste seems to crosscut the former categories: the caste membership of early Tamil immigrants is usually well known among the local people, but in the cases of repatriates, Malayalis or Telugus, the individual caste membership is hardly detectable by outsiders. For most non-Malayalis it is usually sufficient to know whether a Malayali is a Christian, Moslem or Hindu, and any further classification in terms of caste would be of little meaning. Repatriates are generally said to belong to the Harijan castes, but a close look would give a more detailed picture. As further investigation into one of the categories will lead to a more detailed but dispersed representation of the labourers as a whole, I shall focus on their internal links and networks.

Almost every family is tied to agnates and affines somewhere in the hills. Agnates are more likely to live adjacently while affinal relatives either followed from the plains to the same place or live within range of the local market or of the wider working radius. Labourers visit their relatives for ceremonies or occasionally at weekends. Relatives living beyond the Nilgiri Hills are rarely visited since such trips can be expensive. An exception are those plantation labourers who migrated early and are paid the official minimum wages; they usually go annually for a short visit to their native place and many are likely to retire there. Kinship, both agnatic and affinal, serves as a basis for strong solidarity and is usually locally based; factions, however, among close kin are not exceptional. But it must be kept in mind that migration to the hills dispersed families, lineages, and sub-castes. Therefore, the kinship network is comparatively loose and not embedded in a local caste system as in a south Indian village.

Most of the labourers work in their particular locality, i.e. in the plantation, in the bazaar, in the fields of smallholders, or in the surroundings of their colonies; but often not all family members will find work in the vicinity. They try their luck in one of the public places where job-seekers gather in the morning, join neighbours who know about a casual or seasonal job, or go to a remote valley where friends or relatives told them about a job opportunity. In that way, unemployed family members of plantation workers come together with settlers from colonies and bazaar labourers, and they work together under a contractor or under a wealthy landlord. In other cases, workers in colonies are picked up daily by a truck from the plantation and work along with estate labourers. Other plantations (which are family property) are formally divided into smallholdings, maintain a minimal labour force and employ bazaar and colony people on a temporary basis. Occasionally there are openings in house and road-construction work. The economic situation is thus dependent on a variety of factors, and the labourers try to extend their personal, informal networks both to find work and to extend work opportunities to their acquaintances.

The links beyond the locality are daily work, visits to the weekly market, occasional political meetings and participation in annual festivals. These kinds of external relations are important for daily and occasional interaction, they supply individuals with information and are a welcome change. However, such external relations do not offer a network of solidarity and are not important for the individual's identity.

The social and political networks depend to a great extent on the residential pattern. In the bazaars where just a few families live together and in the scattered field-huts of the smallholdings, interpersonal relations are not supported by a formal framework and are thus dependent on individual initiative. In the plantations and colonies usually an elected, nominated or informal leader (*talaivar*), looks after individual affairs, solves disputes and represents the residential group. He coordinates and organizes; under his auspices funds for annual festivals or temple construction are collected. The leaders negotiate with landlords over wages and with the local administration, trade unions and political parties about work, wages, land rights, water supply, electricity, etc. The institutionalized quality of solidarity creates a feeling of security among the settlers or plantation workers and seems to be one of the reasons for the change in residence.

Trade unions became active in the Nilgiri Hills after Independence and found their clientele mainly among the plantation workers. In the plantations, usually the *kanganies* or foremen were the headmen and were affiliated to one of the trade unions. Thus the person was more important than the institution. Later, after the arrival of the repatriates, voluntary associations came to the hills and opened offices in all taluks. In the beginning they were most active near Gudalur; in the mid-'eighties, a Kotagiri-based organization started. A few years later, the latter group became well known in the region. It was involved in various fields from healthcare to land rights, organized public meetings and rallies, and strongly influenced the self-respect and self-confidence of repatriates and their image with the public at large.

The kind of solidarity and identity created by voluntary associations and trade unions is structurally complementary to kinship: it is secular and inter-caste, it emphasizes equality, it is addressed to the local administration, political parties and to the public in general. Ideally the membership is open to all, internal procedure is democratic, solidarity ascribed with the suppressed, and the identity created should unite the landless working class.

The networks suggest that there are different levels of cooperation which correspond to respective solidarity and identity. To sum up, caste formation did not emerge in the hills but fragments exist—more strongly visible among the early immigrants but less clearly among the repatriates. Caste membership is usually known by the in-group (i.e., the colony or plantation) but not by outsiders, and is (still) essential for affinal alliances. Kin solidarity in an individual crisis can be expected. The local formation is a product of migration and settlement; it is weak in the field-huts and strong in the new colonies—where an atmosphere of reconstruction prevails, where a new social structure emerged and a vision is realized. The emic as well as the etic view is that settlers form a united, co-operating group (factions are here neglected). The class formation is a concept which is not shared by all labourers. Among the early immigrants it is a small minority who use this category, usually just among plantation workers, and among the repatriates it is a majority, mainly settled in colonies. The distinction emic/etic cannot be applied to the caste and class formations, since the first is not well known in public and the second is not even shared internally. Moreover, 'class' must be understood as a local syncretism—as those who share the concept of class implicitly (and at times also explicitly) exclude the landless day-labourers from the landowning community.

Identity exists at several levels and cannot be easily classified for a complex group like labourers in the Nilgiris. Migration moved people and ideologies into a new context, where both adapted to the new environment. As compared to the Nilgiris, in the plains the caste ideology, and in the plantations of Sri Lanka the class ideology, was more pervasive, and here, in the last two decades, both interacted and produced a unique ferment in the repatriate colonies. Unlike the general pattern in the Nilgiris—where indigenous (pre-British) groups referred in different contexts to a particular identity which relate to a corresponding layer of the same social organization, usually family, extended kinship, sub-caste/clan, caste/tribe—at least in the colonies the different layers refer to different concepts: family is an aspect of caste, the colony is a territorial unit, the term 'repatriate' refers to a common history, and the broadest category, class, is a transcultural concept.

Labourers in the Nilgiris do not constitute a homogeneous group. They are characterized by the locality of their residence which refers to a particular type of work: more exactly the locality refers to a particular type of relationship between the employer and the labourer. In short, labourers on plantations work according to a codified system, bazaar labourers and field labourers are linked to individual employers, and settlers in colonies sell their labour according to chances. Still, an emic and etic distinction is made between the most heterogeneous early immigrants and the repatriates who, too, are not homogeneous at all. Members of all different groups in the Nilgiris will confirm that repatriates have somehow a different outlook upon life. But this would apply in the same way to the various sections among the early immigrants. The major difference is that repatriates seek a different, a more codified, relationship between the employer and the labour force. They oppose the old working order in the bazaar and the fields, and seek what is found in the plantations. Now, two ideologies interact which had been neatly separated in the past. Therefore labourers are adequately described by the relationship they practice and the one they seek.[3]

Notes

1. According to the Census of 1847 there were 3,045 'Hindoos' and 4,941 'Pariahs' from the plains and 7,674 'Hill Tribes' living in the Nilgiris (Ouchterlony 1868: 51).
2. At the time of my fieldwork in Aravenu in 1984 there were 147 families settled in Thavittumedu, and according to the documentation (TECRAS 316) repatriate families were living in this colony in the early nineties. In 1993 I was informed by the leader of Thavittumedu that now more than one thousand people are permanently settled here.
3. This paper is based on fieldwork on plantation labour, repatriates and Badagas in different parts of the Nilgiris, mainly in Kotagiri taluk. I would like to thank the following institutions for their support: six stays (each for a three-month period) and fieldwork for more than a year were funded by the German Academic Exchange Service (1983, 1984 and 1988–9), the Friedrich Naumann Stiftung (1986, 1987) and the German Research Foundation (1991, 1992).

References

Bhowmik, Sharit. 1981. *Class Formation in the Plantation System.* New Delhi: People's Publishing House.

Center for Research on the New International Economic Order (CRNIEO) 1980. *A Report on the Survey of Repatriates from Sri Lanka.* Madras. Second edition.

Francis, W. 1908. *The Nilgiris.* Madras District Gazetteers. Madras: Government Press.

Fries, Yvonne, and Thomas Bibbin. 1984 *The Undesirables: The Expatriation of Tamil People of "Recent Indian Origin" from the Plantations in Sri Lanka to India.* Calcutta.

Grigg, H. B. ed. 1880. *A Manual of the Nílagiri District in the Madras Presidency.* Madras: Government Press.

Heidemann, Frank. 1989. *Die Hochland-Tamilen in Sri Lanka und ihre Repatriierung nach Indien.* Göttingen: Edition Re.

——— 1992. *Kanganies in Sri Lanka and Malaysia. Tamil Recruiter-cum-Foreman as a Sociological Category in the Nineteenth and Twentieth Century.* Munich: Anacon.

——— and Tsukasa Mizushima 1985. 'Tea Estate Workers in Kotagiri Hills, South India. A Study for Places of Origin'. *Indian Geographical Journal,* 60: 161–72.

Hollup, Oddvar. 1986, Calgary Estate. Social Stratification among Indian Plantation Workers in Sri Lanka. Cand. Polit. thesis, University of Bergen.

Kumar, Lalit. 1977. *India and Sri Lanka. Sirimavo Shastri Pact.* New Delhi.

Mandelbaum, David G. 1989. 'The Nilgiris as a Region'. *In* Paul Hockings (ed.), *Blue Mountains: The Ethnography and Biogeography of a South Indian Region.* Delhi: Oxford University Press.

Omvedt, Gail. 1980. 'Migration in Colonial India. The Articulation of Feudalism and Capitalism by the Colonial State'. *Journal of Peasant Studies,* 7: 185–212.

Ouchterlony, John. 1868 'A Geographical and Statistical Memoir of the Neilgherry Mountains.' *In* J. Shortt (ed.), *An Account of the Tribes on the Neilgherries . . .* Madras: Higginbotham.

Tanna, Kaku J. 1970. *Plantations in the Nilgiris: A Synoptic History.* Wellington: C. D. Dhody & Sons.

TECRAS. n.d. *Repatriates from Sri Lanka. District-wise Settlements.* Madras: The Ecumenical Council for Repatriates and Refugees from Sri Lanka.

Voices in the Forest: The Field of Gathering among the Jēnu Kuṟumba

ULRICH DEMMER

8

Introduction

An overview of studies concerned with the social order of South Indian gatherer-hunter societies such as the Hill Pandaram (Morris 1982), the Palliyar (Gardner 1966) or the Nayaka (Bird-David 1987) suggests that it is inadequate to analyse and describe these societies in terms of a 'group model' of society, one that stresses institutions, corporate groups, etc. The social life of these communities is characterized by fluid and flexible social arrangements to such an extent that an analysis in terms of a reified model results in an image of 'social deficiency'—in negative representations. Thus Bird-David most recently argued that there is a strong case for arguing that the impression of 'social deficiency' is a logical corollary of analysis which dwells upon what hunter-gatherers do not have and do not do. Such analysis in turn derives to a large extent from using the 'group' model, which is not wholly suitable for hunter-gatherers (Bird-David 1987: 152).

The Jēnu Kuṟumba, a gatherer/hunter community on the northern hilly slopes of the 'Blue Mountains', are no exception in this regard. Rather, the problem of coming to terms with our anthropological group models of society was present from the very beginning of the fieldwork. The people I worked with never did represent their social relations or their society to me in terms of such a model. My initial hopes to find anthropological counterparts who were able to speak with me in my own anthropological meta-language (of corporate groups, descent rights, clans, etc.), my hopes to find indigenous interpreters who were able to represent their society to me in terms of a 'surface organization of social relations' (Ortner 1984: 129), were constantly frustrated. In contrast to many anthropologists working in India (Burghart 1991), I could not be engaged with indigenous spokespeople who were able to confirm any group model and thus able to collaborate in my initial attempts of building total models. Indeed, as it turned out, there is no indigenous discourse either, in which the Jēnu Kuṟumba represent their society to themselves in terms of a totalizing model—nor in myth or narrative or in rituals or elsewhere. The question raised by M. Strathern then, 'in what cultural contexts do people's self-descriptions include a represen-tation of themselves as a society?' (1988: 9) had to be answered negatively. There were no such contexts. If I were to keep on any dialogic fieldwork procedures, as I was, an understanding and representation of their community structures in any reified form would be, in fact, counterproductive.

At the same time, however, the alternative approach, as exemplified by Bird-David (1987), namely to concentrate on the role of individuals instead of groups and timeless institutions, appeared equally unsuitable. In the course of participant fieldwork it soon became obvious that the Jēnu Kuṟumba do have a vivid life beyond that of the individual; that they, for example, do form camp-groups while going out into the forest for gathering forest products and for collecting honey. The problem however remained. These camps were not the timeless institutions one could build a model with: they were temporary arrangements. They were transient in the course of time with regard to the persons that constituted them. On the other hand, these camps showed, despite their temporality and seemingly individual basis, a recurring structure.

The social life of the Jēnu Kuṟumba, and their way of representing it *vis-à-vis* the anthropologist during field work, thus points one to a basically epistemological problem: namely, how to analyse and describe a flexible, temporary social life that is nevertheless not arbitrary but structured and inscribed with meaning. Rather than viewing social life as the result of or the absence of the interplay between individuals and a given society, the experience of fieldwork required one to transcend that epistemological pair of Individual–Society. From this point of view, the initial problem, of how the prevalent negative representations of the South Indian hunter-gatherer societies could be superseded by more appropriate approaches is rearticulated as: how to conceptualize social life beyond that episteme of individual society.

It is certainly not fortitious that F. Myers, being confronted with a very similar style of representation among another hunter-gatherer culture, the Pintubi (1986), has outlined the direction for such an attempt. In order to describe Pintubi notions and practices concerning territoriality and the person, he applied the concept of 'social reproduction'. Instead of representing this culture in terms of a reified model, he sought to develop an understanding of the processual character of social life, conceptualized as the 'relationship between cultural meaning and social action' (1986: 14) that constitutes social reality. In the present essay I will try to follow his lead. I will attempt to employ approaches concerned with praxis (Bourdieu, Giddens) or, to use an alternative term, with sociality, understood as the 'way in which "the natives" make their collectivities' (Wagner 1974: 104) or as the 'creating and maintaining of relationships' (Strathern 1988: 13) and 'concrete people's ideas about the nature of relationships' (ibid.: ix).

Leaving aside for the purpose of the present essay the differences between the various proponents, they merge in their common interest in describing the way people configure their social world—in the analysis of the production and reproduction of social forms, as they are brought about by the actors themselves. As is well known by now, such approaches accentuate that *(1)* there exist structures in the social domain, *(2)* that these structures are produced or structured by the actors and *(3)* are realized (either consciously or habitually) through the application of specific knowledge practices, habitual conventions and cultural schemata. Seen in this light the task becomes how to account for the flow of social life, understood as the mediation of meaning and structure in situated contexts of sociality.

Especially relevant here of course is Bourdieu's theory of praxis and his concept of habitus, the latter comprising the various cultural schemes that enable actors to produce and interpret their doings (1976: 80). This habitus, understood as a system of lasting dispositions to action, organizes practices as an 'inherent potential to generate homologous formations across different cultural fields' (Hanks 1987: 677). In this essay I will try to employ this concept with regard to the practice of gathering among the Jēnu Kuṟumba, but with a somewhat extended understanding of the concept. While Bourdieu's conception of habitual conventions enables him to show us the working of habitus as a set of symbolic relations and modes of practice like 'rhythm of execution, sequence, duration and so forth' (Hanks 1987: 677), it stresses most prominently the rather formal and aesthetic aspects of practice. Yet this concept, as used by Bourdieu, its theoretical and analytical importance notwithstanding, almost leaves out those aspects that seem to me most important with regard to the sociality I was confronted with among the Jēnu Kuṟumba: namely the fact, advocated by Harré so aptly, that apart from the formal and aesthetic properties of social life, the 'social world is structured as a moral order' (1990: 346). Whatever practices among the Jēnu Kuṟumba I tried to understand, I had to recognize what especially Harré has made the basis of his concept of sociality and habitual convention, namely, that in analysis the 'moral quality of actions must also be included, since the persons who engage in them are, as has been amply demonstrated, deeply engaged in issues of personal responsibility' (Harré 1990: 349).

As I will try to show, the habitual conventions that lead, among the Jēnu Kuṟumba, to the formation of gathering camps, rest basically on an intersubjective moral system of kinship. This system has to be taken into account whenever one speaks of the configuration of social life there. When speaking of habitus or habitual conventions in the present context then, I wish to include this aspect of morality in the concept and rather think of habitual schemes in Harré's 'social constructivistic' sense, as 'moral orders, local systems of obligation and duty with associated valuation criteria' (1990: 348).

Yet, in the same way as the Jēnu Kuṟumba refused to provide me with a ready-made model of their society, so did they refuse to present me with a ready-made model of their moral conventions and ideas, which led to the formation of their social life; in the present case the composition of gathering camps. Rather I was confronted with a kind of social presentation, described by Strathern (1988: 15–16) with regard to knowledge practices in Melanesia, where we do not 'have to imagine that these ideas exist as a set of ground rules or a kind of template for everything that Melanesians do or say'. Accordingly, in learning about the ideas and principles of social life among the Jēnu Kuṟumba, I was never given a contextless 'crash course' on the concepts and cultural meanings that structured their praxis. In the Jēnu Kuṟumba community that I worked with, ideas and concepts were not given to me as an object that could be contemplated upon or a thing that could be used for mere representation. Rather the ideas and concepts that led to the configuration of social life among the Jēnu Kuṟumba were themselves a kind of practice in the sense Strathern (ibid.) has formulated it with regard to social knowledge in Melanesia, where: 'As an implemented or acted upon theory, we might equally well call it a practice of social action.' Indeed this is one of the basic features of habitus, continuously stressed by Bourdieu too. He conceptualized habitus as neither a formal objective structure nor a subjective concept but as an intersubjective phenomenon that is situated in between subject and object, speaker and hearer, and that emerges in the process of interaction or discourse. Therefore, 'praxeological' approaches (to use Bourdieu's term, 1976: 147) try to trace elements of habitus in the oscillation between symbolic forms and social action as happens in 'objective events' (Hanks, 1987: 677), public discourse or praxis.

In this essay I will likewise look for elements of the habitual moral order as they are given expression to and made a theme in objectified form in specific discourse genres, e.g. in the honey song and the honey narrative of the Jēnu Kuṟumba. Then I will try to relate what is being said there, the moral concepts developed therein, to the contexts of action they belong to, since, as Hanks has pointed out:

> In addition to their thematic orientation, works are also oriented toward the action contexts in which they are produced, distributed, and received. Ideological creations become part of practical reality by being realized in action and this entails adapting them to concrete social circumstances (Hanks 1987: 67).

It is clear that such a work—of successfully relating discourses and the action contexts they structure—requires of our analysis to come to terms with the temporality of social life. This is so because, empirically, ideological creations or moral schemata can be objectified and performed in the very actions they structure. Action and cultural schemata can coincide in the same praxis, in the immediate instance of discourse, but they need not necessarily do so. Cultural concepts can also be performed and voiced at times separated from the action context which they help to structure.

Thus for example the honey song (on pp. 178–81) is a performed discourse, expressive and formative of a specific habitus and a simultaneously related context to action. It is a discourse in immediate praxis and accompanied by structuring actions, because it is sung while gathering the honey. In contrast, the honey narrative, which will be given below too, is a discourse narrated at other times in social life, outside the gathering process itself. But nevertheless, the narrative develops a concept of moral relatedness and structure that is thematically related to the context of the configuration of gathering camps, In internalizing the concepts formed in these discourses, I would argue, people acquire a habitus, a sense of sociality and of meaningful relatedness. The meaning that is voiced in this form of discourse can thus be taken as a formative expression of a habitual convention that becomes formative in the practice in other times, i.e. in the formation of gathering camps.

In order to describe this 'oscillation' between voiced meaning and structured action (Hanks 1987: 670) one has to bridge a time gap and go beyond timeless frozen structures as well as beyond the immediate instance of discourse. The writer's time, it seems, is not the time of the actors (fieldworker and indigenous actors) in the field. Accordingly our written representation seems to require a synopsis of the lived time of our subjects; it requires distance and an objectivity from the immediate instances of discourse and practice.

To achieve this, it seems fruitful to me to employ a further praxeological notion, that of 'field', and to assume with Bourdieu that the production of social forms is taking place in fields of social/cultural praxis. Bourdieu speaks of doings that constitute fields (1990: 88) and of fields as configurations 'of a structure of relations' (1990: 191). Here I will take up this idea of the field in understanding it as a series of thematically related verbal and non-verbal doings, discourses and actions, that contribute to the emergence of objectified recurring structures. Such a notion of field should allow our anthropological objectification to relate and describe various practices (actions and their contexts), that belong to each other thematically, even though they need not necessarily be performed simultaneously. The notion of field may thus allow me to change the frame of time in order to represent to the reader (and only to her/him) the way social life is configured. Though that requires distance, I hope to demonstrate in the present article that this does not necessarily entail dominance and suppression of the Other and his/her voices, as some (e.g. Fabian 1983) seem to fear.

In what follows I will concentrate on one field of social practice among the Jēnu Kuṟumba, namely the field of gathering. I will first show the overall structure of the gathering camps, then will explore some of the habitual moral schemes the Jēnu Kuṟumba employ when bringing forth the structures, in that I will try to trace these concepts in the oral discourses (honey song and honey narrative) where they are voiced and where they are construed discursively by the Jēnu Kuṟumba. My hope is that in that way, rather than suppressing other voices in the course of my interpretation, I can base it as far as possible on them. Finally I will try to throw some light on the agents involved in the production of these structures.

Ethnographic Background

Following the various accounts of the Census of India[2] publications, the Jēnu Kuṟumba, also known as Kāṭṭunāyaka in Tamil-as well as Malayalam-dominated areas, are numerically the largest gatherer-hunter society (around 15,000 to 20,000 people) in South India, located in an area stretching along the western side of the ghat forests which are today part of the states of Kerala, Tamil Nadu and Karnataka.

If the results of my explorations, which are based on work among the Jēnu Kuṟumba in the border area between Tamil Nadu and Karnataka, apply to other regions as well, the Jēnu Kuṟumba are subdivided into a multitude of small, quasi-endogamous networks. The network I worked in embraces between 250 and 300 married people, all related to each other through narrow and extended kinship ties of filiation and marriage, so that one could speak of such a network as of a classificatory kindred, in contrast to Yalman's or Barnett's micro-castes that seem to consist of genealogical kindred formations (Yalman 1962, Barnett 1975).

Since there are no lineages, unilinear or agnatic descent groups, that act or define themselves as corporate units, the social order is not framed in a group model of society, but rather in interpersonal terms of sociality. People in the network are situated in a chain of mutual obligations in a moral order of kinship that stresses, as we will see below, filiative and, most important in the context of this article, affinal bonds.

Within each network certain people regard themselves as people of the *deyivagāru*, i.e. they consider themselves as belonging to or joining (*sēr*) certain male and female deities (*deyiva*). Beyond FF or MM however, genealogical relations with these deities (who are called upon and denoted as grandfather *ettan* or grandmother *acci* respectively) are not remembered. All those who join one deity (between twenty and fifty adults) have in common their relationship *vis-à-vis* their deities, but they do not share any obligations or rights in land, property or knowledge, so that these people neither act nor regard themselves as corporate groups either.

The deities prefer to live in the form of *māya* (i.e. invisibility) in their territories called *jama*, and the living too prefer to live in the *jama* of their deity, however without restricting such a territory to the people of one deity, which would be simply impossible, since the women keep their relationship with their deity after marriage. Accordingly, children are associated with at least two deities, namely the father's deity and the mother's deity; i.e. there is no unilinear prescription for the recruitment of these people. In practice however the Jēnu Kuṟumba will, as they say, 'look after' one deity most intensively; that means they will give offerings to it, speak with it and listen to its demands. The deity in turn looks upon the living as its children, is expected to listen to their demands and to protect them.

Within the network, there are three socio-religious offices: that of the *bandāri*, of the *jajman* and of the *pūjāri*. The *bandāri* acts mainly as a mediator or messenger, informing and calling together all the people that are concerned with and for the two important rituals—the death ritual and the first menstruation ritual. The *jajman* on the other hand conducts the proper, in our Western sense, religious tasks. It is the *jajman* who makes offerings to the deities, the dreadful spirits or spirits of the dead during certain public rituals; he has also to take out the first handful of earth in order that a grave can be dug, etc. The *pūjāri* ultimately arranges and mediates the communication between all those who follow the same and between the followers and this deity itself, every deity having its own *pūjāri*. This communication takes place in rather private settings. Whenever a Jēnu Kuṟumba wishes to speak to her/his deity to ask for its support and presence it is the *pūjāri* who presents the offerings in a small ceremony (*pūja*) to the deity.

The Composition of Gathering Camps

The forest regions of the northern Nilgiri Hills constitute the traditional foraging areas of the Jēnu Kuṟumba I worked with. But since the establishment of Reserve Forest Areas and the wildlife sanctuaries of Mudumalai and Bandipur (in the middle of this century), the Jēnu Kuṟumba are deprived of their rights to forage in these forest regions permanently and are forced to live in settlements at the periphery of the sanctuaries and Reserve Forest Area.

In the forest areas however they are entitled to gather the so-called 'minor forest products' like honey, tamarind, tree moss, soapnuts, etc. and the Jēnu Kuṟumba are engaged throughout the year in gathering these products in the forest. For that purpose the Jēnu Kuṟumba form gathering camps moving through the Reserve Forest Areas. However they return to their settlements (either as the whole camp or simply as single conjugal pairs) in cycles lasting between three and five days, because outside the forest (at the outskirts of Masinagudi village) the state government has established an institution that purchases their gathered products—a branch of the so-called LAMP (i.e. Large Multipurpose Societies), as known by the Jēnu Kuṟumba, and therefore called in what follows simply the 'Society'. That institution has the sole right to purchase the minor forest products. After selling their gathered products to the Society, the Jēnu Kuṟumba, after a stay as short as possible in the settlement, buy provisions for their next gathering trip and return into the forest.

With the exception of rock-honey gathering, which requires the cooperation of at least three people, it is the conjugal pair (*okkal*) that is the basic cooperating unit in the process of economic production, since minor forest products are gathered in cooperation between husband and wife. The conjugal pairs however are supported by their own unmarried elder children and by elder unmarried youths, who are related otherwise, e.g. as terminological children [BS, BD (from male Ego's point of view), ZS, ZD (from female Ego's point of view)] or bilaterally [as ZS, ZD (from male Ego's point of view) or BS, BD (from female Ego's point of view)]. So, taking into account only the production process, the conjugal pair is an autonomous element and indeed it happens quite often that *okkals* go out gathering alone, sometimes accompanied by some unmarried youth (*puṇḍagāru*). But most of the time there will be several conjugal pairs, who move together in search of minor forest products, forming gathering camps. Even though these camps don't cooperate in the actual process of gathering, their members are expected, due to their kinship position, to support and help each other in case this should be necessary (one may detect honey, or somebody has an accident, etc.). Such camps are called *jōdi* by the Jēnu Kuṟumba, a term denoting a 'pair', 'a couple', but also more generally 'those who are one, united and equal' (cf. Kittel 1893).

Yet it should be noted first that the personal composition of these camps is extremely flexible, i.e. they are formed anew each time. Indeed one should speak with regard to these 'formationless groups as temporary objectifications of relations', as Myers has suggested in discussing the nature of Pintubi camps (1988: 60).

This flexibility notwithstanding, the structuring of these camps does not come about fortuitously and it can be clearly seen that the respective camps show distinctive features with regard to their structure. If we look first at the kinship relations the members of these camps stand in towards each other, these features are as follows:[3]

The composition of honeygathering camps:

No.	Agnates	Classif. Agnates	Affines	Classif. Affines
1	F/S			WB/ZH; WF/BDH WFS/FBDH
2		eB/yB		WyF/BDH; ZHDH/WFMB
3		F/S; eB/yB	MB/ZS	MZB/ZS; MZDH/WMZS
4		BS/F		WB/ZH; MBSS/FFZS
5				MBSS/FFZS
6		eB/yB; eB/yB	MB/ZS	ZH/WB; WyF/BDH MB/ZS
7			MBS/FZS	
8		WZH/WZH; eB/yB BS/FB; BS/FB	MBS/FZS	
9		MZS/MZS	MB/ZS MB/ZS	FBDH/WFBS
10				BWB/ZHB; ZH/WB; MBS/FZS

The composition of other M.F.P.-gathering camps:

No.	Agnates	Classif. Agnates	Affines	Classif. Affines
1	F/S	eB/yB; eB/yB F/S	MB/ZS	MB/ZS; ZHyB/BWB WB/ZH;ZHB/BWB;WB/ZH
2		3x eB/yB		
3		2x eB/yB		
4	eB/yB		MBS/FZS	3x WB/ZH
5		3x eB/yB	MBS/FZS	
6		FB/BS; FB/BS eB/yB		ZH/WB; ZH/WB WF/BDH
7	eB/yB	WZH/WZH		ZH/WB; ZH/WB
8		WZH/WZH; eB/yB FB/BS	MBS/FZS	ZH/WB; WyF/BDH
9	F/S	eB/yB	MBS/FZS	BWB/ZHB; 3x ZH/WB ZHB/BWB
10		FB/BS		ZH/WB FZH/WBS
11				2x WB/ZS MB/ZS
12				3x ZH/WB
13				ZHB/BWH; WB/ZH ZHB/BWB
14		eB/yB		WB/ZH
15				ZH/WB

1. What is remarkable at first sight is that only in very rare cases (indeed it happened only twice in twenty-five camps), do 'real' brothers (i.e. those who are not terminological kin) move in the same gathering camp. Agnatic relations are therefore rather exceptional.

2. In contrast to this it can be clearly seen that the structure of all camps is based predominantly on affinal relations.

Yet the structures of the several actual gathering camps are not isomorphic so that two types can be distinguished:

A. One type is characterized such that affines, i.e. those who are related immediately through marriage, join with each other. In particular these are the dyads ZH/WB and WF/DH, thus corresponding to Dumont's subcategory of 'immediate affines' (Dumont 1983: 75).

Apart from these, there are in these type of camps genealogical affines as well, even though less frequently, i.e. MB/ZS or MBS/FZS—those who are not related immediately but whose affinal ties are 'inherited'. All of these related affinally in one way or another are regarded by the Jēnu Kuṟumba as close (*daṇḍe*) relatives (*sontagāru*), and it is typical rather than by chance that this type of gathering camp is configured in the preceeding phases of rituals to be held, that is at times when kinship duties between the above mentioned dyads are actualized. This is for example the case when a death ritual (*pole*) is to be carried out in which the gifts of ZH to respective DH play a significant role, but also when one needs really reliable partners to work with, as for instance in the difficult and dangerous task of collecting rock-honey (*bare jēnu*).

No. 4

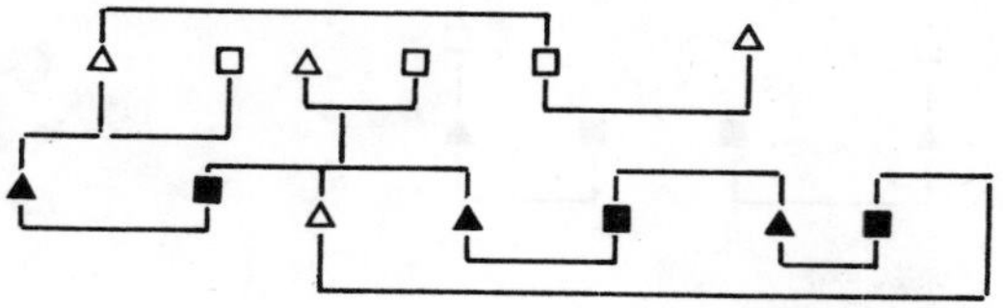

No. 9

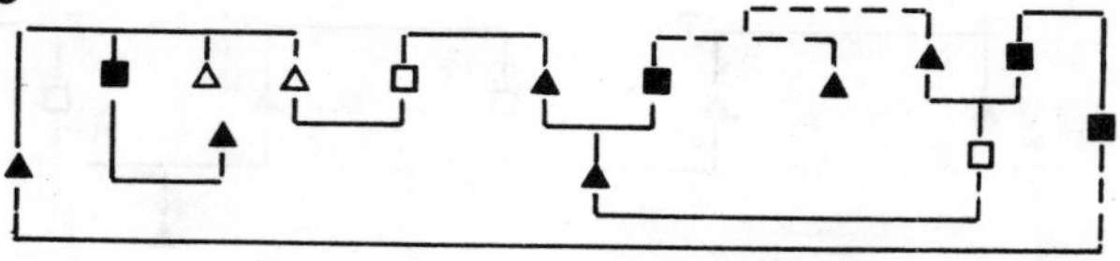

No. 6 (HG)

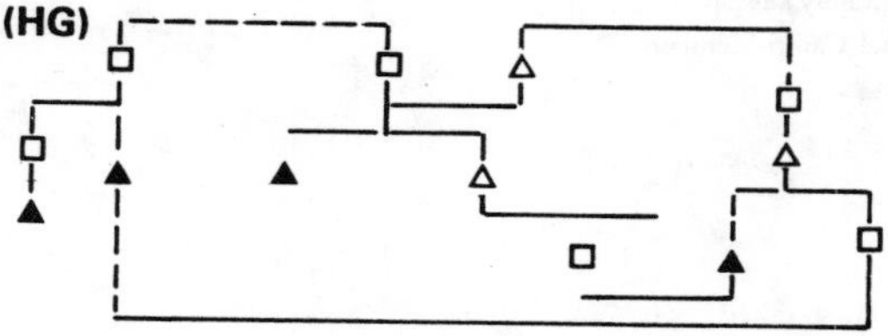

No. 10 (HG)

No. 6

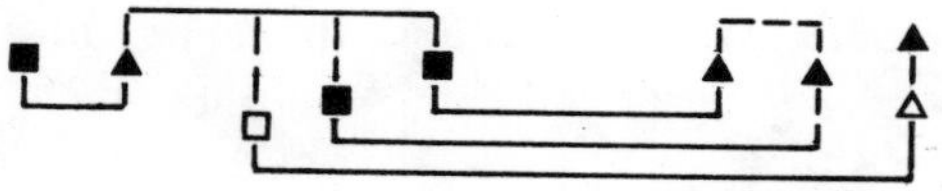

B. The other type of gathering camp is based on relationships between married individuals, i.e. the conjugal pair, as well as on more distant classificatory kinship ties.

No. 2

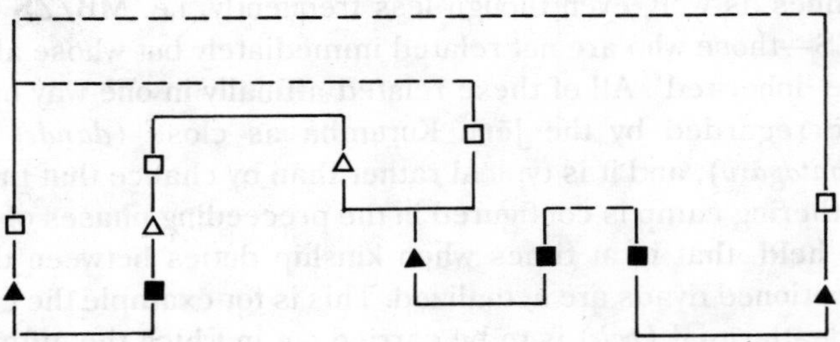

No. 3

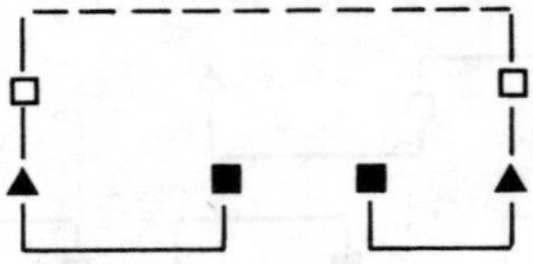

No. 13

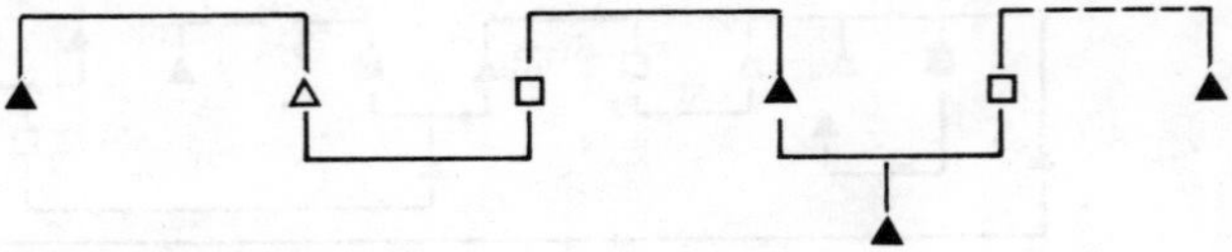

- - - - = Classificatory kinship
▲, ■ = Actual Camp-Members

Habitual Schemata

Now these structures are of course not constitutive themselves but, as outlined above, the outcome of particular practices which, as for example Bourdieu, Giddens and Harré have argued, are based in turn on habitual dispositions and cultural schemata (Bourdieu: 1987: 30, 108 ff., 197 ff.), on a reservoir of 'mutual knowledge about rules and resources' that enables the actors to generate structures (Giddens 1979: 64 ff., 84) and, for Harré, on 'local systems of obligation and duty with associated valuation criteria' (1990: 348).

In the case of the Jēnu Ku̱rumba it seems to me that the practice of configurating gathering camps is based in this sense essentially on a moral order, namely an intersubjective system of meaning and attitudes, that formulates the possible behavioural expectations and attitudes among dyadic relationships on the basis of kinship order (objectified in the terminological system). I will therefore, in what follows, outline in general some of the most important elements of this order, which are relevant in our context.

The above outlined network constitutes the frame for filiative and affinal relationships which in turn determine reciprocity and the flow of ritual gifts and supportive doings, as well as the legitimacy of everyday demands. To begin with, all those who are tied to each other through marriage are obliged to contribute their activity as participation in the course of rituals, particularly the death ritual[4] and the puberty ritual for the young women (the so-called 'Going into the leaf hut', *soppumane ōpodu*), so that these relatives are situated or 'bound'[5] in a complex network of ritualized support-giving and duties. So the husbands of Ego's sisters' respective daughters are obliged to contribute in the death ritual (i.e. ZH has to contribute in Ego's father's *pole* and/or DH has to contribute in Ego's death ritual) and the mother's brother (i.e. the 'real brother' of the mother, *Sōdir māvan*) is obliged to give gifts to his sister's daughter during the latter's maturity celebrations.

This narrower circle of relatives, standing in relationships of marriage and therefore support-giving, is called *bā-mayika* by the Jēnu Ku̱rumba, thus denoting with this term a category equivalent to Dumont's application of affines (Demmer 1993).

But *bā-mayika* are not only situated in a net of obligations with regard to rituals, but are moreover eligible to demand support in everyday interaction. *Bā-mayika*, the Jēnu Ku̱rumba say, should share and distribute (*pirsodu*, the process of distributing) among each other. They should support each other if any one of them runs into difficulties in everyday life, even such difficulties as cloth, money, cigarettes, food or provisions, etc. In everyday life it is ZH and WB (respective BW and HZ), standing in such a relationship, but it should be pointed out here that only marriage legitimizes this kind of demand. That is to say that among genealogical affines of the same generation (MBS/FZS, MBD/FZD), these claims of mutual support and demand, this 'ethic of sharing', does not exist automatically.

These moral concepts are given formative expression in songs and narratives of the Jēnu Kuṟumba. Thus, when listening to the honey song *Jēn-paduna*, we can hear voices that create the meaning of the affinal relationships.

While gathering the rock-honey in the steep and dangerous rocks, the Jēnu Kuṟumba sing a song having as the main theme the mutual obligations among affines. In dramatic phrases the gatherers construct a common identity with the bees, addressing the queen of the bees as mother-in-law whose potential sons-in-law, i.e. the gatherers, have come to take their wives. And how could a mother of one's wife refuse to support her son-in-law in his work, how could she do anything bad to her sons-in-law, her *bā-mayika*? This is the theme of the song.[6]

Honey Song

Jēn-paduna

GATHERER: They climb down the rock and pierce. The honey bees they make rise. I am the son-in-law.

In the storming of the wind he pierces the honey. Your blossoms, the girls, they scare them. The girls arise and dance. They pierce the girls, in the storming of the wind they pierce the honey, in the wind, they pierce the girls. Don't bite children. Rise in the wind and dance, my dear ones.

Baregu eragi kuttidar-alla. Jēn uḷune ē. lsidan-alla. nānu aḷen-alla. gāḷi ōtalu jēnune kuttidanu. ninna ūne eṇṇu makkane jaḍedaru. eṇṇu-makka eddu āḍidaru. eṇṇu-makkane kuttidaru, gāli ōtalu jēnune kuttidaru, eṇṇu-makkane gālilu kuttidaru. kaccāde-ka makkale. gāḷilu eddu āḍunani.

Others: *Kihihi, kihihi.*

Gatherer: In the leaves they climb up, standing steady in the storming of the wind. In this wind they climb. Having come across seven mountains, seven ravines they climb. Having cut the *bōka* blossoms they were asked to bring, they climb. The rock he climbs down, they say. In the rope, in the fibre-ladder he climbs down in the wind. It lifts up the cloth.

I am the son-in-law. The honey bees, they plaster the rock.

soppulu attidaru, gāḷi ōtalu nindu deyira ī gāḷilu attidaru. ēḷu beṭṭa sutti bandu attidaru. bōka-ūne kuydu, tarsida ū kuydu attidaru. baregamba eragidanu. agga, mālulu eragidanu gāḷilu. baṭṭeneella tūkidadu. nānu aḷen nān. jēnu-kunni kallugu metidde.

Others: *Kihi, kihihi, kihi.*

Gatherer: Having cut the *bōka* blossoms, seven mountains, seven ravines. Don't make a fight. Until I take, you remain peaceful.

Having entered the cave they take girls. The girls they restrain. Seven mountains, seven ravines. An empty fortress for the girls who cut and came.

bōka-ūne kuydu, ēḷu beṭṭa, ēḷu aḷḷa. jagala māḍāde-ka. nān eṭṭa ganṭa summag iru.

eṇṇu-makkane ettidar-alla aḷe oḷage ukku. eṇṇu-makkane taḍedaru. ēḷu beṭṭa, ēḷu aḷḷa. kuydu banda eṇṇu-makkagu āku koṭṭe.

Others: *Kihi, kihihi, kihi.*

Gatherer: Remain peaceful for awhile. Still awhile they climb down and pierce. Seven mountains, seven ravines. In the empty fortress. They take the girls. Seven fortesses, seven places. All having cut jasmine blossoms, they climb down in the wind.

Having cut the jasmine blossoms, they pierce the honey. I am the son-in-law.

selpa ottu summag-irnu. selpa ottu eragi kuttidar-alla. eḷu beṭṭa, ēḷu aḷḷa, āku koṭṭelu. eṇṇu-makkane ettidaru. ēḷu koṭṭe, ēḷu jāgalu. mallige-ūne kuydu ellaru, gāḷilu eragidaru. mallige-ūne kuydu jēnune kuttidaru. aḷenu.

Others: *Kihi, kihihi, kihi.*

GATHERER: Children, I am the son-in-law. They pierce the girls. I am the son-in-law. Seven rivers, seven blossoms, seven mountains, seven ravines.
makkalē, nānu aḷenu. eṇṇu-makkane kuttidaru. nān aḷen-alla. ēḷu nīru, ēḷu ū, ēḷu beṭṭa, ēlu aḷḷa.

OTHERS: *Kihi, kihihi, kihi.*

GATHERER: I am the son-in-law, having climbed down in the wind. They bite. They pierce the girls. Don't bite, dear mother. The honey bees who cut the jasmine blossoms and came. On the rope itself I am the son-in-law. In the storming of the wind he climbs down and pierces the girls in the wind. I am the son-in-law.
eṇṇu-makkane kuttidaru. nān aḷenu gāḷilu eragi. kaccidaru. kaccāde-kavva. mallige-ūne kuydu banda jēnu-kunni. aggaleve nān aḷenu nān. gāḷi ōtalu eragi kuttidanu eṇṇu-makkane gāḷilu. nān aḷen-alla.

OTHERS: *Kihihi, kihi, kihihi.*

GATHERER: Having climbed down and having cut *bōka* blossoms. Seven rivers, seven ravines, seven mountains. I am the son-in-law, yours.
Having climbed down in the wind they pierce. For the girls that cut the jasmine blossoms and come, for them there is an empty fortress.
Girls, rise up and dance. Don't bite. Rise up (as) from (old) times in the wind. It is again, you girls. In the wind rise up and dance. I am the son-in-law. Mother, after you gave to us, we, having made your hands empty, we leave you (alone), yes? I am the son-in-law.
eragi bōka-ūne kuydu. ēḷu nīru, ēḷu aḷḷa, ēlu beṭṭa. nān aḷenu, ninna.
gāḷilu eragi kuttidaru. mallige-uñe kuydu banda eṇṇu-makkagu āku koṭṭe.
eṇṇu-makka eddu āḍnu. kaccādenu. eddu kālainda gāḷilu. tirigi idder-alla eṇṇu-makka. eddu āḍidar-alla gāḷilu. nān aḷenu. avva nangagu koṭṭoṭṭu, ningagu bëru kayi mādi, buṭṭeo (n) alla? nān aḷenu.

OTHERS: *Kihi, kihihi, ki.*

GATHERER: Seven rivers, seven mountains they surround. Girls, don't bite. Don't bite children. I. Just a little while more. I am the son-in-law. Those who have trembled your fortress, they did wrong. I am the son-in-law, you made (that we) came together peacefully. I am the son-in-law. A little bit I could not get.

ē̱lu nīru, ē̱lu beḷḷa suttidaru. eṇṇu-makka kaccādenu. makkale kaccādenu. nān. innu selpa ottu gaṇṭa. nān aḷen-alla. ninga āḷa asidavaru mōsa māḍi buṭṭaru. nān aḷen nān. ninga summane sērsi idderu. nān aḷenu alla. kayigu selpa sikkodille.

OTHER: *Ki, kihi, ki.*

As we can see, the honey gatherers construct a context for their actions with this song which rhetorically creates a common identity with the bees as affinal relative. The gatherers regard the bees as potential marriage partners, and in analogy address the mother of the bees as mother of their affinal partners. In the course of this event it emerges too which meaning the category of 'affines', denoted by the Jēnu Ku̱rumba with the term *bā-mayika,* has in this context. *Bā-mayika,* the message of this event is, should care for each other and share among each other; they should not withhold the 'gift' of honey, and among affines the expectation of support can be taken for granted. How could the mother of the girls refuse her affinal support to her unprotected son-in-law? How could she harm him? This seems to be the central message of this song that informs us why the affinal relationship, in the field of gathering, is formative for the structure of the field.

This principle of mutual support among *bā-mayika* is supplemented by another social valuation of this affinal relationship. For *bā-mayika,* the Jēnu Ku̱rumba hold, are those who are 'one' and those who are 'equal'. *Bā-mayika* are *ondeve* and *sāmave,* are those people in whose company one really likes to be, those who are seen likewise with pleasure in one's own company, they are those who are 'close' (*daṇde*) relatives (*sontagāru*), who moreover should preferably keep up marriage ties with each other. In the context of the structure of gathering camps it is especially interesting that this evaluation embraces conjugal partners as well. The women in one's hut, my (male) interlocutors pointed out to me when we discussed these themes, are *bā-mayika,* husband and wife, the conjugal pairs (*okkal*) are *bā-mayika,* and furthermore husband and wife are equal (*sāmave*). Thus it is seen that a shared identity is conceptualized among *bā-mayika,* which evaluates hierarchy as negative and equality as positive. Taking into account this evaluation the obligations of sharing and cooperation between affines become meaningful and grounded, more so as the locus of non-sharing is unequivocally associated with hierarchical relationships.

In fact, this conception of social evaluation of *bā-mayika* as equals stands in opposition to expectations of behaviour in the 'kin' sphere particular to those between brothers, i.e., elder and younger brothers, for there is only hierarchy between brothers. Even though it is commonly held that being in this dyadic relationship they should support each other as well, no Jēnu Ku̱rumba I spoke to thought it appropiate to speak of brothers as equals. Thus it is that this dyad is not only the locus of hierarchy proper, but that this feature dominates this dyad to an extent that excludes sharing and mutual support in everyday life. While in the sphere of affines people can show confidence in the return of given things and in mutual support, counting as it were on 'durable prospects', transactions among brothers appear to be more like a bargain, moreover a suspicious one. Among brothers, the Jēnu Ku̱rumba say, an amount or a thing taken should be returned as soon as possible and above all in equal value and, if I have understood my interlocutors well, this is necessary so as not to provoke the anger of one's 'creditor'.

Moreover, this relationship dyad is of course asymmetrical with regard to claiming a debt because, among the Jēnu Ku̱rumba, the younger brother has in common understanding no right to approach an elder brother in a demanding manner, while an elder brother has a right to do so. In everyday interaction this results in the common state of affairs that brothers regularly avoid each other, do not support each other, and do not cooperate as it were, for example in gathering camps. My collaborators stated explicitly that for example they avoid going for rock-honey gathering with their brothers because they won't trust them.

The Jēnu Ku̱rumba are so aware of this 'structural' problem that they objectify this tense relationship explicitly in a narrative of their oral tradition, the honey narrative (*Jēnu-Parasanga*). There, the relationship between brothers is set in remarkable opposition to the affinal relationship *par excellence*, the conjugal pair. Thus other voices can be heard in the forest too, that construe discursively the meaning of the conjugal pair (*okkal*) and the relationship between brothers, and it is again when listening to those voices that we can also understand something about the configuration of social life among the Jēnu Ku̱rumba.[7]

The Honey Narrative
Jēnu-Parasanga

The story narrates how six younger brothers deceive their elder brother while they go on a honey gathering trip. Having prepared all the necessary work the younger brothers persuade the elder brother to climb up into a huge tree laden with honeycombs. The elder brother pierced comb after comb and let the honey down to his younger brothers who catch it in tins.

As soon as the elder brother has taken all the honey and attempts to climb down, the younger brother cut off the bark ladder, the only way down. Laden with honey they return to their settlement leaving the elder brother helpless to the bees, who return in the evening and sting him terribly.

After the younger brothers return to their huts only the wife of their elder brother cares, and asks them about their elder brother. They lie in turn, pretending that he must have come back already. She however does not believe them, takes her small child on her hip and goes into the forest to search for her husband, even though it is getting dark already.

Ultimately, having faced many perils courageously on her way (e.g. a strange hunter who invites her but whom she ignores, tigers and elephants that cross the tree where she takes rest in with her child, etc.), she discovers her husband, sitting helpless and weeping in the huge tree. He asks her to return to their hut and to bring him his ceremonial utensils. This she does, but after she brings them he asks her to leave him. He himself wants to turn into an eagle and to fly away into the deepest jungle. But that request she refuses with the argument that without him she is nothing and that her place is at his side. Finally her husband gives in and when all three of them are transformed into eagles by and by, they fly into the deepest jungle.

But in the end, after the parents have brought their child up in the jungle, all three return to the settlement of the brothers. There, the old-aged parents of the brothers see the three eagles sitting on a huge tree outside the settlement, and the elder brother discloses his identity and the whole story of his brothers' misdeeds. In the end however he forgives them, even promises to protect the whole family, and then flies away with his wife and child.

I think this narrative exemplifies clearly what a husband (*gaṇdan*) and wife (*ëṇdru*) should mean to each other and what value the conjugal relationship has for the Jēnu Kuṟumba, in that it is imagined as the real locus of solidarity, cooperation and support. In contrast, the agnatic relationship between elder brother and younger brother is represented as being dominated by mistrust, as being unreliable, pregnant with treachery and marked by self-interest. The meaning of the conjugal pair, its social evaluation, is thus brought to light in the narrative by contrasting it with the agnatic relationship. Thus we can see here the same opposition that emerged as the main structuring opposition in the gathering configurations as well.

In turn, through this contrast, the conjugal pair appears further as a relationship that belongs, due to its social evaluation and its content, to the affinal realm of relationships. Like the same-sex affinal bond, with its implications of sharing, unity and support, the conjugal bond too has this implication of reciprocal support and can thus be conceived as an affinal relationship. Both categories in this realm, *bā-mayika* and *okkal*, stand in clear opposition to the habitus within the agnatic realm, that among elder and younger brothers. While among affines conceptually, trust in the return of given support dominates the relationship, transactions among brothers are likened to a bargain, an unreliable one at that. Between elder and younger brother, my interlocutors among the Jēnu Kuṟumba told me, the sum of money or the things once taken should be returned as quickly as possible, and equally important is that the same amount should be returned, because among brothers money and things are counted, listed up (*kanaku*) exactly. By returning quickly and equally, one avoids the anger of one's creditor. Affinal relationships in contrast are never depicted in that language of bargaining but rather in the 'spirit of the gift', where one can trust to longer terms in the return of things and support given, while exact counting is inappropriate and against the expected habitus of generosity.

Furthermore, the agnatic relationship is the locus of hierarchy and inequality proper, since this dyadic relationship is asymmetrical with regard to habitual conventions. The younger brother has conventionally no right to approach an elder brother in a demanding manner, while convention grants this right to the elder brother *vis-à-vis* a younger brother. However, given the absence of agnatic, unilineal or other corporate groups among the Jēnu Kuṟumba that may force brothers together, elder brothers cannot exert constraints on their younger brothers in that sense and accordingly, here in the field of gathering, brothers typically avoid each other, do not cooperate and do not support each other. In contrast to this, the position of conjugal pairs emerges as being in the dominant position in this field.

Its dominant status is further underlined by, and thus can be read out of, the spatial order of the gathering camps. Thus there are among the Jēnu Kuṟumba no communal fireplaces beyond the arrangements of conjugal families. Always the conjugal families will arrange their fires in the gathering camps at some distance from each other. They will make them only for themselves and they will remain there among themselves for most of the time. The pairs will also cook together at their fireplace, will eat together at the same time (not the husband first and then the wife, for example); they even take care of the small children by turns. It is in these moments of social practice that the picture depicted for the Nayakas by Bird-David describes equally well the situation among the Jēnu Kuṟumba, when she writes:

> The couple spend most of their time together—they forage together in the forest . . . they bathe at the same time in the river. They sit mostly by themselves near their fire in the evening and in the night huddle together on one mat. . . . To a large extent they share domestic activities such as cooking, cleaning and in even some ways care for children . . . (Bird-David 1987: 156).

I think these movements, this kind of taking positions in space, can be read as outward signs of the high value that is ascribed to the conjugal pair; and they are also strong expressions of the autonomy that is expected from and claimed by the conjugal pairs, despite their being situated in the close kinship configurations in the camps. This autonomy is clearly underlined by the fact that they are also the main locus of verbal and material exchange in the camps. There is usually very little verbal interchange between the several conjugal families that camp together. Finally, there is also very limited exchange of things among those who camp together. Food and cooked meals are not shared within the camps. Sharing is conventionally restricted to the conjugal families and only if others in the camp are really in need of help are they supported. Conventionally the pairs are expected to look after themselves and to be as autonomous as possible. My informants among the Jēnu Kuṟumba were very clear about this. Whenever we discussed the organization of the camps, the life in the forest camps and the ideas about the conventional conduct among the people camping together, I got answers like: 'Husband and wife, they have to buy and take their things. If others don't have this and that once, that does not matter. They will be supported and given something. But only once. People should take care of themselves. But husband and wife, they share, they are one and the same, right?'

Agents of Configuration

The configuration of social life does not only come about on the basis of cultural schemata employed by actors, but the realization of structuring requires that the production of social structures can be, if we follow for example Giddens, by several different agents. Indeed, the distinctive realizations of the affinal structure in form of the two above explicated types of gathering camps remain, with regard to this aspect, yet to be accounted for. But this can be understood, I think, with regard to the concrete circumstances under which the respective structures are brought forth. That is to say and to be shown that in particular moments of socio-cultural production different agents are recognizable with regard to the specific structures that are configured on the basis of the above depicted habitual schemata.

Thus it emerges from a consideration of contexts, that at certain times in the social production (objectified in type *A*), it is the affines (namely WB and MB) actively bringing forth the structure. So it happens in the weeks preceding a death ritual that relatives of the dead person demand the support of their *bā-mayika* on the basis of the above-mentioned cultural schemata. By joining with their *bā-mayika* in everyday gathering, they seem to be able to achieve a kind of control over the income and labour force of their gathering campmates because the cultural schemata prescribe the unity and equality of *bā-mayika* and thus their corporate contribution to the ritual. So at those times it is apparently these affines, being the main agents, who effect the structure of those gathering camps that are constituted by *bā-mayika*. Thus both 'close' affines, WB and MB, can effectively bring forth the structure of camps at particular moments, being bound in a system of sharing and support and legitimized to raise their demands.[8]

The other type of camp, in contrast, is best understood in seeing the LAMP Society as a structuring agent. Looking at this type, it may seem at first glance that the conjugal pairs exhibit their sole autonomy and sovereign agency. But of course the LAMP Society plays a decisive role in the background. It is the Society that executes the control over the proceeds of the people as well.[9] In fact it is the Society that grants the Jēnu Ku̱rumba money in advance for their future activities and the conjugal pairs are therefore necessarily interested in meeting the demands of the society, thereby intending to reduce their debt. This means in turn that the conjugal pairs try to avoid the demands of their 'close relatives' in everyday life, they avoid their *bā-mayika* as it were. Meeting their demands as well would mean raising ones debt which is equally prevented by the Society. So it can be seen that, indirectly, the demands of the Society as agency appear to determine the structuring of those camps in which the conjugal pairs appear as autonomous units: autonomous only in the sense that they avoid the control of 'close' relatives whenever possible, since it is the Society in the end that controls, to a large extent, the gains of these pairs. I think it is in that way that it could be understood how, despite a background of a sole habitual schemata, two different types of gathering camps are nevertheless configured.

Conclusion

What appears to be decisive for the structuring of gathering camps among the Jēnu Kur̲umba is on the one hand the habitual expectation of reciprocity and sharing among immediate affines, 'the spirit of the gift', among *bā-mayika,* in the positive sense but, I would argue, also in the negative in so far as the attempt to avoid this very same obligating relationship can be seen as constitutive for the gathering camps of the conjugal type. Clearly the latter are formed by relatives having little or no obligations to each other. This indicates the far-reaching independence, autonomy as it were, of the conjugal pairs, being here committed to neither side. In such cases the conjugal pairs appear as autonomous units with regard to the distribution of proceeds as well, it should be added. This structural position of the conjugal pair is in accordance with its valuation among the Jēnu Kur̲umba, where it is to be interpreted as a unit that is essentially an affinal relationship. In fact, as the Jēnu Kur̲umba hold, the woman in one's hut is *bā-mayika* (i.e. an affine). On the other hand, the habitual expectation of non-sharing, non-support and of exact balancing among brothers, as well as the asymmetry in this relationship dyad, seems to inform the avoidance of brothers in everyday life, i.e. here in gathering camps.

Ultimately one could see that in all the cases demonstrated here the affinal structure of the gathering camps of both types rests on the above–mentioned habitual schemata of expectations and corresponding knowledge about the moral order of kinship, as it is expressed by those voices in the forest we could listen to in the discourses above. This knowledge informs the configuration of the camps, informs the specific habitus of the Jēnu Kuṟumba in the field of gathering, characterized by 'affinity as a value', to apply Dumont's words (1983) here—by the enacted unity of affines, their mutual obligations and involvement in a system of mutual support and giving, but also by the antagonistic attitudes of elder versus younger brothers and, last but no least, by the value attributed to the conjugal pair.

NOTES

1. I worked for three years with the Jēnu Kuṟumba of the northern Nilgiris (in stints of twenty three, six, two and four months between October 1987 and December 1994. I wish to acknowledge the support of the German DAAD and the Friedr.-Naumann Foundation whose scholarships made my work possible. I also wish to thank Richard Wolf, who worked with the Kota people in the Nilgiris, for his helpful critique of a previous version of the present essay. Of course, responsibility for remaining shortcomings rests exclusively with myself.
2. cf. Census of India 1961: vol, IX, part V-B(1), Preface, VOL.XI, part V-A, VOL. part V-A, p.125 and Census of India 1971: Series 19, part IX, p.227; Series 9, part II-C(1), p.215.
3. These findings are based on data from twenty-eight gathering camps, the members of which are known to me well enough to trace their kinship relationships.
4. For the social meanings and moral concepts created in this context by other voices, cf. Demmer 1993.
5. To marry someone is called in Jēnu Kuṟumba, as in many other Dravidian languages 'to bind (*kaṭṭale*) someone'.
6. The song is sung like a duet. The gatherer sings the verses, while he is engaged in the rocks. In between, the other members of the gathering party, those who keep the rope tied at the top of the rock and those who remain at the bottom of the rock waiting to take the honey that the gatherer lets down to them in a bamboo basket, repeat his verses joyfully as a chorus refrain. In addition, the honey-gathering party members also exchange information and orders in between the sung phrases. These exchanges are also melodic and concern the work process they are engaged in (whether the honey is good, or whether the gatherer on the rope should let down the basket with honey, whether the members at the bottom of the rock should prepare the grass torch to smoke out the bees, etc.). These exchanges are left out here, even though in the actual situation they contribute to the dramatic atmosphere that characterizes the honey gathering in the rocks.

It should be mentioned here that the Ālu Kuṟumba of the eastern Nilgiris also sing such songs. The material presented by D. B. Kapp shows that their meaning is similar even though they are shorter and do not involve the whole gathering party (Kapp 1983).

7. I give here a synoptical version of the narrative. The complete transliterated text and its translation is to be found in M. Gossel (n.d.).
8. J. Altmann and N. Peterson have shown a similar situation prevailing among contemporary aboriginal groups of Arnhem land. Altmann and Peterson 1988: 78, 93.
9. Here the situation corresponds to the findings of Morris who sees (1982: Ch. 5), among the Hill Pandaram in south India, external agents as being responsible for the structure of gathering camps. Another parallel with Jēnu Kuṟumba is, further, that among the Hill Pandaram too: 'Affinal links seem to serve as a guiding principle in structuring friendships and camp aggregates' (ibid.: 157). Thus certain camps among the Hill Pandaram show a structure very similar to that exemplified here.

References

Altmann, J. and N. Peterson. 1988. 'Rights to Game and Rights to Cash among Contemporary Australian Hunter-gatherers'. *In* D. Riches, T. Ingold, and J. Woodburn (eds.), 2: 75–94.

Barnett, S. 1975. 'Coconuts and Gold.' *Contributions to Indian Sociology:* 133–56.

Bird-David, N. 1987. 'Single Persons and Social Cohesion in a Hunter-gatherer Society'. *In* P. Hockings (ed.), *Dimensions of Social Life: Essays in Honour of David Mandelbaum.* Berlin and New York: Mouton de Gruyter.

Bourdieu, P. 1976. *Entwurf einer Theorie der Praxis. Auf der eth-nologischen Grundlage der kabylischen Gesellschaft.* Frankfurt/M.: Suhrkamp.

——— 1987. *Sozialer sinn. Kritik der theoretischen Vernunft.* Frankfurt/M.: Suhrkamp.

——— 1990. *In Other Words: Essays Towards a Relfexive Sociology.* London: Polity Press.

Burghart, R. 1990. 'Ethnographers and Their Local Counterparts in India'. *In* R. Fardon. (ed.), *Localizing Strategies. Regional Traditions of Ethnographic Writing,* 260–79. Edinburgh: Scottish Academic Press (and Washington: Smithonian Institution Press).

Demmer, U. 1993. 'How to make the Spirit of the Dead (gāḷi) Happy: The Rhetoric of Words and Deeds Ritual'. Paper read in an interdisciplinary symposium (Oct. 1993) at the South Asia

Institute, Heidelberg. Forthcoming in Schoembucher, E. and Zoller, C. P. eds. *The Meaning of Death in South Asia.* New Delhi: Manohar.

Dumont, L. 1983. *Affinity as a Value: Marriage Alliance in South India, with a Comparative Essay on Australia.* Chicago and London: The University of Chicago Press.

Fabian, J. 1983. *Time and the Other: How Anthropology makes it Object.* New York: Columbia University Press.

Gardner, P. 1966. 'Symmetric Respect and Memorate Knowledge: The Structure and Ecology of Individualistic Culture'. *Southwestern Journal of Anthropology,* 22: 389–415.

Giddens, A. 1979. *Central Problems in Social Theory: Action, Structure and Contradiction in Social Analysis.* Berkeley: University of California Press.

Gossel, M. n.d. 'Oral Tradition and Language of the Jēnu Ku̱rumba (south India)'. Unpublished Ph. D. dissertation, Heidelberg.

Hanks, W.F. 1987. 'Discourse genres in a theory of practice'. *American Ethnologist,* 668–92.

Harré', R. 1990. 'Commentary by Rom Harré'. *In* R. Bhaskar (ed.) [*Harré' and His Critics: Essays in Honour of Rom Harré*'. Oxford: Blackwell.]

Ingold, T., Riches, D., Woodburn, J. (eds.), 1988. *Hunters and Gatherers.* 2 Vols. Oxford, New York, Hamburg: Berg Press.

Kapp, D. B. 1983. Honigsammeln und Jagen bei den Ālu Ku̱rumbas. *Anthropos,* 78: 715–38.

Kittel, F. 1988. *A Kannada-English Dictionary.* New Delhi: Asian Education Services.

Morris, B. 1982. *Forest Traders, A Socio-economic Study of the Hill Pandaram.* London. The Athlone Press.

Myers, F. 1986. *Pintupi Country Pintupi Self. Sentiment, Place, and Politics among Western Desert Aborigines.* Washington: Smithsonian Institution Press.

———— 1988. 'Burning the truck and holding the country: property, time and the negotiation of identity among Pintubi Aborigines.' In T. Ingold, D. Riches, J. Woodburn, *Hunters and Gatherers: History, Evolution and Local Change,* 2: 52–75. New York: Hausurg.

Ortner, S. 1984. 'Theory in Anthropology since the sixties.' *Journal of Comparative Studies of Society and History,* 26: 126–66.

Strathern, M. 1988. *The Gender of the Gift: Problems with Women and Problems with Society in Melanesia.* Berkeley, London, Los Angeles: University of California Press.

Wagner, R. 1974. 'Are there social groups in the New Guinea Highlands?' *In* M. Leaf (ed.), *Frontiers of Anthropology*, 95–122. Berkeley: University of California Press.

Yalman, N. 1962. 'The Structure of the Sinhalese Kindred: A Reexamination of the Dravidian Terminology'. *American Anthropologist*, 64: 548–73.

Toda Huts and Houses: Traditional and Modern

WILLIAM A. NOBLE

9

The Nilgiri Hills, where the Toda live, rise spectacularly over 2,100 metres from a plain in the extreme northwestern part of Tamil Nadu, Southern India (Fig. 9.1). The indigenous vegetation of the upper regions comprises temperate grasslands interspersed with patches of upland forest, called *shola*, in hill hollows. Ecological changes, begun by the British who first came to the upper Nilgiris in the 1820s and accelerated since Indian independence have had a profound impact upon the Toda. Most visibly, grasslands were converted to forest on a massive scale through the regimented plantings (row after row) of acacia and eucalyptus from Australia, and of Mexican pines. The Wenlock Downs are now mostly covered by man-made forests, and some of the Kunda grasslands have largely disappeared in like manner.

Numbering 1008 in 1988, the Toda community is best known for its traditional devotion to buffalo herding. Milk from a hierarchy of sacred she-buffaloes is processed in a corresponding spectrum of increasingly sacred grades of dairies, the temples of the Toda. Sacred milk from secular buffaloes, which therefore can only be processed by males, was traditionally churned into buttermilk within spaces next to the front walls of dwelling huts (Rivers 1906: 51, Fig. 15). In independent India, agriculture was more actively promoted among the Toda than ever before. In the mid-seventies, with the Hill Area Development Programme, the Toda's economic base was converted from one of herding to that of farming. By 1978 practically all Toda families were farmers (Walker 1986: 280–2). While agents of the Indo-German Project assisted in the promotion of the latest agricultural procedures, Todas have also turned profitably to the farming models of their Badaga and Kota neighbours. The Badaga, who probably number above 150,000, are among the most progressive

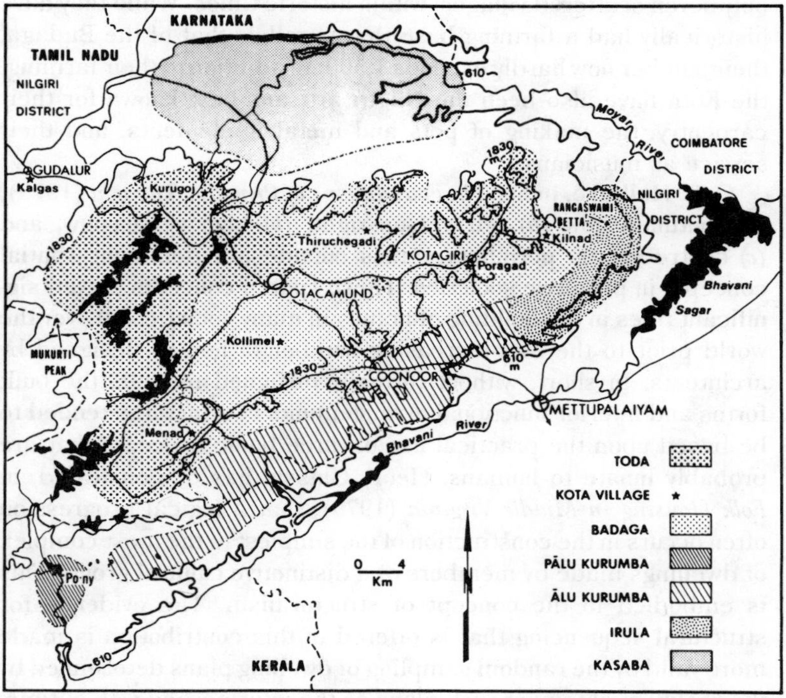

Fig. 9.1 Toda and their Traditional Neighbours: The Main Habitat

farmers in India. It is they who turned to potato cultivation in a big way to meet a World War I demand for potatoes, and in the process they abandoned the use of the plough. They have of late increasingly turned to the planting of tea. The Kota are unique in having occupied only seven scattered villages within historic times. While they have historically had a farming base that parallels that of the Badaga, their number now hardly exceeds 1,500. In addition to their farming, the Kota have also been the Nilgiri artisans best known for their carpentry, the making of pots and metal implements, and their service as musicians.

C. R. Hallpike, in his *The Foundations of Primitive Thought* (1979), has outlined how *(a)* left versus right, *(b)* high versus low, and *(c)* centre versus periphery versus outside are dominant spatial concepts in primitive societies. These spatial concepts played significant roles in the building of homes in many societies all over the world prior to the ever-increasing number of homes designed by architects. In short, without formally designed models, the built forms and interior functional arrangements of structures tended to be based upon the practical use of three basic concepts that are probably innate to humans. Henry Glassie has demonstrated, in *Folk Housing in Middle Virginia* (1979), that a logical progression often occurs in the construction of the simplest to the most complex of dwellings made by members of a distinctive cultural group. This is embodied in the concept of structuralism. The evidence for structural sequencing that is offered in this contribution is made more valid by the random sampling of dwelling plans determined by the reality of obtaining such plans as the intermeshed web of time, immediate social dynamics, individual energy, and weather permitted.

The Badaga, Kota, and Toda of the Nilgiris have dwellings that are fundamentally organized by the concept of right versus left. Much that is significant is related to the interior functional arrangement of the dwellings, and microworlds of reality would thus never have been known if only the exterior features of the dwellings had been recorded. Unless there is a stated departure, the discussion of dwellings that follows is based upon the assumption that the reader is facing toward the front of each dwelling under consideration. For convenience, the traditional barrel-vaulted or front-gabled dwellings with thatching of the Toda are called huts, whereas the later dwellings (typically side-gabled) with wattle and daub walls, or stone and mortar walls, or brick and mortar walls, are called houses. As the Toda abandoned their traditional huts, the housing models provided by the houses of their nearby Badaga neighbours (Fig. 9.1) were particularly influential. Thus, the terms full Badaga style versus half Badaga style of houses are used here.

Traditional Huts

BARREL-VAULTED HUTS

Jacome Fenicio wrote the first description of a Toda barrel-vaulted hut in 1603 (letter from Finicio to the Vice-Provincial of Calicut, 1 April 1603, in part translated by Q de Alberti, in Rivers 1906: 720–30). Barrel-vaulted huts were once the most numerous of traditional huts, and have remained a hallmark of the Toda habitation to those visiting the Nilgiris. The current ten or fewer of them indicate a sharp decline in the number of traditional dwellings. With the exception of Kaxwr̄y with only one surviving hut, not far from the Ootacamund to Gudalur road, the barrel-vaulted dwellings of Po·ṣ and Nü·ḷn occur in the wilder southwestern Nilgiris. Nü·ḷn had the only increase of barrel-vaulted dwellings from 1963 (three) to 1994 (six), and is also remarkable for the rethatching of its dairy in 1994. Because one of the three barrel-vaulted huts at Po·ṣ (the one with the bee-keeper) in 1990 had bundled and bound acacia sticks for the main structural ribs (instead of *te·f* bamboo) and lashed acacia sticks in series (instead of *wa·ṛ* bamboos), it represents a technological departure from the traditional.

The barrel-vaulted huts of the Toda are among the most distinctive dwellings of India. Each entails the remarkable combination of *te·f* bamboo (? *Pseudoxytenenathera monadelpha* Soderstrom and Ellis) from the northern Nilgiri slopes, possessing tensile strength when bent over for the barrel-vaulted supports; rattan (*Calamus pseudotenuis* Becc.) cut in rain forest of the far western Nilgiri slopes and carried afar in bundles for all the ties and bindings; *wa·ṛ* bamboo (*Arundinaria wightiana* Nees and A.w. var. *hispida* Gamble), mainly cut near local streams for the roof base; and grass (*Andropogon polypticus* Steud. var. *deccanensis* Bor) growing in low-lying marshes, for exposed roof thatch. In lower parts of the Nilgiris east of Dodda Betta, and sometimes for higher western huts as well, coarser thatching grasses (*Cymbopogon* spp.) are substituted. In contrast to the first type of grass that is always cut, the coarser thatching grasses are pulled from the ground with their root systems somewhat intact.

Hut ends are constructed with upright planks next to each other in two opposing rows set into the ground (Fig. 9.2, with an example from 1963). While the Toda once felled trees with axes, split tree trunks apart with wedges, and then levelled the rough planks with adzes, sawed planks were later depended upon. *Te·f* bamboo is bundled and bound with split rattan to form the two main series of structural ribs in the vaulting. Ribs in the first series, placed just to each side of the front and back walls, are set into the ground at their ends and lashed to the walls with rattan ties. They are curved over to conform with the wall profiles. One of the main characteristics is that the front vaulting will be slightly broader and higher than the back vaulting. Each completed hut is thus slightly broader and higher at the front. Horizontal poles, spaced equally apart from each other, are lashed onto the main ribs. A second series with more and thinner bundles of bound *te·f* bamboos, set into the ground on each side and bent over for the barrel-vaulting, is lashed onto the poles below. Pairs of *wa·ṛ* bamboos are lashed together, and at even intervals, onto the second series of barrel-vaulted *te·f* bamboos below. Then to hold more *wa·ṛ* bamboos in place, a small series of bent-over *te·f* bamboos is lashed into position to form the outer confining barrel-vaulted ribs. *Wa·ṛ* bamboos are then stuffed, one by one, into the spaces below the outermost ribs and between the lashed on, paired *wa·ṛ* bamboos until there is a continuous covering of side-by-side *wa·ṛ* bamboos. The roof is finally thatched with rows of bundled grass. Starting from the ground on each side and continuing upward, each row of thatch is held down by two *wa·ṛ* bamboos lashed onto the underlying framework. When the top is reached, extra thatching is held down by several substantial poles laid from front to back and then lashed down. Roof ends extending to front and back may both be padded with grass that is neatly and tightly bound into place with rattan, but it is more customary just to bind the front ends. While small windows may be cut out of the front planks, windows can also be formed by leaving small empty spaces between the vertical planks. Chinks between the planks are filled in with small pieces of wood and the final application of a clay and buffalo dung mix.

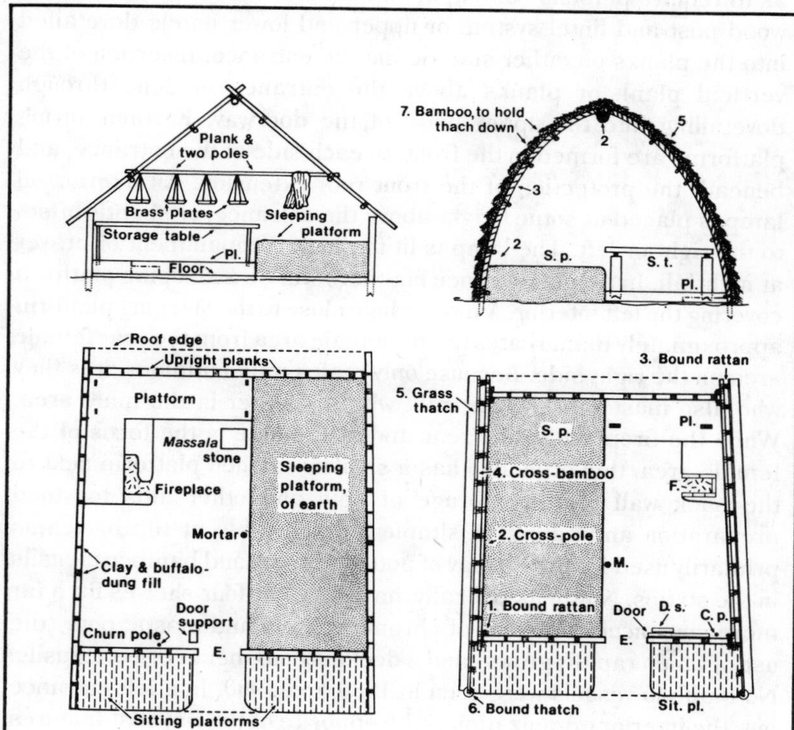

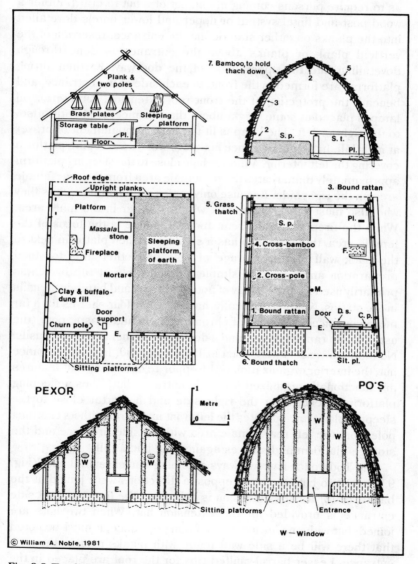

Fig. 9.2 Traditional Toda Dwellings: Two Styles

The functional arrangement of interior hut features is regularly balanced out in the same way (Fig. 9.2). The entrance built into the front wall is placed either slightly to the right or left and is so low as to require persons coming in and out of a hut to crawl. Either a wood post and lintel system or upper and lower lintels dovetailed into the planks on either side define the entrance. Insertion of the vertical plank or planks above the entrance is done through dovetailing into the upper lintel of the doorway. Earthen sitting platforms are formed in the front, to each side of the entrance, and beneath the protection of the front roof extension. An interior oil lamp is placed at some height above the entrance, or slightly offset to the right or left. The lamp is lit to the accompaniment of prayer at nightfall. In a right-entrance hut there will be a sleeping platform covering the left interior. A mortar hole close to the sleeping platform approximately demarcates the front male area from the rear female area on the right side. Because only males milk buffaloes, it is they who also must process the milk with a churner in the male area. While the fireplace to the rear and at the side is the focus of the female area, this area also has a shallow earthen platform next to the back wall for the storage of pots and other aids for food preparation and eating. A simple storage table at the back was primarily used for the display of pottery, brass, and bamboo utensils in the sixties. Now huts typically have three or four shelves for a far more conspicuous display of chrome vessels and plastic pots (the use of which rapidly grows) and a declining number of brass utensils. No bamboo vessels were seen in 1988 and 1990. In a left-entrance hut, the interior organization is the opposite of the way that features are functionally organized in a right-entrance hut. Thus a sleeping platform extends over the right side and a mortar close to the sleeping platform separates the left front male area with its churning pole from the left rear female area with its side fireplace and the storage platform and shelves against the back wall.

The Toda once had two ways of joining barrel-vaulted huts (Fig. 9.3): (*a*) two huts facing in opposite directions were joined at the backs, or (*b*) a back extension is built from the first hut, and side entrance is provided for the extension hut. When two huts are joined, but with one having a side-facing entrance, it must be noted that there will be a side wall made with planks next to the side entrance. Lesser barrel-vaulted ribs for the roof are placed in the ground between the planks, and the roof rising above the planks can

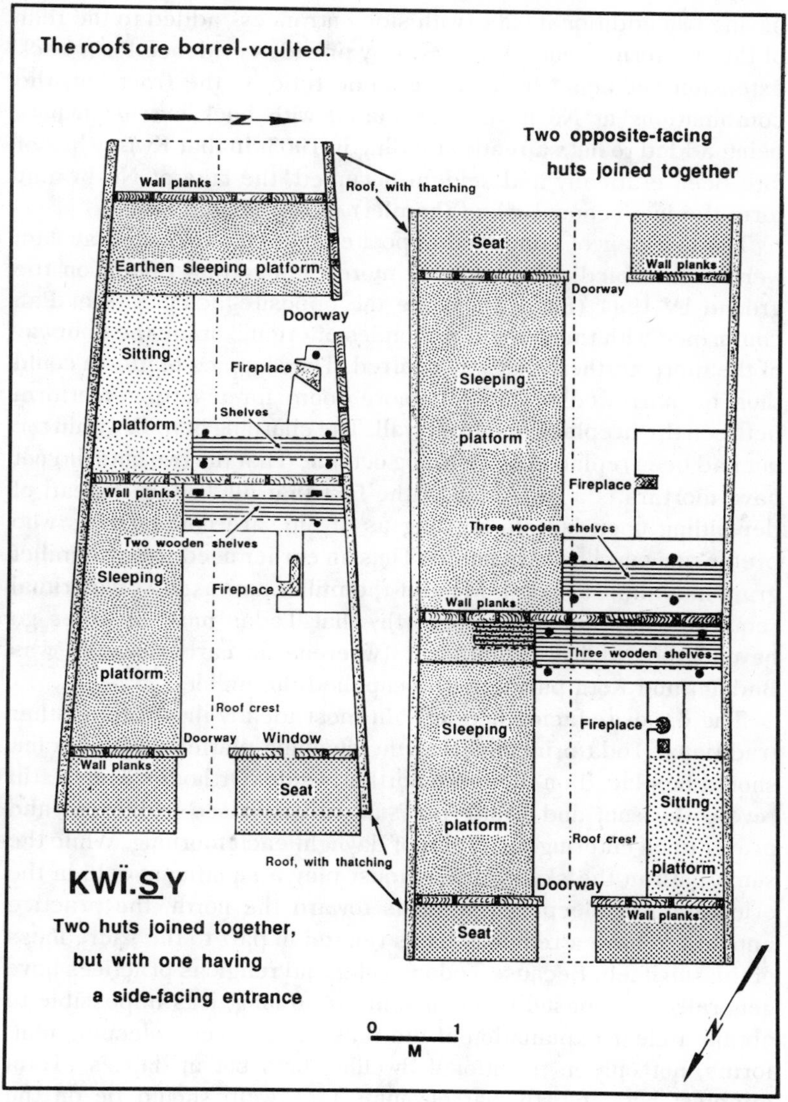
The roofs are barrel-vaulted.
N
Two opposite-facing huts joined together
Wall planks
Roof, with thatching
Earthen sleeping platform
Doorway
Sitting platform
Fireplace
Shelves
Wall planks
Two wooden shelves
Sleeping platform
Fireplace
Roof crest
Doorway
Window
Wall planks
Seat
Roof, with thatching
KWÏ.S̲Y̲
Two huts joined together, but with one having a side-facing entrance
Seat
Wall planks
Doorway
Sleeping platform
Fireplace
Three wooden shelves
Wall planks
Three wooden shelves
Sleeping platform
Fireplace
Sitting platform
Roof crest
Doorway
Seat
Wall planks
0
1
M
N

Fig. 9.3 Pan

thus be made in the normal way. The roof of the single hut with a back extension at Kwï·s̱y had caved in by 1994, and the rest of the hut was disintegrating by then. There was a single hut with a back extension at Nü·ḷṇ in 1990. The hamlet was made unique in 1994 by having two additional huts (with side entrances) added to the rear of the two former huts. While Kwï·s̱y provides evidence for a back extension hut being built at the same time as the front hut, the combinations at Nü·ḷṇ are associated with back extension huts being added to huts already standing in 1963. In that Kwï·s̱y has of late been eratically and seldom occupied, the huts at Nü·ḷṇ may form the last seaonal *mund* (hamlet) of the Todas.

The last pair of combined opposite-facing huts, located at Pan, were a crumbled mess of little more than rotting thatch on the ground by 1994 (Fig. 9.3). While the opposite-facing huts at Pan conformed with the general principles of organization, the doorway of the more northerly hut was centred. The sleeping platform could thus be narrowed to provide more room for a sitting platform between the fireplace and front wall. The churning of milk within the hut had been replaced by churning outside. That the two huts did not have mortars is a reflection of the fact that all Todas, instead of depending upon buffalo herding as of old, are now farmers who prefer rice purchased at shops. Thus an earlier need to crush millet grain has almost ended. Most of the millet now used serves ritual requirements, and it is noteworthy that Todas must at times go beyond the Nilgiris to obtain it (whereas, in early times, it was Badaga and Kota partners who supplied the millet).

The opposite-facing huts at Pan most ideally illustrate another traditional Toda principle: that the sleeping platform within a hut should be placed on the more northerly side. Orthodox Todas still revere the sun, and salute the sun with upraised right arm and prayer upon entering the realm of daylight each morning. While the sun's path in the sky each day must play a significant role in the orientation of sleeping platforms toward the north, the practice appears to have a religious basis related in part to the sacredness of the sun itself. Because Toda secular and religious practices have generally been based upon custom for so long, it is impossible to obtain a clear explanation of the reasons why Toda sleeping platforms, not only in traditional dwelling huts but in dairies (Toda temples: huts, mostly barrel-vaulted) as well, should be on the northerly sides of the huts and dairies. A diagram is provided

(Fig. 9.4) in an attempt to suggest some reasons for the northerly orientation of sleeping platforms. Orientation towards the north is envisioned as attractive and creative because earliest Toda settlement was in the northerly parts of the Nilgiri massif. The creation of the Toda and their buffaloes is believed to have taken place in a northerly area, and is associated with god Ö·n and goddess Tö·kis̱y. Ö·ntöw the place of Ö·n, is on the northern edge of the Nilgiri massif. N·oṣ *mund*, particularly associated with the place where the goddess Tö·kis̱y accomplished her creative acts, is next to the main northern pass with the central *ghat* road dropping down to the Mysore Ditch. By contrast, orientation toward the south is envisioned as repelling because of its association with death and Amuno·ṛ, the main Toda World of the Dead. The entrance to Amuno·ṛ in the extreme southwestern Nilgiris is in a harsh grassland beyond Kwï·s̱y, the last of the Toda *munds* to the southwest. As Ö·n finally became the God of the Dead who ruled over Amuno·ṛ, his dualistic polarity associated with creation (northerly) versus death (southerly) is noteworthy. Such a polarity conforms with right versus left thinking, and the inherent duality it contains is also characteristic of Hindu thinking. We are thus reminded of the Hindu belief in a northerly quadrant toward Himalaya, the Abode of Snow with Mount Kailas, where great deities dwell, versus a southerly quadrant toward a deathly world controlled by Yama, God of the Dead. The Hindu supreme god Siva is both Creator (especially in the form of *Linga*) and Destroyer (especially in the form of Nataraja).

After what has just been said, it is obvious that the two huts at Kwï·s̱y have some marked departures from the norm. The characteristic narrowing and lower height towards the back, in both huts, is the most exaggerated of the Toda huts seen by the writer. The absence of mortars in both huts is due to the fact that Kwï·s̱y is believed to have once been a *ti*·dairy (the most sacred of dairy grades) established and lived in by Kwaṯe·n, the member of the Mö·ṛ patriclan who eventually became a god-mountain. Because the site is still very sacred, the main Toda emblems of femaleness—broom, pestle, and winnowing basket—can never be brought into the hamlet. As this is the closest hamlet to Amuno·ṛ, expectant Toda females must leave the site before they deliver their infants. One would expect Kwï·s̱y to have a high degree of conformity with the locational principle of sleeping platforms toward the north. Instead, however, the sleeping platform in the main front hut lies next to the southern

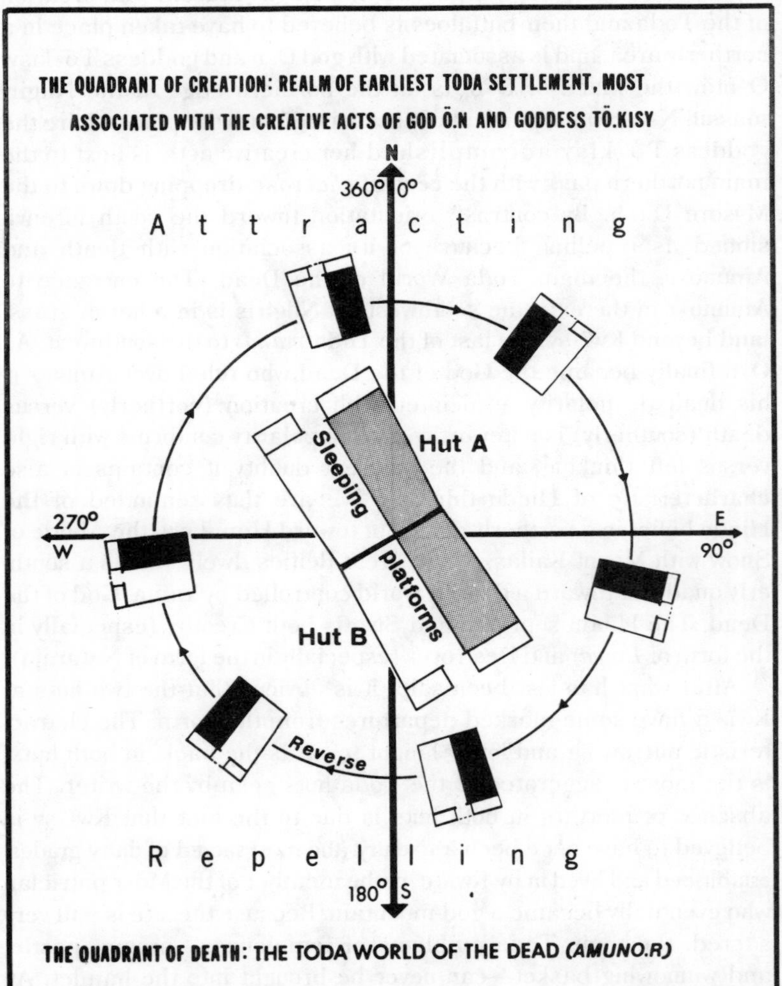

Fig. 9.4 Reasons for the Northerly Orientations of Sleeping Platforms

side (the one closest to Amuno·ṛ), and the sleeping platform in the other hut has an unusual north to south orientation. While there may once have been sound reasons for the departures from the norm, they now remain unexplained. Todas have long since forgotten the reasons behind orientation requirements or their departures from the norm.

The adaptation of barrel-vaulting for more substantial Toda housing has been minimal. An attempt to use barrel-vaulting for a house occurred at Pö·rxas̱. Walls built with bricks and mortar were constructed in the front and back, the interior was organized in the traditional way, and the roof had the final, typical thatching. The dwelling was occupied into the sixties, but has since been in ruin. Professional architects employed by the government in the sixties designed houses with brick and mortar walls, and concrete barrel-vaulted roofs, built in the two urban *munds* of Ka·s̱ and Meḷga·s̱ in Ootacamund. Two or three of the six houses at Ka·s̱ have always been used as buffalo calf shelters, but the rest continue to be occupied by Toda families. The four houses at Meḷga·s̱ were occupied continuously by Toda families until they were pulled down in 1994 and replaced with new side-gabled houses.

Front-gabled Huts

An illustration of a front-gabled hut (Baikie 1834: op. 110) next to a barrel-vaulted hut proves that the two hut types were constructed since at least the 1830s. Because front-gabled huts are never used as permanent dairies (the temples of the Toda), barrel-vaulted huts probably antedate the front-gabled ones.

Front-gabling among the Todas appears to be an adaptation of the side-gabling that is typically seen in Badaga houses (Rivers 1906: 29; Walker 1986: 48). The Badagas had at least one front-gabled temple in 1876, and such construction might also have inspired the front-gabling in Toda huts (Grigg 1880: 226). While Todas have not constructed front-gabled permanent dairies, their temporary dairies are typically front-gabled. Most front-gabled huts have vertical end and side walls formed with upright planks, similar in thickness and width to those in barrel-vaulted huts, set into the ground. Rarely, upright slabs of stone approximating those of wood are used as substitutes. Regardless of materials used, end walls taper down from their centres. Both side walls of equal height are aligned beyond the end walls. An entrance similar to that of a barrel-vaulted dwelling is formed slightly to the right or left of centre in the front wall. An earthen sitting platform (Fig. 9.2) is built up outside, on each side of the entrance and to the front extensions of the side walls. Chinks in all the walls are filled with pieces of wood (and more rarely stone pieces) and a clay and buffalo dung mixture. The front-gabled roof is made with horizontal poles set onto the top of the front and back vertical wall planks (true, too, of the barrel-vaulted horizontal poles, although they also sit on the main rattan ribs), more rarely on stones. Taking advantage of holes cut near the tops of the vertical planks, or stones, the horizontal poles are lashed onto the front and back walls for further strength (also true of barrel-vaulted roof construction). A series of rafter poles, extending slightly beyond the side walls and just beyond the topmost horizontal support pole forming the crest, are lashed onto the horizontal poles below. Horizontal *wa·ṛ* bamboos in tight series next to each other are lashed onto the rafter poles. Then row upon row of thatch is applied, starting from the bottom on the two sides and going to the top. Paralleling barrel-vaulted roof thatching, each layer of thatch is held down by two bamboos lashed into position. Extra thatch layering at the top is held down by poles lashed near their ends and onto the horizontal crest pole below. As regards the position of an entrance slightly to the right or left, the interiors of front-gabled huts are organized in a manner identical to barrel-vaulted huts.

Front-gabled dwellings at Po·ṣ and Piškwašt demonstrate basic technological shifts from hut to house materials for building. Paralleling the case of barrel-vaulting, the retention of front-gabling for Toda house construction was rare. The front-gabled hut at Po·ṣ has a roof with Mangalore tiles and a bargeboard at the front. Mangalore tiles were first produced by the Basel Mission in Mangalore, and some houses built by foreigners in Nilgiri urban centres had bargeboards. The use of a bargeboard at Po·ṣ was a rare choice, but it must be noted that there are now two new side-gabled house with bargeboards on both sides at Omga·s̲. A thatched front-gabled house at Piškwašt has cut stone walls and external front sitting platforms of cut stone. Stone walls in Toda dwellings of any sort are relatively rare.

Barrel-vaulted and Front-gabled Confinement Huts

All pregnant women had to leave Kyu·ṛ and stay in nearby Mo·lkuš, and Rivers (1906: 314) mentions that the front-gabled confinement hut for them there (Fig. 9.13) was about ninety metres from the hamlet. Based upon a lithograph of 1847, showing a confinement hut close to dwelling huts and separated from them by a fence, we also know that Todas once constructed barrel-vaulted confinement huts (Fig. 9.13). A front-gabled confinement hut was usually a miniaturized version of the larger front-gabled dwelling hut. It could also be cruder in construction, with a series of poles set next to each other and vertically in the ground to form the walls (Rivers 1906: 325). A barrel-vaulted confinement hut was made in a very characteristic way, with two vertical and opposing poles that were y-forked at the top. Two barrel-vaulted ribs of *te·f* bamboo, having several bamboos bound together with rattan, were then run over the y-portions of the two poles. The basic frame of the roof was completed by the lashing on of a crest pole from the top of one barrel vault to the other. *Wa·ṛ* bamboos, in sequence right next to each other, were then lashed onto the outer surfaces of the two barrel vaults. In the usual manner, starting with a layer of thatch next to the ground on each side and with each layer held down by two *wa·ṛ* bamboos lashed onto the barrel vaults, the upwards layer upon layer of thatching was in like manner applied all the way to the top. Then, finally, an extra layer of thatch would be applied along the crest line.

It seems likely that each Toda female once stayed in a confinement hut *(pïṣa·ṣ)* during at least her first menstrual period. The Irulas, eastern slope neighbours of the Todas, have continued to use confinement rooms for women undergoing menses (Noble and Jebadhas 1989: 287, end plate 21, C). While Rivers was aware of confinement huts, he does not mention their required use for Toda women during menstruation. Long after the use of confinement huts was ended among the Toda, Walker (1986: 204) mentions that a girl is still excluded from her home for three days when she undergoes her first menstrual period. She stays in a vacated house where no cooking may be done; food is brought to her from her home, and a female companion may stay overnight with her. This girl is not permitted to consume milk, buttermilk, or butter, all linked to the sacredness of even secular buffalo milk. Emeneau (1967: 318) and Walker (1986: 204) are in agreement that women are not expected to confine themselves during all subsequent menstrual periods.

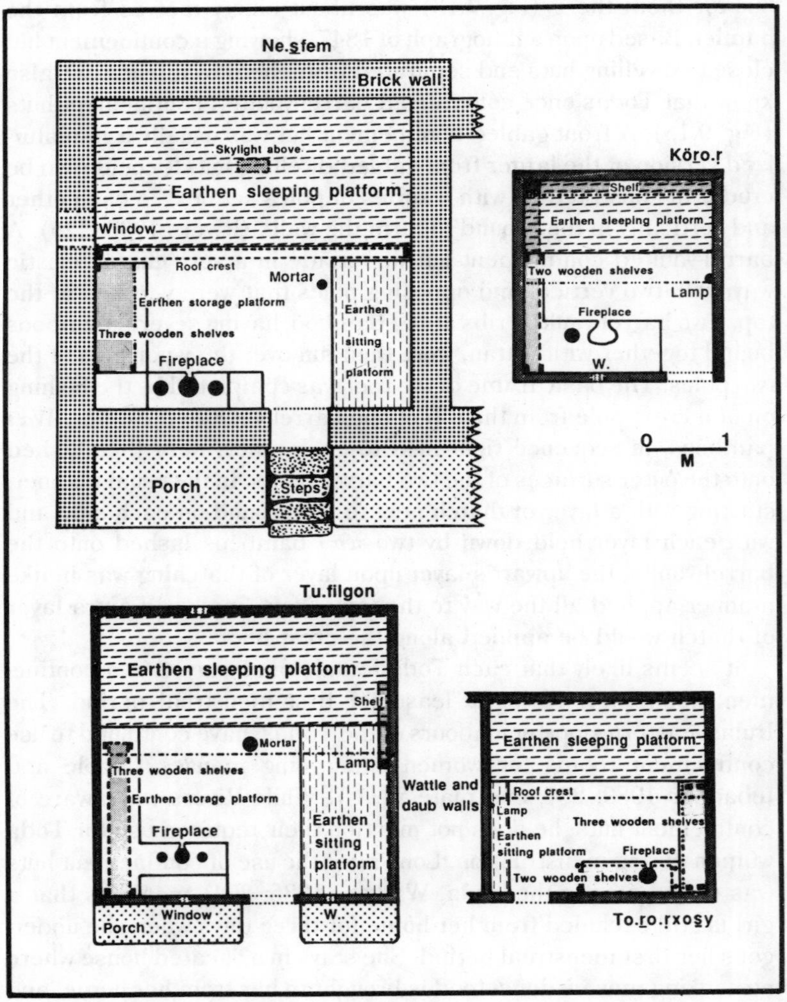

Fig. 9.5 Single Unit Toda Houses

In about the fifth month of her pregnancy, a Toda woman once had to retreat to a confinement hut for close to a month. It was on a new moon day that the pregnant woman first went to the confinement hut. After ritual which was different for women in the two subcastes, a *To·ɽθas̱* or *Töwfiḷy* woman entered the hut after her wrists were burnt (Rivers 1906: 313–9). There she stayed with a female companion until shortly before the next new moon. Apart from eating regular food brought by relatives, the two women were periodically given food by well-wishers who had to stay some distance from them.

With experienced females in attendance, Toda women assume a kneeling position during delivery in their homes. They once had to go to confinement huts a few days later. While, again, the ritual related to women in the two subcastes varied considerably, women in both rubbed ash on their heads and walked to the confinement huts while shaded by their *pu·txuḷy*s drawn over the heads and the leaves of Nilgiri holly (*Ilex denticulata* Wall and *wightiana* Wall.) held above. To avoid the evil influence of a celestial body called *ke·t*, believed to be near the sun, each mother looked away from the sun (Rivers 1906: 323–31). Her infant, always having its head covered by cloth, was carried ahead by another woman. Likewise, and especially for protection against *ke·t*, holly leaves provided shade. Following ritual before the confinement hut, the mother and infant remained in seclusion until a few days before the next new moon if the infant was not the firstborn. If the infant was the firstborn, the period of seclusion lasted until a month after the new moon following the birth. A female companion could stay with the mother, and she was tended in the same way as she was after her wrists were burned.

After one to three months have passed from its birth, the infant's face is finally exposed for the first time. While visiting Pö·rxas̱ in 1988, the writer observed what happened. The oldest male took the male infant, still covered, to the dairy at daybreak. As he bowed to the earth and touched the infant's head to the earth before the dairy entrance, the males present blessed the infant. Upon rising, the elder uncovered the infant's head and publicly named him for the first time. All then went to the buffalo pen, and after the elder and infant bowed to the entrance, the elder said, 'See the buffaloes, see the crows, see the beautiful earth', as he showed these to the infant for the first time. And there was rejoicing, with breakfast food, among all. A later feast that may be provided for members of the Toda community in general was observed at Po·s̲ in 1988. Males and females, seated on grassland in separate rows, were given food on banana leaves. Afterwards, the infant just named that morning was carried around from person to person, and he was lowered toward each visitor, and sometimes to the foot of a visitor. Each person visited uttered a blessing and gave a cash gift. Then, in closing, some men ran far across some still existent grassland to round up the buffalo calf gifted by the male infant's maternal uncle. If an infant is female, the mother simply takes her at daybreak to where the women usually go to collect buttermilk from the priest (Rivers 1906: 331–2). There she uncovers the infant's head for the first time and shows her the dairy, buffalo pen, and the creations of nature. There is no general celebration or gift-giving.

Houses with Traditional Interior Functional Relationships

The Todas had started to build houses by the start of this century. Of the first Toda hamlet with a house that we have record of, at Kī·wīd̲y, Rivers (1906: 671) wrote, 'It has a modern house, the largest and most highly ornamental Toda dwelling which I saw in the hills'. The brick and mortar house with an upper floor was owned by Ti·r̲xar̦, and in 1954 it was demolished and replaced with a house of stone. The dominant factor of side-gabling employed by the Badaga in their houses was adopted by the Toda and used as the norm in the construction of their houses. While Badagas between 1880 and 1935 shifted from houses having wattle and daub or stone walls with thatched roots to walls made of bricks and mortar with roofs of Mangalore or simple concave tiles (Shortt 1868: 58; Grigg *et al*. 1880: 225; Sastri 1892: 757; Ranga 1934: 5), it was not until after World War II and Independence that the Todas underwent a major shift to houses made with the same materials. While the Badagas are increasingly building two-storied houses, only one Toda upper storey dwelling unit was recorded in 1988 (at No·ṣ). A recent Badaga love for external blue wash or paint on houses has thus far had no significant impact on the Toda.

Any evidence for aligning sleeping platforms next to the northern sides of houses seems erratic enough to suggest that the increased complexity of housing and associated difficulties in orienting sleeping platforms may have caused what was once a common practice to be overlooked and replaced by other considerations. There is also a probability that any attempt to follow the ancient practice would be more consistent in the earliest houses and would decline with the passage of time as one house replaced another.

Single Unit Houses

Unless an exception is specifically mentioned, these and all other houses covered in the rest of this article are side-gabled. Single unit houses may stand by themselves, but there is a strong tendency to follow the Badaga precedent and to align these and all other Toda houses into rows. Until a family is economically better off, house walls may be of the wattle and daub type (Fig. 9.5). The most commonly used eucalyptus uprights and acacia horizontals in such walls are covered with mud. Wattle and daub houses are more coarsely thatched than traditional huts, and some may have a layer of pine needles spread over polyurethane sheets. These are laid over lesser horizontal poles lashed onto rafters, in turn tied to a few larger horizontal poles below. More substantial walling and tiling are sure signs of economic progress. With the exception of side entrances rather than end entrances in relationship to their roof crests, the interiors of single unit houses are almost exact functional duplicates of the interiors of traditional huts. Even the lamps are placed approximately where they would be in traditional huts. It is interesting to see how the rightwardness or leftwardness of fireplaces is governed by left-sided or right-sided entrances. As in some traditional huts, but to even a greater degree in single unit houses, earthen sitting platforms are constructed. Quite logically, the sitting platforms are built behind and to either the immediate right or immediate left of entranceways.

Houses with a Front Extension

Toda houses may be extended towards the front (Fig. 9.6) in the next structural step towards increased complexity. The traditional unit at To·r̲o·ṛ, with left fireplace, storage platform and shelves at the far left, rear sleeping platform, and right sitting platform next to the doorway, has a single storage room attached in front. Due to the utilitarian nature of this room, the sacred lamp is positioned above the doorway in the back room. As they continue with farming,

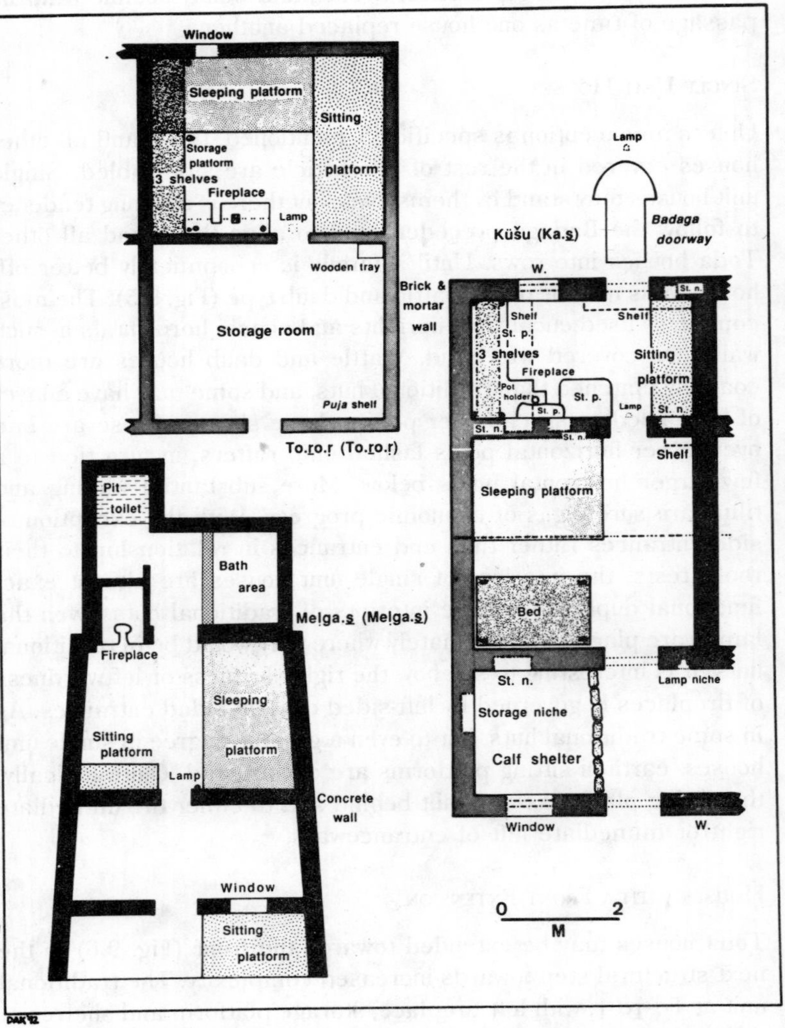

Fig. 9.6 Toda Houses: Front Extension

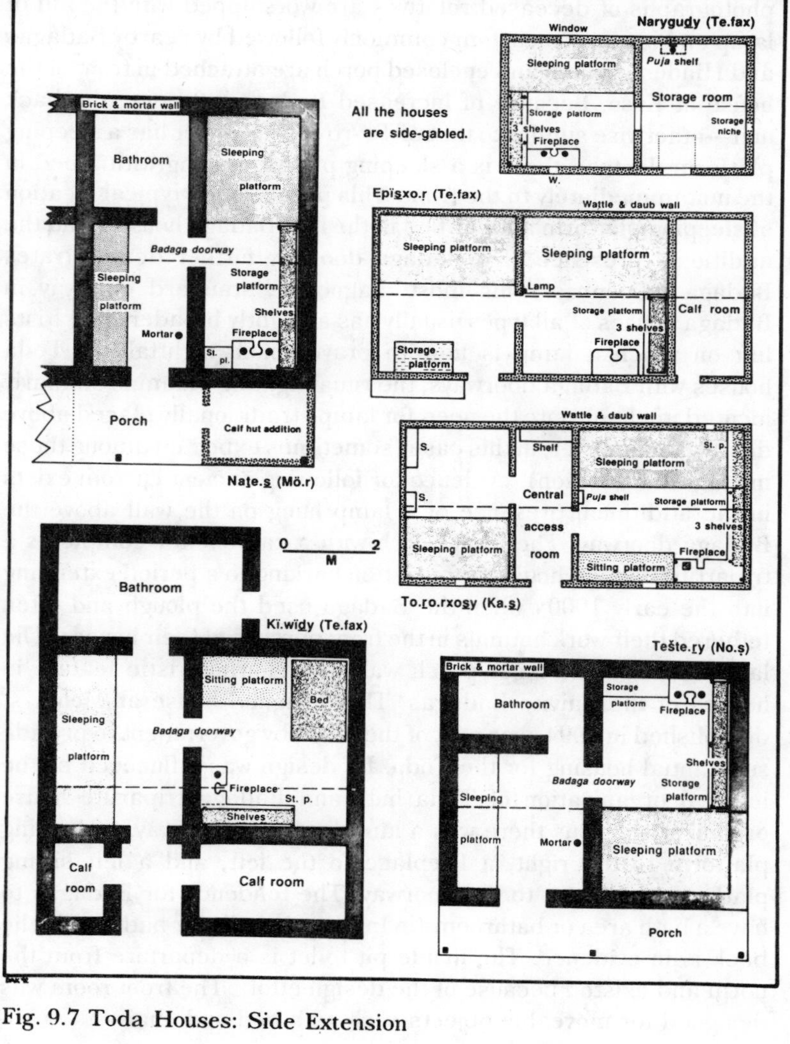

Fig. 9.7 Toda Houses: Side Extension

the Toda need more space. In addition to the storage of farming equipment, fertilizer and pesticide, agricultural produce at harvest time can be processed, dried, and stored in the additional space. The To·r̲o·ṛ storage room also has a *puja* (worship) shelf where the photographs of deceased relatives are worshipped with the aid of lamp and incense, a custom commonly followed by nearby Badagas and Hindus. A room and enclosed porch are attached in front of the house at Küsu. Because of increased Badaga influence, the back unit—otherwise similar to that of To·r̲o·ṛ—no longer has a sleeping platform. Instead there is a sleeping platform along with a bed in the unit immediately to the front. This parallels the typical location of sleeping platform and/or bed in the half Badaga houses, and the additional presence of a Badaga doorway further demonstrates Badaga influences. This most diagnostic, standard doorway in Badaga houses of all types usually has a slightly broader shelf to its left on which a lamp is lit–with prayer–each nightfall. In Toda houses with Badaga doorways, the ritual lighting of lamps similarly located might obviate the need for lamps traditionally placed above doorways. However, in this case (sometimes expected among those in cultural transition), evidence for following ancient custom exists in the additional presence of a lamp hung on the wall above the Badaga doorway. The front porch with a calf shelter completes a tripartite Badaga house organization harking to a period extending into the early 1900s when the Badaga used the plough and often tethered their work animals in the front porches of their houses. The lamp niche in the inner porch wall is a characteristic feature in houses of the Saivite Badagas. The designed house at Meḷga·s̲, demolished in 1994, was part of the effort by government to provide substantial housing for the Toda. Its design was influenced by the internal organization of Toda huts and Badaga tripartite house organization. Thus there was a lamp near the doorway, a sleeping platform to the right, a fireplace to the left, and a left sitting platform right next to the doorway. The tendency for Badagas to have a bath area or bathroom (in India, primarily for bathing) in the back is in evidence. The inside pit toilet is a departure from the norm and existed because of the design effort. The front room was designed for moveable objects such as a bed and chairs.

Houses with a Side Extension

Toda houses may also be extended towards either side (Fig. 9.7) as an alternate structural step toward increased complexity. Houses with wattle and daub walls well demonstrate the process in its simplest stages. A Narygu<u>d</u>y house has a traditional unit with fireplace to the left, a storage platform to its far left with three shelves, rear sleeping platform, and a room serving for storage extended to the right. The *puja* shelf in the rear of the storage room has a lamp and a statue of Ganesh. Calendars honouring the Christian, Islamic, and Hindu faiths hang on the rear wall. The traditional unit with right fireplace, far right storage platform and three shelves, rear sleeping platform, and the lamp next to the doorway at Epïsxo·ṛ has a living and storage room extended to the left. The small storage platform within the room is used to hold a trunk with prized family possessions. The house at To·<u>r</u>o·rxo<u>s</u>y is made more complex with the addition of a central access room. There is a traditional unit to the right of this room, and to the left is a living and storage room. The developmental model suggests that it would be possible instead to have the traditional unit to the left of the central access room and a living and storage room to the right. The houses at Na<u>t</u>e·<u>s</u>, Tešte·<u>r</u>y, and Kï·wï<u>d</u>y reveal a strong Badaga influence. Each is substantially built with brick and mortar walls, and each has a Badaga doorway. Looking through the Badaga doorways into the traditional units, Na<u>t</u>e·<u>s</u> has a sitting platform, then fireplace to the right, a storage platform and shelves in the back, and a large sleeping platform to the left. Tešte·<u>r</u>y has a sleeping platform to the right, storage platform and shelves in the back, and a fireplace to the left. In the not so perfectly conventional Kï·wï<u>d</u>y, there is still a bed to the left for sleeping and a fireplace to the right. All three rooms to the left of the traditional units have sleeping platforms of wood in the Badaga style. In the Badaga way, we start to see clear evidence for right kitchens (where no shoes may be worn) versus left rooms for sleeping, with the characteristic wooden platforms for sleeping. Thus a traditional Toda micro-microworld comes to exist in a larger, interior Badaga microworld. The three Toda houses also help us to understand more clearly the past development of stronger tripartite divisions in Badaga houses. A broader porch is eventually liable to be functionally altered by the addition of a calf hut. An even larger porch might someday be utilized for substantial calf rooms.

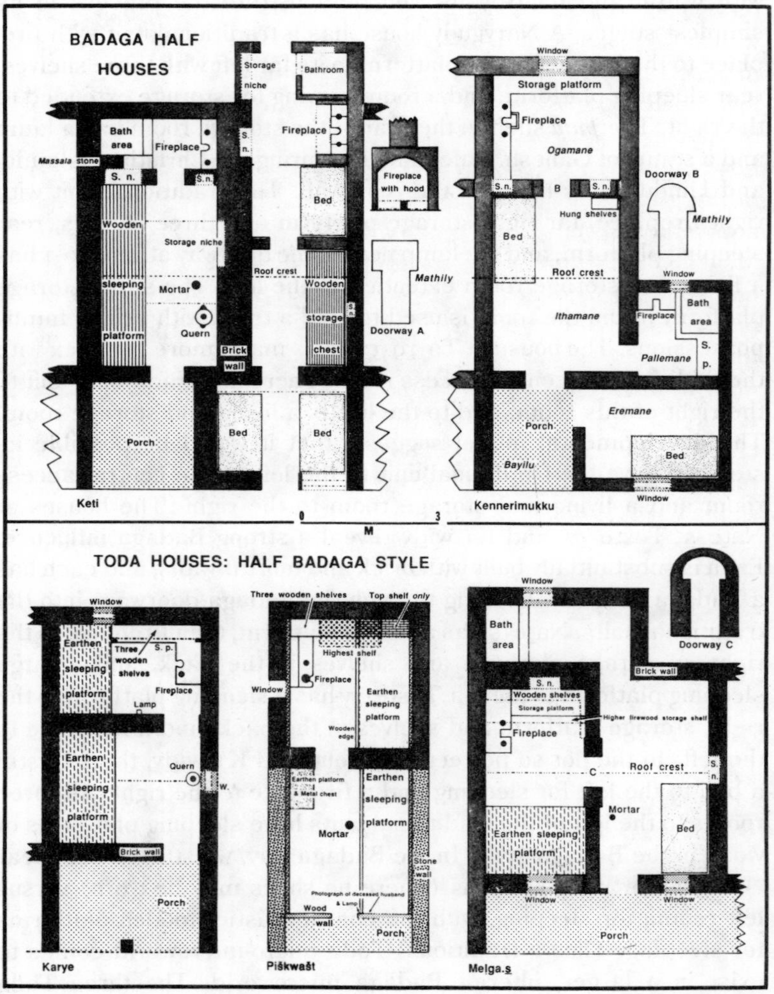

Fig. 9.8 Badaga and Toda Houses

Badaga and Toda Half Houses

Advanced Toda houses are inextricably linked to the houses which the Badaga have built before. While the Badaga have a strong tendency to place their fireplaces next to either the right or left side walls of their houses, they do not invariably do so. In Toda houses most strongly influenced by the Badaga, fireplaces will also be located next to either the right or left side walls. At the same time the ancient traditional interior organization within huts will usually be preserved to an amazing degree. In dealing with the organization in the great majority of Badaga houses, it becomes necessary to adopt the terms of Badaga full houses and Badaga half houses. Most Badaga families live in full houses that are two rooms wide; half houses only one room wide are far less common. While the two types can have separate origins, there are some Badaga full houses that were divided into two half houses by filling of the middle wall doorway and the provision of another entrance. There seem to have been two main reasons for such a division: (*a*) two brothers in conflict who ultimately decide to divide a house into two parts, one for each; or (*b*) mother-in-law domination leading to so much stress that a young couple ultimately decide they must be separated by the same alterations. The Toda have families living in the equivalents of Badaga full and half houses, so built from their inception.

A Badaga half house at Keti (Fig. 9.8) shows tripartite division with a broad front porch, a middle room with a wooden sleeping platform and a mortar plus quern for the preparation of grain, and a fireplace next to the right wall in the back room with a bath area. The adjacent half house also has a basic tripartite division. The front porch area is developed into a bedroom with two beds, the next room has a traditional storage chest (also for sleeping on) which in earlier times played a more vital note in the economy through the storage of grain, and a doorway of earlier style (still more commonly used by the Kota) leads into a back room with hooded fireplace, small bathroom with thin walls in a corner, and a bed separated from the cooking area by a plywood divider. The tripartite house at Kannerimukku is somewhat a variant in having developed to one side. In contrast to the two houses at Keti, its back kitchen has a fireplace next to the left wall (a location said by Badagas to have once been commoner, but now comparatively rare). A regular Badaga doorway leads from the middle multipurpose room with bed into the kitchen. The side extension from the

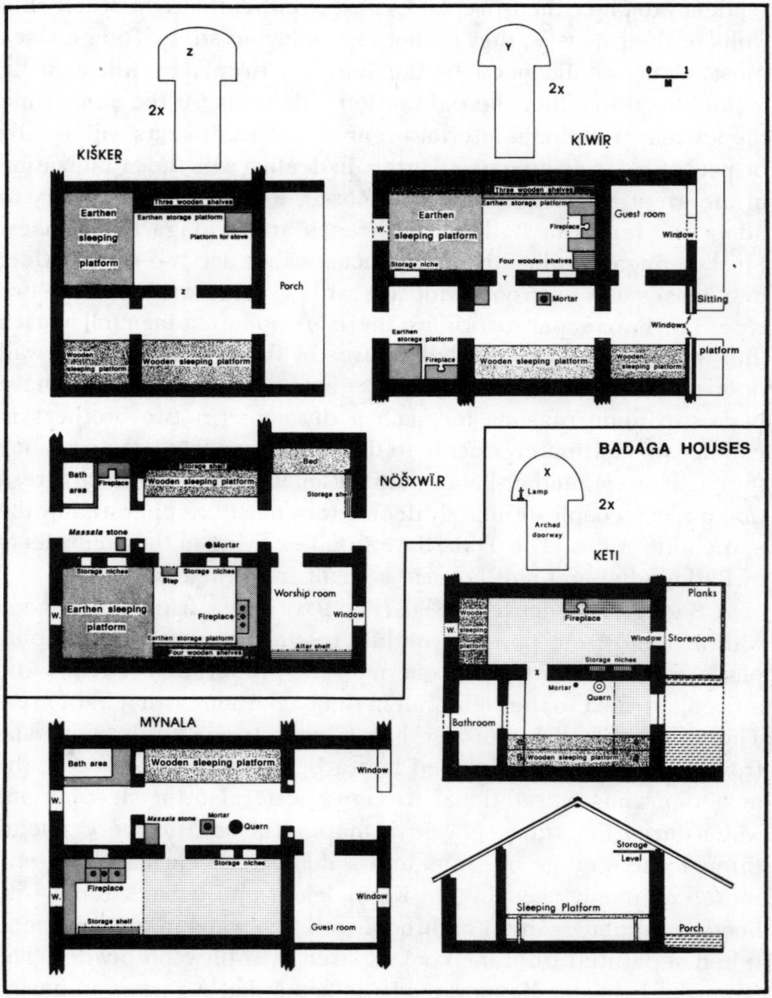

Fig. 9.9 Toda Houses: Full Badaga Style

middle room has a bath area and fireplace to heat water for anybody taking a bath. The front porch extension serves for the development of an extra bedroom.

While the tripartite Toda houses at Karye· and Piškwašt have fireplaces either next to the right or left side walls, they are also remarkable in having the ancient traditional unit preserved. Thus, if we associate the lamp in the back room at Karye with a slightly to the right entrance in a traditional Toda hut, all is in order: the fireplace is to the right, a storage platform and shelves are to the back, and an earthen sleeping platform is to the left. While there is a quern for grain preparation in this house, note that a Badaga locational factor was used in its placement. The quern thus stands next to the right wall in the middle multipurpose room with another earthen sleeping platform. If we compare the left rear doorway at Piškwašt with a traditional Toda hut, the left fireplace, rear storage platform (from the floor base) and shelves, and right earthen sleeping platform are also all in full conformity with the traditional functional arrangement. Notice too, however, the existence of Toda micro-microworlds within Badaga tripartite microworlds, for the traditional Toda units correspond with back kitchens in Badaga half houses, and there are also the equivalent of Badaga central multipurpose rooms and front porches.

The house at Meḷga·s̱ (demolished and replaced with another house by 1994) with a side development as well, is quite fascinating in that it clearly shows the influence of full Badaga houses. The Badaga doorway is correctly placed, for in a full Badaga house such a doorway leads from the multipurpose room to the kitchen. The mortar close to the middle wall is also in conformity with Badaga locational precepts. When we look through the Badaga doorway, remembering that the lamp at its side functionally replaces the traditional Toda lamp affixed higher on the wall, we find the left sleeping platform versus right fireplace to conform with traditional Toda precepts; however, the right storage platform and shelves do not. The tripartite division in a Badaga full house is usually associated with a back bathroom, true too in the case of this Toda house. There is also a porch at its front.

BADAGA AND TODA FULL HOUSES

A house at Keti (Fig.9.9) demonstrates how the traditional Badaga full house is typically two rooms wide, with a kitchen on one side, a

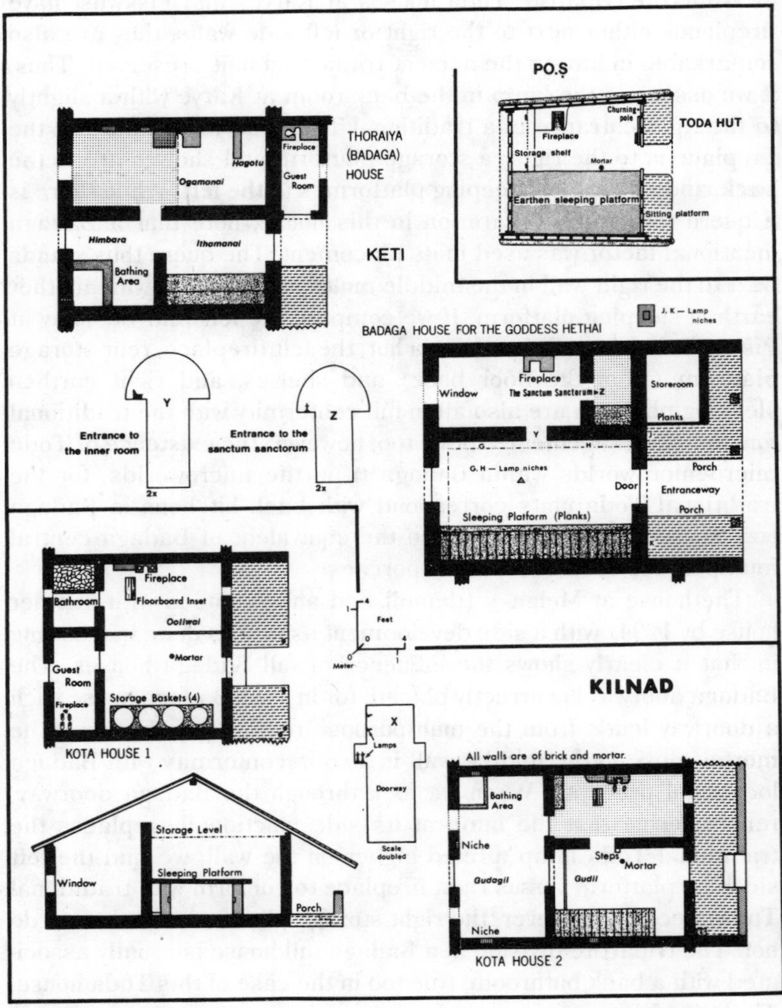

Fig. 9.10 Functional Parallels between Toda, Badaga and Kota Dwellings

multipurpose room with a wooden sleeping platform to the other side, and an arched Badaga doorway between these two rooms. The multipurpose room has a mortar (and sometimes a quern) close to the central wall. Right versus left generally relates to the entrance, as in Toda huts. If the entrance is to the left, one enters a multipurpose room with its wooden sleeping platform to the left. After going through a Badaga doorway into the right side kitchen, the fireplace will ideally be next to the side wall. Conversely, if the entrance is to the right, one enters a multipurpose room with wooden sleeping platform to the right. After going through a Badaga doorway into the left side kitchen, the fireplace will ideally be next to the side wall. In the case of the house at Mairele, the fireplace in the kitchen is not next to the side wall. Tripartite organization in Badaga full houses, demonstrated at Ke:ti and Mainele, generally has the sequence of a front porch to a multipurpose room to a bathroom. The first description of a Badaga full house, given by Jagor in 1876 (193–4), shows that the basic two rooms width and tripartite division which existed then have remained unchanged. Badagas then using ploughs stored these and other agricultural implements on front porches next to entranceways. Stalls to the other side of entranceways sheltered buffalo calves. The front division of the great majority of current Badaga houses now has a room for sleeping (often a provision for guests), or a storeroom, or a *puja* (worship) room, or some combination of these.

The existence of Toda micro-microworlds within Badaga microworlds is most clearly demonstrated in Toda houses of the full Badaga style. In such Toda houses with a left entrance and therefore a wooden sleeping platform next to the left side wall (in the Badaga style), and looking through a Badaga style doorway into what would normally be the kitchen in a Badaga house, a person will see (as in the examples aṭ Kišker̲ and Kï·wïr, Fig. 9.9) a Toda earthen sleeping platform to the left, a storage platform and shelves above to the rear, and a fireplace to the right (in one example, a platform for kerosene oil stove instead). In a Toda house of the full Badaga style, with right entrance and therefore a wooden sleeping platform next to the right side wall, and looking through a Badaga doorway into what would normally be the kitchen in a Badaga house, a person will see (as in the example at Nösxwï·r) a Toda earthen sleeping platform to the right, a storage platform and shelves above to the rear, and a fireplace to the left. Thus traditional functional relationships within Toda huts are maintained within the functional relationships of traditional Badaga houses, while the standardized concepts of right versus left are also adhered to. These houses also reveal the Badaga tripartite division with front porch or room, multipurpose room with sleeping platform, and back room, which to a lesser degree among the Toda (because they are more likely to still bathe in a stream) is a bathroom.

Functional Parallels between Toda, Kota, and Badaga Dwellings

It is only when we compare the plans of Toda, Kota, and Badaga dwellings (Fig. 9.10) that we are able to comprehend the most amazing reality of all: that the dwellings of the three groups seem to have their origin in a hut similar to that of the Toda. Most ancestors of the Saivite Hindu Badagas ('Northerners'), in part fleeing from Islamic political domination, may have settled mainly on the Nilgiris after the fall of the Vijayanagar Empire in AD 1565. Although there is some possibility of archaeological excavations someday assisting in the determination of how long the Toda and Kota have inhabited the Nilgiris, it is now impossible to say whose ancestors came first. Both groups may have been around far longer than the Badagas.

The Kota House 1 at Kilnad has only a wooden partition between the two main rooms, and thus it does not seem that far removed from the probability that in earlier times the Kotas also had single room huts. The interior functional arrangements of such huts would in all likelihood have been identical to those of Toda huts, including determination of the functional arrangements relating to right versus left entrances. To make huts larger in a conventional way, it was necessary that the entrance should be shifted to the side with the mortar, so that the mortar would remain as the basic divider between the kitchen half and the sleeping half further enlarged into a multipurpose half with a level for sleeping and/or storage next to the side wall. A later stage in development would be related to the building of a central wall with a doorway to separate formally the multipurpose room from the kitchen. The place for the dividing mortar had to be set close to the middle wall. While the doorway between the multipurpose room and the kitchen in Kota House 1 is plainly rectangular, a next stage doorway was cruciform—as in Kota House 2—so that the left side niche could serve as a setting for a sacred lamp lit each evening. The higher porch sections to each side of the lower entranceway in Kota House 1 are reminiscent

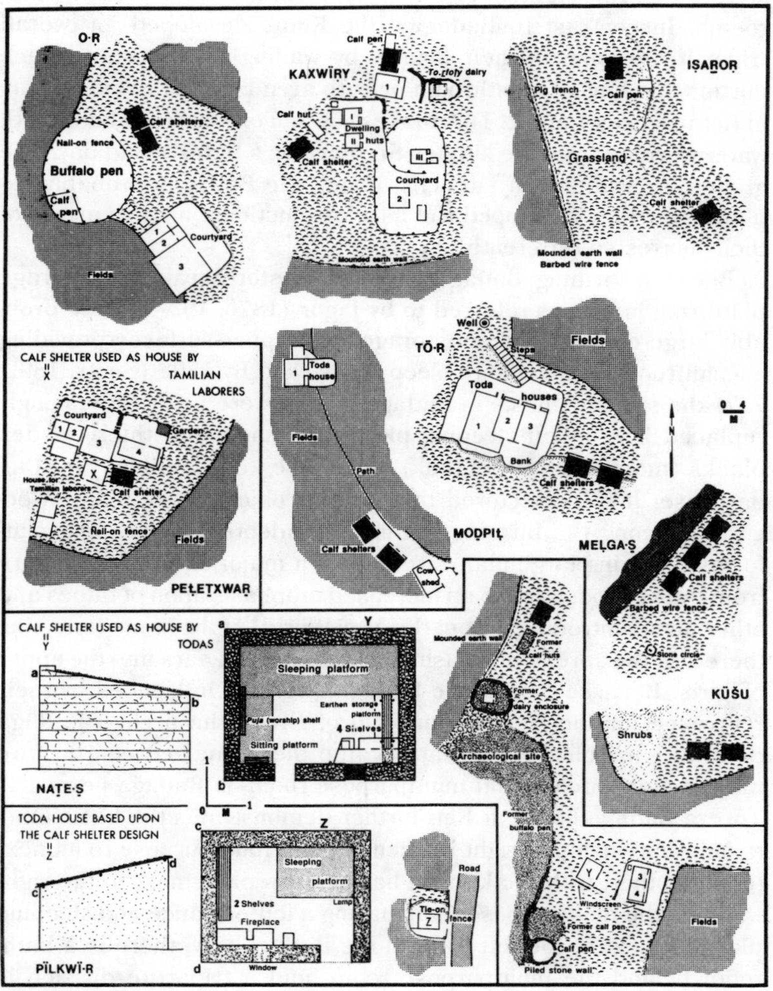

Fig. 9.11 From Calf Shelters to Toda House

of the front seating platforms of Toda huts. From what we know historically, the Badaga and Kota have characteristically aligned most of their houses into house rows, a custom that finally contributed to the development of raised and continued porch areas into rooms. In contrast to Badagas, the Kotas developed an overall tripartite division in their houses by walling off the entire back portion and having a bathroom or bath area behind the kitchen, as in Kota Houses 1 and 2. This makes sense if one wants to bathe with water warmed from the kitchen fireplace on a bitterly cold day. The greater sacredness of kitchens among the Badagas probably explains why they developed the interior functional arrangements of their houses so differently.

Because farming Badagas needed to store grain, the storage platforms in houses referred to by Jagor (1876: 193–4) were probably large chests for grain storage, with upper surfaces providing enough room for people to sleep on as well. By 1892 (Sastri 1892: 757) the storage chests in Badaga houses were being increasingly replaced by wooden sleeping platforms made with thick wooden planks (most desirably of teak), and these were eventually in standard use. It is conjectured that similar objects and changes occurred among the farming Kotas. The adoption of sleeping platforms requiring large planks relates to a major shift in agriculture from millet production to an increased emphasis upon potatoes and other plants introduced from the New World. At the same time, too, there was the spread of a cash economy with bazaars into the upper Nilgiris. Because the Saivite Badagas were so influenced by their reverence for the sun (an emblem of Siva), the arched Badaga doorway symbolizing the sun became the norm between the two main rooms–kitchen and multipurpose room–in Badaga houses. A Toreya Badaga house at Keti further demonstrates the basic functional relationship of right kitchen and left multipurpose room next to each other, with the kitchen having a fireplace next to the right wall and the multipurpose room having a left entrance and sleeping platform next to the left wall. In the Badaga way, there is a bathroom behind the multipurpose room, and a tripartite division is developing through the porch and guest room with fireplace in the front. However, the most revealing feature in this house, representative of an earlier time in which milk from livestock was routinely processed in many houses, is the small and secluded area called the *hagotu* where milk is processed. This area matches that part of a Toda hut where the churning of milk was done by males (likewise, a less common practice now, with sitting platforms sometimes located there instead). The potential sacredness of this corner, sacred in the past because of its association with milk, is further demonstrated by the location of the sanctum sanctorum in the Badaga house for the goddess Hette at Keti. Whereas the Kota always have free-standing temples for their deities, temples that are interesting in having no interior images, the Saivite Badaga customarily have separate temples for well-known Hindu deities and more personal houses built into their house rows for their own deities. The House for Hette: in its simplicity due to the belief that a deity has no need to bathe, it is strikingly similar in its functional relationships to the Toda hut. A sleeping platform next to the left side wall is provided for the deity, and food for the deity is cooked over the fireplace next to the right side wall. As *prasadam*, the food is first offered to Hette and is then distributed among the worshippers present (a common Hindu practice). The Hette image is kept on the shelf in the sanctum sanctorum, located in a roomed section which is the counterpart of the area used for processing milk in a Toda hut. As the sanctum sanctorum requires a sacred doorway with lamp, this and other houses for deities will be the only Badaga houses with two such doorways.

With the discovery that a hut similar to the Toda traditional hut was probably the internal functional inspiration for Kota and Badaga houses as well, we have returned full circle to origins. When the Toda adopted Badaga half and full houses for their own, note how they typically used each kitchen for their expression of the functional relationships in their traditional huts, and thus created Toda micro-microworlds within Badaga microworlds. Of all features, it is the earthen sleeping platform that is the most characteristic of the Toda.

From Calf Shelters to Toda Houses

Government efforts toward improvement are sometimes institutionalized through campaigns. By 1990 there was a campaign to build wells for the Todas, but in 1988 there was a campaign to construct calf shelters. The calf shelters approximate each other in size, are constructed with stones and cement, have two entranceways, and frequently have ridged asbestos sheeting roofs. In that each costs Rs 10,000, it is no wonder that humans eventually eject buffalo calves from these substantial structures and appropriate them as houses for themselves. We thus have an illustration of how structures designed for one purpose may eventually be used for altogether another purpose by quirky, unpredictable people.

Calf shelters built thus far are aligned or scattered in some Toda hamlets (Fig. 9.11, in which not all calf shelters are shown). Designers probably never realized how their calf shelters would provide ideal frameworks for conversions to housing and introduction of the functional relationships in traditional Toda huts. The year 1988 identifies the start of a diffusion wave involving calf shelters among the Toda. The start took place at Peleṯxwaṟ, where Tamilian labourers appropriated one of two calf shelters for a house. In 1988 the first Toda family occupied a similar shelter at Naṯe·s̠. To create a single unit Toda house, a family simply closes off one of the two entranceways in a calf shelter. In the example at Naṯe·s̠, with a left side entrance, an earthen sleeping platform was formed in the back, the fireplace was placed to the right front, and a storage platform and shelves were built next to the right wall. The spacing of entranceways in calf shelters also enables the construction of sitting platforms, one being next to the left wall in this example. The *puja* shelf with lamp at Naṯe·s̠ is also located where the lamp in a traditional hut should be. Note, however, that a repeated design flaw is also present in the house at Naṯe·s̠: the tilting of the roof toward the front, so that monsoonal rain falling on the roof is diverted towards any human entering the house. Both 1988 calf shelters at Kaxwïṛy and the 1988 northernmost calf shelter at Iṣaṟoṛ were converted to houses before the end of 1990.

It is remarkable that, in 1988 and at Pïlkwï·ṛ, an inventive Toda actually designed and built a house based upon the calf shelter design. Notable too is his construction of a front wall that is higher than the rear wall, so that monsoonal rain falling on his roof is shed backward and thus away from any humans entering his house. It 1988, in conformity with what one expects to find in a single unit Toda house, there was a right entrance, left front fireplace, left wall storage shelves, a rear sleeping platform, and right lamp where it would be in a hut. A fascinating change related to the creation of a non-traditional interior had taken place by the end of 1990. So that foreigners and non-Toda neighbours would not have to remove their shoes upon entering the house, a separate and enclosed mini-kitchen was formed next to the right wall. To accommodate it, a new sleeping platform was built in from the left wall. The former fireplace area was converted to smooth flooring, so that guests

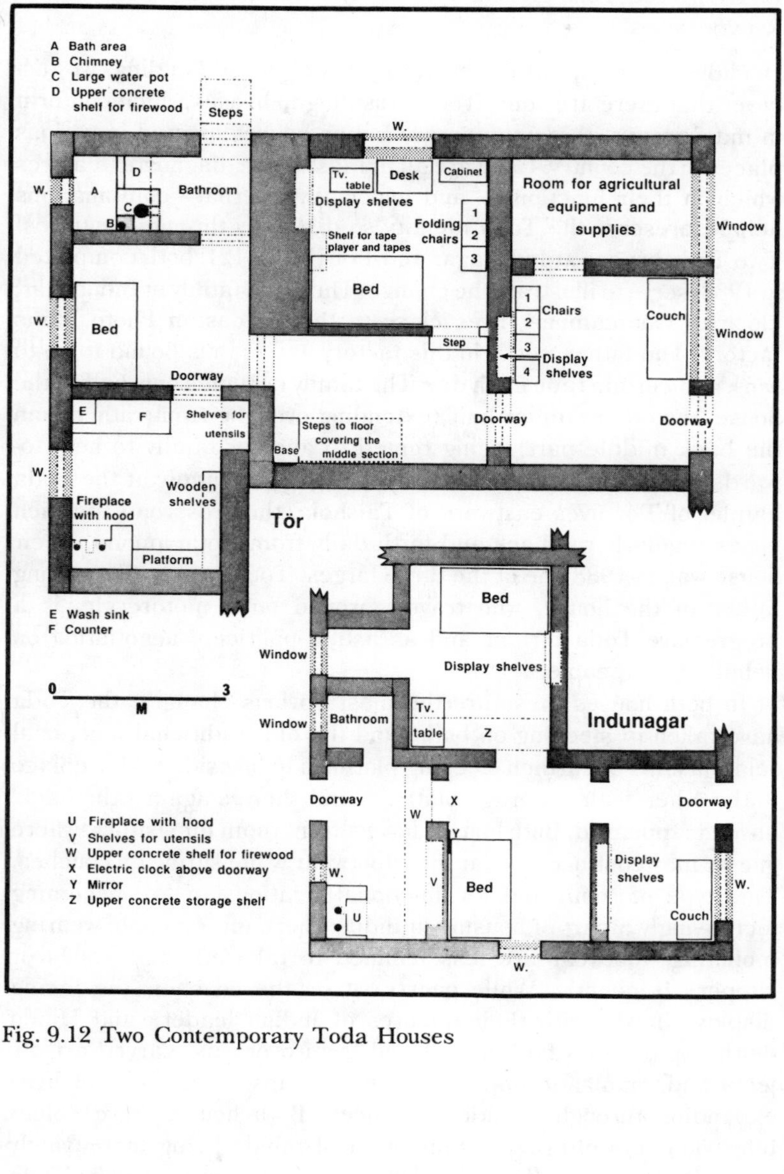

Fig. 9.12 Two Contemporary Toda Houses

could have unimpaired access to the sleeping platform, sometimes a sitting platform.

Contemporary Toda Houses without the Earlier Functional Relationships

Decades later, and after several cycles of house building, we discover that there are some Todas residing in houses which conform in many ways with contemporary Indian houses located in various places in the country. Gone are all or most of the diagnostic features which in their functional—and especially internal—combinations helped preserve the Toda identity so distinctly through centuries! Two Toda houses at Indunagar and Tör (Fig. 9.12), both completed in 1988, serve to illustrate the change. The Toda family at Indunagar, close to Ootacamund, lives close to the Hindustan Photo Films factory. The father works in this factory and is thus bound to go to work at a certain time each day. The family occupies only half of the house, the other similar half (extending over the front rather than the back middle part) being rented to another family to help towards the payment of the monthly mortgage. A family at the Toda hamlet of Tör lives eastward of Taishola, the crossroad to which buses regularly run back and forth daily from Ootacamund. Their house was in 1988 one of the three largest Toda houses. The young father of the house, who travels around on a motorcycle, is a progressive Toda farmer and an astute politician negotiating on behalf of his people.

In both houses these are the most obvious changes: the Toda have taken to sleeping on beds, and the old traditional functional relationships of earthen sleeping platform to one side and fireplace to the other, with a storage platform and shelves against the back, have disappeared. Both houses have a front room for visitors, where guests may continue to wear their footwear while sitting on couches. This type of room and its functional relationship are becoming increasingly a part of housing in India, where more people wearing 'polluting' footwear are less inclined to take off their shoes or slippers frequently. While guests sit on the couches, the facing display shelves with their pictures of Indian leaders and Hindu deities, postcards both inland and from overseas, carved art objects and/or plastic objects bought on trips, offer proof of lives expanding through outside influences. Both houses have colour television sets offering further proof of minds being increasingly opened to outside influences. Within less than five years, the Toda

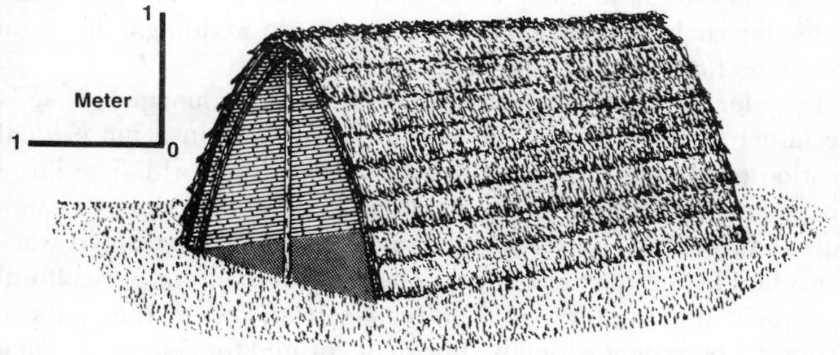

Suggested by an illustration in Barron, 1837, *Views in India*.

From Royal Anthropological Institute of Great Britain and Ireland, photo. 6546; and Rivers, *The Todas*, Fig. 45 on pg. 314.

Fig. 9.13 Toda Confinement Huts

have shown an amazingly rapid transition from the use of black and white to colour television. While both houses have fireplaces that are low-lying, there are hoods and chimneys above for the containment of smoke and its dispersal to the outside. Past to present Toda culture in both houses is most solidly reflected by the sets of shelves upon which utensils are so conspicuously displayed. The growing popularity of chrome utensils varying in size and easily bought in bazaars is evident in many Toda houses. It has become customary to display such objects conspicuously at Toda weddings, the main occasions for the gift-giving of such things.

The electric clock above the doorway of the Indunagar house is the latest icon, replacing the ancient lamp, and in a more ideal position to mingle symbolically with the outside world. The large mirror next to the door bespeaks fresh commitment, hasty examinations of self for appearances' sake before rushing off to work controlled by the master of time. The special room for agricultural equipment and supplies at Tör results from recent demands in farming. Equipment within had been decorated for Saraswati Puja, a Hindu event involving much festivity. The chairs reflect the increased raising of human bodies above ground level. The desk relates to a growing sense of agricultural business as a pursuit worthy as an object to work at and think of. The shelf for the tape player and tapes proves an interest in the new dimensions of sound. Steps to the floor covering the middle section in the Tör house lead to an upstairs *puja* room with the images and pictures of Hindu deities. The bathroom is unique among the Toda in having a special device to heat bath water. Lastly, the unique washing sink and counter further contribute to the raising of human bodies above ground level, for they enable individuals to stand and wash at the sink or prepare food at the counter.

Conclusions

Toda dwellings are functionally organized in relationship to a right versus left entrance, and there is a logical structural progression in development from the simplest hut to the most complex Toda full-Badaga houses. The word 'Badaga' is used here because Toda houses, especially those with brick and mortar walls and Mangalore tiles, are inextricably influenced by the houses which the Badaga have built before. Right versus left organization, which is maintained throughout, albeit in slightly modified form in full Badaga houses, is based upon the traditional Toda functional relationships within huts of sleeping platform to one side, the fireplace to the other, and storage platform and shelves located in the back of the hut. The functional relationships in the two basic traditional hut plans with right or left entrances are particularly well preserved in the entire spectrum we have examined, with the kitchens of the more advanced houses serving as the units in which the two plans are retained.

Thatched Toda huts with two traditional interiors thus generally have a right or left entrance and are either barrel-vaulted or front-gabled. There are also combinations of two huts that are either (*a*) back-to-back or (*b*) with the back extension hut having a side entrance. At Nü·ḷn there is the only combination of front hut with three back huts having side entrances. A model that attempts to explain the custom of orienting sleeping platforms toward the north in traditional huts suggests a symbolic system based upon an attracting northerly quadrant versus a repelling southerly quadrant.

Toda houses with traditional interior functional relationships range from single unit houses, to houses with front extensions, to houses with side extensions, to half Badaga houses, to full Badaga houses.

When we return full circle to origins, there is clear evidence for Kota and Badaga houses being derived from simple huts having one or the other interior functional relationships. The traditional Toda right versus left functional relationship is consistently retained by the Toda when they adapt to the use of Badaga half and full houses, in turn based upon the traditional functional relationships. Thus there are in these Toda houses Toda micro-microworlds within Badaga microworlds.

Calf shelters built by government are constructed in such a way as to be easily adapted to single unit houses with the two Toda traditional interior functional relationships. The basic form of the calf shelter has already been creatively adapted by a Toda who then went a step further to devise a non-traditional interior in which the main secular room was separated from a sacred mini-kitchen.

Finally, there are now some Toda who live in contemporary pan-Indian houses without the Toda traditional interior functional relationships. Even the earthen sleeping platform, the single most diagnostic feature in Toda dwellings, is missing in these.

Note

Field work undertaken in the Nilgiris was enabled in 1962–3 by the Office of Naval Research, in 1988 by the Faculty Research Council of the University of Missouri, in 1990 by the National Geographic Society, and in 1994 by the Research Board, University of Missouri. The 1988 and 1990 work could not have been accomplished without generous assistance from Muthicane Toda, Catherine C. Noble, and Jennifer D. Noble, to whom the writer is extremely grateful. Thanks are also extended to the ever patient and generous Badagas, Kotas, and Todas who permitted the invasion of their privacy so that the plans of their dwelling could be drawn.

References

Baikie, Robert 1834 *Observations on the Nilgiris.* Calcutta: Baptist Mission Press.

Barron, Richard 1837 *Views in India, chiefly among the Neilgherry Hills.* London, Havell.

Emeneau, Murray B. 1967 *Dravidan Linguistics, Ethnology, and Folktales: Collected Papers.* (Linguistics Dapartment, Publication 8.) Annamalainagar: Annamalai University Press.

Glassie, Henry 1979 *Folk Housing in Middle Virginia.* Knoxville: University of Tennessee.

Grigg, Henry B. *et al.* 1880 *A Manual of the Nilagiri District in the Madras Presidency.* Madras: Government Press.

Hallpike, C. R. 1979 *The Foundations of Primitive Thought.* Oxford: Clarendon Press.

Jagor, Fedor 1876 Die Badagas im Nilgiri-Gebirge. *Verhandlungen der Berliner Gesellschaft für Anthropologie, Ethnologie und Urgeschichte* 8: 190–204.

Noble, William A., and A. William Jebadhas 1989 'The Irulas' *In* Paul Hockings (ed.) *Blue Mountains: The Ethnography and Biogeography of a South Indian Region.* Delhi: Oxford University Press 281–303, end plates 21, 21.

Ranga, N. A. 1934 *The Tribes of the Nilgiris: Their Social and Economic Condition.* Madras: Bharat Publishing House.

Rivers, William 1906 *The Todas.* London: Macmillan & Co.

Sastri, S. M. Natesa 1892 'The Badagas of the Nilgiri District'. *Madras Christian College Magazine* 9: 753–64.

Shortt, John (ed.) 1868 *An Account of the Tribes of the Neilgherries and a Geographical and Statistical Memoir of the Neilgherry Mountains.* Madras: Higginbotham & Co.

Walker, Anthony R, 1986 *The Toda of South India: A New Look.* Delhi: Hindustan Publishing Co.

Rain, God, and Unity among the Kotas

RICHARD KENT WOLF

10

Father god who, with the black cow,
  set the first pillar
Where are you?. . .
Lamp lamp where are you? come god!
Are you in *toḍba·l*? come god!
Are you under the *ne·rl* tree? come god!
. . . Are you in *ponic*? come god!

'*veḷke· veḷke·*', a Kota song from Kolme·l

In the story behind the epigraphical song and others like it, a community finds that divine presence depends on communal harmony, unity, and righteous living. Among the Kotas it is a formulation found in various guises: the folklore of devotional music, stories of divine locales, and the ritual structure of worship. In this essay I will analyse all of these forms in a rain-making ceremony the Kotas perform every summer, just before the monsoon.[1] The rain ceremony and the eclectic approach I have employed to discuss it will, I hope, allow us to explore in depth what unity *means* in Kota society, how Kotas have interpreted its relative absence as they have assessed their past and present, and how these questions may have been affected by notions of 'tribe,' Hinduism, and morality projected upon the Kotas from without. I adopted the tactic, now well established in anthropology, of gleaning central cultural issues through the analysis of one event in critical detail. What I hope to accomplish, on a broader methodological level, is a successful narrative synthesis of diverse elements: historical-anthropological, ethnomusicological, personal narrative (with several voices), descriptive, and symbolic-analytical.

The first part of this essay provides a broad context for the analysis of the ceremony. There are three subsections. The first considers what it means for the Kotas to be a 'tribe' in south India. The second provides historical background on two anthropologists studying the Kotas in the thirties: Murray B. Emeneau and the late David G. Mandelbaum. The third section introduces K. Sulli, a Kota reformer and a salient voice in the anthropological record of the tribe. The second part of this paper is a discussion of how the music of the rain ceremony derives meaning from rituals and mytho-historical events extrinsic to it. The third part is a narrative analysis of the ceremony as it unfolds, alternating between a macroview of the whole ceremony in performance and microviews examining the significance of each part in some detail. Finally, I offer a broad analytic view of the entire ceremony, including suggestions as to its origins.

To begin with, I will provide a rather rarified survey of the arguments and issues that will emerge, fleshed out and hopefully lucid, from the analysis. The ceremony is one among several Kota ceremonies which *institutionalize* an association between village unity, righteousness and the efficacy of the Kota gods. The trope of unity is evidenced at several analytical levels. In analysing the overall form, we note first that the rain ceremony consists of a procession to all the 'god places' that border the village and the sequential performance of a special repertoire of twelve 'god tunes'. I would suggest that, by virtue of belonging to one ceremony, the constituent places and tunes belong to one category—albeit a ritually constituted one—and thus establish a 'unity' as regards ritual function.[2] Why this should be the case, and how this bears on behaviour and religious efficacy, will become clear as we consider what these places and musical pieces mean to the Kotas.

Unity in the physical space Kotas occupy is another variation on this trope. Spatial unity is affirmed as the procession traces village boundaries and thereby secures the presence of divinity within them. Phenomenologically, the ceremony would seem to create an experience of temporal unity, by 'binding' the past with the present,[3] and psychic unity, by attempting to insure that all the Kotas are of 'one mind'. It can thus be considered an argument that the Kotas perform for themselves, asserting fundamental social-cultural harmony.[4] The ceremony exemplifies what James Fernandez has described as 'returning to the whole' (1986: 188–213) in that, like revitalization movements and 'perhaps all religions', it is 'fundamentally interested in restoring the relatedness of things' (1986: 191).

When the integrity of the village landscape is recreated in procession, the power of and belief in the gods affirmed through prayer, and the association between land, place and person further established through the power of musical performance and the divine stories this music recalls, rain will come, as they say, 'without fail'.[5] Stated more generally, when unity and righteousness have been 'achieved' (ritually, at least) the Kota gods behave as Kotas would have them behave and the community thrives: rain falls, crops grow abundantly, cattle multiply, children are born and survive, diviners divine and ritual leaders stay alive.

The theme of unity in the ceremony as a whole is mirrored in constituent domains such as verbal discourse, in the ritual phrase, 'Is everybody joined?' and gesture, in the formal sharing of tobacco. In addition, while the enactment of the ceremony establishes a series of analogies and correspondences between its components, the landscape and music involved in the ceremony are, not surprisingly, symbolically loaded in and of themselves. 'Gods' places' (*devrd eṛm*) and 'god tunes' (*devr koḷ*) generally encode perspectives on multiple pasts which seek to preserve the equation of divine efficacy with righteous living as a 'Kota'.[6] Encoding and re-encoding occur in the recounting of stories connected with these places and tunes: each story recalls an event in which divine beings appear to have 'come to the rescue' in moments of stress.

The need to restore wholeness is felt 'particularly in times of stress—where literal routines break down and where we are constrained by false or moribund categories' (Fernandez 1986: 205–6). The tension between the collective creation of the whole, as embodied in the rain ceremony (and, in other ways, in other rituals as well), and the tendency toward community disintegration, embodied in disagreement, the negotiation of modernity, and physical disasters (disease, drought, or inability to complete a ritual), constitutes one of the enduring problematics of Kota society. This tension, I believe, provides an overall clue to understanding the rain ceremony.

The problems of disunity, breaking of rules, changing of norms, and so forth, which are in a sense ritually countered by the rain ceremony, are at the same time presupposed by the very need for its yearly performance. During my investigation of the history of the ritual, I came across materials that may allow us to speculate about the creation of the rain ceremony. At the conclusion of this paper I will consider evidence suggesting that the ceremony may have been invented (or modified into its present form) in 1933, in response to a particular set of modern circumstances which threatened the community.

As a strategy designed in a sense to mirror and in a sense to exemplify and evoke the disunity that I describe as a *raison d'être* for the ceremony, my account includes conflicting statements the Kotas have provided us about the ceremony. I also include conflicting accounts in order to avoid erasing the problems inherent in attempting to abstract, from situations 'on-the ground', coherent cultural systems. One is constantly reminded that *individuals* are involved in that peculiar process of culture-making which unfolds during ethnographic research.[7] It seems important, therefore, to consider situations in which people argue over the details of what occurs in a ritual as well as what it means.

On the other hand, not all individuals can be represented, and not all voices are invested with equal authority to speak for the community. Thus, even though I feel compelled to counter implications that the Kotas, who number only 1,500, are an undifferentiated whole, I will not discredit the value of understanding 'the Kotas' through the thoughtful and creative products of unusually talented or otherwise unconventional individuals.

Striking a meaningful balance (or synthesis) of synoptic, holistic views (*the* Kotas, *the* ceremony, *the* structure) with analyses of how meaning is actually created in specific times and places becomes, then, a central task. Understanding a cultural unit like the rain ceremony in structural terms, for example, must be broadened through a situational perspective—a perspective which recognizes that individual agents (the men who perform the ceremony, decide how the ceremony is to be performed, or argue about what a particular gesture means) create an event while at the same time subtly registering broad macroscopic cultural schema within it—here, the grammar of 'unity' and the discourse of 'tradition'.[8]

This situational perspective involves not only actors of the present but also figures from the past, particularly because some accounts and interpretations of the rain ceremony are historical, appearing in the fieldnotes of the late David G. Mandelbaum. To use

Mandelbaum's material critically it will be necessary to examine the dynamics of fieldwork during his first trip to India (1937-8); and, more generally, the problems associated with using other people's fieldnotes (cf. Smith 1990; Lutkehaus 1990; Sanjek 1990, *passim*), and the multiple histories which are produced when ethnographies of the past are introduced into frameworks based on fieldwork of the present.[9]

A practical problem follows from attempting to combine these diverse sources into a single account. The dimensions of the problem include:

(1) My observations of the rain ceremony in 1991 and 1992;
(2) Kotas reporting on how the ceremony is 'supposed' to be done;
(3) Kotas reporting on how the ceremony has actually been done, based on their memory;
(4) Kotas reporting on how the ceremony has actually been done, based on what they have heard from other Kotas;
(5) Kotas, no longer alive (like Sulli), whose reports are preserved in David Mandelbaum's fieldnotes or publications;
(6) Kotas commenting upon what other Kotas have reported or what I have observed.

The differences between these six perspectives are not merely problems of narrative, of course, but interesting problems in and of themselves. By sifting through, juxtaposing and comparing the histories, descriptions and interpretations I encountered in the process of understanding the rain ceremony, I hope to lead the reader through an epistemological journey that is in some ways like fieldwork (confusing, open-ended, difficult to control). But multiple perspectives, disagreement, and the contestation of 'history' itself are not only in the nature of fieldwork, they are embedded in the ways the Kotas view themselves as a people.

Views of the Kotas: Inside and Outside, Then and Now

The Kotas as a 'Tribe'

The Kotas number about 1,500 (by their own estimates in 1990) and live in seven villages scattered widely across the Nilgiri Hills. The government of India lists the Kotas as a 'Scheduled Tribe'—a designation which purports to safeguard the community against 'exploitation' and to make it eligible for government welfare programmes. The Constitution however does not specify what constitutes a 'tribe',[10] and as a result the label does little to characterize the Kotas as a people. I do not wish to enter into a lengthy discussion about what a 'tribe' in India is, or whether such a term is applicable[11]—clearly the term is a polythetic one (cf. Needham 1975).

Instead, I want to explore the popular images inspired by the word 'tribe,' and its vernacular equivalents. The Hindi word *ādivāsi*, meaning 'original inhabitant', and the Tamil term *paḻaṅkuṭi makkaḷ*, 'ancient race people', are of fairly recent origin. To my knowledge there are no terms in ancient Tamil or Sanskrit which indicate that modern notions of tribe were ever operative in ancient Indian principles of classifying people (George Hart 1993, pers. com.). Even though individual tribe-like (by modern standards) communities were named in many early texts, there were no terms for identifying 'tribe' as a unit of classification.

What, then, does that term 'tribe' conjure up in the minds of Indians today? In a popular construction, the tribe is hypostatized and somehow equated with the primeval Indian.[12] 'The Scheduled Tribes are the real sons of the Indian soil. They are the original people of India who have variously been known as backward tribes, primitive tribes, criminal tribes, *Adimjati* and everything else' (Mehta 1991: 9)

The image ramifies: as 'sons of the soil', the tribals are, if left to their own devices, at one with nature, self-sufficient. They hunt and gather, excel in crafts, are experts in the use of traditional medicines and are capable of sorcery. Tribal gods too are somehow seen to possess an abundance of divine power. Although, or perhaps because, these tribals are more imagined than real, the myth prevails. Many people assume that the tribes of today live in an eroded state, corrupted by modern society from some pre-modern natural state.

In modern India, these populist notions of tribe cannot be considered in isolation from the way any community—a 'tribe', so called—constructs itself as a tribe. And among the Kotas many of these notions do indeed dominate discussions about tribalness. Some brief examples may clarify what I mean. R. Mathi and S. Cindamani, two women in their late forties with whom I had developed a relatively familial relationship, were concerned with attempts by another community to claim tribal status.[13] Their rhetorical questions expressed exasperation, 'How can they be tribal? Do they know blacksmithing? Do they know how to make pots? Are they musicians?'

Many Nilgiri tribals think of themselves in similar terms. R. Mathi's son, Duryodana[14] (my research assistant, close friend and companion), used to enjoy meeting other tribals and enthusiastically accompanied me whenever I visited other tribal villages. In such situations I observed him engaging in lively conversation with other tribal men about honey-collecting, hunting and trapping, and the characteristics of the local flora and fauna. He felt, and believed that other tribals felt, that the Nilgiri tribes share authority in domains of knowledge connected with the forest, craftsmanship and music. These feelings can be said to separate the ways tribal communities view each other from the ways they view non-tribals.

The image of the tribal as the 'primeval Indian' is refashioned and reaffirmed in public displays such as Republic Day, when in the town of Ootacamund the Todas, Kotas, and Irulas are called to sing, dance, and play in full costume. The image tribals themselves construct of intertribal communities is affirmed in similar performances, both participatory and for display, in modern revitalization movements.[15]

MA·MU·L AND OCMU·L

Moving now to a discussion of how Kotas construct themselves as a community, it is possible, and indeed desirable, to deal with concepts growing directly out of Kota discourse. Once such concept is associated with the word, *ma·mu·l*, a term (ironically) of Arabic origin, meaning for the Kotas 'the old way', or 'tradition, custom'.[16] Its opposite, *ocmu·l*, has connotations of foreignness and inauthenticity on one hand, and progressiveness, modernity and vitality on the other.[17]

The Kota word *ma·mu·l* frequently refers to practices of the past—both the 'everyday' variety and those formalized ritually: games, rituals, songs, dances, language, dress and ways of threshing can all be discussed in terms of their *ma·mu·l*-ness. The term is also applied to people who support the old ways or who are themselves very old.[18] A related term is *kaṭ* (*DEDR* 1147), which means 'knot', and by extension 'custom'—that which has been 'tied,' or established firmly.

Ocmu·l practices are regarded ambivalently: at times enthusiastically by those who regard new practices as somehow inauthentic, or threatening to the integrity of the Kotas; and at times sceptically by those who regard new practices as somehow inauthentic, or threatening the integrity of the Kotas. Those who introduce new practices are sometimes regarded with suspicion as well (see, e.g., Mandelbaum 1941; 1960), especially if these people are seen to benefit personally from such new practices.

It seems reasonable to speculate that as the primevalist view of the tribal became increasingly disseminated in the popular media, and as it seems to have grown into one of the informal philosophical bases of public policy, tribes like the Kotas became increasingly self-reflexive about themselves not only as a distinctive ethnic group, but also as a tribal ethnic group. This reflexivity, at least currently, is expressed in the relationship between and the values assigned to *ma·mu·l* and *ocmu·l*.[19] This all becomes relevant to the rain ceremony because the form and content of the ceremony itself point to a conscious awareness of tradition, and the past, that calls for some explanation.

Ma·mu·l and *ocmu·l* are of course very close to what English speakers call tradition and modernity and indeed the issues involved with the tensions between them tend toward cultural universals. My intention here is to bring into focus how the Kotas deal with these issues within their cultural framework. But to do this it is necessary, of course, to recognize the complex historical matrix which gave rise to Kota culture in modern India in the first place.

Anthropologists among the Kotas: David G. Mandelbaum and Murray B. Emeneau

It is often difficult to evaluate in anything but general terms the dynamics of influence between communities in contact (let alone broad entities like Hindu and tribal, Indian and English), the specific ways in which particular communities have responded to colonial and other rulership, or the impact of individuals (writers, administrators, scholars, or cultural leaders) on the history of a community, without considering suggestive historical moments, periods in which persons, places and events intersect in ways that impress upon the cultural history of a community a configuration that appears unique and lasting. Here I wish to consider one such consequential period, both because this consideration will facilitate a critical assessment of data from this period and because it will help situate the history of the rain ceremony itself.

In the period beginning some ten years after a disease decimated Kolme·l village, two scholars arrived to study the Kotas: the Canadian linguist Murray B. Emeneau (b. 1904), who had by then (early fall of 1935) already earned a Ph.D. in Latin, Greek and Sanskrit (1931) and studied ethnological linguistics with Sapir;[20] and the late David Mandelbaum (1911–87), who had written a doctoral thesis (1936) on the Plains Cree, under the direction of Edward Sapir. Mandelbaum arrived in the Nilgiris in April 1937 after a brief stint in Kerala among the tribes of Travancore and the Jews of Cochin (Mandelbaum 1939a; 1939b).

Emeneau was the first philologically trained North American scholar to take an anthropological interest in Indian culture, and certainly the first to apply philological methods to unwritten Indian languages. Mandelbaum was the first American cultural anthropologist to conduct fieldwork in India. By virtue of these circumstances along, both scholars were staking out new ground for American anthropology.

But significantly new events were taking place among the Kotas as well. The thirties was a time of stress for the Kotas of Kolme·l because after the lice-borne 'relapsing fever' struck, the village was left without ritual specialists (*ca·trṅga·rn*) to conduct ceremonies in the traditional fashion. Partly in response to this devastating event, which was believed to be evidence that the Kotas were committing some terrible wrong, and partly to improve their social status in relation to their Hindu and other tribal neighbours, a movement arose to advocate worshiping a new set of deities and another movement arose attempting to modernize Kota ways—particularly as regards the slaughtering of bovine, the seclusion of women during menstruation, and the male style of wearing the hair long.

K. Sulli in Time Perspective

Leading in some of the reforms was a Kota school teacher, K. Sulli,[21] a man schooled by missionaries and who, as a child, even wished to convert to Christianity; although prevented from doing so by his father, Sulli maintained a life-long interest in Christianity and belief in Jesus Christ.[22] Emeneau's contacts in Ooty summoned Sulli, the only English–speaking Kota at the time, to facilitate his study of the Kotas' language. Emeneau had established a routine and style of working with Sulli before Mandelbaum arrived. For a rupee a day, Sulli would come to Emeneau's room in Ooty and dictate stories. Sulli took leave of his teaching job throughout the period of employment with the Americans.

When Mandelbaum arrived in the Nilgiris after three months of exasperating fieldwork with informants (in Travancore) whom he felt to be singularly lacking in volubleness, Sulli seemed to harbour a change in luck. But soon, judging from comments in Mandelbaum's field journals (Mandelbaum n.d.), Mandelbaum became frustrated with Sulli's unfocused loquacity: Sulli was a tap that could not be turned off, wandering from topic to topic, tangent to tangent, and embellishing stories and events with elaborate detail.

Neither Emeneau nor Mandelbaum knew or learned Tamil while they were in India,[23] and neither of them actually learned to speak the Kota language with any fluency. Although Sulli was the only Kota with whom either scholar could communicate directly,[24] Mandelbaum did work with other Kota informants with the help of Christian Badaga interpreters.[25] And he was careful to collect alternative interpretations and points of view from non-Kotas.[26] If Mandelbaum was forced to rely heavily on Sulli, it was not uncritically, however, as this account of Sulli's traits as an 'ethnological respondent' illustrates:

> One is that his recollection tends to be neater and more integrated than was the historical actuality. His narrative artistry is apt to gloss over inconsistencies or irregularities and to make one episode follow another in logical, abstracted sequences that may have more aesthetic symmetry than historical exactness. Sulli has the kind of integrating, abstracting mind which one may consider to be more properly the prerogative of the ethnological theorist than of the ethnologist's informant.
>
> Secondly, he is like any gifted narrator of events in which he took part and of which he finds reason to be proud. He tends to figure much larger in his account than he may have in the event. *But when he gives an impersonal account of, say, ceremonies, these traits do not prevail.*
>
> Sulli, in turn, was influenced by his work with the linguist and the anthropologist. In the first instance, the association with two whom he called 'our Europeans' added to his prestige. It is not unlikely that this association gave him the final impetus, in 1937, to take the decisive step of cutting his hair (Mandelbaum 1960: 307; emphasis mine).

I emphasized the sentence concerning Sulli's accounts of ceremonies to make the point that informants, or 'native collaborators' (Clifford 1988: 49), may position themselves (or may be viewed by others) in different ways as regards what they describe, teach, or interpret (a ceremony, an incident, a song). Sulli figures himself prominently in village events but not in ritual.

But the annotations to Mandelbaum's fieldnotes of the thirties suggest Sulli's narration of ritual suffered from a different problem. Sulli used the English verb 'to say' both for actual utterance and for what Sulli *presumed* actors to be thinking. Dravidian languages contain a verb which is used both to mark the quotations of a speaker and to indicate what a speaker is thinking: in Kota the verb is *in-* (*DEDR* 868); I suspect Sulli's idiosyncratic tendency to confuse what was said from what was thought may have occurred as Sulli translated Kota thoughts into English sentences.[27] But in some ways the bigger problem was that Sulli tended to volunteer explanations of and intentions behind rituals in the first place. Sulli, like other informants described in Casagrande's *In the Company of Men* (1960), 'understood, often with real subtlety, what an *ethnographic* attitude toward culture entailed' (Clifford 1988: 49). Yet his role in controlling the kind of information Mandelbaum ultimately collected cannot be understimated.

For fourteen months out of my two-year fieldwork in the Nilgiris I lived in Sulli's home village, Kolme·l. The accounts I collected (1990–2) differed from those Mandelbaum and Emeneau reported in the thirties and forced me to think about my own informants and their memories, motives, and reliability in ways that presumably would have been different if these writings did not exist.

Because the Kota memory (actual and/or legendary) of Mandelbaum was a positive one, Mr K. Pucan (an eighty-year-old man who was highly regarded in the village, both as an elder and as a musician) and other Kotas who disputed what I had learned from Mandelbaum's notes, would tell me that Sulli was lying about one matter, ignorant concerning another, or inventing data concerning yet another—rather than blame Mandelbaum for what they believed was inaccurate.

Some of my elderly friends in Kolme·l had personal reasons for discrediting Sulli. For example, one lady in her eighties, Pa. Mathi, claimed that Sulli had kept a Kuṟumba man (member of a tribe feared for its sorcery) in his attic and through him killed her ten children and her brother. She further claimed that Sulli's abundant wealth was a result of sorcery. Sulli is not remembered, other than by his family, for positive contributions to the Kota community. In fact, by some he is remembered as a self-aggrandizing trouble-maker. His status outside the community in some ways weakened his authority inside the village.[28]

Despite the fact that Sulli was trying to 'modernize' Kota culture, despite an apparent interest in Christianity, and despite his familiarity with European ways,[29] it appears that Sulli still commanded a detailed knowledge of Kota history, stories and ritual. He may not have been considered any more 'right' in his day than he is now (if one were to conduct a poll), but neither can all the differences between accounts by Sulli and by others be understood as only ideological differences.

The Music of the Rain Ceremony

The following cultural analysis of music in the rain ceremony will consider first the overall structure of the musical repertoire and how it functions within a ritual framework. Then I will consider in turn the symbolism of each constituent 'god tune,' numbering each set of paragraphs for convenient cross-reference later in the text.

Instrumental tunes, or *koḷ*.[30] of the Kotas differentiate, mark, and partially constitute ritual occasions.[31] There is a repertoire for dancing, a repertoire for funerals and a repertoire for 'god'. Each is characterized by broad stylistic features, but the criteria for distinction between repertoires are to a greater extent contextual and singular (piece by piece) than they are musical.

Within each repertoire, a particular tune may be associated with a particular action (in a funeral, for example, one tune is associated with lifting and carrying the bier to the cremation ground). In general, the ways in which the structure of instrumental melodies coarticulates with ritual structures can be analysed as a system of indigenous classification in and of itself.

Melodies are accompanied by one of two basic rhythmic patterns, each of which may be elaborated in different ways. In Kolme·l the rhythms are called *ca·da da·k* ('ordinary variety') and *tirugana·ṭ da·k* ('turning dance variety'). Unlike the complex rhythms performed for various occasions by *Paṟaiyar* or *Cakkaliyar* ensembles on the plains in Tamil Nadu, rhythms performed by Nilgiri tribes are not used to differentiate ritual occasions—although they do differentiate dances.[32]

The twelve 'god tunes,' performed in the Kolme·l rain ceremony are found also in the yearly god ceremony, *devr.*[33] Pragmatic considerations have rendered obsolete ritual practices originally associated with some of these tunes, and in other cases, stories and other contextual material concerning these tunes have been forgotten.[34] The effect of these contextual changes has been, in one sense, an objectification of these tunes as independent musical objects—objects which can be employed in new contexts related, in principle at least, with the contexts for which they are named.

§1. The longest and decidedly most important tune among these is called the *o·la·gicd koḷ*[35] or *guṛy terdd koḷ* ('temple opening' tune). It is used during the annual ceremony of opening the three Kota temples and during other rituals associated with this act. Although the opening of the temple itself is not among the rituals that have been discontinued over the years—it is one of the central features of the god ceremony—many accompanying activities have been abbreviated. For example, the *mundka·no·ns* (ritual leaders) throw grass onto the roof of the temple to suggest symbolically the ancient practice of rebuilding the temple each year. The 'temple opening tune', which is performed to call god regardless of whether or not the temple is directly involved, is in a sense the hypostasis of divine music. As such, this tune also constitutes a necessary beginning of the rain ceremony.

The other eleven *kols* are named as well. These names are one of the means through which each *koḷ* comes to recall a particular context, story or bit of Kota history or a deity, when the original practice which gave rise to these associations has been lost. Knowledge of these *koḷs* and their stories is rather esoteric and for this reason it was difficult to cross-check some details. Because Mr K. Pucan is one of the most widely respected musicians, his conception of instrumental music should be of interest to us. But we must not accept Pucan's authority unconditionally: Mr S. Raman, another respected *koḷ* player, insists that some *kols* do not have names (for example the difference between the 'goddess' *koḷ* and 'father god' *koḷ* he believes, is factitious).[36] Nevertheless, the *devr koḷ* 'lore' was not invented for my benefit[37] and provides useful insights into Kota cosmology and the rain ceremony.

The general point is that the god tunes are 'meaningful' to Kotas in different degrees, not so much in different ways. A few Kota men and probably even fewer, if any, Kota women recognize each tune, know one or more alternate names for it, and know whatever story may be connected with it. More Kotas know that the tunes have names, and know some of the names, but do not know which tune is which; they may or may not know any extramusical associations. Finally some people may or may not recognize that tunes are god tunes by listening, but know that such a repertoire exists and know, because of the performance context, when the tunes are being performed. To them, the tunes are simply associated in some way with the gods.

The Stories behind the Devr Koḷs

§2. Some of the *devr koḷs,* or 'god tunes,' can be characterized as such because they are literally named after deities. The origin of the shortest such tune, the *ni·lgiri co·ym koḷ* or 'Nilgiri god tune', is obscure, as is knowledge concerning the deity. According to Mr Valmand Kamatn of Kolme·l, a former *mundka·no·n,*[38] the 'Nilgiri god' is a primordial Nilgiri divinity who resides in a place called Talko·r[39] at the top of a hill where buffaloes were tended (*mala·ṛ impayṭ*). After some unspecified conflict or ritual misconduct the deity moved to Rangasami Peak.

The *ayṇo·r mundka·no·n* (the ritual leader for worship of the 'father god') of Kina·ṛ village recalled a legend in which the Nilgiri *co·ym* revealed himself to a Kota and an Irula who were walking together. Both Kotas and Irulas began to worship the Nilgiri god at that same spot until some quarrel separated them: the Irulas began to worship on Rangasami Peak and the Kotas near their village—both at the same time of the year (May). The Irulas are priests for 'Nilgiri Ranga,' the deity of Rangasami Peak.[40]

It appears there is some identity between 'Rangasami' worshipped by the Irulas and 'Nilgiri God' of the Kotas.[41] Though Kotas from Kina·ṛ village and Porga·ṛ village worship at and attend Rangasami festivals it is doubtful that the deity is popularly identified with their own Nilgiri *co·ym.* The location of the 'original Nilgiri God' (that is, of the origin stories) was probably the environs of Kina·ṛ village (as opposed to other Kota villages) because this village is relatively near Rangasami Peak. Today a small shrine for Nilgiri God stands just at the border of Kina·ṛ village, where a festival honouring it is held each March.[42]

Koḷ players say they play the Nilgiri God tune while walking to and from places of worship because it is short and easy. In Kolme·l, since no shrine exists there for the Nilgiri God, the performance of the tune is not associated with any particular place. But inclusion of the Nilgiri God tune in the divine repertoire also marks the deity itself as a Kota one. Incorporating the Nilgiri God in the Kota pantheon is a gesture tying the Kotas of all seven villages to the land they inhabit: that is, the Nilgiri God is somehow seen to be, as its name suggests, a primordial divinity connected with the physical place of the Nilgiris, a numen. To the extent that the tune itself recalls stories of the god—in this case fairly unlikely because detailed knowledge of this deity is rare—the tune recalls a former relationship between Kotas and Irulas that was broken, resulting in worship of the same deity in different places. In a sense, then, the Nilgiri God is associated with both a pan-Nilgiri tribal identity and the division into different tribes, each in its locality, and each with its styles of worship.

§3. Another incident of divisiveness, this time disunity within a village rather than disagreement between two men, is associated with a god tune that resembles the Nilgiri God tune, called the *Ki·rpuṭn meyṇ gubḷk oygd koḷ* ('tune for going to the herd of Kirputn's son'). Its story is rather suggestive:

A long time ago many cows were kept in Kolme·l. A terrible disease, affecting the throat and causing diarrhoea, began killing off the cows. The village diviner (*te·rka·rn*) was consulted and became possessed. The 'diarrhoea goddess' (*be·ydamn*), the diviner related, was affecting the cows because the men of Kolme·l were not of one mind—each was out for himself. *Ayṇo·r* (the Kota 'father god'), promising to send the goddess away from the village, began to sing this tune. The song mentions the names of the places along a route to the southwest on the way to the house of a Badaga—the son of one Ki·rpuṭn. This man was apparently branding as his own any cow or buffalo that strayed into his herd—he also had a reputation for cruelty. Within 'eight to fifteen days' the disease left Kolme·l and killed off the Badaga's cattle.[43]

This story exemplifies how divine favour depends on community solidarity. The story teaches, by example, that villagers should value the interests of the community over the interests of the individual: disunity had caused the cows to become ill. It further establishes the Badagas as an 'out group' and reinforces certain negative stereotypes of Badagas that some Kotas hold. The tune, ostensibly composed by *Ayṇo·r* ('father god') himself, is significant both as a divine 'product,' and as the aural reminder of a story and the cultural values that story encodes.

§4. A fourth tune, called the *padnet devr a·td koḷ* or 'eighteen god calling tune', is a bit puzzling. Thus far I have found reference to 'gods' only in Emeneau's *Kota Texts* (1944, III: 17), but the eighteen gods were not named. Mr Pucan suggested that eighteen refers not to gods but to feast days (*u·ṭm*) of the god festival. Nowadays the Kotas of Kolme·l alternate one-day and three-day feasts each year—although it is widely known that the feasts have been shortened over the years.[44] Whether the tune is named after eighteen gods, or as many feasts, or both, the tune seems to have previously had further significance or extrinsic association. Nowadays, to the extent that Kotas reflect at all upon the 'meaning' of the tune, the eighteen god tune is tied to vague notions of divinity, bygone practice, and tradition (*ma·mu·l*), but not to a particular story.

The lengthy feasting may have been connected, in a rather instrumental way, with the arduous process of temple reconstruction. Cane and bamboo collected from the forest were fashioned into a thatched enclosure. Supporting beams for the temples were collected from a 'milk tree' (*pa·l marm*, unidentified botanically, see *DEDR* 4100) in the 'shola' forest[45] called *kuy te·l* (lit.: 'hole forest'), about four kilometres southwest of Kolme·l on the route to Me·na·r village.

§5. The *kab ercd koḷ*, or 'post-cutting tune', originated in an event connected with collecting this 'milk tree'. Because somebody committed a ritual fault during the god ceremony one year, the Kotas could not locate a milk tree from which to cut a pillar for the temple. The diviner, consulted on this matter, put his wrists together behind his back (the characteristic posture for possession among the Kotas), shook and hopped backwards to the shola and revealed a milk tree.

As he hopped, he hummed a tune which the *koḷ* players memorized and subsequently adopted as the 'post-cutting tune'.[46] Like the *Ki·rpuṭn meyṇ koḷ*, (§3) this tune was ostensibly composed by god himself; and also like the *Ki·rpuṭn meyṇ koḷ*, this tune is a metonym for Kota religious values. Proper worship cannot be conducted without the cooperation of all Kotas: if one Kota violates a taboo, it constitutes an obstacle for the whole village. In subsequent years the musicians played the post-cutting tune at some time during the actual process of gathering posts.

In modern times when a permanent structure was erected the post-cutting ritual was unnecessary. But the post-cutting tune remains a nod to the past; whether understood as a reference to building the temple (a reference perceived by all because the name itself gives a clue), or whether understood in terms of the story (a less accessible reference because not all Kotas know the story).

§6. The stories associated with the *Ki·rpuṭn meyṇ* tune and the post-cutting tune suggest that the Kota gods respond favourably to Kota pleas for help. At one time, music was itself used for supplication. Each of three tunes, called *moyr paṭd koḷs*s (complaint experiencing tunes), were used to petition a deity, 'big father god' (*doḍayṇo·r*), 'little father god' (*kunayṇo·r*),[47] 'mother god[dess]' (*amno·r*). Among these, the *kunayṇo·r moyr paṭd koḷ* bears a strong melodic resemblance to the 'eighteen god calling tune' but is supported by a different rhythmic pattern.[48] Although these tunes are no longer used individually to petition particular deities they retain a sacral potency as part of the *devr koḷ* repertoire. They are, like several of the *devr koḷs,* sonic components of bygone rituals which have come to be preserved in a new context.

§7. Kotas 'make god' when they enact the god ceremony and part of this creative act used to include rebuilding the temples. But a more literal 'making' includes the fashioning of the 'faces' of the gods by pasting gold coins and silver ornaments (which were offerings to the god) on patties of cowdung. One man from each of three 'families' (*kuyts*s) is responsible for arranging these coins in the manner of a face on the right entrance-pillar of each of the three temples (one man per temple). Some Kotas think this practice is of recent origin and thus consider it inauthentic (*ocmu·l,* see above). This sentiment is of some consequence since some Kotas define themselves differently from Hindus (though not all do) by emphasizing the idea that Kotas do not represent their deities anthropomorphically. To diffuse the significance of the 'face' as something comparable to a Hindu idol, they explain that coins and ornaments had long been pasted on the temples as offerings to the gods, but over the years people had begun arranging the many ornaments into a decorative pattern, a face. For many of the Kotas who consider themselves Hindu, the face *is* an anthropomorphic representation of the god and, in this sense, *is* like a Hindu idol. For these Kotas the age of the practice is not the issue—new or old, it is a practice culturally valid—and the responsibility of fashioning the face is also an honour. The two perspectives on making the god's face are but a simple illustration of how politically charged and open to interpretation the concepts of *ma·mu·l* ('tradition') and *ocmu·l* ('new rule') themselves are.

Leaving aside the question of how the ornaments are arranged, and what that means, we should recognize that the practice of offering money or precious metals to a deity is itself a widespread and ancient religious practice in India. Among the Kotas, the coins used to be heated in a smithy within the temple premises and fashioned into small bows and arrows and other tools associated with the Kota gods.[49] Since these quintessential Kota skills, blacksmithing and hunting, were said to have been taught to the Kotas by their gods, icons of these practices were also considered holy. Forging these icons was thus another way of 'making god'.[50]

Before the faces are fashioned during the god ceremony, the first three coins must be placed on each of the three temples by the two ritual leaders (*mundka·no·n*s). It is this initializing process which is elaborated ritually, rather than the subsequent arranging of the coins. While the ritual leaders paste the coins, the brass trumpets (*kob,* literally 'horn', always played in pairs) are sounded and the *paṭm pacd koḷ*,[51] or coin placing tune, is played.[52]

Before discussing the next *devr koḷ*, let us further consider the significance of blacksmithing and hunting. Recall for a moment that tribals in India are 'sons of the soil' in the popular imagination and that Indians attribute to the tribal a pre-modern self-sufficiency—all part of the more general idea that tribes are 'at one with nature.' The Kotas quite consciously think of their gods as having something to do with nature (writ large, in the Western sense): the gods are embodied in fire, water, stones, special bows and arrows, and in the blacksmith's shop. During the god ceremony diet is restricted to what used to grow in the Nilgiris (even if it was cultivated) and no intoxicating substances are supposed to be ingested.

But the idea of 'nature' is itself culturally constructed (cf. Schneider 1968) and to my knowledge there is no Kota word for 'nature' as an abstract concept. Kotas use the English word as well as the Tamil equivalent *iyaṟkai*.[53] I strongly suspect that the Kota tendency to associate Kotaness and Kota gods with nature is tied up in a modern self-reflexivity that comprehends the general way tribals are viewed in India. I am not claiming a modern origin for the *practices*, but rather for the *interpretation*. It is in part this interpretation, I believe, that allows the Kotas to think of diverse cultural and religious practices as belonging to a whole.

§8. Hunting is associated not only in a general way with the Kota 'father god',[54] but also in a specific way with a deity named *ve·ṭka·r co·ym* ('hunting god'), worshipped just outside Gudalur town (near the Kota village of Kala·c) by several Nilgiri and Wynaad tribes and castes. The origin stories of this god vary depending on the community telling the story. Kotas of Kurgo·j and Kala·c village still attend the yearly festival for *ve·ṭka·r co·ym* (sometime around October each year), and the men play instruments and dance.[55] Several Kota villages have god tunes named after the hunting god.

In Kolme·l, the hunting god tune was once used in a god ceremony ritual (it has since been abandoned). At the end of the god ceremony the *mundka·no·ns* used to lead a procession to the sacred place called *toḍba·l* and shoot an arrow, symbolically to kill a bison believed to be connected with their gods. This bison had repeatedly disturbed the Kotas during worship.[56] It is believed that, for many years, a bison would come to that place at the end of the god ceremony. More recently, after a bison no longer appeared every year, the practice was formalized into a ritual of renewal called *devr kaytd* ('god washing'). Except during the god ceremony, the deities are believed to reside in the back rooms (*kakui*) of the two ritual leaders' houses (*doḍvay*, 'big house') in the form of a bow and arrow. For the 'god washing' ritual, the bow and arrow were brought to *toḍba·l* under tight security: if women or non-Kotas were to see the deity, the consequences, it is said, would be deadly. Along the way an arrow was shot toward Doddabetta Peak (north) and to the west. When they reached *toḍba·l*, the silver points of arrows were washed, new bamboo was collected for the bow, *tavṭ* ('hill guava,' *DEDR* 3112) wood for the shaft of the arrow and new twine (*pobit na·rl*) were extracted from tree bark for the bow string,[57] The hunting god tune, which was part of this (now abandoned) god washing ritual, is now performed more generically as part of the god tune repertoire.

My impression is that the 'hunting god' is known to most Kotas as a deity in some way connected with their hunting past. As one of the god tunes, it evokes a history and self-identity congruent with the lore of the other god tunes—a history that valourizes a tribal way of life (hunting) in an environment that is substantially their own (the Nilgiris) where divinity is associated with and evident in nature (the bison, the forest materials which the bow and arrow are created as well as in the capacity to control the environment (success in hunting, the use of fire to forge metal arrowheads).

§9. The last two god tunes are *aṛca·yḷ koḷs,* tunes played while men sit under the rough-hewn hut (*aṛca·yḷ*) erected in the temple area during the god festival. All the god tunes are known generically as *aṛca·yḷ koḷs* by those who do not know the individual names or stories.

The Significance of the God Tunes in the Rain Ceremony

Each of the god tunes is named after a particular practice or story whose theme or use is part of 'making god' during the god festival. The fact that the god tune repertoire is also used in the rainmaking ceremony suggests a strong association between the two. All gods of the god tunes are called to participate in a community attempt to bring rain. All these tunes, some from diverse origins, are combined in a single, pointed effort to invoke god. This act of combining suggests that all these tunes are of one category.[58] Bringing these diverse god-related (whether in ritual, origin story, or merely in name) tunes together is a gesture that establishes 'the relatedness of things' (cf. Fernandez [1986: 191], in regard to 'returning to the whole'): the relatedness of different divinities, the unity of the Nilgiris as a region, the importance of right conduct and social harmony, and so forth. Collecting different tunes together into a single repertoire is a musical equivalent of what happens in the procession, which is like a miniature pilgrimage.[59] By incorporating sites of divine presence into a single ritual, the Kotas constitute a spatial unity within the village.

Description and Analysis of the Rain Ceremony

The description that follows will alternate between a macroview of the whole ceremony in performance, and an extended macroview discussing the significance of each part. The micro sections will be marked with smaller type to facilitate reading. I will begin with a personal narrative that harks back to the epigraph of this paper.

Learning About the Rain Ceremony

One day in May 1991 I went to Indu Nagar[60] to meet my Kota friend L.Gunasekaran, an English literature student who was helping me learn the Kota language. He planned to help me interview Mr K. Pucan, a senior instrumentalist and village elder (*doḍa·ḷ*). Fortunately for me, Mr Pucan and his wife were next door visiting their son, Dr Varadharajan, and even more fortunately, Mr Pucan had agreed to sing for me—a significant breakthrough because he had until now insisted that only women could sing. The halting, slightly out-of-tune quality of Pucan's voice, affected as it was by an age of eighty years, was more than compensated for by his way of making performance into a story.

Pucan chose to render two songs which Kolme·l women sing during important festivals. Women sing these songs while dancing in a circle and clapping hands. The songs share much stylistically with women's *kummi* songs of Tamil Nadu and Kerala. Women's singing and dancing are necessary and auspicious endings to entire festivals and to structural units such as specific rituals within festivals; they are considered *ca·trm,* or rituals. One of these ritual songs, from which the epigraph is extracted, has its Kolme·l origin preserved in a well-known story.

In the beginning, a black cow called Basavan led the Kota people to the place called *naṭkal* and indicated that a village should be founded. The first post for the first house in the village was erected there. The Kotas milked the cow and built a temple. Now there are three temples. Big father god temple, little father god temple, and mother goddess temple. The *mundka·no·n* (ritual leader) does *pūja* for these temples. One time the *mundka·no·n* made a mistake and the temple oil lamp disappeared, cloaking the temple in darkness. He could not do *pūja* and, singing this song, went in search of the lamp. The song mentions the names of holy places and trees.[61]

While telling about each of these holy sites Pucan informed us that on the coming Monday, *ka·ṇky* (monetary offerings to the deity) were to be given at each site as part of a ceremony to bring rain. Going from site to site the twelve *devr kols*, or 'god tunes', are performed, and for these tunes, he explained, 'there is meaning' (*artm*, *DBIA* 20). The process of learning and what he meant by 'meaning' was one of the most fruitful and rewarding as well as frustrating activities in my ethnomusicological fieldwork. Ultimately, what I learned about the 'god tunes' has been summarized above. The sites themselves, also of some significance, led me to consider the rain ceremony in a broader Kota context.

The Rain Ceremony in Other Villages and in Relation to Other Ceremonies

The rain ceremony (*may ca·trm*) of four of the seven Kota villages, Kolme·l (eight kilometres south of Ootacamund), Ticga·ṛ (fifteen kilometres northeast of Ootacamund), Kurgo·j (twenty-five kilometres northwest of Ootacamund), and Me·na·ṛ (thirty kilometres south-southwest of Ootacamund), is a procession to trees and stones associated with divinity. Through prayer, monetary offerings, 'jumping' (chanting sacred syllables while stepping rhythmically around a circle), and instrumental music, Kotas beseech their gods to remain in the village and look after their well-being.[62]

The rain ceremonies in each village are composed not only of musical elements but also of other ritual elements found in *devr* (lit. 'god'), the annual god festival. Celebrating the god festival is called *devr gicd*, that is 'doing' or 'making' god; suggesting, I think, that the constitution of divinity is a creative act: it lies in performance.

The god ceremony is also sometimes called *paca·l devr.* The placename *paca·l* refers to the green grassy area around the three central temples. This reference to place is diacritically important: it distinguishes the original god ceremony from another which is devoted to the god Raṅgrayṇ—the Kota version of the Hindu god Ranganathan, worshipped at Karamadai (a town that lies between Coimbatore and Mettupalaiyam).[63] The name for this latter ceremony, *ko·jka·l devr*, 'Ko·j area god',[64] is also qualified by a placename, *ko·jka·l*, the former location of a *ko·j* tree.[65] Placenames are not merely convenient reference points in these contexts. They reflect the fact that Kota gods, like many 'village gods' of South Asia, are numens: they inhabit particular places.

The Rain Ceremony

At about 9:45 in the morning on 20 May 1991, men and boys of Kolme·l village assembled at the set of two upright stones (*naṭkal*) northwest of the temple area (*guṛyva·l*).

The *naṭkal*, a location for village council meetings (*ku·ṭm*) and place of assembly before ritual, is significant as the site on which a divine 'black cow' (*ka·ra·v*) was said to have indicated to the Kotas that they should found a village—as told in the story associated with the epigraph.

As people arrived, the *koḷvar* (band of musicians)[66] prepared their instruments. The drummers tightened their drum heads by heating them by a fire and the *koḷ* (double-reed instrument with conical bore) players adjusted their instruments, dampening the reeds and testing the sound. Elders and *koḷ* players sat with their backs against the stones and faced east, while the other musicians sat to their left in a semicircle. Other men sat on the right.[67] All were dressed in the white clothing appropriate for worship: a cloak called *vara·ṛ* and a waistcloth called *munḍ*. Pucan led as the musicians played three of the god tunes (*devr koḷ*), starting with the tune usually associated with the ritual of opening the temples during the god ceremony.

The Procession

Briefly, the procession begins at the *naṭkal* (stones marking a meeting place); proceeds southeast to a place called *ponic* where three god tunes are played and coins are offered to the deity; returns through the village and proceeds northwest to *toḍba·l* where god is worshipped in similar fashion; returns toward the village via the *arckal* ('king stones'), where three more tunes are played; and finally, all meet at the *naṭkal* again and share tobacco.

After Pucan and Raman played the *o·la·gicd koḷ* and two other tunes,[68] two men sounded the brass horn, called *kob*, another beat a large half-coconut-shaped drum (roughly 2.5 feet in diameter) called the *e·rtabaṭk*.

From this point onwards, the narration of the rain ceremony proper is indicated in regular type; in smaller type are extended explanations of what individual actions, places, or other elements mean.

Both instruments sonically highlight moments when the procession leaves and arrives in a place. Calling attention to important moments is the general function of these instruments, whether those moments are distressing, as in the announcement of a death, or joyful, as in the opening of the temples.[69]

The processional order was loosely structured: a man carrying the *e·rtabaṭk* on his back led the procession while a boy struck the drum from behind. The ritual specialists lagged behind the rest of the group. Pucan and Raman played the first three *kols*, but as Pucan was too old and infirm to keep up with the group, Raman and his son Duryodana played for the rest of the ceremony.

The men walked from the *naṭkal* about half a kilometre southeast to a place about fifty metres above the village and paused to worship at a place called *ka·dmankaṇḍy*, one of several 'raised level grounds of worship' (*kubiṭ kaṇḍy*) surrounding Kolme·l village.

These 'worship places' are significant in that they are the last places from which the village can be seen when leaving and the first places from which the village can be seen when returning (Emeneau 1944, II:245). Just as Hindus value *darśan*, Kotas value the visual interaction between deity and person (Babb 1981; Eck 1981)—although other parallels between Hindu *pūja* and Kota worship are few. In this case, the view of the village *is the* view of the deity, since Kota deities are seen to be especially effective, active, and present within the village boundaries.

The idea that divinity is accessible through vision is expressed in a number of everyday activities, especially in coming and going from the village. Kotas pray facing the temple before commencing any excursion beyond the village. They may even pray before someone else begins an excursion, as did R. Mathi, whenever her son and I would leave town. Upon returning to the village Kotas pray first at the nearest *kubiṭkaṇḍy*, then at holy sites along the way, and finally at the temple. These are not special activities for special days; rather they are ingrained and habitual. Praying at a particular spot includes clasping the hands together in an *añjali* (*kay mu·vd*) and turning to one direction or another while uttering 'god' (*co·ym*). These directions are frequently believed to be the locations of other important deities or shrines—although a given person may not have visited all the locations. It is enough to gives respect by facing the directions in which the deities reside.[70]

The men reached *ka·dman kaṇḍy* and bowed and prayed in the southerly direction, saying 'god' (*co·ym*).[71] Although two ritual leaders (*mundka·no·ns*) and three diviners (*te·rka·rns*) are supposed to lead in this worship, in 1991 only one diviner was alive, and in 1992 there were none.

Sulli narrated to Mandelbaum a prayer which is no longer recited at *ka· dman kaṇdy,*[72] but adds to our understanding of the ceremony (full text and translation in appendix).[73]

Gods *kamaṭraya, amno· r, ayṇo· r, ra· mco· mi, raṅgco· mi* and *beḷdamn*! We are your sons, children of god. Having finished sowing, we are experiencing hardship without any rain. Letting tears fall at god's feet, we come to bring you along. Since[74] *kamaṭraya* lives in *venveṭm* and *raṅgrayṇ* lives in Karamadai how are we to prosper? For that we come, elders and youngsters, with our musical instruments and horns, saying 'we will catch hold of you and go'. So that you don't forget us, we come in the manner of supplicants and grab (*i.e.* bow at) your feet.

The idea contained in the phrase 'since *kamaṭraya* lives in *venveṭm* and *raṅgrayṇ* lives in Karamadai how are we to prosper?' is that since Kota gods are originally from areas outside of Kolme·l, they might return to these places of origin because the Kotas of Kolme·l are not living righteously.[75] We have seen similar themes in the stories behind the god tunes and the song *veḷke· veḷke·* (in the epigraph) as well: a goddess caused cattle to become ill because the village was becoming factionalized (§3); the 'milk tree' was rendered invisible because the people were not living righteously (§5); and the lamp disappeared because the ritual leader had committed some fault.

kamaṭraya, ayṇo·r and *amno·r* are names for the three Kota gods associated with three temples in the centre of the village.[76] But the other three gods, *raṅgco· mi, ra· mco· mi* and *beḷdamn* are the new trinity of gods (shared by Hindus and other tribals) introduced from Karamadai town in 1925 (Mandelbaum 1960: 226). Since there are no longer any diviners alive for the three gods (for whom the Kolme·l temple called *ko·jk· l* was constructed), these gods are not currently represented in the rain ceremony.[77]

After worshipping by clasping the hands together, turning to the right or to the left,[78] and bowing down (*aḍmuṛtd*), the men walked east-southeast for just over a kilometre to the first of a series of stone circles that are part of the place called *ponic*[79] (one of the sacred sites mentioned in the song *veḷke· veḷke·*) or *eṛtvaṇ* ('place fruit').[80] This first place is called the *parykm vecd eṛm* or the 'offering keeping place'.

Although the history of *ponic* has not been maintained in legend, the place remains significant because Karamadai and other divine localities are visible from there (K. Pucan, pers. com.). Once again the *visual* accessibility of the divine proves to be important.

Before offering money to the deity,[81] the ritual leaders asked if everybody had joined and all responded, 'we have joined', because all men of the village must be present for important supplicatory functions.[82] Then the village headman (*gotga·rn*) unwrapped a coin from a cloth wallet, placed it on a piece of cowdung, and both ritual leaders lifted it together with their right hands, left thumb placed upon the coin, and placed the offering under the *va·ce·ry* bush growing in the stone circle, a gesture which summarizes the oneness for the which this ritual strives.[83] Together everyone prayed in the easterly direction (*ki·mu·l*).

A few notes on the significance of plants: The *va·ce·ry* bush under which the offering is placed in not, according to K. Pucan, particularly significant *per se.* But C.K. Tetn of Kurgo·j narrated a ritual, practised in Kolme·l as well, in which seven thorny plants are combined and burned in seven fires. After a woman gives birth to her first child she must cross these fires before returning to her home. And during the Kurgo·j god festival, menstruating women must bathe in the river and cross these seven fires before returning home. Two of the seven plants are *tak* and *va·ce·ry.*[84] The *tak* plant is of central purificatory significance at the beginning of the god ceremony: the youngest male of each household must clean his house ritually by brushing branches of *tak* along its walls and floor. Thorny plants are generally used in Kota rituals to remove menstrual difilement (*ti·ḷ*), ward off evil, and purify living spaces (the house and surrounding area and the temple). Thus the association of *va·ce·ry,* one such thorny plant, with the presence of divinity at *ponic* is a logical one in the Kota scheme, although there is no indication that it plays a purificatory role.

Sulli indicated in his 1937 account that the plant growing in the stone circle was a *ne·rl* plant (not *va·ce·ry*). Whether or not *ne·rl* plant was once in *ponic,* it does belong to a class of plants serving similar purificatory functions and is frequently a plant under which coins are offered to the deity.[85] During the 'milk ceremony' (*pa·l ca·trm,*)[86] for example, the ritual leader makes his cow ritually clean by running two or three feet of *ne·rl* branches along its back. In particular, the *ne·rl* is said to remove *ti·ḷ,* the defiling effects of menstruation or childbirth.[87] This purifying property of *ne·rl* may also explain why it is also used, along with two other types of wood, to fashion pillars supporting the frame of a new house.

The song quoted in the epigraph, 'lamp', where are you?' includes a line 'are you under the *ne·rl* tree?' I asked a few Kotas about the places mentioned in the song, once again, about a year after the incident in which Puccan first mentioned the rain ceremony. Duryodana suggested (he had reflected on this question himself), and others concurred (but not necessarily because they had independently come to the same conclusion), that the trees and plants mentioned in *veḷke· veḷke·*, and those which are generally considered to be of religious significance, are those which yield flowers or fruits.[88] The *ne·rl* plant does bear fruit (as does *tak*) and even the seed of this fruit seems to have been important at one time. Emeneau (1944, II:361–3) recounts a story in which a Toda girl, born after her parents made a vow to the Kota gods of Kolme·l, makes an oath on a dried seed of a *ne·rl* fruit.

After the ritual leaders placed a coin under the bush, the men left the *parykm vecd eṛm* ('offering keeping place') and walked north-northeast, about sixty–five metres in distance and about seventeen metres lower in elevation, to another stone circle.[89] At this second circle, the men faced northwest and prayed.[90] About 14 metres southeast of the circle they lit a fire and heated the drums. Then the young men held hands and danced counterclockwise around the stones chanting '*ho·ko·*' in the characteristic Kota form of worship, *edykd* (lit., 'jumping').[91]

Sulli stated in his first, very elaborate, account of the rain ceremony (Mandelbaum n.d., 1937 May 14), that a diviner used to become possessed at *ponic*. Another informant told Mandelbaum that although possession might occur, it was not a necessary part of the ritual.[92] Possession did not occur in 1991 or in 1992.

Sulli explained the monetary offering as a fine[93] for failing to offer god 'rice and beans and ghee' after the festival (*pabm*, *DBIA* 256) in March; they ask the gods not to go to Karamadai and *venveṭm*.[94]

After the dance was completed, men and boys gathered branches of the purple ellipsoidal berry called *tak* (*Berberis tinctoria*—*DEDR* 3096—the same plant mentioned above in connection with cleaning the house during the god ceremony).

It is unclear whether this berry collecting ever had any particular meaning attached. Pucan said that the boys pick the berries, which are ripe at that time of the year, take them home and eat them. Sulli mentioned nothing about the collection of *tak*. The question of ritual (*ca·trm*) boundaries (is possession part of the ritual? is *tak* collecting part of the ritual?) is an interesting one to explore. Kotas may sometimes disagree about what is and what is not part of a ritual, and if the question is important enough, they will call a meeting and argue about it until a decision is reached—and a few weeks later they may change the decision.

While boys collected *tak*, other boys and men gathered near the fire and the musicians played three more god tunes.

According to Pucan, the *paṭm pacd koḷ* (coin placing tune [§7]) should be performed on arrival at *ponic*; an association one might expect since the tune is named after the action of offering coins to god. But this conceptual link is not necessarily maintained in practice. I asked Pucan to further explain which tunes are played at which places. He indicated that any three of the twelve were to be played in each of the four places; or as many as they could remember. Raman, who played at *ponic* when I witnessed the ceremony, said that 'for the tunes there are no names, they are for calling god'; that is, he thought of the god tunes as a single entity used in a generic way to call god.

When the activity at *ponic* was completed the men returned toward the *naṭkal* along a different path, spreading flowers of various plants on stones along the way. Later I was told that these flowers invite and lead the god into the village.

Sprinkling flowers: more on the boundaries of ritual: Learning about the significance of sprinkling flowers was another opportunity to observe how various activities are included or excluded from rituals, by whom, and when. On another day I was casually discussing the rain ceremony with A. K. Rangan, one of three men who, in addition to Sulli, were outcasted for such modern practices as cutting their hair. Rangan, a philosopher and popular composer of Kota-language songs, has remained estranged from the community. He has a remarkable memory for details of ritual and aspects of Kota culture despite the fact that he has not participated in community activities in at least forty years.

Rangan knew nothing of the sprinkling of flowers and in fact claimed this practice was new and inauthentic (not *ma·mu·l*) if it was practiced at all. Taking this difference as a challenge we walked about the village and consulted men and boys at random. Several men said they had been going to *ponic* since they were children and there was absolutely no such practice. Finally we found one forty-five year old man, S. Easwaran, who provided an explanation (the flowers form a path to lead the god) he had obtained from his own father, K. Tu·j—but Rangan still doubted the 'traditionality' of the practice. I remember thinking how odd it was that many men, like Rangan, *personally* separated themselves in some ways from the old ways (thinking them old-fashioned); but when others began to change, would scoff and become concerned over what was and what was not called for according to 'tradition.'

Pucan, who during the previous year had disclaimed any knowledge of the flower path, this year offered an explanation along the lines of Mr Easwaran's. I took this experience as paradigmatic. The Kota attitude towards practices not known is 'it doesn't exist'. And even the most forthcoming teachers may not reveal what they know, even if the knowledge involved is not particularly secret. My inability to second-guess my Kota friends and teachers reminded me how indeterminate the whole process of learning another culture really is. Why did Pucan not tell me what he thought the flowers meant the first time I asked him? Was it the way I asked the question? My language skills? Was he just tired?

Worshipping with flowers and creating a flower path are widespread Hindu practices as well,[95] and there is no reason to assume that the practice has been in existence since the 'first' rain ceremony. Rituals are changing all the time. Even while I was in Kolme·l a new element was added. In 1991, the procession headed directly back to the village and beyond it to *toḍba·l*, but in 1992 another stone circle had been erected. This circle was called *kuneṛtvaṇ* ('little place-fruit'). It was located about 350 metres west-northwest of the last stone circle. The procession stopped and they prayed facing the village temples (west-northwest).

According to Dr Varadharajan, this new circle was erected because a community of stonemasons (*bo·yar*, see *BED*, p. 440), who had purchased nearby land from the Badagas, were encroaching on what was considered to be a divine area. By building the stone circle and demarcating the region through this ritual, the Kotas made an effective boundary against further encroachment.[96]

Leaving the set of stone circles and returning to the village, the procession continued to another numinous site, the *toḍba·l* or 'bison place'. In Kolme·l *toḍba·l* is located about 700 metres west of the central temple area, outside the village.

The significance of toḍba·l: Since miracles demonstrating the power of god were said to have occurred at this site; the place is considered a 'god's place' (*devrd eṛm*) and Kotas of Kolme·l worship at the *ne·rl* tree in the *toḍba·l* whenever they pass it. In the four Kota villages of Me·na·ṛ, Kolme·l, Ticga·ṛ and Kurgo·j, the *toḍba·l* (or cognate term) originated with the presence of a bison (*toḍ*) disturbing worship. In some cases the bison was shot, and in other cases it ran away. Because the bison reappeared at the same time each year, the place was thought to be divine.[97]

In Kolme·l, the *toḍba·l* used to provide a point of reference and boundary in ritual games (Emeneau 1944, IV: 319). Emeneau reports a story of a cow who raises the children of a man at *toḍba·l* (1944, III: 2–23). Mandelbaum recorded a story in which two boys, in secret, fashioned a statue of god in clay and kept it at *toḍba·l* (2 May 1937), feeding it rice. Later they brought the statue to the temple and fed it meat. This angered the village because the Kota gods are vegetarians. They entered the temple and disappeared along with the image. Mandelbaum also recorded a practice of ritual stone-lifting at *toḍba·l* (6 June 1937). The practice was discontinued when the stones disappeared; according to Sulli, when menstruating women went to the place.

The stones of *toḍba·l* were also significant in the founding of the new temples (*ko·jka·l*). A man became possessed, and acting as the god, indicated where a new temple should be built (Mandelbaum 1941) by placing a stone from *toḍba·l* on the spot (Mandelbaum n.d., 23 October 1949). K. Pucan tells a story in which his ancestor, Kaṇmi·rve·ri·ṇ ('eye-hair grandfather'), prophesied his own death; predicting that he and his three brothers, after dying, would grow as four connected trunks of the *ne·rl* tree at *toḍba·l* (as it grows today).

The place clearly has a history of significant activity surrounding it. Consequently, it is no wonder the rain ceremony includes *toḍba·l* and that the ritual leader who sang 'lamp, lamp', looked there for the god.

In 1991 and 1992 the ritual leaders offered a coin at *toḍbal* just as they did at *ponic*, without uttering any prayers in particular, although once again they asked 'have we all joined?' The men faced west (*i.e.* facing the *toḍba·l* with their backs turned towards the village), each with hands clasped and held to his forehead; they turned to the left, then to the right, and then back again (there was some variation in this); then they bowed down on their knees and elbows, some on their stomachs. Then they all relaxed for a short time while Raman played three more god tunes.

Sulli mentioned in his 1937 account that diviners became possessed and prayers were spoken at *toḍba·l*. Once again, the prayer beseeched the gods to stay in the area and not to stray beyond the village until the crops had been reaped. It expressed thanks that the Kotas had never been in want of food and the wish that the Kota population increase. Nowadays, according to Pucan, there is no elaborate prayer and no possession.

Leaving the *toḍba·l*, the procession returned towards the village. The *ko·jka·l* temple, founded in the 1920s, lies along the route back to the village, just beyond the half-way point. Within the temple premises is a place of significance, the *arckal* ('king stone'), that predates the temple—in fact, today the *ko·jka·l* temple itself is not considered to be connected with the rain ceremony. The *arckal* are two stones on which a minister of Tipu Sultan and a Kota king were said to have sat as they transacted tax payments.[98]

In earlier times the Kotas used to collect taxes (Mandelbaum 1989: 158) for the Mysore Raja from nearby Badagas and others in the sub-district. If the significance of the two stones originated in marking a place for transaction, I did not understand why the place would be included in the rain ceremony. Sulli told Mandelbaum (n.d., 14 May 1937) a story which provides a more understandable reason for inclusion; although the specifics, even as a story, are probably inaccurate. Tipu Sultan, according to Sulli, instructed one of his men to build a house on the site of the *arckal.* When the man began digging, the tool disappeared into the ground. This story, and others like it, locates the power of Kota gods in specific localities. These gods demonstrate power only when their space is somehow violated.[99]

At the *arckal* the men performed the 'jumping' (*edykd*) dance and the musicians performed three more god tunes. Finally all men returned to the *naṭkal* and gathered in a semicircle; several performed 'jumping' to the northeast of the stones. Then the village headman brought bundles of tobacco and gave them to Pucan, who, having rejoined the group at *arckal,* was sitting in the centre. Pucan asked if he should break the bundles saying, *kaba·l oṛdve·ra·,* (and the men answered) 'untie the bundle'. Each man took a little piece of tobacco and chewed it. I could not understand what they had said and asked my friend Gunasekaran to repeat it. Gunasekaran asked Pucan, and instead of repeating the words, explained what the action *meant,* saying 'it's like eating something off one plate'.

Eating off one plate is one of the major symbolic means of expressing unity and equality among the Kotas,[100] and in this case was a metaphor for the sharing of tobacco.[101] Sulli, in explaining the meaning of tobacco, used another metaphor: 'we enter as one under a big cloak':

> The big cloak allusion means that there is peace among us so we all lie down together under the same big cloak. When a visitor comes to the village we send our wife away to the other part of the house and we sleep together with out visiting friend under one cloak (Mandelbaum n.d., 18 May 1937).

Following the distribution of tobacco in 1991 there was a meeting during which, among other things, the headman raised a concern about the paucity of good *koḷ* players. All agreed that more boys should be encouraged to learn the *koḷ.* A similar concern dominated the rain ceremony of 1992 when Raman turned up late and his son Duryodana was forced to lead the procession. Such events underscore the community value ascribed to music.

This concludes the detailed description of the rain ceremony as I witnessed it. The remaining discussion concerns the context of the rain ceremony as a whole.

Reflections upon the Whole

THE RAIN CEREMONY AND THE HARVEST

On the Tuesday following Monday's rain ceremony, the village diviner was once obliged to climb the temple *tak*[102] tree and announce '*ind ma·p iḍuge·*' 'today take leave'.)[103] The following two Tuesdays were and are also supposed to be such formal days of rest. Until the recently deceased Va. Kamaten called an end to the practice, the Kotas would also refrain from working for three Fridays after the three Tuesdays and then for three Sundays after the three Fridays. When this final day of ritually calculated leave had passed, it would be time for the harvest to begin. According to my calculations, based on these days of leave, the rain ceremony would have occurred nearly six weeks before the harvest. Va. Kamaten changed the rules to suit the tea harvest, which must continue throughout the rainy season.

Just as Saturdays are religious holidays to Jews, and Sundays to Christians, Mondays, and to a lesser extent, Saturdays are traditional days of ritual observance for the Kotas.[104] The days of leave associated with the rain ceremony, taken to show respect for the gods, do not fall on these traditional weekly holidays.[105] I would suggest that, since the ceremony marks however the formal beginning of the monsoon season, these special days of ritual leave in a sense 'stand for' the long monsoon periods which people would have at one time spent in their homes anyway. In the old days, they say, the sun would not shine for months on end. And, as I interpret them, the three sets of three one-day-a-week vacations, which interlock and yet exclude other holidays, provided continuity and a means of practically reckoning time between the sowing season and the harvest season.

SUMMARY: VILLAGE UNITY CONSTITUTED IN THE RAIN CEREMONY

I suggested that the performance of god tunes is a musical parallel of the procession to holy places. *Ponic* and *toḍba·l* are in some ways eastern and western boundaries of the village: not of the village interior, where the houses are built, but the village boundaries as ritually constituted in prayer to village deities; borders of ritual games; demarcation of land; and incorporation in 'god' stories and songs. They are the borders within which all sorts of ceremonies for the Kota gods are contained. By offering coins at these places, invoking god, praying, performing music and so forth, the Kotas affirm the geographical integrity of the village landscape in specifically deity-oriented and community–oriented terms.

Like the twelve tunes, which together constitute the musically divine, the four places, *ponic, toḍba·l, arckal,* and *naṭkal,* enshrine and contain within their borders the spatially divine. Both the places and the tunes are meaningful, in part, because they remind Kotas of stories about the power of the gods. In this sense, they encode a kind of positively valued past, a past in which the gods worked to the Kotas' benefit. The rain ceremony combines these elements in a uniquely Kota *bricolage,* drawing upon the 'remains and debris of events . . . fossilized evidence of the history of an individual or a society' (Lévi-Strauss 1966: 21–2; de Certeau 1984: 29–42). Rather than relegating the rain ceremony to that mystical, universal phenomenon which Lévi-Strauss calls 'mythical thought', I prefer to think of it as a 'strategic' (de Certeau 1984: 35–6) use of the past, a performance aimed, in part, at delimiting a 'place as its own'.[105]

The temporal remove of 'a past' is only relevant in relation to a later period, let us call it a 'modern' period, from which a 'disjuncture' from the past can be experienced and reflected upon.[106] Put in another way, modernity, in my usage, is relational rather than temporally fixed: it marks a community's self-awareness of the gap between the present and an 'authentic' past (for the Kotas, that constructed authenticity called *ma·mu·l*). For the Kotas, it is a modern period in which one might expect the integrity of the landscape, the memory or faith in the gods, and the unity of the people to be a trenchant issue; trenchant enough to urge a 'return to the whole'. It is possible to locate one such moment of disjuncture (it happens to be in the twentieth century)—there may be more—but to what extent is it reasonable to search for origins of the rain ceremony in this period? What would constitute evidence of such origins?

Kota Views on the History of the Rain Ceremony

Significant new features of rain propitiation may have come about during a period of drought:

In 1933 there was no rain at all in the district. They asked the god and the diviner said, 'Go to *ponic* and call the god with your flutes [*koḷs*], then come to *toḍba·l* (there they bow down and pay a rupee to the god), then come and sit in front of the *ra·mayṇo·r* temple, at the *arckal* . . .'

When they reached there, a big storm and heavy rain came. *It fell only in Kolme·l not across the boundary*. [Sulli's account in Mandelbaum n.d., 14 May 1937, 3–4; my emphasis added].

The first passage is puzzling. Did Sulli mean that the *first* rain ceremony of this form (the procession and coin offerings), in Kolme·l, occurred in 1933? If the ceremony was already a yearly occurence, as it is now and as it was in 1937,[107] would the diviner have needed to tell them to enact a ceremony they already knew? Were there gaps in Mandelbaum's account (did he ask, 'give me an example of a time when the rain ceremony needed to be performed' or 'when was the first rain ceremony?')[108] Even if the first ceremony was in 1933, where did the form come from? Can we assign Kota gods (the purported inventors of all ceremonies) the same agency as human *bricoleurs*? Parallel ceremonies exist in other villages now and some did in 1937 as well, according to Mandelbaum's Kurgo·j Kota informants and a Badaga interpreter.[109] What does it mean for a ceremony to 'originate' in a place, by divine decree in a sense, if it exists in similar form elsewhere?

Between my two years of fieldwork in the Nilgiris I came back to the United States, began studying Mandelbaum's fieldnotes, and discovered Sulli's (14 May 1937) account. When I returned to the Nilgiris I asked Pucan and Raman when the rain ceremony began. Both insisted that it originated long ago (*ma·mu·l ca·trm*, 'traditional ritual'). I mentioned Sulli's account and they both scoffed. Sulli could not be trusted, they told me. Pucan told me on several occasions that he felt Sulli was misinforming Mandelbaum. But since Pucan did not know English, he could not intervene. How Pucan perceived Sulli to be giving misinformation is a different question—his English was insufficient to understand discussions between Mandelbaum and Sulli and he would seldom have been present during their work sessions. Rather, I think, Pucan's overall distrust of Sulli prompted him to think Mandelbaum was being misled.

Pucan indicated the ceremony originated very long ago, during a year when there was no rain in the district. In quite another context I asked the late Va. Kamaten about the significance of *ponic* as a place and he replied with this interesting answer,[110] 'Once drought hit Kolme·l and people went [there] and built a stone [structure] and were praying [to] it. When they were praying it started raining, *and from then onwards it became a custom.* This happened more than a Century ago'; [interview, Va. Kamaten, 9 January, 1992; my emphasis].

Sulli, Pucan and Va. Kamaten agree that the *ponic* ceremony originated one year when there was no rain. It seems unlikely that Sulli would have mistaken the year of drought since his 1937 discussion with Mandelbaum took place only four years after the remembered drought. But what might cast suspicion on Sulli's dating of the first ceremony is his support for the new gods and the possible desire to show their role in bringing rain. Púcan and Va. Kamaten, as two of the oldest members of the village, either may have forgotten that the ceremony began in their lifetimes or may have wished to make the ceremony appear more 'traditional' by asserting its origin to be earlier than it actually was. Sulli and Mandelbaum discussed the rain ceremony on other occasions, and Mandelbaum recorded another Kolme·l man's description of the rain ceremony, but no mention was made of the ceremony's origins: this also seems suspicious to me, if the ceremony was indeed four years old. The matter of when the ceremony originated will have to remain unresolved.

Can we approach the problem from the other side? With due respect for the limits of such speculation, let us ask: if the ceremony, in its present form, did originate in 1933 or thereabouts, why that form at that time? What was special about the 1930s that might have called for historical reflection, reaffirmation of boundaries and reassertion of social unity? I alluded already to the social and religious upheaval of the period, beginning first with the epidemic of 1924. Let us examine that period in more detail.

One of Mandelbaum's major articles on the Kotas, 'Social Trends and Personal Pressures', is part of the 'culture and personality' discourse of his generation. Here he describes the 1924 'epidemic of relapsing fever' which decimated the Kotas. In Kolme·l, all the ritual leaders and diviners for the three *ayṇo·r* and *amno·r* temples died, as did many others.[111] In 1925 the Kotas began their yearly god ceremony without any ritual specialists; and when the villagers prayed to the gods to indicate successors for these men, 'as had not happened before in the memory of the people, no man was supernaturally propelled to the temple pillar to be diviner; none was seized as priest' (Mandelbaum 1960: 226).

Mandelbaum goes on to explain, as I confirmed recently with other Kotas, that a rather irresponsible and untrustworthy man by the name of Kucvayn became possessed by what he claimed was the god Ranganathan of Karamadai. Kotas have had long-standing involvement with worship of this deity, at least according to Kotas today.[112] But still, the community was slow to accept a new addition to the village pantheon. But in 1926, when new priests were still not chosen, the community heeded the words of Kucvayn when Ranganathan spoke through him demanding a temple be built. Only then, he claimed, would diviners for the old temples be chosen. Two other men were possessed by Rama and Betdamn respectively and Kucvayn chose a priest for the three new gods (Mandelbaum 1941).

Indeed the next year all five vacant posts were filled as prophesied by Kucvayn. But ambivalence over the new temples was still not erased. Two factions in the village remained bitterly opposed until around 1960 (S. Raman, pers. com.). A well-known mourning song (*a·ṯḻ*) captures, with emotive richness, the atmosphere of hostility of the period; since it also illustrates the way in which value can be negatively assigned to village spaces, it is worth including here.

The song was composed by Tu·j, S. Raman's father, in mourning the loss of a young girl named Rangumathi (a name, incidently, which combines the prototypical female Kota name Mathi with the name of the new deity, Ranga). Rangumathi was the daughter of one K. Payrn (older brother of the K. Pucan of this paper).

My mother[113] Rangumathi, what will I say Rangumathi?
Kolme·l village, where umbrellas hardly fit[114]
'the middle-street people's cremation site we want,' they say, Rangumathi![115]
My mother Rangumathi, what will I say Rangumathi?
'that-street people's cremation site we don't want,' they say, Rangumathi!
My mother Rangumathi, what will I say Rangumathi?
Kolme·l village, village where umbrellas hardly fit
My mother Rangumathi, what will I say Rangumathi?

Payrn angered the *ma·mu·l* people ('traditionalist' faction who did not support the new gods) of his own exogamous division, which occupied one segment of the village (*a·ke·r* or 'that street'), by agreeing to fill a ritual position for another exogamous division (occupying *naṟyke·r*, 'middle street'). The vacancy was left by a man who became a diviner for one of the new deities. When Payrn's daughter Rangumathi died, a quarrel arose in the village as to where the daughter should be cremated, whether in the site reserved for the 'middle-street' people, or the site used for the rest of the people.

This story illustrates how village factionalism is tied not only to different deities but also to the space on which Kota culture is inscribed. It is ultimately irrelevant whether this particular event occurred before or after the rain ceremony was instituted (almost definitely afterward, if it originated in 1933 or before), rather it characterizes a relatively extended state of disunity among the Kotas of Kolme·l, beginning with the arguments over new deities in the middle 1920s, and continuing for several decades.

Now, although a few families still tacitly avoid worshipping at the *ko·jka·l* temple (the single temple erected for the three new gods), the new deities have generally been embraced . The new gods were only one of a number of changes occurring at the time—sartorial changes and changes in hairstyle, a movement to do away with the menstrual seclusion hut—all modern in outlook but also contrary to Kota cultural conventions. These conventions were brought into clear focus when they were challenged. Kotas were compelled to reconsider practices they had never previously needed to question.

Believing that the gods had or would leave the village and return to their places of origin, the Kotas became acutely aware of their ineffectiveness in coping with a deadly epidemic; and they associated this ineffectiveness with the exigencies of modernity: they needed new gods for the new times. But new gods created new problems of village divisiveness. In this sense, for several decades after the plague of 1924, the 'literal routines' of the Kota community broke down and the community was made to believe, by new factions in the village, that the traditionalists (*ma·mu·l kaci*) were causing the community to be 'considered by false or moribund categories.'[116]

Then, in 1933, there was no rain. Kota stories like those associated with the cattle of Kirputn's son (§3) and the milk tree (§5) demonstrate that divination in Kota society locates a physical problem (sick cows or inability to find a particular tree) in a societal one (violation of a taboo or social dissonance). A Kota deity responded, through a diviner, to this 'time of stress' and outlined a course of action to restore rain whose ritual vocabulary and grammar constituted a discourse of holism. It is therefore not unreasonable to suggest that the rain ceremony may have served a *revitalizing* function in the 1930s.

Conclusion: Performed Identities in Space and Time

By juxtaposing tunes and places of religious significance, the rain ceremony establishes a common context through which the interrelatedness of music, people, places, the gods and community memory is *performed*. The rain ceremony is in this way an argument—not a verbal argument, but an expressive one—which links the notion of unity or wholeness to the efficacy of the gods and the continuity of the Kota community. Here rain is transformed into a key symbol: a literal nourisher of the Kota people and an indicator that the Kota community is still vital—spiritually, socially, and physically.

By ritually reinscribing the landscape, the rain ceremony persuades the gods to remain in the village and defines the 'Kota' realm against that of the 'outside'. We may regard as a case in point the recent introduction of the *kunerṭvaṇ* (the new shrine, 'little place fruit') to prevent encroachment by the *bo·yars.* Based on this principle of inclusion and exclusion, Sulli's assertion that rain fell 'only in Kolme·l, not across the boundary' is logical, even if not literally true.

This analysis of the rain ceremony suggests that Kota constructions of what we might call 'spatialized subjectivities' meaningfully parallel those found on the plains. Margaret Trawick has suggested in a recent paper, for example, that Tamil Paraiyars identify so strongly with the places they inhabit that 'place' and 'people' become virtually equated (Trawick 1991: 224). 'Place' emerges as a rhetorical substitution for 'people' in the verbal style that Cevi, a Tamil agricultural labourer, employs in her performance of song (1991: 236–7). The parameters of Tamil identity with the land, in this example, are manipulated through language use.

Through a series of carefully framed questions, E. Valentine Daniel explored shades of meaning and semantic penumbrae of Tamil terms of place. He found that *āṟu nāṭṭu Veḷḷāḷars* conceptualized territories described by Sanskrit-derived terms (*tēcam, kirāmam*) in a manner systematically different from those described by Tamil ones (*ūr, nāṭu*). He argued that the Tamil terms provided a 'person-centric definition of space . . . in keeping with the person-centric orientation of Hindu culture'.[117] The Sanskrit-derived terms were 'relatively context free, universal, and fixed' (Daniel 1984: 70). Tamils located *ūr* boundaries in landmarks: first the shrine for a sentinel deity, Karuppu, and then other shrines, intersecting roads, and other points of significance.

We will recognize that the *āṟu nāḷḷālar* conception of 'the village' is virtually identical to the Kota conception of the village as constituted in ritual.[118] Perhaps Kotas are affectively attached to features of the landscape, in part, because they strongly value the latter close to their gods. On a spatio-social level, the integrity of Kolme·l village thus comes to depend upon keeping the gods within its borders. These borders, like those of the Tamil *ūr*, are divine locales. The constituent rituals of the rain ceremony designed to please the gods residing there thus achieve, in effect, a 'binding' of the village.[119]

Divine localities in South Asia are almost always associated with origin stories that explain or illustrate their power. To state that 'place-histories' are 'a unique Tamil expression of Hinduism' (Gonda 1962, 2: 40; cited in Harman 1989: 25) would be stretching a point because 'many of the histories of particular Tamil temples appear, either originally or exclusively, in the Sanskrit language' (Harman 1989: 25), and the phenomenon is certainly not confined to India.[120] But in the Nilgiris many places are not just locations of divinity but are *themselves* divinities—among the Kotas and even more so among the Todas,[121] mountains are a principal example of this phenomenon. But once again, as Zvelebil warns us,

> One must . . . be cautious in ascribing an 'areal status' to this cultural trait. Hinduism in general, particularly in the South, knows of mountains which *are* gods and are worshipped as such: the best-known example is probably Arunacala-Tiruvannamalai, which is worshipped as the 'solidified' form of the fiery Linga (Zvelebil 1979, III:149n.).

Thus we find that the Kotas assign significance to places and organized spaces in manners akin to those found in other parts of South Asia, and particularly South India. It may be that what makes Kota space 'Kota' is indeed the particular claims on the landscape rather than the forms these claims take.[122]

The claims of morality and spiritual power placed upon the landscape and the musical repertoire are *qualitative* claims about the past. In fact, rather than referring to 'the' past, these claims refer to 'a' particular past. The past is selected: it is a favourable past, a strategically significant past. The particular past is emphasized in the present, under sacralized conditions. To support and sustain selection and symbolic manipulation of the past is not a phenomenon confined to the Kotas: it is characteristic human behaviour, particularly in the context of social and political movements. But as Arjun Appadurai has argued, there are important culturally imposed limits on the past as a symbolic resource (Appadurai 1981). The many 'pasts of an Indian village' (cf. Cohn 1987 [1961]), or any other cultural unit, must be understood in culturally specific and historically situated terms. The Kota method of linking place, past and identity is as much South Asian in character as it is Kota.

We have seen that the god tunes function in much the same way as place in this place-past-identity equation. The type of musical sign in operation here is what Christian Kaden has termed a 'detached or loosened symptom' (1984: 126; cited and translated in Stockman 1991: 329)—that is, when the context and function of music are 'loosened from their contextual conditions (a lament from actual death and its rituals, a march or dance from a situation of real marching or dancing), they refer to the original reality more in the sense of a symbol' (Stockman 1991: 329). Thus the temple-opening tune and other god tunes come to have more richly nuanced meanings when they are incorporated into contexts other than those for which they were named. They also accrue meaning when conceptualized as a unit rather than as units. Instead of merely being copresent during isolated rituals, they are inscribed in a musical genre called the 'god tunes'.[123] Their sequential performances during the god ceremony and the rain ceremony are musical rituals unto themselves. But the meanings of the music reach deeply into other ritual and historical values.

Postscript

The Kotas have managed in course of time to maintain a remarkably strong sense of uniqueness within India while at the same time adjusting to and incorporating both modern and Hindu features of Indian society around them. Most Kotas find no contradiction in stating they are Kota and they are Hindu; that they belong to a tribe and have their *own* deities and that these deities are also 'Siva' and so forth. What Mandelbaum wrote in 1941 is perhaps even more true today.[124]

> The new ways are so much with the tide of the times that even the most obdurate of the surviving conservatives have yielded to them in some

degree. For a time, there was a possibility of fission in Kota society, through a process which has often occurred in Indian village life when the devotees of a new dispensation form themselves into a new endogamous group. But the reforms now seem quite right to most Kotas who have grown up in the past twenty years; and the integrative forces—including their apprehensions about the Badagas—are strong enough to avert any split in the Kota community . . .

They can happily worship two sets of gods because, like most peoples of India, they find no necessary contradiction in doing so, as long as their social practices and identity do not suffer thereby. And as has commonly happened in India, the new deities are being amalgamated with the older gods. Many of Sulli's fellows agree with him that the new gods are just the old ones who have decided to take new names, new forms, and to prescribe new ritual practices (Mandelbaum 1941: 254).

This phenomenon of inclusion is so widespread in India that for some people it, along with caste, has been erroneously thought to be somehow a defining feature of Hinduism.[125] But this does not mean that the Kotas do not strive to establish and maintain a certain 'Kotaness.' Within this modern Indian context, the rain ceremony strives for a rather special kinds of Kotaness. Unlike the unfortunate ritual leader who lamented as he searched all the holy places of the village 'god, god, where are you?' the Kotas celebrate on these holy places and beseech the gods for rain, asserting by their actions, 'god, god, here you are' and, by extension, 'so are we.'

Notes

1. The data for this paper derive from ceremonies I witnessed in 1991 and 1992 in Kolme·l and Ticga·ṛ villages, and from historical and contemporary descriptions of the ceremony in these and other villages. Kota village names, rather than equivalents in English, Tamil or Badaga languages, have been employed throughout this paper. Common English spellings for the seven Kota villages are given below:

Kota	*English*
Kolme·l	Kollimalai
Ticga·ṛ	Trichygady
Me·na·ṛ	Kundah Kotagiri
Porga·ṛ	Kotagiri
Kina·ṛ	Kil Kotagiri
Kurgo·j	Sholur Kokal
Kala·c	Gudalur

I have retained the English word 'Kota' instead of the Kota word *ko· v* however, to facilitate English indication of gender and number, i.e. 'Kota woman' rather than the linguistically correct *ko· ty*, and 'Kotas' rather than *ko· vgu· ḷ* All spellings accord with Emeneau's phonology in *DEDR*, etc.

2. Nancy Munn suggests that iconicity between symbol vehicles and meaning is a generalizable phenomenon: 'the form of the vehicles is intrinsic to the message carried, and certain qualities of the referents are put into social circulation as part of this form' (1974: 580). That is, the overall organization of the ceremony, its formal features (the way in which the places and tunes are used or presented), should structurally replicate the meaning of its constituent elements (the places and tunes themselves).
3. 'Time-binding' is Fernandez's skillful turn of phrase for 'one of the chief contributions of culture', its ability to knit together, to unify, and to bridge the apparent dichotomy between past and present (Fernandez 1966:69).
4. Central concepts in Victor Turner's work on ritual are particularly revelant here: the capacity of ritual to unify apparently disparate significata, and to condense many ideas and relationships into a symbol vehicle that would require considerable exegesis if expressed verbally.
5. David Lan's subtle analysis of the Zimbabwean revolution notes an analogous relationship among people, land and rain among the Shona of Zimbabwe, where proper regard for the spirits of dead chief's was necessary to ensure rain, 'peace and plenty'. Furthermore, 'amongst the Shona the right of ownership in land is demonstrated and proved by the ability of a particular set of ancestors to control its fertility. The people whose ancestors bring the rain own the land' (Lan 1985:98). In this regard, Kota gods are to Kotas what Shona ancestors are to the Shona. Lan's book served as an inspiration in my own analysis, as in my initial field investigation.
6. Although the meanings behind sacred sites and musical tunes could conceivably be manipulated in new and different ways, they generally are not. That is to say, all ceremonies directed towards the gods involve a similar style of 'selectivity', the process of 'constructing around the dominant symbol a context of symbolic objects, activities, gestures, social relationships between actors of ritual roles, and verbal behaviour (prayers, formulas, chants, songs, recitation of sacred narratives, and so on) that both bracket and underline those of its referents deemed pertinent in the given situation' (Turner 1977:187).
7. *See* Daniel (1984:13) on a use of the term 'culture' which comprehends this creative process.
8. For more on this 'representational hypothesis' concerning the relationship between macro- and micro-sociological perspectives see Knorr-Cetina's introductory essay in *Advances in Social Theory and Methodology. Toward an Integration of Micro- and Macro-sociologies* (1981: 30–40 and *passim*). *See* also Marcus' concise summary (1986:169 n.6).
9. For a critical analysis of the use of history in ethnography see the essay 'Ethnography and the Historical Imagination', and other essays appearing in the book of the same name (Comaroff and Comaroff, 1992). My present article does not, however, aspire to be the new 'historical ethnography' which the Comaroffs propose—particularly because my subject matter is, on a gross level, easily circumscribed.

10. Rather, it empowers the President of India, in cooperation with a State Governor, to designate which 'tribes or tribal communities' are to be scheduled (Mehta 1991:29).
11. For a broad spectrum of arguments see Mehta (1991), Thapar (1977). Singh (1972), and for a review, Babiracki (1990).
12. For a discussion and critique of a related idea, 'primordialism', in the discourse of ethnic identity and nationalism, see Brass (1991:16 and *passim*).
13. If a community is officially classified as a 'tribe' it is eligible for various forms of government sponsorship.
14. Duryodana is a Tamil name (actually a Sanskrit name drawn from the *Mahābhārata*, pronounced as if it were Tamil). At birth, all men and women are given one of several Kota names. First born males in Kolme·l, for example, are named Kamaṭn. Nicknames are used to distinguish among those with the same name. These include 'flat-nose', 'eyebrow', 'shit' and other which relate either to some distinctive physical features or to some funny childhood story. Nowadays it is common to give a child Tamil or other Indian name in addition to a Kota name.
15. The tribes in the Gudalur area of Tamil Nadu and in the Wynaad of Kerala are currently working together under the auspices of ACCORD—Action for Community Organization, Rehabilitation and Development. They hold an intertribal gathering every year which features traditional sports, games, music, dance and drama as well as newly created ceremonies expressing intertribal solidarity.
16. The word probably entered Kota through Tamil: see the *Tamil Lexicon.*
17. The term results from a 'false' etymology: *ma·mu·l* is interpreted as a combination of the prefix *ma,* from the Tamilization of the Sanskrit *mahā,* great, with the Kota word *mu·l,* 'direction' (metaphorically extended to 'way or manner'). *oc* is a Kota prefix meaning 'new'—but the connotation, often negative, is foreign or forbidden, '*oca·ḷ cet̠*' for example, refers to the stench of a 'new' (i.e. non-Kota) man.
18. *See* Mandelbaum (1960; 1941) on village factionalism based on attitudes towards *ma·mu·l.*
19. What may seem even more obvious, at least on the surface, is that since both terms are not Dravidian, the concepts themselves may not be indigenous. The assignment of such social-cultural meanings to linguistic phenomena is very tricky, however, and would warrant consideration of a kind I am not equipped to carry out.
20. Although over his three years in the Nilgiris Emeneau worked primarily on the Toda language, he also made the first significant contributions to the study of the Kota, Kodagu and Kolami languages.
21. Sulli's life is discussed at length in Mandelbaum's article, 'A Reformer of His People' (1960).
22. Very few Kotas converted to Christianity and those who have are effectively separated from the community. Reverend Metz's disparaging account of Kota attitudes toward missionaries in 1864 captures the spirit, if not behaviour, of Kotas today: 'when I endeavour to address them they drown my voice with their dreadful music, or compel me to retire by abusing me in the most obscene and offensive language or barking at me in the style of their own half-wild dogs.

Thus I have often had to leave their villages, with a heavy heart at their apparently hopeless condition' (Metz 1864: 134).

23. Emeneau feels that his lack of familiarity with Tamil allowed him to learn the structures of Kota and Toda without a Tamil bias (1993, pers. com.).
24. Intensive learning from a few knowledgable informants is a common, pragmatic, and perhaps necessary component of fieldwork. The problems engendered by relying on a small number of informants are not so much those of 'getting it wrong' or creating lacunae, since completeness is a fiction anyway, as they are the silencing of the dialogic process which ultimately informs an ethnography. Some recent ethnographies still explore the possibilities of understanding culture through the individual (e.g. Crapanzano 1980; Shostak 1981). But the significance of these ethnographies, Clifford notes, 'is the transformation of 'cultural' text (ritual, an institution, a life history, or any unit of typical behaviour to be described and interpreted) into a speaking subject, who sees as well as is seen, who evades, argues, probes back'. This is effected by 'staging dialogues or narrating interpersonal confrontations' (Clifford and Marcus 1986: 14). Mandelbaum represented Sulli in such interactive settings—although seldom with the anthropologist in broad view.
25. The Badagas (lit. 'northerners') comprise a number of castes who migrated to the Nilgiris from Mysore, probably in the sixteenth century. They participated in a close system of reciprocal obligations with the Nilgiri tribes until the middle of this century when imbalances in population, the rise of a cash economy, and political fractionalism led to the gradual breakdown of this system. *See* Hockings' *Ancient Hindu Refugees* and other references in *Blue Mountains* (1989). The role of a Badaga, Christian or otherwise, as an interpreter or an informant in research about the Kotas is a precarious one, given the distrust some Kotas have and do harbour towards them.
26. Particularly from the Badaga M.N. Thesingh, a man who served as an informant to subsequent scholars, including Paul Hockings.
27. On Sulli's ability to speak English and Emeneau's role in improving it, see Emeneau (1940, I: v).
28. I have not been able to ascertain what Sulli's position was *vis-à-vis* others in the community before he became active in pushing for reforms. To the extent that present-day observation can illuminate the problem, Kotas tend to hold members of their community who have succeeded in the modern world (education, salaried, urban jobs, etc.) in high esteem provided they do not try to use this success to bolster their power within the village.
29. This familiarity was undoubtedly gained through his missionary education. But he also gained experience as the lone Kota, who, by virtue of knowing the English language, could mediate between Kotas and the English (Sulli n.d.).
30. An identification of the idea of 'tune' with the instrument it is played on is indicated by the use of one term, *koḷ*, for both. The word *koḷ* could also be translated as 'melody,' but I prefer 'tune' because 'tune' seems to convey the notion of a musical unit, a song without words; ('Do you know that tune?' means 'Do you know that composition?' 'Do you know that melody?' could refer to a particular part of a composition). 'Composition' might also be suitable, but the term carries with it Western notions of invention that are not appropriate.
31. This practice is common to most of the Nilgiri and Wynaad tribes who maintain traditions of instrumental music and dance: these include Iruḷas, Beṭṭa

Kurumbas, Ālu Kuṟumbas (and probably Pālu Kuṟumbas as well), Kāṭṭu Nāyakas and Paṇiyas.

32. Although two *koḷs* may in rare cases be distinguished through their accompanying rhythm (*da·k*), the melody alone is usually diacritical.

33. The origin of the number twelve is unclear. Pucan claims to have learned only twelve of what were once sixteen *devr koḷs.* Each time we (myself and other interested Kotas) have attempted to count the *koḷs* as they are performed sequentially (whether in ritual context or isolated for performance), we have arrived at a different number. The number twelve has no particular significance in Kota culture.

Sulli, in Mandelbaum's notes on the rain ceremonies, mentions that eighteen 'songs' are played, some sung and some on instruments. In other contexts, Sulli and other informants have mentioned nine god tunes and twelve god tunes. Because there seems to be some question as to what is counted within the special repertoire and what is excluded from it, I hesitate to conclude that the repertoire has shrunk, although it does appear that fewer men are competent to play these tunes now than were able to in the 1930s. Most of the special twelve *devr koḷs* are generically called *aṛca·yḷ koḷs* as they are played together as a set underneath an enclosure called *arca·yḷ.*

34. These processes have been discussed systematically, e.g., Tambiah (1981) on ossification in ritual and Kaden (1984) and Stockman (1991) on semiotic aspects of decontextualization in music. Manuel (1993: 131–52) devotes a chapter to a related process through which melodies become 'resignified' in Indian popular music.

35. Although I have not been able to figure out the morphology exactly (and it was not readily apparent to Emeneau either, when I asked him), the term *o·ḷa·gicd* apparently refers to the making (*gicd*) of the sound of the holy syllable '*o·Iy*' as is commonly the practice during peak moments of worship.

36. Raman, the husband of R. Mathi and father of Duryodana, is also the classificatory younger brother of Pucan. Deep respect mixed with competitive feelings and moral and ideational differences characterize their relationship. Pucan and Raman, as my closest musical and cultural teachers and friends, encapsulate for me the absolute contestability of cultural meaning and content.

37. This lore also appears in passing throughout many of Mandelbaum's fieldnotes—from several informants, from several villages, and through different interpreters. Toward the end of his 1930s fieldwork period, Mandelbaum began eliciting stories connected with these tunes. He obtained information similar to what I collected. I had not seen these stories before my fieldwork ended, although I had read a version of the rain ceremony as Sulli dictated it.

38. Va. Kamatn, who died in February of 1992, had lost his position as *mundka·no·n* when his wife died. Among the Kotas, ritual leaders and diviners must be married and their first wives (who have important ritual roles) must be living.

39. *Talko·r* (also *talkavr* and *talku·r*) is a place near Me·na·ṟ village that lies along the route to the Kota land of the dead (located near the Toda land of the dead, near Mukurti Peak; see Emeneau 1944, II: 195). It is the site at which the culture hero Koṯe·rveyki·ṇ was said to have shot an arrow into a stone and released a spring. A version of this story, recorded by Emeneau in the 1930s (1944, I: 137) is also told today, and is preserved in a well-known mourning song. Mr Raman, in the context of discussing the spirits of the dead (*a·na·ṭo·r,* literally 'those

of that land'), mentioned *talko·r* as the name of the place that the dead go to. He may have been confused: he also thought the place may be called *dodde·r vetm,* which means 'big god peak'. *Dodde·rvetm* is also a holy place near Me·na·ṛ. Neither place, however, is considered to be the land of the dead.

40. Zvelebil provides an account in which two Irula brothers quarrelled and parted. The next day when they met, the older brother asked what the younger had eaten. Both claimed to have eaten fruit and milk, but in fact the older had eaten meat. They quarrelled again and vomited to prove what they had eaten. Through magic of the older brother, the younger vomited meat. He was sent to settle in Karamadai on the plains and the older brother went to settle on Rangasami Peak. The account continues to relate how the divinity of each brother was discovered. What is significant here is the association of the Karamadai deity and Rangasami as brothers (Zvelebil 1988: 137–8) The Karamadai temple is now considered Tamil Vaisnava (*i.e.* Hindu), but an Irula priest also plays a role in the *pūja,* the details of which I do not know. Zvelebil reports, misinterpreting Emeneau somewhat, 'Kotas worship the god at Karamadai in the Vaisnava temple there including him in a prayer which is said by the Kota priest and the diviner in the field before they begin to plow . . .' At the time of Emeneau's research, the prayers including the names of older Kota gods were apparently extended to include the newly arrived Karamadai gods. The Kotas used to visit Karamadai and participate in the festival there; after bringing the god(s) to Kolme·l they no longer actually went to Karamadai. Zvelebil identifies *Beṭdamn* ('peak goddess'), the goddess included in the 'new' Kolme·l trinity, with *Raṅgamma beṭṭ* ('Ranga mother peak'). Although there was reluctance to admit the Karamadai gods into Kolme·l village, there was and is a belief that the deity in Karamadai was originally a tribal one. A Kota origin story for the temple (provided by K. Pucan) is similar to the one reported by Zvelebil (1979 III: 137), but the protagonists are a Kota and a Kurumba. If the Irula story of two brothers is merely a transformation of the Kota story of a Kota and an Irula (the Kina·ṛ *mundka·no·n's* story), the Koṭa Nilgiri *co·ym* may actually be the deity now called *Rangasami* (or Rangasvami, Ranganathan, etc.). This conjecture is also supported by Emeneau's story of *koṯe·rveky maṯe·rveky,* culture heroes and best friends who have been memorialized (and apotheosized) in stones on hills near Kina·ṛ village and Me·na·ṛ village (*talko·r,* see previous footnote) respectively. A variation on this story, found today, maintains that both sites are parts of the same parts of the same deified man: the head near Me·na·ṛ (thus justifying the *tal* morpheme of *talko·r,* meaning head) and the rest of the body near Kina·ṛ.

41. *See* previous note for an extended discussion of this identity.

42. Although the people from Kinaṛ village also have (or had) a Nilgiri god tune, I was unable to hear or record an example to compare it with that of Kolme·l.

43. This is a version told by K. Pucan. I found two other versions of the same story in Mandelbaum's 1937–8 fieldnotes, one by a musician and one by Sulli. Sulli's version did not mention that a tune was associated with the story.

44. The 'eighteen songs' to which Sulli refers in Mandelbaum's notes might also have some connection with this. *See* also Emeneau's *Kota Texts* (1944, II: 337, n.5), where eighteen days of the god festival are mentioned, and eighteen gods are also mentioned (1944, III: 17).

45. 'A "shola" is . . . an evergreen forest of the elevated Nilgiri Plateau, located along stream banks or in hollows and surrounded by large tracts of savanna' (Lengerke and Blasco 1989: 54).
46. Mandelbaum collected a version of the same story from Kurgo·j village. I recorded a version of the *kab ercd koḷ* in Kurgo·j, played on the *bugi·r* (a five-holed bamboo trumpet, not a 'flute' as in *DEDR* 4239) by K. Mundan (brother of S. Cindamani). His version of the tune is quite different from that of S. Raman and K. Pucan. It may be an entirely different tune with the same name and story attached. Comparison is difficult in part because I did not ask the musicians themselves to compare the tunes and because versions of the 'same' tune on the *bugi·r* and on the *koḷ* will sometimes differ because the latter has six holes and the former only five.
47. Since *kunayṇo·r*, according to one story, is said to have come to Kolme·l from Porga·ṛ village out of attraction for the music, the last day of the Kolme·l god festival, 'dance day,' is celebrated in honour of him.
48. This is one of the few instances in which the accompanying rhythmic pattern, or *da·k*, is a diagnostic feature of a *koḷ*.
49. Before the lamp was introduced, the only objects in the temple were a few large stones within which the fire was built. Ornaments are no longer forged within the temple. A stock of ornaments and coins is kept with the ritual leader or another trusted member of the community.
50. Here the question of how Kota 'icons' relate to Hindu 'icons' is relevant: modern Hindu gods often look like people. Kota icons like the bow and arrow are different in that they embody divine practice. In a way this is comparable to the way the musical instrument, the *viṇā*, or any book, *is* the goddess Sarasvati.
51. Also called *paṭm kacd koḷ*, or 'coin offering tune'. The tune is rhythmically different from but melodically similar to the *amno·r moyr paṭd koḷ*. These observations of similarity and difference are Pucan's: he thinks about the tunes in this way to keep track of which ones he has played and which ones he has yet to play at a given time.
52. The period during which Dr Varadharajan and the other two men arrange the coins into faces is one of the loosely structured periods during which young boys can practice playing the musical instruments without fear of reprimand. The instruments are loud and should not be played in the village at other times unless a particular occasion calls for it.
53. It is difficult to determine when the Tamil word *iyaṟkai* began to take on Rousseauistic meanings. The word is derived from the Tamil verb *iyal* meaning 'to be possible'; *iyal* as a noun means 'nature' in the sense of 'property' or 'quality.' The abstract noun *iyaṟkai* has meant not only 'nature, disposition, inherent quality' but also 'that which is natural', as opposed to that which is made (*ceyaṟkai*). This latter meaning has been traced to the *puṟananūra* (written circa first century BC-AD first century; cf. *Tamil Lexicon*). But even in this opposition we should not read 'nature' versus 'culture'. The absence of a Kota word for 'nature' is not conclusive evidence that the concept is foreign; but neither is the presence of a word for nature in modern Tamil usage evidence that the concept is ancient. It seems likely that the modern *iyaṟkai*, when it is used in the sense of Nature, with all the romantic connotations, is the result of

syncretism–but how, when and if this occurred really cannot be traced. I thank Dr James Lindholm for providing insight into some of these points.

54. *Ayno·r* is also known in Kolme·l and some other villages as *Kamaṭraya*, a name for which M. B. Emeneau has not yet been able to discover a satistactory etymology.

55. A god of the same name is important to the Todas as well, as I have found this deity mentioned in one Toda song I recorded. Vasaumalli, a Toda woman who translated the song for me, commented predictably 'they [the Kotas] copied it [worshipping the hunting deity] from us'.

56. Several other villages have a site of divinity called *toḍba·l* and an associated origin story similar to that told in Kolme·l.

57. This is the description S. Raman (age fifty-seven in 1992) recalls hearing when he was a thirteen year-old boy. A village diviner described the ritual to him. Even at the turn of the century when Thurston was collecting information on the Kotas the shooting of the bison was a bygone practice, but 'what takes place at the present day is said to be unknown to the villagers, who are forbidden to leave their houses during the absence of the hunting party' (1909, IV: 16).

58. I made this point in a paper entitled 'The apotheosis of a Musical Repertoire: Identity and History in the 'god tunes' of the Kota Tribe (Nilgiri Hills, south India)' (Wolf 1993).

59. Schechner constructs a similar argument about the Ramlila processions of Ramnagar, which 'condenses much of the Indian subcontinent into a comprehensible single sacred space with nine main stations . . . ' (1983:257).

60. Indu Nagar, the headquarters of Hindustan Photo Films, lies just outside Ootacamund.

61. This version of the story is modern and fashioned for my understanding in several ways. For one thing, Kota worship is not called *pūja: pūja* is a specifically Hindu ritual which usually involves worship of an anthropomorphic deity with fire, incense, flowers and coconut. Kota worship is much simpler in form. Mr Pucan did not disclose the 'mistake' committed by the *mundka·no·n* and, as I feel other Kotas may not want this information revealed, I leave it out of my account. The modernity of this version of the story also lies in its location. The introduction of a lamp into the temple is a phenomenon of the last half-century or so, and some villages still reject this Hindu influence. A version of the story related by Mrs Cindamani of Kolme·l identifies the *mundka·no·ḷ*, wife of the *mundka·no·n*, as the singer of the song. In this version she attempts to coax the god back after her husband committed a ritual error. In this version it is the lamp in the house that disappears: this makes a bit more sense since the lamp is lit in the temple only once a year. She finally finds the lamp at *ponic*, one of the numinous sites involved in the rain ceremony.

62. The rain ceremonies of Kina·ṛ village (fifty-five kilometres north-northeast from Ootacamund) and Porga·ṛ village (on the edge of Kotagiri town, thirty kilometres east of Ootacamund) and an additional ceremony at Ticga·ṛ are different. They involve young unmarried girls circling the temples and the village while sprinkling water. Kala·c village (on the edge Gudalur town) practices no ceremony for bringing rain, in part, I gather, because rainfall is timely and abundant.

63. See Mandelbaum (1941) for the story of how this Karamadai deity came to be worshipped in Kolme·l.

64. During the time of Mandelbaum's and Emeneau's research, the new gods were referred to in relation to an adjacent area called *ke·rva·y*—literally 'street mouth', presumably an entryway into the village. Why the point of reference has changed I have not been able to determine.
65. For the word *ko·j* see Emeneau in this volume, par. 17 and footnote 15.
66. This term is a contraction of *koḷpartabaṭk*, or *koḷ*, the double reed instrument, *par*, the barrel drum, and *tabaṭk*, the frame drum.
67. This arrangement was undoubtedly more orderly than it would have been had I not been present and videotaping the event. But in general, at gatherings at the *naṭkal*, elders are seated as has been described and others in a group to the east, either circled around or loosely facing the rest of the group.
68. In this case they played the 'eighteen god calling tune' (§4) and 'Nilgiri god tune' (§2). The order is not fixed, but Pucan keeps a general sequence in mind in order to remember which tunes have been played and which have not.
69. See Needham (1967) on the role of percussion in association with 'the formal passage from one status or condition to another'.
70. I did not note the exact direction while the ceremony was being conducted. While mapping the area later, my assistant Duryodana pointed to the direction and I noted it with my compass. On another occasion I asked Pucan's son, Dr P. Varadharajan, and he said the direction of prayer was east, 'facing the sun'.
71. The *ka·dman kaṇḍy* may be significant as a marker of the past in two respects. It is near a tree where Todas used to offer clarified butter at Kota god ceremonies and would sit to watch the proceedings. Todas were not permitted (by their own 'pollution' rules as well as by Kota orthodoxy) to enter Kota villages. The general region of the *kaṇḍy* also encompasses an abandoned buffalo or cow pen (*to·y*) which may have had a significance which is now lost.
72. It may never have been a formal prayer; see earlier part of this essay on Sulli's tendency to verbalize thoughts.
73. Mandelbaum (n.d., field notes from 14 May 1937 [misdated 13 March], p.7). I have revised the transliteration system and standardized the spelling to conform with my system. I have also translated directly from the Kota, rather than reproducing Sulli's English which, in this case, overlooks important subtleties.
74. I used 'since' to translate a conditional tense in Kota that could also be translated as 'while'. There is a slight possibility that I misinterpreted what Mandelbaum had written as '*itme·l*', since vowel length was not indicated. The 'e' should be long for '*itme·l*', to mean a conditional form of the verb 'to exist in place' (*DEDR* 480). If the 'e' is short, the words should be separated and the 'el' is short for '*elm*'—'all'. In this case translation would read 'O Kamatraya who lives in . . . and Rangrayn who lives in... and all [in the sense of etcetera]'. This is close to the rough translation that appears in Mandelbaum's notes, but I think it is in this case an unlikely one based on my experience with the language.
75. S. Raman has repeatedly told me that the gods left Kolme·l long ago and that is why no new diviner has become possessed in the last several decades. See also Mandelbaum (1941).
76. *Kamaṭraya* is another name for *ayno·r* (see p. 270, nt. 54). There are two *ayno·r* temples, one for 'big' *ayṇo·ṟ* and one for 'little' *ayṇo·ṟ*.

77. It is not clear the extent to which the new gods ever played a role in the rain ceremony. In other, less elaborate descriptions by Sulli and in those Mandelbaum collected from other Kolme·l informants, the new gods appear less prominently than they do throughout the May 1937 account.
78. I think 'left' is normative but I know no reason for it.
79. The same place as *ponac* in *Kota Texts* (Emeneau 1944, III: 131–2). Here a man/demon would wait and attack men by swallowing them through his anus, until conquered in *te·lo·yna·r* by a man named Ciṅg ra·jn. Although I was not able to learn any more about *ponic* during fieldwork, Mandelbaum noted that stones used to be taken from *ponic* to the village during the god ceremony to be used in the construction of the shed (*aṛca·yḷ*) (Mandelbaum n.d: 27 October 1937).
80. This first stone circle is about a metre high and two metres in diameter. One must remove footwear if entering within an area of about seven metres in radius from the circle. The stones of the first two circles in *ponic* are supposed to be of ancient origin, but the structures themselves are periodically rebuilt and painted white.
81. Pucan said three coins, *mu·nd paṇm*, are offered to the deity but I only noticed one rupee coin and in Sulli's account only one rupee was offered.
82. During the most important days of the god festival, for example, attendance is taken and those not present are punished with additional or unpleasant tasks. Women are usually involved in other activities during ceremonies. If the presence of all women is required in any ceremony connected with Kota gods, the women must not be menstruating. During the god ceremony, the potential problem this creates is solved through a ritual in which all women are symbolically secluded in the menstrual hut for one day (they all go to one area below the village: they cannot actually fit in one house). By doing this they are considered free from the effects of menstruation (*ti·ṭ*), which, as in Hinduism, must not come in contact with the gods. But this temporary fiction is only partially accepted: the women who are actually menstruating cannot dance on the *pacaḷ* (grassy area between the temples). The rain ceremony is conducted on a Monday, a day on which working in the fields is prohibited. Women are busy on this day cleaning the house, purifying the house and the area around it with cowdung, cooking and other domestic activities. They play no direct part in the procession, offering of coins, or music making.
83. Unified action by the ritual leaders is, in an extended sense, a performed version of what Ortner (1979: 94) calls a summarizing symbol; although it would be more accurately termed a summarizing icon, in the Peircian sense of icon (Peirce 1955: 102): a sign which resembles its object. More precisely, it is what Peirce terms an iconic legisign, 'any general law or type, in so far as it requires each instance of it to embody a definite quality which renders it fit to call up in the mind the idea of a like object'. Unified action by the ritual leaders is a 'type', even a Kota 'law' of behaviour, which suggests similar unified action be followed by the rest of the Kotas.
84. Sulli and several other of Mandelbaum's informants described versions of the same ritual and a version was also documented by Thurston (1909, IV: 23). I am told the ritual is still practiced in Kolme·l today when a woman gives birth to her first child, but I have not had the opportunity to witness it.

85. The *toḍba·l* is a site of a *ne·ṛl* tree in Kolme·l, and to my recollection, in each Kota village which has a place of similar name.
86. In this ceremony the power of the Kota gods is affirmed in a spontaneous overflowing of milk. This milk is milked in secret by the ritual leader and kept in the *kakui* (back room) of his house, the same room in which 'god' in the form of a bow and arrow resides. 'May milk overflow', or '*pa·l poṅgum*', is a redolent image in many Kota prayers which means to Kotas, 'let our population increase'. It is a metaphor for community vitality. For an account of the milk ceremony, see Emeneau's *Kota Texts* (1944, IV : 300–9).
87. In Tamil the word *tiṭṭu* also refers to the lasting and defiling effects of death. In Kota the word *ke·ṛ* is reserved for this 'death pollution'. I have in general avoided the English word 'pollution' because it tends to lump different concepts into one category. The effects of death and menstruation are dealt with in very different ways. The verbal root of *ti·ṭ* (*DEDR* 3274) in many Dravidian languages means 'to touch' or to defile by touching; *ke·ṛ* is related to the Dravidian verbal root *keṛ-*, 'to perish or be spoiled'. The noun form *ke·ṛ* and related forms in other Dravidian languages mean 'ruin, death' or 'evil'. Although menstruation is defiling to men and to the gods, it is not 'evil' or the same thing as death.
88. The divine value accorded fruit helps explain why the other name of *ponic*, *erṭvaṇ,* or 'place fruit', may be significant as a place name. Nowadays people think of *ertvan as* a name, not as a word with a significant etymology.
89. 1.48 metres in height, 2 metres in diameter, with a 30 cm. high rectangular block on top.
90. As was typical in many ritual situations, in 1992 there was considerable disagreement about which direction was correct. One village elder, Mr Motakambaten, claimed prayer must be in the direction of the village temples, i.e. West. The previous year's headman, Mr Bullan, argued that worship should be directed to the north, towards Doḍḍabeṭṭa. Pucan, who was considered the ultimate authority, said that prayer should be directed northwest. Pucan's son, Dr Vaṛadharajan, who recounted this dispute, suggested, with some doubt, that northwest might be the direction of *ve·ṭka·r ayṇ* (see previous discussion of the *ve·ṭka·r co·ym koḷ* or 'hunting god tune' [§8]). The notion that the direction be connected with some sort of significant place or deity is important. It is also interesting that questions of what should be done, and why, are open for debate. Northwest may have been ultimately arrived at as a compromise but the 'reason' may have been invented after the fact.
91. Other Nilgiri tribes and the Badagas chant similar syllables in a similar style. The Toda 'dance songs' documented by Emeneau are executed in this style. The Kota chants have no semantic content.
92. On other ritual occasions possession is desirable and its failure to occur is a bad sign. In Ticga·ṛ, possession of the diviner was (in 1991) a formal part of the rain ceremony.
93. Kotas of today sometimes describe the offerings in similar terms. Dr. Varadharajan—not without a note of humour—described offerings to the god as 'bribes'.
94. Since the text is not given in the vernacular, it is unclear here, as it is at times elsewhere, whether Sulli was explaining his interpretation or whether a prayer is recited during the ritual.

95. In *pūja* flowers have at least two major classes of meanings. As a fragrant offering to the deity, flowers are a form of honour, welcome and beautification. In this way, they support other activities like the offering of incense, fruit and music and the dressing of the deity [see, e.g., extended description of *pūja* in Babb (1975: 31–67)]. At times the colour of the flowers is important, red flowers being associated with certain deities and yellow flowers with others. Hanchett (1988: 121) reports how villagers' interpretations ('the goddess likes it') differ from an educated Brahmin's interpretations of the *tala* flower: the tight buds are a model for chastity and the yellow color is fitting for the goddess of wealth. Daniel (1984: 190–223) describes a divination ritual in which the meaning of flowers hinges on the correlation between colours and personal 'qualities' (*kuṇam*), hot vs. cold, past, present and future, and so forth. Gold (1988: 124, 190–261 and *passim*) shows how the word 'flower' is used by Rajasthani pilgrims to denote (and suggest identities between) 'icons embodying spirits of dead children, bone remains of cremated adults, womb, and unborn children'. These are but a few examples which suggest flowers are 'elaborating symbols' (Ortner 1979: 96) in Hinduism.
96. Setting off an area as 'sacred' is a common strategy in India for protecting land.
97. Further details concerning this legend can be found in Mandelbaum's fieldnotes, e.g. his 11 February 1938 annotations to notes of 24 April 1937.
98. There is considerable variation in accounts of this process. Many Kotas talk of Tipu Sultan without really knowing when and where he actually ruled.
99. The numinous quality of gods and their association with particular spots is, of course, a widespread religious theme in India. Such spots often become pilgrimage sites, representing in broad geographical terms what the sites in the rain ceremony trace, as a processional route, in and around the village.
100. During *pabm* ('festival'), for example, the entire village eats off the same plate in every house of the village (Emeneau 1944, IV: 294–301).
101. Tobacco sharing as a strong symbolic statement of unity is also indicated by Sulli's description of occasions in which tobacco was not accepted by all male members of the village: these men were permitted to voice their grievances, and tobacco was shared only after the disputes were settled.
102. The diviner did not climb the *tak* tree in 1991 because he could hardly walk.
103. 'Leave' does not mean refraining from work, but refraining from certain kinds of work: in particular, agricultural work.
104. Kotas told me that their weekly days of leave were signs of respect for their gods. Sulli provided an alternate explanation for the observance of a holiday on Monday (Mandelbaum n.d.). Apparently the Kotas used to work for their Badaga 'partners' (those with whom they had established reciprocal obligations) on Mondays. After the Kotas and Badagas discontinued their relationship, the Kotas continued to recognize these days as out of the ordinary by refraining from working in their own fields.
105. I draw upon de Certeau's special use of the word 'strategy', 'the calculation (or manipulation) of power relationships that becomes possible as soon as a subject with will and power (a business, an army, a city, a scientific institution) can be isolated. It postulates a *place* that can be delimited as its own and serve as the base from which relations with an *exteriority* composed of targets or

threats (customers or competitors, enemies, the country surrounding the city, objectives and objects of research etc.) can be managed'.

106. 'Disjuncture' is a key word in a current anthropological discourse about modernity. In a recent, rather influential article, Arjun Appadurai argues that displaced communities and intensive cultural transactions constitute an interactive system which is 'strikingly new' (Appadurai 1990). I would argue that such disjunctures are apparent even among communities like the Kotas, whose recent geographical ('ethnoscapes') displacements have been minimal but who are inextricably entangled in national and global 'finanscapes,' 'technoscapes,' 'mediascapes' and 'ideoscapes'. I would locate the primary disjuncture, among the Kotas, as temporal rather than territorial; but as we have seen in the rain ceremony, a self-awareness of inhabited space is an important (but not necessarily new) cultural value. What has occurred musically, the collection of tunes from diverse sources into a single repertoire (broadly encoding a positively valued past), is an example of 'reevaluation' (Slobin 1992: 70) which has occurred within the community and *not* for outsiders.
107. That the rain ceremony was a yearly event in 1937 is indicated in Mandelbaum's handwritten annotations to his typed notes from 14 May 1937.
108. From the way the notes tend to include questions and answers, and from how they were annotated from inquiries on later days, I tend to think Sulli volunteered this information without prompting.
109. Timothy, one of Mandelbaum's Christian Badaga interpreters, said, 'These fellows know how to make rain at the end of April. They are lazy and do not fork their fields in March and April as do the Badagas, or they hire someone to do it for them, so at the end of April their ground is as hard as stone. They go around their boundaries one day with music and by three o'clock that day an inch of rain must fall' (11 July 1937).
110. The English gloss for the Kota is provided by L. Gunasekaran. The actual interview was conducted by Gunasekaran's father, Lakshmanan, because the family wanted a record of his speech, stories, and general knowledge of the old days. Va. Kamaten was literally on his deathbed, his conversation was very difficult to understand, and his narratives were interspersed with frequent gaps in memory.
111. The recently deceased diviner of Kolme·l, who became diviner after the plague, said forty of the eighty people living in the village at the time succumbed to the disease.
112. See more on this deity in the discussion of the Nilgiri God tune (§2) and above, note 45.
113. Term of affection for a girl.
114. This phrase refers to a golden age in which the village was more populated. 'The houses at Kolme·l were so many and so closely spaced that the old-style leaf umbrella, which cannot be folded, could not be carried through the village' (Emeneau 1944,1:81).
115. The streets or *ke·rs* correspond to exogamous units in the village. The 'middle street' people use a cremation site separate from that used jointly by the other two exogamous divisions.
116. Here I return to these quotations to reiterate the relevance of Fernandez's arguments, 'Particularly in times of stress—where literal routines break down

and where we are constrained by false or moribund categories—do we turn to figurative language and the argument of images for a wider and more transcendent view of things. These are the times with which ritual and revitalization are most associated' (1986: 205–6).

117. Ramanujan's *Interior Landscape* provides a very different, ancient Tamil conception of peace which coarticulates with emotions, time periods, flora and fauna, and music.
118. Incidentally, *u.r* is also a Kota word, referring generically to non-Kota villages. A Kota village is termed *ko·ka·l*, or 'place of Kotas'. Kotas use specific words for the places Badagas, Todas and Kuṟumbas inhabit as well, i.e. for the communities with whom they have had extended contact.
119. In the adjoining Coimbatore district, Beck (1976) provides an analysis of an entirely different sort that demonstrates a relationship between spatial orientation, person and the cosmos itself.
120. Stories of Australian aboriginal places (this 'singing into existence' is captured nicely in Chatwin's 1987 novel, *The Songlines*) and Christian European pilgrimage sites are prominent examples. Keith Bassoa has written suggestively on the use of placenames and stories in everyday language among the Apache (Basso 1990). Writings on South Asian place-histories are extensive and need not be enumerated here. For further reference consult Harman (1989: 25–7).
121. Although as Walker (1986: 156) notes, the 'gods of the sacred [dairy] places' are considered much more important than the mountain deities.
122. Pilgrimage is a common structure through which diverse identities may be simultaneously instantiated. Gold (1989), for example, shows how individual life aspirations are projected into pilgrimage, and Fuller (1992: 211), the symbolic role of pilgrimage in Maharashtrian cultural unity. For a more general discussion of Indian regionalism, *see* Bernard Cohn's (1986) essay 'Regions Subjective and Objective: Their Relation to the Study of Modern Indian History and Society,' and the comments that follow in the volume.
123. Actually, the tunes that belong to this 'detached' category are the 'twelve god tunes' (or *aṟca·yḷ kols* , tunes played under the rough-hewn hut [§1-§9]). They form a sub-genre of a more general genre of 'god tunes' which are still tied to the contexts for which they are named.
124. I am told the factions remained until about 1960. Sulli may well have exaggerated a picture of social harmony to bolster his own image as an effective reformer.
125. Inden's recent (1990) critique on Indology and histories of India puts such essentialisms in their place.

Appendix

1. Text to *veḷke· veḷke·* as sung by K. Pucan, 16 May 1991

ka·r a·vo·ṛ kabiṭvd ayṇo·r e·y o·ḷi·ro
co·ym e·y o·ḷi·ro veḷke· veḷke· e·y o·ḷi·ro co·ymḷ
(these first two lines were not lined up well with the tune and are not strictly characteristic of the verse-form of this song)
veḷke· veḷke· e·y o·ḷi·ro va· co·ym
toḍba·le o·ḷi·ro va· co·ym
veḷke· veḷke· e·y o·ḷi·ro va· co·ym
ne·rl marka·l o·ḷi·ro va· co·ym
vile marka·l o·ḷi·ro va· co·ym
veḷke· veḷke· e·y o·ḷi·ro va· co·ym
ne·rl marka·l o·ḷi·ro va· co·ym
ponic lie o·ḷi·ro va· co·ym
veḷke· veḷke· e·y o·ḷi·ro va· co·ym
veḷke· veḷke· e·y o·ḷi·ro va· co·ym
viky marka·l o·ḷi·ro va· co·ym

2. Prayer at *ponic* as Sulli dictated to Mandelbaum
(I have standardized the spelling)

co· mi kamaṭraya amno· r ayṇo· r ra· mco· mi raṅgco· mi beṭdamn
(calling gods, three old Kota deities and three new ones, Ramaswamy, Rangaswamy and Betdamn).

a· m nin mog kunj vitaṇ el vitṯ may
we're your sons[1] sowing and all having completed rain

i· la· d kactm paṭr co· ym ka· lk
being without difficulty experiencing god's leg at

copni· r viglk a· m elm ni· mn pacrvaglk vade· m
to fall in prayer we all you to grab and come came

kamaṭr ayṇ venveṭd itlme· raṅgrayṇ
Kamatr father (god) living in Venvetm and Rangr father (god)

ka· rmo· ṛḷume· itme· l a· m ennm varkvd[2]
in Karamadai also since you are living we how prospering

adnk· yṛ a· m doḍa· ḷo· r kuna· ḷo· ṛ emd par
for that reason we with big men and small men our barrel drum

tabaṭk koḷo· ṛ kobo· ṛ ni· m paco· ko· m iḏr
frame drum with shown with horn with you we grab and go thus

vade· m emn marva· d a· m a· to· n da· kl
we come us without forgetting (?) one who calls like

va· ve· rm ad nimd pa· dtn a· m pace· m
? (we come?) that your feet we grab

1. *Mog* means 'soni' and *kunj* means 'men as children of god' (*DEDR* 1646).
2. Probably variant conjugation of *DEDR* 5372 (*vadky-*)—to prosper—is perhaps pronounced more like Tamil *vāḻ*?

3. Song composed by Tu·j (father of S. Raman) for Payrn's daughter Rangumathi, as sung by Kembi of Kurgo·j village, 7 June 1992.

la la la . . .
en av raṅguma· dy enke· ngo raṅguma· dy
kolme· l ko· ka· l ko· r a· ṛad ko· ka· l
la la la . . .
naṛyke· ro· r du· vk ve· ku· d̲a· re raṅguma· dy
la la la . . .
en av ranguma· dy enke· ngo raṅguma· dy
la la la . . .
a· ke· ro· r du· vk ve· ṛa· d̲re raṅguma· dy
en av raṅguma· dy enke· ngo raṅguma· dy
kolme· l ko· ka· l ko· ṛ a· ṛad ko· ka· l
en av raṅguma· dy enke· ngo raṅguma· dy
la la la . . .

REFERENCES

Appadurai, Arjun 1981. 'The Past as a Scarce Resource'. *Man* n.s. 16: 201–19.

——— 1990. 'Disjuncture and Difference in the Global Economy'. *Public Culture* 2, no. 2: 1–23.

Babb, Lawrence A. 1975. *The Divine Hierarchy: Popular Hinduism in Central India.* New York: Columbia University Press.

——— 1981. 'Glancing: Visual Interaction in Hinduism'. *Journal of Anthropological Research* 37: 387–401.

Babiracki, Carol 1990. Musical and Cultural Interaction in Tribal India: The Karam Repertory of the Mundas of Chotanagpur. Unpublished Ph.D. dissertation; University of Illinois, Urbana-Champaign.

Basso, Keith H. 1990 *Western Apache Language and Culture: Essays in Linguistic Anthropology.* Tucson: University of Arizona Press.

Beck, Brenda 1976. The symbolic merger of body, space and cosmos in Hindu Tamilnadu. *Contributions to Indian Sociology* n.s. 10: 213–43.

Brass, Paul R. 1991. *Ethnicity and Nationalism: Theory and Comparison.* New Delhi: Sage publications.

Burrow, T., and M. B. Emeneau 1984. *A Dravidian Etymological Dictionary* [*DEDR*]. 2nd edition. Oxford: Clarendon Press.

Chatwin, Bruce 1987. *The Songlines.* New York: Penguin Books.

Clifford, James 1988. *The Predicament of Culture: Twentieth Century Ethnography, Literature, and Art.* Cambridge, Mass.: Harvard University Press.

——— 1990. 'Notes on (Field) Notes' *In* Roger Sanjek, *Fieldnotes,* 47–70. Ithaca: Cornell University Press.

Clifford, James, and George E. Marcus. (ed.) 1986. *Writing Culture: The Poetics and Politics of Ethnography.* Berkeley: University of California Press.

Cohn, Bernard S. 1966. 'Regions subjective and objective: Their relation to the study of modern history and society'. *In* Robert Crane(ed.). *Regions and Regionalism in South Asian Studies: An Exploratory Study.* Durham: Duke University.

——— 1987 [1961]. 'The pasts of an Indian village'. *In* Bernard S. Cohn. *An Anthropologist Among the Historians and Other Essays,* 88–99. Delhi: Oxford University Press.

Comaroff, John, and Jean Comaroff. 1992. *Ethnography and the Historical Imagination.* Boulder: Westview Press.

Crapanzano, Vincent 1980. *Tuhami: Portrait of a Moroccan.* Chicago: University of Chicago Press.

Daniel, Valentine 1984. *Fluid Signs: Being a Person the Tamil Way.* Berkeley: University of California Press.

de Certeau, Michel. 1984. *The Practice of Everyday Life.* Steven Randall trans. Berkeley: University of California Press.

Eck, Diana L. 1981. *Darsan: Seeing the Divine in India.* Chambersburd, PA: Anima Books.

Emeneau, Murray B. 1937-8. 'Ritual games of the Kotas'. *Bulletin of the Sri Rama Varma Research Institute* 5: 114–22; 6: 1–6.

——— 1944. *Kota Texts.* 4 parts. Berkeley: University of California Press.

Emeneau, M.B., and T. Burrow 1962. *Dravidian Borrowings from Indo-Aryan.* [*DBIA*]. Berkeley: University of California Press.

Fernandez, James W. 1966. 'Unbelievably subtle words: Representation and Integration in the Sermons of an African Reformative Cult'. *History of Religions: An International Journal for Comparative Historical Studies* 6, no. 1: 43–69.

——— 1982. *Bwiti: An Ethnography of the Religious Imagination in Africa.* Princeton: Princeton University Press.

——— 1986. *Persuasions and Performances: The Play of Tropes in Culture.*

Fuller, C. J. 1992. *The Camphor Flame: Popular Hinduism and Society in India.* Princeton: Princeton University Press; New Delhi: Penguin Books India.

Gold, Ann Grodzins 1989. *Fruitful Journeys: The Ways of Rajasthani Pilgrims.* Delhi: Oxford University Press.

Gonda, Jan. 1962. *Les Religions de l'Inde.* 3 vols. tr., L. Jospin. Paris: Payot. (Cited in Harman 1989).

Hanchett, Suzanne 1988. *Coloured Rice: Symbolic Structures in Hindu Family Festivals.* Delhi: Hindustan Publishing Corporation.

Harman, William P. 1989. *The Sacred Marriage of a Hindu Goddess.* Delhi: Motilal Banarsidass.

Hill Fox (Pseud. for A. K. Ranganathan) 1960. *Nīlakiri Carittiram* (*mūṉṟām pākam*). [Nilgiri History (third part)]. Ootacamund: Ṭi kiraṇṭ Indian Publications.

Hockings, Paul 1980. *Ancient Hindu Refugees: Badaga Social History* 1550–1975. The Hague: Mouton Publishers.

——— (ed.) 1989. *Blue Mountains: The Ethnography and Biogeography of a South Indian Region.* Delhi: Oxford University Press.

Hockings, Paul, and Christiane Pilot-Raichoor 1992. *A Badaga-English Dictionary.* [*BED*]. Berlin: Mouton de Gruyter.

Inden, Ronald 1990. *Imagining India.* Cambridge, MA: Blackwell.

Kaden, Christian 1984. *Musiksoziologie.* Berlin: Verlag Neue Musik. (Cited in Stockman 1991).

Knorr-Cetina, Karin, and A. V. Cicourel 1981. *Advances in Social Theory and Methodology: Toward an Integration of Micro- and Macro-sociologies.* Boston: Routledge and Kegan Paul.

Lan, David 1985. *Guns and Rain: Guerillas and Spirit Mediums in Zimbabwe.* Berkeley: University of California Press.

Lengerke, Hans J. von, and Franois Blasco 1989. 'The Nilgiri environment'. *In* Paul Hockings (ed.) *Blue Mountains,* 20–78. Delhi: Oxford University Press.

Lévi-Strauss, Claude 1966. *The Savage Mind.* Chicago: University of Chicago Press.

Lutkehaus, Nancy 1990. 'Refractions of Reality: On the Use of Other Ethnographers' Fieldnotes. *In* Roger Sanjek (ed.) *Fieldnotes,* 303–23. Ithaca: Cornell University Press.

Mandelbaum, David G. n. d. *Field Notes.* Bancroft Library collection no. 89/129cz. Berkeley: University of California.

——— 1939a. 'Agricultural Ceremonies among Three Tribes of Travancore'. *Ethnos* 4: 114–128.

——— 1939b. 'The Jewish Way of Life in Cochin'. *Jewish Social Studies* 1: 423–60.

——— 1940. *The Plains Cree.* Anthropological papers of the American Museum of Natural History (New York), 37 part 2.

——— 1941. 'Social Trends and Personal Pressures'. *In* Spier, Hallowell and Newman (eds.) *Language, culture and personality: Essays in Memory of Edward Sapir,* ed. Menasha Wisconsin: Sapir Memorial Fund. Repr. *in* Charles Leslie (ed.). *Anthropology of Folk Religion,* 221–55. New York: Vintage Books (1960).

——— 1960. A reformer of his people. *In* Joseph Casagrande (ed.). *In The Company of Men.* New York: Harper.

——— 1966. 'Transcendental and Pragmatic Aspects of Religion'. *American Anthropologist,* 68: 1174–91.

——— 1989. 'The Kotas in Their Social Setting'. *In* Paul Hockings, (ed.) *Blue Mountains,* 144–85. Delhi: Oxford University Press.

Manuel, Peter 1993. *Cassette Culture: Popular Music and Technology in North India.* Chicago: University of Chicago Press.

Marcus, George E. 1986. 'Contemporary Problems of Ethnography in the Modern World System'. *In* Clifford and James Marcus, (eds.), *Writing Culture* George E. *The Poetics and Politics of Ethnography*, 165–93. Berkeley: University of California Press.

Mehta, P. L. 1991. *Constitutional Protection to Scheduled Tribes in India: In Retrospects and Prospects.* Delhi: H. K. Publishers.

Metz, Johann Friedrich 1864. *The Tribes Inhabiting the Neilgherry Hills: Their Social Customs and Religious Rites.* 2nd edition. Mangalore: Basel Mission Press.

Munn, Nancy D. 1974. 'Symbolism in a Ritual Context: Aspects of Symbolic Action'. *In* J. J. Honigmann (ed.) *Handbook of social and cultural anthropology*, 579–612. New York: Rand McNally.

Needham, Rodney 1967. 'Percussion and Transition'. *Man* (n.s.) 2: 606–14.

———— 1975. 'Polythetic Classification: Convergence and Consequences'. *Man,* (n.s.) 10: 349–69.

Ortner, Sherry. 1979. 'On key symbols'. *In* William A. Lessa and Evon Z. Vogt. (eds.) *Reader in Comparative Religion: an Anthropological Approach,* 4th edn.; 92–8. New York: Harper and Row.

Peirce, Charles S. 1955. *Philosophical Writings of Peirce.* Justus Buchler, (ed.). New York: Dover.

Ramanujan, A. K. n.d. *The Interior Landscape: Love poems from a Classical Tamil Anthology.* Delhi: Clarion Books.

Sanjek, Roger, (ed.) 1990. *Fieldnotes: The Makings of Anthropology.* Ithaca: Cornell University Press.

Schechner, Richard 1983. *Performative Circumstances: From the Avant Garde to Ramlila.* Calcutta: Seagull Books.

Schneider, David 1968. *American Kinship: A Cultural Account.* Englewood Cliffs, N. J.: Prentice Hall.

Shostak, Marjorie 1981. *Nisa: The Life and Words of a !Kung Woman.* Cambridge, Mass.: Harvard University Press.

Singh, K. Suresh 1972. *The Tribal Situation in India.* Patna: Indian Institute of Advanced Study.

Slobin, Mark 1992. 'Micromusics of the West: A Comparative Approach'. *Ethnomusicology*' 36, no.1: 1–87.

Smith, Robert J. 1990. Hearing Voices, Joining the Chorus: Appropriating someone else's fieldnotes. *In* Roger Sanjek. (ed.) *Fieldnotes,* (ed.) 356–70. Ithaca: Cornell University Press.

Stockman, Doris 1991. Interdisciplinary Approaches to the Study of Musical Communication Structures. *In* Bruno Nettl and Philip V. Bohlman. (eds.) *Comparative Musicology and Anthropology of*

Music: Essays on the History of Ethnomusicology, 318–41. Chicago: University of Chicago Press.

Sulli, K. n. d. 'Culliyin varalāṟu' (Sulli's life history). Unpublished handwritten autobiography (in Tamil).

Tambiah, Stanley 1981. 'A Performative Approach to Ritual'. *Proceedings of the British Academy* 65: 113–69.

Tamil Lexicon. 1982. Madras: University of Madras.

Thapar, Romesh (ed.) 1977. *Tribe, Caste and Religion in India.* Meerut: G. Wasani for Macmillan India, Ltd.

Thurston, Edgar, and K. Rangachari (eds.) 1909. 'The Kotas'. *Castes and Tribes of Southern India,* 4: 3–31 Madras: Superintendent, Government Press.

Trawick, Margaret 1991. 'Wandering Lost: A Landless Labour's Sense of Place and Self'. *In* Arjun Appadurai, Frank J. Korom and Margaret Mills (eds.) *Gender, Genre and Power in South Asian Expressive Traditions,* 224–66. Philadelphia: University of Pennsylvania Press.

Turner, Victor 1977. 'Symbols in African Ritual'. *In* Janet L. Dolgin, David S. Kemnitzer, and David M. Schneider (eds.) *Symbolic Anthropology: A Reader in the Study of Symbols and Meanings,* 183–94. New York: Columbia University Press [Reprinted in *Science* (1973), 179: 1100–5.

Walker, Anthony 1986. *The Toda of South India: A New Look.* Delhi: Hindustan Publishing Corporation.

Wolf, Richard K. 1993. 'The Apotheosis of a Musical Repertoire: Identity and History in the 'god tunes' of the Kota tribe (Nilgiri Hills, South India)'. Unpublished paper read at the Midwestern Meeting of the Society for Ethnomusicology, Ann Arbor, MI.

Zvelebil, Kamil 1979. *The Irula (Erla) Language.* 3 parts. Wiesbaden: Otto Harrassowitz.

———— 1988. *The Irulas of the Blue Mountains.* Syracuse: Maxwell School of Citizenship and Public Affairs, Syracuse University.

Badaga Epic Poetry

PAUL HOCKINGS

11

Nilgiri Literature

The extensive literature on the Nilgiri Hills has been scholarly for the most part, and since the early nineteenth century has not actually included much Literature. Until half-a-century ago one could be forgiven for assuming that, since the indigenes were unlettered, writing about the Nilgiris was essentially a European undertaking. But then in 1944–6 M. B. Emeneau published the four volumes of his *Kota Texts,* and it immediately became apparent that even non-literate people could have their own folk literature without a medium of literacy. In 1971 Emeneau made the same point again, and perhaps even more tellingly, with the publication of his massive *Toda Songs.* This was to be followed in 1984 by *Toda Grammar and Texts.* Clearly a second Nilgiri community was creating a lively folk literature too.

Prior to Emeneau's gargantuan efforts in this field, the only creative literature associated with the Nilgiris was in the field of the English novel. Though not well known—and perhaps deservedly so—there were in fact four British authors active in the Nilgiris, three of them writing mediocre novels that are perhaps only worth reading today for their local colour.

The first of these, Florence Marryat, was a daughter of the famous Victorian writer Captain Marryat. She is now something of a bibliographer's nightmare, having at different stages in her life been known as Mrs T. Ross Church and Mrs Francis Lean. Her *Véronique* is a classic example of the three-volume Victorian novel that Oscar Wilde inveighed against; but it was evidently a successful one, for it ran to four editions during 1869–72, in London, Leipzig and Boston. Her heroine is a Roman Catholic girl from a village just south of Ootacamund, who is dishonoured by a perfidious Protestant. The next writer, Fanny Emily Penny, was the wife of a Protestant minister, who evidently lived most of the time in Coonoor, to judge by the setting of several of her very numerous novels: *Love in the Hills* (1913), *Get on with the Wooing* (1931), and *Chowra's Revenge* (1937), among others. A third writer, somewhat more polished and less romantic than these two, was C. Hilton Brown, who published several volumes of verse as well as novels; among them were *Dismiss!* (1923) and *The Second Lustre: A Miscellany of Verse* (1923). Some of his novels were set elsewhere in Southern India, or in Africa, where he died in 1961. In 1933–4 he was Collector of the Nilgiri district, and during 1940–6 he was a fixture in the Talks Department at the BBC. A fourth writer, who published little beyond the duography *We Two Together* (1950) to be set in the Nilgiris, with his well-known wife Margaret, was the art critic James Cousins. He had been a small part of the Irish literary establishment at the beginning of the century, linked with such figures as Joyce and Yeats in Dublin. He is known for writing a play, *The Racing Lug* (1902), but having spent most of his adult life in India, and his final years in Kotagiri, he is mainly remembered for his writings on Indian art.

More durable in its impact than any of these writers was the work of a local coffee-planter, Edwin Lester Linden Arnold (a son of Sir Edwin Arnold). This Arnold wrote only one, quite non-literary, work dealing with the Niligiri area, *On the Indian Hills: or, Coffee-Planting in Southern India* (1881); but he has been described as the 'inventor' of science-fiction writing because of his *The Wonderful Adventures of Phra the Phoenician* (1890), and as said by a recent (1995) critic to 'continue to have an influence on science fiction and fantasy.'

A more tenuous connection with world literature is the figure of Johannes Hesse, a missionary who lived at Ke:ti during the 1870s and wrote nothing of any note. His son Hermann Hesse, on the other hand, was to become one of the most influential writers of the twentieth century.

It is certainly time to recognize that throughout the entire period covered by the activity of these scribblers and the more serious investigations of M.B. Emeneau, there was also to be found in the Nilgiris a body of epic Badaga poetry which is still alive today (thanks in part to modern tape recordings). This poetry has not been examined previously, although one example has been presented in translation by Gover (1871), and has also been presented in Badaga by Hockings (1988: 560–87). This poetry is of such vibrant quality that an article on the subject is long overdue.

Epic Defined

The field of epic poetry is vast. The genre goes back at least 4,500 years to the *Epic of Gilgamesh*, a Babylonian tale that has come down to us in a dozen different versions in several languages, one being the biblical story of Noah and the flood. While all other epic poems known to us are more recent than that one, they are not necessarily confined to the literate civilizations, and have been recorded by anthropologists and folklorists across a wide field from Iceland to Africa and New Zealand. Such an immense geographical distribution suggests the possibility that epic poetry was more widespread in times long past, but that for want of any means of permanent transmission down to the present whole oral literatures have been totally lost to posterity again and again.

What do I mean by epic poetry, however? It is a story which is sung, a narrative song, perhaps even a slice of history retold again and again for public entertainment. The consensus among scholars is that an epic is narrative, poetic and heroic: as Felix Oinas expressed it, 'folk (or oral) epic songs are narrative poems in formulaic and ornamental style dealing with the adventures of extraordinary people' (Oinas 1972:99). Epic poetry normally has protagonists in the third person and past tense. It is true that a narrator may depart from the third person very occasionally, as if to keep his audience on their toes: in a Badaga example,

> Now Ma:di took some food and went to the outer room, where she ate it. She washed the plate: do you know what she's going to do next?

Such exceptions apart, epic contrasts with lyric poetry, which is typically in the first or second person, present tense.

Music seems nearly always to have been an integral part of the performance, whether it be vocal or instrumental. In fact, it has been found in various parts of India that 'the language of the epic is more influenced by song rhythms than by poetic metres... Indian poetic metres do not necessarily correspond with the rhythmic structures found in music and it is these rhythmic structures that prevail in many Indian epic performances' (Blackburn and Flueckiger 1989:3). The native term used for 'epic performance' in Badaga, Tamil and some other languages is the one we translate as 'song' *kaḍe.* Brenda Beck, in her study of *The Three Twins*, has demonstrated just how important a musician is in setting the rhythmic pattern of the performance and thus giving the Indian bard a framework within which he elaborates the tale he is to tell. Incidentally, I say 'he' throughout all this, because female bards are virtually unheard of. But in so far as epic poetry has been recorded for posterity, it is the verbal content which has commanded the greatest attention of folklorists, literary critics and ethnohistorians alike. It is only over the past half-century that effective means of recording music in the field have been available to some of us. Nonetheless the music is of great importance in setting the rhythm and regulating the tempo of the performance, and Beck rightly argues that it is these factors which allow the bard to get the whole story out—rather than his prodigious memory. She studied one performance in Tamil Nadu which ran for forty-seven hours, spread out over a three-week period; and she adds that 'One popular paperback version of the Brothers story, for example, has about 4,700 lines of text. A more literary variant, published more recently, contains over 9,500. The version dictated by the bard I commissioned has about 11,500 lines' (Beck 1982:6).

Oral Technique

So can we really believe the bard remembered every word of that epic by rote? No; in fact, Beck noted that, of the various bards she encountered in her study of *The Three Twins* epic, 'Each said he consciously added new bits of the story picked up from others, and subtracted things that seemed less popular. No bard interviewed claimed that he worked with a fixed text' (Beck 1982:85). The same is true of the Badaga bards I worked with: I recorded several versions of *Ka:ge Gauda* from two singers, and they were very different.

The singer's craft is a most demanding one. He has to sit before a critical, sleepy, perhaps even an unruly or drunken audience of his fellows, and rapidly tell a tale in a restrictive verse form, for a more or less continuous period ranging in the Badaga case from maybe ten minutes to eight hours. Even when running into a duration of some hours, this might be a relatively easy task for one who had memorized a precisely fixed text, such as a written one. Yet what the oral poet does is vastly more difficult, for he is in effect composing a more or less new song of great length and with virtually no pause for contemplation. It is therefore not surprising that this style of oral literature commonly includes large phrases or repetition. The man is remembering and versifying, rather than memorizing his material beforehand. This stems from the obvious fact that not only the singer but some generations of his predecessors in this task were unlettered people—either non-literates or men who wrote and read too haltingly to use a written text as an aid in their endeavour. In short, as the epic singers have no concept of a fixed text, I don't think we should be looking for one. The thematic content is fluid.

In the Badaga poems it is usual for the singer to begin his performance with a synopsis of the plot, or at least an outline of who the characters are. This is quite important, as some of the epics involve a large number of characters. Here, for example, is the opening of *Ka:ge Gauḍa*:

Mutta Gauḍa is a headman who was getting on well.
He owned Gudda:ṇi Estate, and was looking after it.
He died, and after his death a bad time began for Ka:ge Gauḍa.
Another man, Beḷḷiya Ka:ḍa, is a prominent person on the Hills.
Ka:ge Gauḍa was in distress for a dozen years with his misfortunes,
But Beḷḷiya Ka:ḍa encouraged him, saying 'Don't be afraid!'
Ka:ge Gauḍa approached Cikkana Dore . . . (and so on).

As the story develops, attention to detail is, along with repetition, what makes the Badaga epic so infernally long: this quotation from *Kadare Gauḍa* is absolutely typical. It is the advice of a mother to her daughter on meeting her suitor for the first time.

I know you like him very much, so when you go to bow down your head to their hands, go very carefully:
For if you take mincing steps they'll say you are like a hen;
And if you take big steps they'll say your legs are very broad.
So you must look at the ground very carefully when you walk.
[This line is actually a Badaga saying]
'As you walk you shouldn't trip'. So she counselled her daughter.
Wearing a distinctly coloured strip of cloth supplied by Mala Cetti and tied to her loincloth,
The coloured border of which had also been woven by Mala Cetti;
Her headdress given by Cinna Cetti had a panel like gold;
So she just came along, passed through the door, and came onto the threshold,
And just peeped out to see them.
She trod with milky steps, and when she lifted each foot it was just like clarified butter.
She went near to them on the embankment, and welcomed them, saying,
'Uncle, have you come then?' and they blessed her with pearly hands,
Saying 'you be good!'

But here the singer gets into the formalities of greeting, which tend to be worded the same way every time people meet formally in the poem. Incidentally, one will notice here and elsewhere the many references to dairying. It is a curious and historically interesting feature of the entire Badaga corpus that Badagas are regularly portrayed as cattle-farmers, and very rarely is there any reference to agriculture, which is in fact and long has been their primary mode of subsistence. It looks as though they see a certain glory in herding cattle, fending off tigers or other marauders and so on, which far outshines the dull daily routine of farm work.

The social and artistic functions of epic performances are quite varied: they may serve as panegyric, as family, community or national history, as political propaganda, as a form of education for the young, and last but certainly not least as night-time entertainment. Aware that so much can hang on his performance, the epic singer as we have seen carries the tradition in his head and recomposes the songs as he goes along. Thus the singer must be aware of the occasion and the nature of his audience, people who must ultimately be moved to action, to tears or laughter, or at least be instructed, through the skills of his total performance. The fate of the song is in the hands of the singer: he may corrupt a good and worthwhile story, or he may perhaps improve and elaborate one that had been in a corrupt state. But since he does not slavishly repeat the same words on every occasion, he becomes a creative artist who by the very nature of his work denies later critics the possibility of establishing a 'correct' text or an 'original' version of the tale. This fact was, of course, well known to many generations of Homeric scholars.

Epics and History

It is commonplace that epic poems might be used as historical evidence, as indeed the Homeric ones have been, but that they do not nowadays stand up to rigorous scrutiny as historical documents. That at least may be the view of modern historians and ethnohistorians, but it is almost beside the point. For those often unlettered hearers of an epic performance believe that the poem is faithful to history, and accept it as willingly as, over the past seventy years, they have been able to accept the truth of mythological films.

Although English is one of a few European languages that use the word 'history' for a factual account of past events, other languages use *historia* to mean a story, a tale well told. English evidently needs to keep the boundary between history and myth distinct. Anthropologists and historians know of several ways in which the two differ, and one of these is in the count of characters: a history of the Indian independence movement has no set number of participants in it, and the number could easily be expanded a great deal at each re-analysis. But the *Æneid* and each text of the *Morte d'Arthur* have a definite cast of characters. The telling of Badaga epics is not so rigid, and extra characters do sometimes slip in and out of the action at successive retellings. Not only that, but additional historical information—gossip or commentary, if you like—is available to the bard which is not always incorporated in his poem. It is as if the archaeologists could tell us how King Arthur actually lived at Glastonbury in the first half of the sixth century—something additional to the texts of the fourteenth century Arthurian cycle—which would make them seem more historically valid. A simple Badaga case of this is the *Lament of the Grieving Mother*, a short song sung first after her mother's brother died, and following the death of all her sons: it ended with the despondent line.

'Though I gave birth to eight sons, the worst drought came to me.'

But people can also tell you that following her uncle's funeral the woman found she was pregnant and gave birth to yet another son, who grew up and prospered. They say that because of her great sorrow her dead mother's brother returned to be reincarnated as her son, and gave his name to the boy. But none of this is in the song as I recorded it: it's oral history.

In summary, the four elements common to all narrative find themselves presented in even measure in the epic poem: these are action, character, setting, and theme. In other kinds of oral literature, such as the short ballad, one or more of these features is usually given short shrift.

Content

In many of the world's earliest epics, such as *Gilgamesh* and the *Odyssey*, we find the hero seeking knowledge or power, commonly magical power, over the forces of the unknown, especially death and malicious spirits. So many of these epics take the hero into the underworld on some such crucial quest. In more recent times, however, this concern is not nearly so prominent in epic poetry as is the struggle against enemies and other evil human forces, as we can see in the Gaelic, Slavic and Badaga epics. Nonetheless there is one eighteenth-or nineteenth-century Badaga epic that indeed takes the heroine and her dim-witted guide on a tour through purgatory. I might quote a small part of that poem for the benefit of smokers:

'But elder brother Simpleton,
In a collapsed grave in the dirt of a ditch,
One person is lifting a bundle of tobacco and
People are letting out a little smoke:
Who are those people, O elder brother Simpleton?'
'Don't you know, O younger sister, Haṭṭi Tippe?
On the Nilgiri Hills those who have struck widows
And taken away their pocket-money,
On the Nilgiri Hills, those who did wretched things,
Those who caused injuries,
They are put into a collapsed grave,
Tied together, and one person gives them
A little smoke to puff, it is said.'
'Don't you know, it's the headmen.'
'On the Nilgiri Hills, all those wretched ones who have done evil
Remain in a ruined grave, don't you know?
Let the headmen be, younger sister.
Didn't you know, younger sister?
On the Nilgiri Hills, the headmen have done so much evil:
Hasn't Haṭṭi Tippe seen it with her own eyes?' (Hockings 1988: 562–5)

Morality is embodied in these works, even at the most basic level of separating good from evil. The accumulated wisdom of a culture must be transmitted to the younger generation, and artfully embedding it in a putative history of one's people has always been a part of epic poetry, not only among non-literate singers, but also in the work of poets like Virgil, Dante and Milton, who of course wrote everything down (or had a daughter to do it). In the Badaga corpus we have a particularly good instance of the didactic epic in something called *The Quarrel over the Boundary*. This is a ballad lasting nearly two hours which shows how it is better to have a headman mediate a dispute than fall to blows over it. The actual quarrel concerns a tree growing precisely on the boundary of two territories;

no problem over land, but one over the tree which contains eighty bees' nests full of honey, and so there are rival claimants for this. No doubt there was already friction between the two sides, but at least in this instance they did not get to the point of throwing rocks and wasps' nests at each other, as sometimes did happen.

Some Badaga Epics

Unige Ma:ḍa, one of the shorter epics I have recorded so far, is also one of the two already published (Hockings 1987). It deals with relations between the members of two very different Nilgiri communities, the Badagas and the Kuṟumbas. As has been pointed out many times before, and as other ballads like *Kadare Gauḍa* make clear, these two groups have traditionally had very strained relations, arising from the fact that the Kuṟumbas are taken to be the most dangerous sorcerers, and the Badagas, accepting this for unquestionable fact, bought the Kuṟumbas off with annual gifts of grain, cloth, and other goods. An orderly countenance was put on this transaction, Badagas going so far as to employ a particular Kuṟumba sorcerer to protect their village from the presumed supernatural attacks of other Kuṟumbas. For his services this village watchman, as I call him, was paid protection money in the form of food and goods that were levied from every Badaga household. Such at any rate was the traditional picture, although the institution has become moribund. But running counter to this stereotyped view of what Kuṟumbas can do, *Unige Ma:da* is a touching poem about goodness towards one's fellow men, and in particular the deeds of one particular Badaga in rescuing and befriending Unige Ma:da, a Kuṟumba, who was weakened to the point of death by starvation. The poem makes no reference to the fear Badagas regularly felt towards all Kuṟumbas or to the sorcery which ought to have been at Unige Ma:da's command. He belonged to a notorious Kuṟumba village, but one year the drought was so desperate there that it carried off his wife and eight sons. Keeping himself alive on honey and wild plants, he wandered to a Badaga hamlet where he collapsed, but was soon to be rescued by Jo:gi, a Badaga who also had eight sons. He and his wife nursed Ma:ḍa back to health, and in thankfulness Unige Ma:ḍa spent the rest of his life tending Jo:gi's buffaloes, whose curd had been his first food there.

This uplifting poem has a happy ending, but many do not. Another short song, *The Ghost who Asked for Milk*, is rather more typical of the tragic muse in Badaga poetry. It purports to be the words which a ghost sang to her living brother. He was out on the Downs, far from home, tending the buffalo herd, and thus did not know that his sister had died in her village. The song opens with the line,

'O Brother, elder Brother!—the apple of my eye!
I—your sister—have come here: please open up the door!'

But knowing that she could not have come there, least of all at nighttime, the young man refused to open the door although his sister's ghost was outside singing lines of a song in which she described which particular buffaloes she wanted. In the morning he went outside to find ten of his buffaloes dead—his sister's spirit had come in the night and taken them off to heaven with her. And then he met two men coming from the village with the dreadful news.

Death is omnipresent in the Badaga literature; indeed there is a short devotional song on the inevitability of death which quickly says it all:

What use is it if little ones, daughters and sons, are born?
What is the use if you build a thousand houses for your sons and daughters?—
Death awaits you.
For you, there will be death one day; there's death for you.
What's the use of milking a barrelfull of milk?
What use is it if extra food is grown?
For you, that is the last thing:
One day it will be the last thing for you.
What use is it to have a pearl necklace?
That is the last thing for you.
One day will be your last.
What use is it if for you to experience joy?
What if you have thousands and thousands of everything?
There will be death for you one day.

Taken as a whole, the Badaga epics have a distinctiveness that places them quite apart from Tamil epic poetry, from even that of the neighbouring Coimbatore district where Brenda Beck worked. This distinctiveness is more than just a matter of language difference, or Badaga vs. Tamil. For in the Tamil epics, such as the one studied by Beck, the gods loom large, and even the characters of the earthbound heroes are writ large, with exaggeration of their strength and far-fetched exploits being a constant feature. A major theme in most Indian epics is the relationship between men and gods; but the Badaga epics speak of another world than that, and no gods are there: there is relatively little by way of supernatural intervention. True, there is some sorcery and ghost possession, but this has nothing to do with the gods anyway; and it is notable that gods never make a dramatic appearance amidst human events, as they so often do in Tamil epics, and indeed in Tamil films.

So a feature that sets the entire corpus of Badaga epics off from epics elsewhere in India is their secular way of proceeding. I know of no corpus in another Indian language which so eschews gods and miracles as devices for advancing the plot. In a Tamil tale, for example, we can see by way of contrast the importance of miraculous events. A man is wrongfully accused of trying to elope with a dancing girl. Although the accused person, a military hero who has adopted a disguise, is taken before his king, the latter fails to recognize him, and gives him the gruesome sentence of being taken to the forest where an arm and a leg would be amputated. This was done, and the unfortunate man was left there, to be found by his grieving wife. But then the king learnt the true identity of the man he had punished, and in his grief prayed to the goddess Mīnakshi to give the poor man back his limbs. In answer to these prayers, the arm and the leg grew back... And so the story goes on (Shulman 1985:358). This is a relatively mild example of the miracles in Indian epics, but it would never occur in a Badaga one. The only spheres of the supernatural into which the Badaga poet steps concern ghosts and sorcery. And both are taken not as marvellous events but as regular facts of life. When the unfortunate heroine in *Kadare Gauḍa* goes down the mountain slopes, is bewitched and dies, modern people would suggest she had contracted malaria in that area and succumbed to it. But the traditional explanation was Kuṟumba sorcery, and so the poet elaborates on just how this was done.

I would also suggest that the characters of the Badaga heroes are not dramatically developed in their psychological features, as they would be in most European epics. *Kadare Gauḍa* again provides an example to support this view. For much of that poem is not about the hero Kadare but about his brother and the sister-in-law who are killed by sorcery. Until we near the end, Kadare's role in the overarching structure is perhaps to give continuity to the poem;

rather like the chorus in a Greek tragedy. This opinion becomes firmer if we look at the summary of the characteristics of epic heroes that has been provided by Jan de Vries.

TABLE 1

The Indo-European Heroic Life Cycle

1. A. The mother of the hero is a virgin.
   B. The father of the hero is a god.
2. A. The birth of the hero is physically 'unnatural' in some way.
3. A. The young child is exposed or abandoned by its parents.
   B. The young child is fed by animals.
   C. The young child is found by shepherds.
   D. The young child is raised by a mythical figure.
4. A. The hero reveals his strength, courage, or other peculiar features at an early age.
5. A. The hero acquires some kind of invulnerability.
6. A. The hero fights with a dragon or other monster.
7. A. The hero wins a maiden after overcoming great dangers.
8. A. The hero makes an expedition to the underworld.
9. A. The hero is banished from his realm but returns to become victorious over his enemies.
10. A. The hero often dies young.

Source: de Vries, *Heroic Song and Heroic Legend*, 1963

He has listed ten features generally found in the life cycle of the Indo-European hero; and these features are even found, all ten of them, in the Tamil epics; though Tamil, like Badaga, is not an Indo-European language (both are Dravidian). But when we look at the life of some such Badaga hero as Kadare Gauḍa we find *none* of these heroic features is present. One might argue that I have chosen the wrong poem for comparison and perhaps I have; yet if I pick out the one Badaga epic which is ostensibly more like an Indo-European epic, what do I find? Look at the poem called *Haṭṭi Tippe* or *The Song of Heaven* (Hockings 1988), which contains the nasty bit about smokers in purgatory. On the face of it I thought this one was reminiscent of Dante's *Inferno.* But if we glance at the poem we find only one correspondence with de Vries' list: Item 8—the hero (in this case a heroine) makes an expedition to the underworld. It is the only epic in the Badaga corpus where something like that happens.

Clearly then we are dealing with a new and original literature here. Superficially it seems to derive nothing from other regions, or from the two most famous, most widespread and most translated of Sankrit epics, the *Mahābhārata* and the *Rāmāyaṇa.* But is this really so?

Kadare Gauḍa

Since I have mentioned the poem *Kadare Gauḍa* more than once, I would like to examine it in some detail here. The story opens on a very happy note. Kadare and his younger brother Beḷḷi go off to another village, where they ask the headman for his daughter as a bride for Beḷḷi. Father and daughter accept the proposal, and soon she is brought in procession from her village to Beḷḷi's, and the wedding is completed. Almost immediately she becomes pregnant, and a son is born, little Jo:gi. So far the story has proceeded with charming details along just the lines that every Badaga would wish for himself. But now there enters the character of Senna Modaḷi, a Kuṟumba sorcerer. He got very angry as he hadn't been invited to the grand wedding, even though he was associated with Beḷḷi's family in a formal exchange relationship. When he visited their village, he found that the young wife Solema:di was alone at home, but her husband was off working in a tea estate. Solema:di politely offered the visiting Kuṟumba a simple meal of millet gruel and pea curry, but because he was still angry about her wedding he demanded a more costly meal of table rice and curried chicken. As she could not comply with this, he snubbed her.

Later Solema:di went off with a group of girls to gather wild gooseberries in the jungle; while doing this, they were watched by Senna Modaḷi. He turned himself into a mock-tiger (a favourite Kuṟumba trick), roared at the girls, and then took Solema:di's basket of fruit and threw it into the bushes. Not having seen this herself, she accused the other girls of having taken her fruit. An argument followed, and the girls went off leaving her alone. The poem immediately becomes foreboding, as these girls explain to Kadare Gauḍa the circumstances under which they had left his sister-in-law behind in the jungle. Knowing all about the tigers, elephants and sorcerers that live there, he begins to talk about how his brother will soon be going into mourning:

He prayed to god, to Brahma: 'What have you written on my head?
I've spent a thousand coins, even three thousand coins as earnest money for my brother Kumme Beḷḷi.
Spending so much, I've gained you only after a good selection.
When can I see your pearly face again? What can I say to my brother Beḷḷi?
Before all the beard has appeared on his face, he has to take a knife to it;
And is he to turn towards the street with a golden earring?
Is he to do the funerary earring ceremony?
Why haven't you come with the group? why were you alone out there?'
Meanwhile the Kuṟumba was terrorising Solema:di:
That man poured the fruit out again and was filling her with fear.
Anyhow, when she stepped off the slope with some fruit,
He turned into a snake with five heads, and came and wrapped round her legs.
She was terrified of the snake—but then there was no snake.
And, filled with fear, when she took some four steps forward,
He again turned into a mock-tiger and stood before Ma:di.
Then she was very fearful, and leaving that spot she took four steps.
He turned himself into a bear, and since she was afraid,
Leaving that spot, she again took some four steps forward.
Then he turned himself into a little pig and was running round her in circles, and she was afraid.
Leaving that spot, she took some four steps forward.
He turned himself into a black dog: it was running round and round her legs.
Leaving that spot, she took some four steps forward;
Leaving that spot, she took some four steps forward.
After that, when she reached Micciha:ḍa,
Now with a turban like a big basket and a hair-knot like a small basket,
That man jumps from the upper part of the slope, with a bamboo stick.
And now, doesn't the So:lu:ru girl Solema:di's face turn like anything?
Her plate-like face became severe.

After Senna Modaḷi appears now as a man, they have a conversation which does nothing to assuage her fears. He invites himself to supper at her house that night, and after finishing it refuses to leave. She is alone there with her baby, and she moans to the child, 'Now the murderer is near me, and my husband isn't to be found,' But his brother Kadare Gauḍa comes along at that moment, and so the Kurumba sorcerer hides. She goes to the door and the poem moves forward dramatically:

. . . Kadare Gauḍa came along:
He came to the yard, and asked the girl to open the door.
As she opened the door, the Kuṟumba climbed up into the loft.
When he came into the house, he saw the girl's face by the light of the oil-lamp:
Her face looked most vexed. 'Why has your face become so dour, just like a plate?
I've spent a thousand coins and three hundred coins as earnest-money for you, Solema:di;

I brought you here after making the best selection for my brother Beḷḷi.
Things are getting bad for him now.
When shall we see your glittering teeth? When can we see your pearly face?
Whenever we come here, Ma:di, you'll be smiling; but now, what's the matter?
Whenever we come here, we see your front teeth; what's wrong with you now?'
'There's nothing to ask about now, O Brother-in-law: what's the use?
O Brother-in-law, Kadare Gauḍa, what's to be done now?
O Brother-in-law, you needn't worry yourself about the death of a female: think of her as an old lump of food:
That old lump is carried off by a black dog; think of it like that.
If Kadare Gauḍa is dead, we'll think one side of the district has been damaged;
If you die, one household of the gentry will be destroyed.
But if I have to go, then let me go: so please go away from here.'
As she said these words, Kadare Gauḍa was leaving in confusion.
'Today, O Brother-in-law, I'll be the wife of the Kuṟumba whom you've kept as a guard;
So I'm going away, and please let me go! Go away safely yourself!'
Then he said to her, 'When then can I see you, Solema:di? How can I bear this?'
And so saying, he went off with a gun;
With a gun which was then tied in knots by the Kuṟumba.
When he got to the end of the lane, then the Kuṟumba knew she had told Kadare Gauḍa everything.
He played all his tricks, and set fire to the water-tank.
He took a kidney, nurtured with milk, and ate it.
Thus he caused the girl to die within three days. Then he removed the bolt of the door,
He opened the wooden door, and sprang off into the jungle.

The Badagas know that they have no answer to Kuṟumba sorcery, unless perchance they can mobilize the resources of a yet more powerful Kuṟumba, as they sometimes think they have. That does not happen here, and the audience senses the inevitability of the situation: once a sorcerer becomes so angered, the death of his victim is just a matter of suspenseful time. In this instance it occurred because of the classic act of sorcery, his abstracting one of her kidneys and eating it. And, as if to underline just how evil this man Senna Modaḷi is, he evidently passes the night with the bewitched Solema:di, and then goes off to find her husband on the tea plantation, to bring him false news about his wife, brother and son:

Thinking you're away in the Estate for about three months,
They don't care at all for Fair Jo:gi (the baby), and they're having an affair . . .

Thus he made things far worse. Beḷḷi of course went storming off to his home, barely in time to see his wife die. She knew very well what was happening, and asked her father to describe her funeral. Then having identified Senna Modaḷḷi to Beḷḷi as the culprit, she sets the scene for the rest of the story, when she will be dead and when Beḷḷi must seek his revenge. And after the pre-planned funeral, Gauḍa searches out another bride for his brother, as indeed he should do.

Sometimes the action moves very fast, to reach a monumental climax. Thus the final passages in *Kadare Gauḍa* tell how he arranged this second marriage; how the marriage was performed but not consummated when the bride was twelve; how the Kuṟumba sorcerer Senna Modaḷi, having seen her at a festival, came during the night, drugged her new husband, and raped her too; soon after this she too died, whether from shame or sorcery one cannot tell. Yet finally a day of reckoning came:

'But I'll go to Meṭṭukallu
And I'll burn the whole place down.' So saying, off he went.
When he reached Meṭṭukallu he closed all the doors there,
But he couldn't know that one woman was outside the village answering nature's call.
After setting fire around the village, he happened to notice the woman standing beyond.
At once he hit her with a big stick, giving many blows, and thinking her dead threw her aside.
Once the fire was burning, all the people in the houses were incinerated.
But unfortunately the murderer [i.e. the sorcerer] had gone to Ni:rgunḍi at that time.
After a while, Kadare came to know he was in Ni:rgunḍi estate.

Well, this dramatic event actually occurred in 1875, as police records show. Beḷḷi's employment on a British–owned plantation, and the mention of a shotgun, also suggest this story was an interpretation of actual events of about a century ago. But one notices that Senna Modaḷi escaped the fire, and when Kadare Gauḍa heard this, he went after him with a shotgun. Finally he caught up with the sorcerer:

He caught hold of the hair of his head, and angrily exclaimed:
'Without your even asking, I've been giving you double tribute.
Although I've given you such presents, you made my house empty and finished off our two wives.'
When he was caught like this by the hair Senna Modaḷi began to wrestle too.
But he threw the Kuṟumba down on the earth, and holding him there firmly he put his toe to the trigger.
And one shot went off. But the Kuṟumba grabbed hold of an axe.
Then Kadare took this axe from him and chopped him with it.
Being thus wounded, the Kuṟumba was nearing death,
But he didn't die, and was much troubled, saying:

'Please take the knife and cut my thigh:
There is some potion inside my thigh.
You must take it out and burn it, for only then will I die.'
When he said that, Kadare cut his thigh with the axe.
After he took out the potion and burnt it, Senna Modaḷi died,
The poor man departed!

But the dénouement was still to come, and it was equally gripping. Kadare's arson had wiped out the entire labour force at Ni:rgunḍi Estate, and so its European proprietor brought a legal suit against him. This led to the conclusion of the epic:

To the man who had burnt the entire village, judgement was given that he should be hanged.
And giving such a judgement, the magistrate informed the Queen about it [i.e. the British government].
Anticipating that his sentence would be confirmed, he made ready the arrangements and asked Kadare Gauḍa his last desire.
Kadare was so asked, and replied that he wanted to chew betel leaves;
And so the betel leaves were given to him,
'And is there anything more you want?' they asked.
With a gob of betel leaves and nuts in his mouth, he said,
'I want to see your lady near me' [i.e.the magistrate's wife].
When that lady came to him, he spat the betel in her face.
Immediately the judge got very angry, but Kadare Gauḍa said:
'If you wash this, it will disappear, yet for this you're getting so angry.
But *he* has killed my two wives, whom I can never get back.'
And then he asked the judge, 'please make a re-enquiry, so that I may win this case'.
But because the magistrate had been disgraced in this way, he ordered
Kadare Gauḍa to be hanged before even receiving his orders from the Queen.
After he was hanged, orders did reach the magistrate, to the effect that if there is such a brave and strong man, you should not hang him:
He will be useful to our government.
These were the orders that came from the Queen.
After receiving them, he sent back word that he had already hanged Kadare.
And again orders came from the superiors, saying,'How could you hang Kadare before receiving the orders?
For doing so, you have been fined one pie' [the smallest coin].
So, after receiving these orders, he thought he could not pay this one pie fine, and could not live with the shame either.
Saying as much, he got on the back of a white horse, and rode off along the track that leads to Avalanche.
Until this day the whereabouts of that European and his horse are unknown.

And so only at the end do we realize why Kadare and not his brother is presented as the tragic hero of the epic tale.

Are Badaga Epics Indian?

While the heroes of Tamil and Sanskrit epics may go out into the forests to do their valiant deeds, they are usually urban-based people. Just like the heroes in Shakespeare, who never do a day's work, the Indian heroes regularly live in palaces and enjoy an elegant lifestyle that is something far beyond the reach of all village audiences a bard might encounter. I may here mention an interesting cultural feature in some Tamil as well as Indo-European epics, namely dicing. This occurs most memorably in the *Mahābhārata,* where the five Pāṇḍava brothers play dice with the god Vishnu. Madeleine Biardeau has suggested that the incidence of dicing in these epics is to emphasize the randomness of human events. The *Three Twins* story certainly amplifies that general idea too: after each of six separate games with Vishnu, dramatic twists in the fortunes of the heroes occur. After game 1 'the heroes are cajoled by their mother into unwanted marriages; 2 their parents die; 3 war is declared against their rival cousins; 4 the Chola king demands back taxes in an insulting manner; 5 news is received by the younger male that the elder has been put in jail; and 6 their sister requests a parrot, which leads to a war with the Veṭṭuvas and eventually to the heroes' death' (Beck 1982: 143).

You'd think they would have stopped playing long before that! But perhaps ancient Indians, like modern psychologists, recognized that gambling is an addictive malady.

None of this is to be found in the lives of the Badaga heroes: no palaces, no dicing, no elegant lifestyle, no gods as companions. Indeed, the Badagas never had palaces or dice, and always kept their distance from the gods. So misfortunes, which come repeatedly in their longer epics, are explained by some other factor than the random occurrence of ill fortune that comes in the *Three Twins* epic of the Tamils and is symbolized by the outcome of dicing. For Badagas that mechanism seems to be a malicious fate which is triggered by the machinations of evil Ku̱rumba sorcerers who don't have an ounce of goodwill in them.

I should point out here that Hindu mythology generally makes the gods the origin of all evil, which they have unceremoniously dumped on man in this mortal world. We can find this theme as far back as the *Black Yajurveda,* composed about the ninth century BC. It occurs again and again in the sacred texts; but not in the Badaga epics, where the Kuṟumba sorcerers, like sorcerers in West Africa, are shown to be the source of evil. This is not to say that the Badagas lack a concept of fate: indeed, when the sorcery of a Kuṟumba is seen to strike home, the hero or heroine commonly says something like: 'O what a miserable fate has befallen me!' In other words, fate is a pan-Indian feature of oral epics, but sorcery is the specific mechanism through which it operates in the Badaga case. As John D. Smith has said in his useful comparative study of the ideology of the Indian epics, '...an epic hero is subject to two distinct controlling forces: the causal pull of a fated future plan and the causal push of past human events' (Smith 1989: 185). This concept is of course a useful poetic device, for it enables the audience to think they know what is going to happen, which keeps their attention rivetted. A tension arises between fated action and free action, and it leads the listeners on to anticipate the dénouement.

The Badaga epic heroes are simple peasants, and they live in ordinary, named, still extant villages; when they go from one place to another, they do not use decorated elephants, nor even horses: they simply walk along the footpaths. And unlike so many heroes, these put in a hard day's work. They are less ideal for a modern audience than ancestors of the real people who live in their villages today. And here perhaps we begin to get closer to what these men and women are *doing* in the Badaga epics: they are emphasizing the cultural identity of the Badaga people, recalling some items of ethnohistory for their modern descendants, and in the telling blocking out all of the perplexing, non-Badaga world around them. The Badaga bards are singing a cultural tradition; constructing it, some would say.

I don't wish to stress the distinctive, non-Indian character of the Badaga epics too much. During the 1980s a panoply of folk epics from all over India was studied and published, sufficient to support a tripartite classification of them into: (1) martial, (2) sacrificial, and (3) romantic. The Badaga epics fit into all three slots fairly well.

In the important matter of structure, too, Badaga epics can be seen as falling into an Indian framework. In a provocative paper Beck (1989) showed that the Sanskrit and more recent folk epics of India reflect a tripartite characterization of heroes at the core: (1) a lead hero or heroine; (2) a secondary male; (3) a secondary female (Fig.1). This obviously is the pattern in such a Badaga poem as *Kadare Gauḍa* or *Unige Ma:ḍa.* But whereas martial and sacrifical epics are in general associated with ritual, the Badaga ones have nothing whatsoever to do with ritual: indeed they are only martial in the sense that violence is occasionally used to obtain an end; or sacrificial in the sense that a fairly decent or well-meaning hero or heroine is sacrificed to the whims of an anti-Badaga fate, not a deity but an unseen, unwarranted fate typically implemented by some Ku̱rumba sorcerer.

We should of course expect the Badaga epics to be different from other corpuses. I say this not just because they are in a distinct language; but because, as Stuart Blackburn has succinctly put it, 'Oral epics in India have that special ability to tell a community's own story and thus help to create and maintain that community's self-identity' (Blackburn & Flueckiger 1989: 11).

Brenda Beck, in showing that one standard pattern of heroic alliance in Indian epics is the triangle formed by two brothers and the wife of one of them, reminds us of the archetype which might have provided the template for *Kadare Gauḍa*. It is none other than that national epic, the *Rāmāyaṇa*. First composed in North India some 2,500 years ago, this enduring tale in 24,000 *ślokas* or distichs has been retold, re-enacted and translated from one end of the subcontinent to the other. There are three main written recensions, and any number of regional variations. Even illiterate people—such as the Badagas until the last century—have been exposed to versions of this story as told by itinerant entertainers through the ages.

Books II-VI, which embody the original version of the tale, deal with the adventures of Rāma and his wife Sīta; her scandalous abduction by Rāvaṇa, the demon king of Lanka or Ceylon; her rescue twelve years later with the help of Rāma's devoted brother Lakṣmaṇa; her subsequent estrangement from her husband, despite her protestations of faithfulness to him; her appeal to the Earth-goddess (her mother) to attest the truth of this declaration, which is followed by the appearance of that goddess on a golden throne; and a dramatic finale in which Sīta and the Earth-goddess return to the underworld. It is probably irrelevant here to draw the parallel with Persephone, but we may mention the fact that *Sīta* in Sanskrit also means 'furrow in a field'.

One century ago Albrecht Weber (1892: 192) suggested that Sīta represented Aryan husbandry, hence her name, and that this husbandry had to be protected from the depredations of aboriginal tribes of India who had been displaced by the Aryan invaders. (Modern worship of Sīta indeed treats her as an agricultural goddess.) Along these lines we find the long drawn-out struggle between the two sides: Rāma and Lakṣmaṇa, on the one hand, and Rāvaṇa and his hordes, on the other. The *Rāmāyaṇa* certainly draws a clear line between good and evil in this struggle; and so portrays Rāvaṇa as cruel, lecherous and unscrupulous, while Rāma and Lakṣmaṇa are the epitome of manly virtue and Sīta of wifely devotion. What is important for us here is that the *Rāmāyaṇa* has provided the Badaga poet unconsciously with a paradigm in which Rāma can be equated with Beḷḷi, Lakṣmaṇa with Kadare, Rāvaṇa with Senna Modaḷi, and Sīta with Solema:di.

There is perhaps a greater historical dimension to this parallel too. For if Sīta is named 'furrow' because she stands for civilized agriculture, she finds her Badaga parallel in fertile women like Solema:di who will raise up sons like Jo:gi to become the farmers and cattle-keepers of future generations. It was these men who, generation after generation since the first Badaga settlement on the Nilgiri Hills in the Sixteenth century, seized land from the forests and tamed it through slash-and-burn cultivation. But whose forests were they?—the Kuṟumbas', if anybody's. No wonder that they, like Rāvaṇa and his hordes of Rākṣāsas, used sorcery to protect themselves from intruders. This reading of an underlying theme in the *Kadare Gauḍa* story finds support in an unlikely source, namely placename analysis. For there are a number of Badaga villages whose names refer specifically to the Kuṟumba hamlets which had previously been there: Arekombe and Manjakombe, which include the suffix–*Kombe,* meaning 'Kuṟumba hamlet'. Then there is Kolekombe, 'Magical murder hamlet'; and Uḍiyakombe, 'medicine-bag hamlet'. These are not all.

In short, I am suggesting here that some of the Badaga epics function for that community rather as *Beowulf* did for the early English, or the *Æneid* for the Romans: as an embodiment of territorial conquest and national identity.

References

Beck, Brenda 1982. *The Three Twins: The Telling of a South Indian Folk Epic.* Bloomington: Indiana University Press.

——— 1989. 'Core Triangles in the Folk Epics of India'. *In* Stuart H. Blackburn, Peter J. Claus, Joyce B. Flueckiger, and Susan S. Wadley, (eds.) *Oral Epics in India* 155–75. Berkeley: University of California Press.

Blackburn, Stuart, & Joyce B. Flueckiger 1989. 'Introduction'. *In* Stuart H. Blackburn, Peter J. Claus, Joyce B. Flueckiger, and Susan S. Wadley, (eds.) *Oral Epics in India* 1–11. Berkeley: University of California Press.

Brown, Charles Hilton 1923. *Dismiss*! London: Methuen & Co. Ltd.

——— 1923. *The Second Lustre*: *A Miscellany of Verse.* Oxford: Basil Blackwell.

Cousins, James Henry Sproull 1902. *The Racing Lug.*

Cousins, James Henry Sproull, and Margaret E. Cousins 1950. *We Two Together.* Madras: Ganesh & Co.

Emeneau, Murray Barnson 1944–6. *Kota Texts.* University of California Publications in Linguistics, vol 2–3. Berkeley: University of California Press.

Emeneau, Murray Barnson 1971. *Toda Songs.* Oxford: Clarendon Press.

——— 1984. *Toda Grammar and Texts.* Memoirs of the American philosophical Society, no.155. Philadelphia: American Philosophical Society.

Gover, Charles E. 1871. *The Folk-Songs of Southern India.* Madras: Higginbotham & Co.; London: Trübner & Co.

Hockings, Paul 1987. 'The Man Named Unige Mada (Nilgiri Hills, Tamilnadu)'. *In* Brenda E. F. Beck, Peter J. Claus, Praphulladatta Goswami, and Jawarharlal Handoo, (eds.) *Folktales of India* 125–29. Chicago: University of Chicago Press.

——— 1988. 'The Song of Heaven'. In *Counsel from the Ancients, a Study of Badaga Proverbs, Prayers, Omens and Curses* 560–87. Berlin & New York: Mouton de Gruyter.

Marryat, Florence 1869. *Véronique: A Romance.* London & Guildford: Richard Bentley; 3 vols.

Oinas, Felix 1972. 'Folk Epics'. *In* Richard Dorson, (ed.) *Folkore and Folklife* 99–115. Chicago: University of Chicago Press.

Penny, Fanny Emily Farr 1913. *Love in the Hills.* London: Chatto & Windus.

——— 1931. *Get on with the Wooing.* London: Hodder & Stoughton.

——— 1937. *Chowra's Revenge.* London: Hutchinson & Co., Ltd.

Shulman, David M. 1985. *King and Clown in South Indian Myth and Poetry.* Princeton: Princeton University Press.

Smith, John D. 1989. 'Scapegoats of the Gods: The Ideology of the Indian Epic'. *In* Stuart H. Blackburn, Peter J. Claus, Joyce B. Flueckiger, and Susan S. Wadley, (eds.) *Oral Epics in India* 176–94. Berkeley: University of California Press.

Vries, Jan de 1963. *Heroic Song and Heroic Legend.* Barbara Catharina Jacoba Trimmer, trans. London: Oxford University Press.

Weber, Albrecht 1892. *The History of Indian Literature* John Mann and Theodor Zachariae, trans. 3rd edn. London: K. Paul, Trench, Triibner & Co.

The Construction of the Nilgiris as a 'Tribal Sanctuary'

MARIE-CLAUDE MAHIAS

12

In modern anthropology, the case of the Nilgiris has been used to construct very different sociological models. It has been equally easy to prove that the inhabitants were isolated tribes or that they were part of a *jajmānī*-like system of interdependence, with either the Todas or the Badagas as the dominant caste. Although the weakness of the data from remote times has indeed something to do with this, the same data were still sufficient to lend themselves to divergent elaborations, which clearly points to theoretical and ideological bias in the construction of those models.

Nevertheless, I do not want to enter this debate which has, to my mind, been skewed from the start. The bases of the British distinction between 'caste' and 'tribe' were never clearly defined. These terms have a history in which scientific and political considerations have always been intertwined. When the Indian National Census endorsed the distinction and created exclusive categories in 1871–2, it placed before the administrators endless difficulties and soon compelled them to look into the transformation of tribes into castes (Sinha 1980: 2, 7). By adopting these same sociological labels, the Constitution of 1949 established them as political dogma, inseparable from Indian independence and unity, and turned them into stakes. Since then, as Paul Hockings (1993: 351) reminds us, 'the academic question has been overtaken by the political ramifications of being identified with one or the other'. Challenging these labels is therefore interpreted, *ipso facto*, as a political issue.

For my part, I would rather question the perception and the definition of the Nilgiri peoples during the nineteenth and the beginning of the twentieth centuries. First of all, I shall examine what was initially written about the Nilgiris.[1] To a certain extent one can follow Hockings when he writes, concerning the words, 'caste' and 'tribe': 'there is no point in our seeking for consistency in the early use of these various terms. It was only after the anthropological writings of E. B. Tylor and Herbert Spencer had had some impact on the public, and the Census of India was getting itself organized (1871 and later), that these terms began to lead separate lives' (Hockings 1993: 352). But leaving aside their intrinsic meaning or sociological relevance, a formal analysis of the frequency and the evolution of these words can throw some light on their authors and their time. The choice of what today we call sociological concepts was never discussed. But that does not mean it was wholly arbitrary.

I shall consider only eyewitness accounts, leaving out all the compilations, despite their interest. The analysis of these texts allows us to identify three main periods, or rather trends, which emerge one after the other and go on to develop without becoming entrapped by specific temporal limits.

Variability of the Terms Used with a Preference for 'Caste'

The first reports we are able to consult were written by civil servants on assignment, and more precisely by surveyors. After the cession of the Coimbatore district, in 1799, the first task of the British was to abolish the ancient revenue system and establish a new one. Hence it was felt necessary to make a careful survey of the new territories. Three of these reports, written between 1812 and 1821,[2] have come down to us:

(*a*) William Keys, Assistant Revenue Surveyor, sent, in June 1812, 'A Topographical Description of the Neelaghery Mountains' to the Collector of the Coimbatore District, W. Garrows.

(*b*) Lieutenant Evans Macpherson, 1820, Superintendent, Neelgherry Road, transmitted a brief report to John Sullivan, the next Collector of Coimbatore, who had entrusted him with the construction of the first road and the survey of the lands.

(*c*) Lieutenant B. S. Ward, Deputy Surveyor-General, was the author of a more substantial *Geographical and Statistical Memoir of a Survey of the Neelgherry Mountains. . . .*, 1821.[3]

As Evans Macpherson wrote to John Sullivan, who pressed him to state his opinion, they were 'In humble situation in this country'. Being technicians who spent from one to three months in the Nilgiris, they were 'little in the habit of writing on any subject', and wrote 'with pleasure but with much diffidence'.

These first three reports, written independently, described physical, commercial and agricultural conditions more carefully than human aspects. They presented the inhabitants, with their respective names, but the generic terms keep changing. In addition to 'people', 'population', and 'inhabitants', the term 'caste' was used in the majority of cases. In these three reports, I have found seventeen instances of 'caste', six of 'race', five of 'class', and one of 'tribe'.

This last report referred to the Todas,[4] in the space of a few pages, as 'a migratory race' and 'a migratory tribe'. 'Class' always referred to a sub-group in a broader whole.

'Race' had, at this early date in the nineteenth century, a very general meaning close to the old acceptation connected with European feudalism, and one understands that it could have been equivalent to caste. Indeed it emphasized appearance, a difference, either from the people of the plains or within the Nilgiri people themselves, but it did not stress physical features alone.

For instance, the region is 'inhabited by a race of people differing in language, appearance, and doubtless in origin' (Macpherson). Although they are a caste, the Todas 'are evidently a distinct race' and the Mullukurumbas 'a primeval race'; with regard to the Kotas: 'This caste of people are the most industrious race'; and to the Irulas: 'These are a distinct race of people from the other highlanders' (Ward).

But, as I said, the term 'caste' was most frequently used. The first visitors to discover and explore the region were prepared to see castes with occupational specializations, interrelations and even differences of status.

Of course, the context contributed to their preference for the use of 'caste'. The region was discovered rather late in the history of British colonization. Therefore these civil servants had been in India long enough to be familiar with the caste society and its features (such as classification of economic activities, sharing of food, etc.). Moreover, they were accompanied by Indians—Tamils, servants and followers, who translated what they encountered according to their usual way of thinking. Lastly, as Rivers (1906:15) and Emeneau (1963:191) have shown, 'outsiders have usually communicated with the Todas through the Badagas', and through the Badaga language, if not Tamil or Kannada. We know today that the Badagas were the most recent newcomers in the hills, the closest to the world of the plains, and the most interested in differentiating themselves from other hill peoples. The first accounts were definitely biased in favour of castes.

What was observed confirmed this opinion:

1. All these surveyors discerned a subdivided human whole: 'These (nauds) are inhabited by a race of people . . . , and divided into twelve castes' (Macpherson).

2. The occupational specialization was immediately apparent for them. The Todas were exclusively herders, and migratory. The Kotas were cultivators, and very industrious craftsmen. The Irulas cultivated the slopes, gathered forest-products, 'fell[ed] large trees and conveyed the timber down to the plains' (Keys). The Badagas were the principal cultivators.

3. This specialization entailed a certain interdependence, and involved economic as well as ritual relations.

On the one hand, the Todas received a part of the crop from the Badagas 'and others', who could only be the Kotas (Keys, Macpherson), which made up their only source of cereals. The same held for the Mullukurumbas, because 'the produce of their fields . . . seldom affords them a sufficiency for consumption' (Ward). The Kotas got unserviceable old animals from the Badagas for a trifle. The lrulas 'often come down to the plains to dispose or barter plantains and other hill productions at the market villages' (Ward).

On the other hand, the Mullukurumbas (nowadays identified as Ālu or Pālu Kuṟumbas) served as priests to the Badagas, especially at ploughing and harvesting time. The Mullukurumba began the ploughing in each field, for which he received from each *ryot* a few measures of the ripe grain. And at harvest time he was required to reap the first handful of the grain, and 'is then permitted to take as many sheaves as he can bear away on his shoulders' (Ward). As for the Todas, they received 'from quarter to half a Rupee as a present' whenever wealthy Badagas celebrated a marriage (Ward).

4. Stratification[5] was supposedly based on criteria such as hereditary land rights, annual gift of a certain portion of each crop, commensality, free entrance into the house, and on comparisons with the low country.[6] The Todas 'appear to be the aborigines of the hills; they are acknowledged lords of the soil by other castes'

(Macpherson); they are 'the hereditary claimants of the soil' (Ward), as attested by their providing a portion of the harvest. The Kotas form 'the lowest class' among the three who live in the upper hills' (Keys). 'They are of a very inferior caste, and by their neighbours considered in the same light as the chuckler in the low country; and none of the other castes will eat with them or even enter their houses'. (Macpherson).

In short, the first discoverers encountered distinct, named groups which they identified as 'castes'. They recognized features they had already observed in the plains and which would later be systematized as characteristic of the caste society. For them, South Indian human diversity could easily put up with a few additional groups with their own distinctive features. This trend did not suddenly vanish, and traces will be found in later works.

'Tribes' Take the Place of 'Castes'

The next group of authors still used such terms as 'race', 'class', 'tribe', 'caste', but their frequency as well as their usage changed. Except for Harkness, all used 'tribe' in the title of their publication. I shall follow the chronological order in presenting five of them, who seem representative and who have shaped this trend.

(*1*) In May 1819, Louis-Théodore Leschenault de la Tour, a French naturalist, spent a short period in the hills along with John Sullivan. He was very busy gathering 2,000 plant and 156 animal samples which he was to send back to France, and probably did not actually meet many aboriginal peoples. On his return, he wrote an account in a Ceylonese paper; then on 9 September 1822, he read *Relation Abrégée d'un Voyage aux Indes Orientales* before the Académie des Sciences, in which he explained:

> Les habitans sont peu nombreux, ils paraissent fort doux, ils mènent une vie heureuse et indépendante; ils sont divisés en trois tribus: les boggers, les cotters et les totters: les derniers qui habitent les régions les plus élevées, sont regardés comme les habitans primitifs, ils ne sont que pasteurs; ils possèdent de nombreux troupeaux de buffles. Les deux autres tribus cultivent la terre ou exercent des métiers utiles (Leschenault de la Tour 1822:16).

So it was a French savant, 'naturaliste du Roi', endowed with the prestige of his office, who deliberately used the word 'tribe' in this region for the first time. He knew nothing about the Indian population and society, and was also ignorant of the connotations this term carried in the context of imperial India. One should know that, from the seventeenth century onwards, the word 'tribe' had been in common use (in English as in French) in the natural sciences, and particularly in zoology, to designate the intermediate level in the systematic classification, between the family and the genus.

(*2*) In 1832, Captain Henry Harkness, of the Madras army and Secretary to the Royal Asiatic Society, published the first book devoted entirely to the Nilgiris and their inhabitants. He spent at least nine months travelling throughout the area, and apparently knew something of the Toda language (cf. p.43).

The word 'race' appears first in the title of his book, *A Description of a Singular Aboriginal Race Inhabiting the Summit of the Neilgherry Hills,* which refers to the Todas. It then is used in the book to refer to each group. It indicates a particular appearance, made up of a set of morphological and behavioural features. So for the Todas, the height, the eyes, the teeth, but also the bold bearing, the expressive countenances 'lead to the conclusion that they must be of a different race to their neighbours'. The Kotas are 'a strange race and differ as much from the other tribes of the mountains as they do from all other natives of India'; the Kuṟumbas 'another race', the Irulas 'a race of people', and the Badagas 'a timid race'.

Yet these same groups were above all tribes. At the same time, and even though he classified three of them (the Kuṟumbas, Irulas, and Badagas) as Hindus, Harkness denied the existence of caste. For him, the Badagas were divided into eight different classes, and the Irulas into two; the Kotas have 'no distinction of caste' (Harkness 1832: 30); the Todas do not know of 'any difference of caste among themselves' (Harkness 1832: 31), even though he distinguished between two branches which, 'till within the last few generations, kept themselves quite distinct, and never intermarried' (Harkness 1832: 32).

Still this author did not isolate these new tribes, and in his opinion comparison was required if for no other reason than to further knowledge: 'In order to come to any definite or satisfactory conclusion concerning the Todas, or their language, it is necessary, however, to know the prominent features, and history of the other tribes who dwell on these mountains' (Harkness 1832: 27).

(*3*) The Reverend J. Friedrich Metz published several articles in English in the *Madras Christian Herald* in 1856, then in German in

1857 'Die Volkstämme der Nilgiri's', before a friend later edited his notes into a book in 1864: *The Tribes Inhabiting the Neilgherry Hills.* Perhaps more than by his writings, this missionary of the Basel Evangelical Missionary Society played an important part as an intermediary (and, one may well imagine, informant) for all visitors over a long period in the mid-nineteenth century.

There is again much confusion between the notions of race, class, tribe, and caste in his book, and no specific meaning or use can be distinguished:

'There are five different races'. 'The Kotas are the only one of all the hill tribes who practice the industrial arts, and they are therefore essential almost to the very existence of the others classes'. 'They are, however, a squalid race . . . and are on this account a byeword among the other castes' (Metz 1864:127).

Yet a new phrase appears—'hill tribe'—in which 'hill' becomes a qualifier: that is, one must be from the hills to be tribal. That is why the Irulas cannot be called a hill tribe, 'partly because they reside so low down, and partly because their language . . . is a dialect of Tamil' (Metz 1864: 11). The same held for the Badagas, as their history and relatively recent migration were better known. It should be pointed out however that Metz worked almost exclusively among the Badagas, whom he encouraged to break off relations, especially ritual, with the other groups.

(*4*) Among those who helped diffuse the notion of tribe, special mention must be made of James Wilkinson Breeks, of the Madras Civil Service, who was the first Commissioner of the Nilagiris[7], from 1868 till he died in 1872, and who made a study on orders.

In May 1871, the India Museum of Calcutta decided to open a section to illustrate 'the state of the arts among the aboriginal and other jungle races in India'. To this end, the curator sought to obtain 'collections of their arms, ornaments, dresses, household utensils, tools, agricultural implements, musical instruments . . . , that will serve to illustrate the habits and modes of life of those indigenous races that have remained but little affected by foreign civilization'. Breeks replied promptly (in July 1871) and enthusiastically. It was obvious that he was already well acquainted with the question. He would be glad to procure a collection:

to illustrate the habits and modes of life of the jungle tribes of the Nilagiris . . . for the Nilagiri tribes at any rate are abandoning their distinctive customs. For example, among the Todas infanticide has been put a stop to; polyandry is on the decline; their buffalo sacrifices at the dry funeral are curtailed, and create comparatively little interest . . . Amongst a people in so low a state of civilization, a very few years serve to efface all trace of a custom that has been given up; whilst a careful examination into their existing condition and habits, affords the only hope of arriving at their origin and past history.

It was a matter of collecting and buying objects in order to document peoples that had remained 'little affected by foreign civilization', and to acquire 'materials for a comparative study of the arts practiced by races in an early stage of social development'—in other words, primitives, in the original sense of the word, with a view to an evolutionist history of humankind. The long series of quotations that precedes has no other purpose than to highlight the gap between local and imperial knowledge and the fact that the latter is bound to prevail. In its search for peoples left behind by civilization, the Museum of Calcutta was not listening to the man in the field, despite his title of Commissioner, when he said that the traditional customs had been seriously transformed by colonization and were doomed to vanish within a short time.

J. W. Breeks proposed an inquiry 'as exhaustive as possible', bearing on 'the four Nilagiri, jungle tribes, viz.: 'the Todas, the Kotas, the Kurumbas and the Irulas'. It should be noted that the Badagas were no longer an aboriginal or jungle race, and the Irulas had been restored by him to their status of tribals, because they lived in the jungle. His P*rimitive Tribes and Monuments of the Nilagiris* was published in 1873, one year after his death.

(*5*) The same year, Colonel W. E. Marshall published *A Phrenologist amongst the Todas, or The Study of a Primitive Tribe in South India.* For him, the Todas were a case for studying how 'savage tribes melt away when forced into prolonged contact with a superior civilization'. This book is highly significant, since it falls unequivocally into the field of anthropology, which was just being created, and shows just how influential were ideas discussed in Europe. It attracted immediate review from one of the prominent French physical anthropologists of the time, Jean-Louis-Armand de Quatrefages de Bréau.

To summarize, this pro-tribe trend was impelled by authors with a sound educational background (naturalists, medical doctors, military men, administrators and museologists), who were also members of various scientific societies. To this list must be added: the philologist B. H. Hodgson, member of the Asiatic Society, who, on the basis of lexical information provided by Metz and other missionaries from Kaity, argued (in opposition to Harkness) against the Todas' singularity and affirmed the close relationship between and the common origin of hill and plains languages; J. Shortt, physician and surgeon, member of medical, anthropological, ethnological and zoological societies in Great Britain and India; Lieutenant later also Colonel W. Ross King, member of the Anthropological Society of London. The first tendency was continued by the missionary Metz, by probably less educated James Hough, chaplain in the Madras establishment, and by occasional authors publishing in wide-circulation newspapers ('Rifle' 1873).

For writers of the second trend, each group was a tribe, which had (Hough 1829: 109) or, more often, did not have caste (Harkness 1832: 30, 31; Shortt 1868: 57). Notice that caste has changed levels. For the preceding 'humble men', 'caste' referred to each group; now it is located within each group. What then did they mean by the term?

At first these tribes were never considered in isolation. Their mutual relations, even though not studied in depth, were always pointed out. The same tribes were then qualified as hill-tribes, which excluded the Irulas and the Badagas, and later as jungle, primitive, and even savage tribes, which led to the reintegration of the Irulas, but not the Badagas. At this point economic or ritual relations were no longer noted. In any case, the qualifier chosen for the word 'tribe' became determining. No thought was given to the notion of tribe in itself, rather it was as a function of its hill or jungle character that a group fell into the category 'tribe'.[8]

'Tribes' Redefined in Terms of 'Castes'

A third trend became apparent at the beginning of the twentieth century and continued until well after independence: it was the turn of the professional scientists. There were few of them: W. H. R. Rivers (1906), M. B. Emeneau (from 1935), and D. G. Mandelbaum (from 1937). All of them nearly always used the word 'tribe', but carefully avoided the image of jungle or primitive tribe.

W. H. R. Rivers' monograph, recalling the Todas as 'picturesque and, in many ways, so unique', does not forget that they had never been isolated, and that they had particular relations with the other tribes. In addition to an entire chapter devoted to 'Relations with

Others Tribes', many notations relativized even the isolation of the Plateau. Rivers went on to suggest that a more exact knowledge of Indian customs and ceremonies could show their difference to be slighter than they seem to be at present (Rivers 1906: 4, note 2).

Murray B. Emeneau, a linguist and Sanskritist, was the great decipherer of the languages and oral literatures of the Nilgiris, and in particular those of the Todas and Kotas. It may be presumed then that he had the most intimate knowledge of these groups. Although he did not specialize in political or social organization, he set out expressly to supplement Rivers' account and found the existence of a system of matrilineal clans which Rivers had missed (1938, quoted in Rooksby 1971: 114–15). For him the Kotas were 'a small tribe or caste'. He entitled the first Kota myth: 'How Kitu·rpayk . . . originated the three castes'.[9] But he still used a formula which brought sharp reactions from an American anthropologist: 'For a long time . . . these tribes formed a local but not too aberrant version of the Hindu caste system' (Emeneau 1944: 1). The specialization and the interrelations led him to write: 'The communities are symbiotic economically and even, to some degree, religiously'. He was even firmer in his 'Introduction' to the *Toda Songs* (1971: xxiv): 'The Toda community is often referred to as a tribe. It is in reality part of a local caste-like system, the Nilgiris system, which includes also Kotas, Kurumbas, and Badagas'.

David G. Mandelbaum arrived in India in 1936, and almost immediately went to work with Emeneau. At first he did not question the notion of geographic isolation, the idea of a social and cultural 'enclave' constituted of several tribes living in economic and social symbiosis. But from 1952, he described their economy as 'geared to a caste-like division of labor', then in 1954 as 'a caste-like interdependence'. In 1955, he even went so far as to write: 'Yet for all their differences from the usual south Indian patterns, all the Nilgiris peoples accorded, in fundamental ways, with the prevalent village tradition'. He made the comparison even clearer in 1956 (1989) : 'Kotas are, and were, decidedly more akin to what Sinha calls the Hindu peasantry of the plains than they are like the tribesmen of the central hill belt'.

Apparently, it was his interest in the modern change that led him to new interpretations and expressions: 'If the Kotas have not been a caste before, they are becoming more and more like the lower castes of the plains below their homeland' (Mandelbaum 1989:

184). But one can also believe that he evolved as he came to know Indian society better, as he could compare his data and analysis with other South Asian scholars, whereas he had arrived in India after writing a dissertation on the Plains Cree, 'An Indian Tribe'.

The Scientific Issues: For Further Research

In the Nilgiris, far from being immediate, the notion of primitive tribe was a romantic,[10] administrative, and scientific construction: three aspects which could be found in the same person. The notion of tribe prevailed as the British settled there, as roads were opened on every side of the plateau,[11] as markets were organized, making it possible to send off local products as well as to acquire goods from outside, as villages of immigrants from the plains grew up (Hockings 1989: 337). The more the region opened up geographically, socially, and economically, the more the aboriginal people were seen as being different, primitive, associated with the jungle (or savage), and consequently as the epitome of a tribe. This was aggravated as the description and organization of the region was taken out of the hands of local administration to depend on decisions made at the higher levels of British India (e.g. the orders from the India Museum), or on concerns having little or nothing to do with India (as will be seen, ideas relevant to European scientists).

The needs and interests of the British authorities and administration in India have always been advanced as an explanation, and of course they must be taken into account. By the second half of the eighteenth century, the East India Company had already developed an administrative system, with its own categories and ways of dealing with them. But once the Europeans adopted the word 'caste', and throughout the seventeenth and eighteenth centuries, the terms 'caste' and 'tribe' were used interchangeably, 'caste' sometimes being taken for the vernacular term and 'tribe' for its translation (Yule and Burnell 1903: 171–2). The two terms were still approximately equivalent at the turn of the nineteenth century.[12]

In the Nilgiris, both trends (pro-caste and pro-tribe) left their mark on, and in turn were influenced by, debates on the matter of land tenure and revenue. These discussions set at odds different parties. On one side, people like John Sullivan, the founder of Ootacamund, who had paid the Todas for the land he took from them, 'endorsed the absolute proprietary rights of the Todas to the entire Nilgiri plateau, on the presumption that they were the earliest settlers there'. On the other side, those like Stephen R. Lushington, Governor of Madras, or the Military Commandant of Ootacamund, argued that 'throughout India proprietary right in land belonged to the Government' (Hockings 1989: 340; Grigg 1880: 314–43). One party insisted on their being particular and called the hill people 'tribes', whereas the other wanted to consider them to be just like other South India, castes.

But I would like to emphasize the influence of scientific issues on the designation of the Nilgiri groups. Bernard S. Cohn (1968: 16–17) pointed out that the administrative-official view of caste reflected the anthropological interests and theories of the period between 1870 and 1910. I believe that this influence made itself felt even earlier, before the birth of anthropology as we know it today, in other words, basically social and cultural anthropology. But this can only be outlined within the scope of this essay.

This influence can be surmised by the swiftness with which publications circulated, and by the interest they raised in Europe. Leschenault de la Tour was read by his English contemporaries and quoted as an authority. Marshall's book was reviewed at length (three articles for a total of forty-three pages) the next year by A. de Quatrefages, one of the founders of French physical anthropology. He had already read King's publication (1870) and had seen photographs and cranial measurements of the hill people brought back by Mrs Janssen, wife of the astronomer Pierre-Jules-César, who had gone to India to observe the great solar eclipse in 1872. De Quatrefages was also an admirer of Adophe Pictet, Sanskritist, inventor, in 1859, of an ethnology of the Aryas, whose perfect language could only be the reflection of an ideal state of humanity (Olender 1989: 127–34). Elisée Reclus, and his brother Elie, both libertarian French geographers and tireless travellers, showed in the *Nouvelle Géographie Universelle* (1883) and in *Les Primitifs* (1885), that they were astonishingly well documented on the Nilgiri people. At a later period, Emeneau's *Kota Texts* were discussed by Marian Smith, an American folklorist and linguist, two years after they had been published.[13]

Conversely, learned writers who described the Nilgiri people were probably well informed and nourished the discussion in European scientific circles. Since the study of Sanskrit began, India had been an exemplary place in which to investigate various issues of the human sciences to come, all of which were connected and associated with the attempt to trace the origins of mankind, with the old dream of discovering the roots of humanity, religion, language. All depended on the notion of race as an 'explanatory framework'; races which, in Renan's words were of an 'intellectual and moral mould' (Laurens 1988: 376). For the new discipline of anthropology,[14] the heir to zoology, one of the main issues was the classification of human races, which opposed monogenists and polygenists, and encouraged the search for autochthonous, unknown races. The Nilgiris constituted a true laboratory for observation and experiment. They presented salient features allowing the observers to infer that some of the Nilgiri people were either a 'hardly modified sample of the first human races' (Marshall), or 'representative of an exceptional type, remained in a pure condition' (de Quatrefages).

The relations between observers in India and new fields of research can throw a different light on the use and evolution of words like 'race, 'caste', 'tribe', which were not yet sociological concepts. They may explain the omission of caste, by some writers in the mid-nineteenth century. Caste did not exist outside India. It did not exist for the European anthropologists, who only knew the tandem 'race and tribe.'

'Race', an extremely common word having no precise definition, was the object of a variety of interpretations coloured by tendencies and persons. Moreover, the term has evolved considerably over the course of the nineteenth and twentieth centuries, and one must be wary of anachronistic interpretations. Until sometime around 1875, a race was defined not only by physical features, but also by way of life, intellectual and social state, and above all by the language spoken.[15] The nineteenth century witnessed the triumph of comparative philology. For scholars of this time, it was language that guaranteed a people's identity over time, which revealed the people's fundamental features and even authorized one to speak of 'linguistic race'. This reminds me of an aspect of the descriptions of the Nilgiris that I overlooked in presenting the texts, which was the attention given to linguistic resemblances and differences, and the collection of vocabularies for comparative purposes. The notion of 'race' was applied to all mankind and either did not carry a value judgement . . . or carried the idea of progress on the path to the perfection that was Christian civilization.

The notion of 'tribe' was less extensive. It applied only to particular races, to which nineteenth-century evolutionism assigned a particular stage in human evolution, leading from the simple primitive to the complex civilized. Geographical and social isolation (up on a hill or out in a jungle) vouched for their primitiveness, original purity, and scientific value. European scientists looked for correlations between the different criteria to constitute distinctive entities and typologies. Their method increased the isolation of each group.

In the early twentieth century, social anthropology had developed in India as elsewhere. The caste society was now sufficiently recognized to give rise to attempts at synthesis and explanation. The choice between 'tribe' or 'caste', terms inherited from the past, then referred to and had to agree with the prevailing historicist view of Indian society, and particularly of South India. According to this perspective, the Dravidian population was originally comprised of tribes that had been either transformed into castes by integration into the population of Indo-European origin and Hindu religion, or remained unchanged.[16] To fit with this view and to confirm it, Nilgiri people had to be isolated, non-Hindus, tribals. Considering the inhabitants of the Nilgiri as castes would have upset this model. While researchers in the field tended to see castes or something resembling them, they were held back by bigger interests (bigger than the researchers or the field of Indian studies) which they were neither ready nor disposed to confront.

Conclusion

By its interest in content, in the manufacture of scientific facts and not only in the framework or the sociocultural context, the history of sciences has shown long ago that it can be nothing if not social, and even anthropological. The perception and the constitution of sociological reality are inseparable from the concepts which express them, and these concepts are not given in advance. They are often the outcome of a controversial epistemological construction and have evolved over the course of time.

The elements at stake go well beyond the main forces at play and the research trends generally recognized in Indian studies. Combining and comparing these elements has given rise to various solutions shaped by local contexts and historical periods. We have no right to regard these as arbitrary or inconsistent without examining them, unless, that is, we assume that our predecessors were less well endowed with logical capacities than we. These solutions only seem arbitrary or inconsistent because we project contemporary meanings onto past periods, forgetting that the elaboration of these very meanings took several centuries of observation, reflection and evolution. The logic of these discourses cannot be assessed or appreciated using meanings crystallized at a later time. To state baldly, as for example Surajit Sinha does (1980:1), without indicating the period, that the British discovered a rigid system of castes and tribes 'outside the Brahmanic *Varna-Jati* hierarchy' is one such anachronistic interpretation and inevitably leads to the discovery of inconsistencies. These terms were being used well before they were constructed as two sociological poles structuring Indian society. Exactly when and how did the transformation come about? This remains to be studied. The case of the Nilgiris cannot be generalized as it stands. Nevertheless it invites care in the reading and interpretation of texts from the past and the multiplication of analyses localized in space and time.

Notes

An earlier version of this text was presented at the 13th European Conference of Modern South Asian Studies, Toulouse 1994.

1. I will restrict my investigation to the writings of this period, with the exception of a few references to be found in earlier texts.
2. There is said to be a report by Colonel Mackenzie, written in 1808, which Grigg (1880: 278) was already unable to see in his time.
3. It was apparently not submitted to the government until July 1826 (Grigg 1880: 285).
4. In the nineteenth century each author had his own system for transcribing names. I have unified the spellings in accordance with present-day practice.
5. The British in India did not need anyone to teach them about hierarchy. In the Nilgiri region alone, 'there was an almost caste-like discreteness, a separate life-style and a minimum of intercommunication between the administrative officials, the army officers, the planters, the tradesmen, the teachers, the Protestant missionaries, the Catholic priests, the retired and the tourists' (Hockings 1989: 342).

6. The Office was held before him by the judge of Coimbatore, who was in charge of the administration of justice both in the lowlands of Coimbatore and on the Nilgiri Hills (Grigg 1880: 309).
7. This seems to have been true for the 'criminal tribes' as well. Among the groups on this list (who were not found in the Nilgiris) some were there purely because of the need to survive in times of famine or war, because of the scission of or exclusion from a caste, sometimes a high one. These groups recruited from all segments of society, bringing together a diversified membership, and their organization sometimes resembled that of a sect with rites of admission and founding heroes. It was their nomadic life style and their legally reprehensible activities that turned them into tribes, a category ratified by the Criminal Tribes Act of 1871 (Pouchepadass 1982). This is a far cry from a sociological or even an ethnic definition of the notion of tribe.
8. This is not a translation; there is no title in the Kota myth.
9. This aspect, particularly the representation of the Todas as an example of the good, noble savage, has been developed by Dane Kennedy (1991). The demonstration is, however, based on a too narrow selection of information to be fully convincing.
10. The first road was reported completed on 23 May 1823. There others were opened in 1823–4 (Grigg 1880: 286).
11. See, for example, Buchanan 1807. A sampling from this text reveals that 'caste' is used to designate first of all the four *varṇa,* the subdivisions being termed 'tribes'; but the two levels may be shifted without disturbing the relation of order. Furthermore it appears that 'tribe' is used more often to designate groups with a very low status.
12. A more thorough inventory needs to be made of the interactions with scientists in the different European countries as they entertained strong ties with each other, in particular for Germany, on which I lack the actual documentation for the moment. My bias towards French sources is clear, but these relations are all the more significant in that this country no longer had at the time any particular interests in India.
13. Anthropological societies were founded in Paris 1859, London 1863, and Berlin 1869.
14. Maurice Olender (1989: 49) places the beginning of the ideological and political exploitation of this notion around the 1870s. A great deal has been written on this subject, and we will not go into it here. For a partial review, see Laurens 1988.
15. This interpretation by conquest no doubt comes from an earlier time and expression like 'the low caste tribes of the plains' (Shortt 1868: 56). In fact, it merely displaces and repeats that of the European peoples (Laurens 1988).

REFERENCES

Breeks, James W. 1873 *An Account of the Primitive Tribes and Monuments of the Nilagiris.* Delhi: Cultural Publishing House (1983).

Cohn, Bernard S. 1968. 'Notes on the History of the Study of Indian Society and Culture'. *In* Milton Singer and Bernard S. Cohn, (eds.) *Structure and Change in Indian Society.* Chicago: Aldine Publishing Co.

De Guatrefages, Armand 1873–4. 'A Phrenologist among the Todas . . . By William E. Marshall, Lieutenant Colonel of Her Majesty's Bengal Staff Corps, London'. *Journal des Savants,* Décembre 1873: 729–45, Janvier 1874: 5–22, Février 187: 96–106.

Emeneau, M. B. *Kota Texts.* (University of California Publications in Linguistics). Berkeley and Los Angeles: University of California Press. 4 parts.

———— 1963. 'Ootacamund in the Nilgiris: Some Notes'. *Journal of the American Oriental Society,* 83: 188–93.

———— 1971. *Toda Songs.* Oxford: Clarendon Press.

Grigg, H. B. (ed.) 1880. *A Manual of the Nílagiri District in the Madras Presidency.* Madras: E. Keys, Government Press.

Harkness, Henry 1832. *A Description of a Singular Aboriginal Race Inhabiting the Summit of the Neilgherry Hills, or Blue Mountains of Coimbatoor, in the Southern Peninsula of India.* London: Smith, Elder, and Co.

Hockings, Paul 1989. 'British Society in the Company, Crown and Congress Eras'. *In* P. Hockings. (ed.) *Blue Mountains. The Ethnography and Biogeography of a South Indian Region,* 334–59. Delhi: Oxford University Press.

———— 1993. 'Ethic Identity in a Complex Society: The Badaga Case'. *Bulletin of the National Museum of Ethnology,* 18, no.2: 347–63.

Hodgson, B. H. 1856. 'Aborigines of the Nilgiris'. *Journal of the Asiatic Society of Bengal,* 25, no.1, 31–8; no.6: 498–522.

Hough, J. 1829. *Letters on the Climate, Inhabitants, Productions, etc., of the Neilgherries, or Blue Mountains of Coimbatoor, South India.* London: J. Hatchard and Son.

Kennedy, D. 1991. 'Guardians of Edenic Sanctuaries: Paharis, Lepchas, and Todas in the British Mind'. *South Asia,* 14, no.2: 57–77.

King, W. Ross 1866. *The Aboriginal Tribes of the Nilgiri Hills.* London: Longmans, Green, and Co. (A paper read before the Anthropological Society of London, 3 May 1870, and published by the Society in the *Journal of Anthropology*).

Laurens, H. 1988. 'Le concept de race dans le *Journal asiatique* du XIXe siècle'. *Journal Asiatique,* 276, nos.3–4: 371–81.

Leschenault De La Tour, L.-T. 1822. *Relation abrégée d'un voyage aux Indes Orientales.* Extrait des Mémoires du Museum d'histoire naturelle, t. 9, 5e année, Paris: Imprimerie de A. Belin.

Mandelbaum, D.G. 1952. 'Technology, Credit, and Culture in an Indian Village'. *Human Organization* 11, no.3: 28. Reprinted in 1960 'Technology, Credit, and Culture in a Nilgiri Village'. *In* M.N. Srinivas, (ed.) *India's Villages,* 103–5. Bombay: Asia Publishing House.

——— 1954. 'Form, Variation, and Meaning of a Ceremony'. *In* Robert F. Spencer, (ed.), *Method and Perspective in Anthropology. Papers in Honor of Wilson D. Wallis*; 60–102. Minneapolis: University of Minnesota Press.

——— 1955. 'The World and the World View of the Kota' *In* McKim Marriott, (ed.), *Village India. Studies in the Little Community,* 223–54. Chicago: University of Chicago Press.

——— 1989. 'The Kotas in their Social Setting' *In* P. Hockings (ed.), *Blue Mountains. The Ethnography and Biogeography of a South Indian Region:* 144–85. Delhi: Oxford University Press. (Also in R. Redfield and M.B. Singer (eds.), 1956. *Introduction to the Civilization of India.* Chicago).

Marshall, W.E. 1873. *A Phrenologist amongst the Todas, or the Study of a Primitive Tribe in South India. History, Character, Customs, Religion, Infanticide, Polyandry, Language.* London: Longmans, Green, and Co.

Metz, J.F. 1864. *The Tribes Inhabiting the Neilgherry Hills; their Social Customs and Religious Rites.* Rough notes of a German Missionary. Second enlarged edition. Mangalore: Basel Mission Press.

Olender, M. 1989. *Les Langues du Paradis. Aryens et Sémites: Un couple providentiel.* Paris: Gallimard/Le Seuil.

Pictet, A. 1877. *Les Origines Indo-Européennes ou les Aryas primitifs. Essai de paléontologie linguistique.* (1ère ed. in 2 vol. 1859 and 1863), Paris: Sandoz et Fischbacher.

Pouchepadass, J. 1982. 'The 'Criminal Tribes' of British India: A Repressive Concept in Theory and Practice'. *International Journal of Asian Studies,* 2, no. 1 : 41–59.

Reclus, Élisée 1883. *Nouvelle géographie universelle. La terre et les hommes; XIV Inde méridionale: Madras, Maïsour, Courg, Cochin, Travancore.* Paris: Hachette et Cie. (511–78.)

Reclus, Élie 1885. *Les Primitifs. Etudes d'ethnologie comparée.* Paris: G. Chamerot.

'Rifle' 1873. 'The Hill Tribes of the Neilgherries' (*Madras Standard*, 18 October). *The Indian Antiquary*, 2, January: 32.

Rivers, W.H.R. 1906. *The Todas.* London: Macmillan & Co.

Rooksby, R.L. 1971. 'W.H.R. Rivers and the Todas', *South Asia*: 109–21.

Shortt, J. (ed.) 1868. *An Account of the Tribes on the Neilgherries* and *Geographical and Statistical Memoir of a survey of the Neilgherry Mountains*, by J. Ouchterlony [1847.] Madras: Higginbotham and Co.

Sinha, S. 1980. 'Tribes and Indian Civilization: A Perspective' *Man in India*, 60: 1–15.

Smith, M.W. 1948. 'Kota Texts: a Review of the Primitive in Indic Folklore'. *Journal of American Folklore*, 283–97.

Biographical Notes

NURIT BIRD-DAVID was born in 1951 in Beersheba, Israel. She studied economics and mathematics at the Hebrew University, Jerusalem (BA, 1974), and then specialized in social anthropology at Cambridge. Her field research on the Naikens of Gudalur Taluk was conducted in 1978 and 1979. She was awarded the Ph.D. in social anthropology by Cambridge University in 1983, and now teaches anthropology at the University of Haifa.

ULRICH DEMMER was born in 1956 in Frankenberg, Germany. He studied anthropology and comparative religion at Freiburg University and then at Heidelberg, where in addition he studied Tamil. His fieldwork among the Jēnu Kuṟumba has continued from 1987 until the present, and in 1993 he received a Ph.D. in anthropology from Heidelberg University. At present he is a research fellow at Heidelberg University, and is working on forms of ritual discourse among the Jēnu Kuṟumba.

MURRAY B. EMENEAU was born in 1904 in Lunenburg, Nova Scotia. He had a distinguished undergraduate career at Dalhousie University, Halifax, Nova Scotia, and at Balliol College, Oxford, before studying linguistics and anthropology at Yale, under Edward Sapir, E. H. Sturtevant and others, in 1926–31. His Nilgiri fieldwork in 1935–8 pioneered in the analysis of the Toda, Kota and Badaga languages. Since 1940 he has been Professor of Sanskrit and General Linguistics at the University of California, in Berkeley. He has produced a lengthy series of studies on the Dravidian languages, including a *Dravidian Etymological Dictionary* (with T. Burrow, 1984). His latest book is *Dravidian Studies: Selected Papers* (1994).

FRANK HEIDEMANN was born in Bochum, Germany, in 1957, and is now *Wissenschaftlicher Mitarbeiter* at the Institute of Ethnology, Free University of Berlin. He has worked in development projects in Sri Lanka before studying social anthropology, sociology and rural development at the universities of Marburg, Göttingen and Madras. His Ph.D. thesis focussed on the up-country Tamils of Sri Lanka and their repatriation to India, and was published in German (1989). A later work, *Kanganies in Sri Lanka and Malaysia* (Munich, 1992) deals with the Tamil recruiters-cum-foremen. He has conducted four years of fieldwork in south India, has produced films for the Institut für den wissenschaftlichen Film at Göttingen, and since 1988 has been working on the religion and politics of the Badagas.

PAUL HOCKINGS was born in Hertford, England, in 1935, and studied at the Universities of Sydney, Toronto, Chicago, Stanford and California. He is the author of numerous articles on the Nilgiri Hills as well as several books: *Ancient Hindu Refugees: Badaga Social History 1550–1975* (1980), *Sex and Disease in a Mountain Community* (1980), and *Counsel from the Ancients: A Study of Badaga Proverbs, Prayers, Omens and Curses* (1988). He has also edited *Blue Mountains: The Ethnology and Biogeography of a South Indian Region* (1989), *Principles of Visual Anthropology* (1995) and two volumes of the *Encylopedia of World Cultures* (1992–3). He teaches anthropology at the University of Illinois, Chicago, and is currently editor of the journal *Visual Anthropology.*

MARIE-CLAUDE MAHIAS studied anthropology at the University of Paris-V (Sorbonne), specializing in the cultures of South Asia, and gaining the Doctorate in Ethnology in 1981. She is the author of a detailed analysis of Jain cuisine, *Délivrance et Convivialité: Le système culinaire des Jaina* (1985), and also edited *Techniques et culture: Inde* (1989). Since 1982 she has been Chargée de recherche at the CNRS in Paris, and has been doing research on Indian traditional technology and gender specialization. In the Nilgiris she has recently been studying Kota pottery production.

WILLIAM ALLISTER NOBLE was born in 1932 in Nagercoil, Tamil Nadu. He received most of his primary education in the Nilgiris, before going to the United States. He began field research on five Nilgiri communities during 1962, and has returned to India a number of times since, mostly to work in Kerala, Punjab and the Nilgiris. In 1968 he was awarded the Ph.D. in geography and anthropology, by Louisiana State University, and has since published many articles on the ethnography, architecture and human geography of the Nilgiris and Kerala.

CHRISTIANE PILOT-RAICHOOR was born in 1951 in Fontainebleau, France. She studied linguistics at the Université La Sorbonne Nouvelle of Paris and gained the Doctorate for her study of Badaga grammar and syntax. She began field research on the Badaga language in 1975 and has subsequently visited the Nilgiris several times. Since 1988 she has been attached to the Laboratoire de Langues et Civilisations et Traditions Orales (LACITO) of CNRS. She has published several articles on the Badaga language and is co-author with Paul Hockings of *A Badaga-English Dictionary* (1992).

ANTHONY RUPERT WALKER was born in 1940 in London. He was educated at Tonbridge School, Osmania University, Hyderabad, and St. John's College, Oxford. After an initial field study of the Todas in 1962–3, he studied at the Institute of Social Anthropology, Oxford, under E. E. Evans-Pritchard, David Pocock, Edwin Ardener and others, and presented his Toda material there (M.Litt., 1965). During the late sixties he was constantly with the Lahu Hill people of northern Thailand, and in 1972 was awarded the D.Phil. by Oxford University for his dissertation on the Lahu has published over sixty articles and three books on the upland peoples of northern Thailand. At the same time he has been returning repeatedly to the Nilgiris, and has been studying the Toda people fairly continuously for twenty-five years. His book *The Toda of South India: A New Look* was published in 1986. He is currently Associate Professor and Fellow, Institute of Pacific Studies, University of the South Pacific, Suva.

RICHARD KENT WOLF was born in 1962 in Chicago. He studied mathematics and music at Oberlin College and spent several years in Madurai, Tamilnadu, learning to perform the South Indian *vīṇā* before beginning graduate studies in Ethnomusicology at the University of Illinois, Urbana-Champaign. There he completed a Master of Music thesis on *vīṇā* style. His doctoral dissertation, entitled 'Of God and Death: Music in Ritual and Everyday Life. A Musical Ethnography of the Kotas,' was based on research with the Kotas conducted in 1990–92. After returning from his Kota fieldwork, he taught music and ethnomusicology at the University of Illinois, Northwestern University, DePaul University and Columbia College, Chicago. Currently residing in New York, Wolf is a visiting scholar at Columbia University's Southern Asian Institute, and Director of the Folk Arts Programme at the Brooklyn Arts Council.

ALLEN ZAGARELL, formerly an electrician, studied at the City College of New York and the Oriental Institute at the University of Chicago. He received his doctorate from the Vorderasiatische Altertumskunde Institut of the Freie Universitāet of Berlin, Germany in 1977. He is Associate Professor of Anthropology at Western Michigan University in Kalamazoo. His early research dealt with the emergence of a highland way of life in the mountains of southwest Iran. Since 1983 he has been working in southern India.

Index

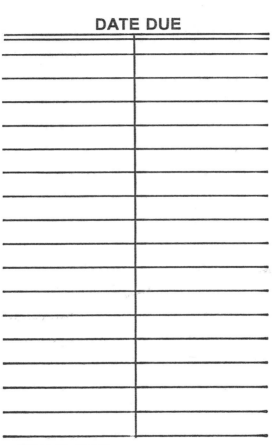